Conversations:
Selected Papers of Arnold D. Richards Volume 6

Conversations: Selected Papers of Arnold D. Richards Volume 6

with Introduction by Merle Molofsky

IPBOOKS.net
International Psychoanalytic Boo
International Psychoanalytic Books (IPBooks)
New York • http://www.IPBooks.net

Conversations: Selected Papers of Arnold D. Richards Volume 6

Published by IPBooks, Queens, NY
Online at: www.IPBooks.net

Cover Picture: *Beat the Whites with the Red Wedge*, Soviet Propaganda Poster, El Lissitzky, lithograph print, circa 1919.

ISBN 978-1-956864-82-3

Dedicated to Barbara and Ernest Kafka, MD

Contents

Introduction by Merle Molofsky[1]

During the many decades of his professional lifetime, Arnold D. Richards has made a notable contribution to psychoanalysis, as an exemplary gifted clinician, theoretician, educator, editor, and writer. Five previous collections of his papers have been published, and I am honored and privileged to be introducing the sixth volume of his collected papers.

In addition to his dedication to psychoanalysis, Dr. Richards has been deeply involved in preserving Yiddish culture and language. He was a

---

1 Merle Molofsky is a New York State-licensed psychoanalyst; a psychoanalytic educator; and a poet, fiction writer, and playwright. She has served on the Editorial Board of *The Psychoanalytic Review* for many years, including as Associate Editor when Michael Eigen was Editor, and when Gerald Gargiulo was Editor. She also serves on the Editorial Board of *The Journal for Controversial Discussions*. She is former Editor of *Other*/Wise, the online psychoanalytic journal of the International Forum for Psychoanalytic Education (IFPE).

Merle Molofsky serves on the faculty of the Training Institute of NPAP, and on the faculty and Advisory Council of Harlem Family Institute. She is former Dean of Training, NPAP; former Director of Education, the Institute for Expressive Analysis (IEA). In 2012 she received the Gradiva Award in Poetry from the National Association for the Advancement of Psychoanalysis (NAAP). Her play, "Kool-Aid", was produced in 1971 at the Forum Theater of Lincoln Center, New York City,

Her recent publications include four books published by IPBooks. She served as Editor for *Jew-Hating: The Black Milk of Civilization* (2023); and is the author of a collection of poetry, *Sh'Ma, I Hear Voices* (2024); *Necessary Voices: A Collection of Short Fiction* (2019); a novel, *Streets 1970*, (2015). She has other notable publications, including many psychoanalytic articles and chapters in psychoanalytic books, such as "Permission and Gratitude: Michael Eigen's Gateway to Possibility and Freedom", in *Healing, Rebirth, and the Work of Michael Eigen*, edited by Ken Fuchsman and Keri S. Cohen, Routledge, London and New York: 2021; "To Be a Therapist and To Be a Psychoanalyst: That is the Answered Question", in *Rage and Creativity: How Feminism Sparked Psychoanalysis*, edited by Lucille Spira, IPBooks, New York: 2020; "Pedro Almodóvar: Women Searching for a Man Searching for What Women Want, in *What Have I Done to Deserve This? And Julieta*", Chapter 5, *Pedro Almodóvar: A Cinema of Desire, Passion and Compulsion*, edited by Arlene Kramer Richards and Lucille Spira, with Merle Molofsky, IPBooks, Queens, New York: 2018.

Board member and former chair of the YIVO Institute for Jewish Research, which is entwined with his knowledge of psychoanalysis. He has written about reading the Yiddish newspaper, *The Forward*, when he was a five-year-old child in Brooklyn, and, in 1939, seeing an article about the death of Sigmund Freud, which became crucial in his discovery of a fascinating discipline, psychoanalysis. Thus, Yiddish culture and psychoanalysis are interwoven for him since childhood.

One of the articles in this collection of papers is not written by Dr. Richards, but, rather, is a commentary on an article Dr. Richards wrote, "The Need Not to Believe", in which Dr. Richards discusses the role of Judaism in Sigmund Freud's life. The author praises Dr. Richards's article as comprehensive and insightful. In particular, the commentator cites Dr. Richards's identification of three strands of Freud's sense of his Jewish identity: commitment to cultural assimilation, the tradition of Bildung (essentially personal and cultural development); his response to anti-Semitism; his "militant godlessness." "Militant godlessness" implies a dedication to science and rational thinking that involves rejection of religion. Psychoanalysis reveals that a belief in a supreme being, a deity, as delusional, derived from an infant's wish to be taken care of by all-powerful parents.

Another paper, by Dr. Marco Conci, is a review of *Growing Up Orthodox* by Dr. Richards, and describes his experience meeting Dr. Richards at a conference, perhaps in 1993, and being impressed, perhaps awed, by meeting such a distinguished psychoanalyst, "a bearded man looking like a Jewish prophet." Dr. Conci also addresses Dr. Richards's reading of Freud's death in the Yiddish language Forward, at the age of five. He comments that Dr. Richards, now 90 years old, was the child of Eastern European Jewish immigrants, and thus grew up bilingual. He cites Dr. Richards's interest in Ludwig Fleck's concept of a thought collective, and observes that Dr. Richards addresses a variety of alternative psychoanalytic theories from a perspective of a contemporary Freudian analyst. He notes that Dr. Richards chose to study psychoanalysis at the Menninger Clinic in Topeka, Kansas, rather than in New York City. He appreciates that Dr. Richards has a dialectical approach, builds on Theodor Reik's *Listening with the Third Ear*, hearing unconscious process, and then, listens with "the fourth ear", as he "tries to listen from various vantage points of competing theoretical schools." Dr. Richards does not accept the idea of an orthodox Freudian monolith, therefore ably represents his own concepts, an aspect of a distinguished career with many achievements, earning awards.

Similarly, this collection includes a review Richard Tuch wrote of Volume 1 of Dr. Richards's Selected Papers, stating that "Richards has a bone to pick with analysts who make a habit of dismissing, to the point of condemning, the work of colleagues whose approach is largely informed by modern conflict theory." He describes Dr. Richards as a "publisher extraordinaire", recognizing his generosity. I agree that Dr. Richards indeed is generous, including this review in Volume 6 of his collected papers.

Equally generously, Dr. Richards includes a review that Nathan Szajnberg wrote of Volume 5 of his selected papers. Fittingly, Dr. Szajnberg also is generous. He addresses Dr. Richards's first essay, "Dreams and the Wish for Immortality," beginning by saying that the essay brings to mind the Passover song in the Haggadah, sung at the end of the seder, "Dayenu", which means "Enough." He praises Dr. Richards, noting that he has made so many contributions, that what has been offered would be enough.

Yet enough could never be enough! Dr. Szajnberg identifies Dr. Richards's wish for longevity, Dr. Richards, writing about the vicissitudes of being part of his once and perhaps still beloved New York Psychoanalytic Institute, indicates a wish that he could be young again. He calls this wish for longevity "a moment of writing that is personal, vulnerable and moving." Indeed, in citing this phrase, he captures Dr. Richards's approach to writing!

Speaking of Dr. Richards's approach to writing, I now will focus on his articles in this collection.

The first article I will comment on is "Holes in the Door Post." Dr. Richards eloquently addresses, poignantly laments, the death of Yiddish language and culture in Europe, due to the Shoah, the Holocaust, focusing on what can be seen in Warsaw today. The holes in the door post are all that remains of what had been mezuzahs affixed to the door posts in Jewish homes. He calls us to cry out against the murderers, and bear witness to the evils of the Holocaust. He also reminds us to "celebrate the enduring power of life." He asks, who are the witnesses? He answers, I am. I am a psychoanalyst. I help people to find their own histories.

This article avidly discusses the efforts of YIVO to memorialize the lost Jewish writers, the lost Yiddish culture, 11 and ½ pages long, a lengthy but incomplete list of names. Of note: YIVO was founded in Vilna in 1925, and Albert Einstein, Sigmund Freud, and Edward Sapir were trustees. Documents found by a United States Army officer in a freight car were sent to New York, and were the foundation of the YIVO collection. Dr. Richards says that his mother said, "Better they had saved fewer papers and more people." Heartbreaking.

Dr. Richards, who, is a psychiatrist as well as a psychoanalyst, has a strong foundation in medicine, in neuroscience. His review of *Gray Matters*, by Theodore Schwartz, is both personal and academic. He acknowledges that they have known each other since the neurologist's childhood, when Dr. Schwartz was two years old, calls Dr. Schwartz "Teddy," and credits Dr. Schwartz's exemplary knowledge and skill, saving Dr. Richards's life by operating on a "massive subdural hematoma in one side of the skull." He rightly describes Dr. Schwartz as "one of the most foremost neurosurgeons in the United States", and discusses the book itself as an overview of Dr. Schwartz's medical training, "an in-depth history of the development of the field of neurosurgery itself."

We continue to learn more and more about Dr. Richards in another article, an interview of Dr. Richards conducted by Dr. Moises Lemlij, psychoanalyst and professor at the University of Lima, Peru. The interview was published in *Face to Face*, a compilation of interviews of psychoanalysts by Dr. Lemlij. The two met in 1994 when attending the Latin American Congress of Psychoanalysis. One from an English-speaking country, one from a Spanish-speaking country, they discovered they shared a mother tongue, Yiddish, living in bilingual households, sharing certain similar backgrounds regarding sociopolitical family values.

In the interview, Dr. Richards discusses his memories of puberty and adolescence, his concept of orthodoxy, and contemplates why he became a psychoanalyst. Orthodoxy is central. Should he have become a psychoanalyst, or a rabbi? Dr. Richards discusses the impact on him when he studied psychoanalysis at the Menninger Clinic, when he wondered, why am I in Topeka, Kansas, in the middle of nowhere, and not in Brooklyn, in NYC. He also discussed the impact he and his wife, Arlene Kramer Richards, had while in Topeka, saying that they brought culture to Kansas, such as choosing movies to show there. He reflects on his family's cultural influence on him, his father's influence. He says he wasn't a "red diaper baby", since his father was not politically active, yet acknowledging that as an adolescent in his household he became concerned with social justice. Being Jewish always was an important theme. Yes, he mentions seeing the article in the Yiddish newspaper *The Forward* about the death of Sigmund Freud when he was a little boy. Such a significant moment in his life! It still resonates.

Once again, he discusses his involvement with YIVO, and once again he visits anti-Semitism and Freud's struggle with being Jewish. During this part of the interview, Dr. Lemlij raised the issue of being "too Jewish."

In an Afterword, written a full decade since the interview, Dr. Richards describes the present as a time of consolidation of professional, clinical, and pedagogic identity, that he stays active professionally in a particular way, writing, and publishing International Psychoanalytic Books.

Dr. Richards is so interesting that it is not surprising that other major thinkers are drawn to interviewing him. Sara Israel, deeply involved with the National Yiddish Book Center, conducted an interview with him that touched on major elements of his life, themes that are interwoven in his narrative, such as his family background; the importance of Yiddish culture and language, including stories and music; orthodoxy; Sigmund Freud and psychoanalysis—a tapestry of memory, nostalgia, and creativity.

Responding to Ms. Israel's sensitive questioning, Dr. Richards describes his family background as a "mixed marriage", describing his father as a Russian Bolshevik, his mother coming from an Orthodox Jewish household in Eastern European Galicia, a region comprising part of Ukraine and Lithuania. Dr. Richards has pointed out elsewhere that so many of the original psychoanalysts in Freud's inner circle were Jews from Galicia. Yet in this "mixed marriage", both parents spoke Yiddish (which was my mother's first language but may not have been my father's first language). He proudly speaks of a photograph of his mother as a little girl gracing the cover of a Yiddish-language novel, *Oyf Zeydn's Felder* (English title, *In Grandfather's House*), by Isaac Metzker, famous for being the revered writer of "Dos Bintele Brief", an advice column in *The Forward*, replying to letters written by readers of the Yiddish newspaper. Thus the importance of Yiddish once again is in the foreground, important both to the interviewer Sara Israel, herself involved in YIVO, and Dr. Richards.

Ms. Israel elicits from Dr. Richards many of his treasured early memories, his sense of the history of Brooklyn neighborhoods, his discovery of Sigmund Freud when Freud's death was reported in *The Forward*; his learning about World War II, and the Holocaust, from news articles; his singing lessons with Sholom Secunda at the secular Workmen's Circle, where Sholom Secunda taught the class a new song he had written, soon to become a well-known song, "Dona"; his turning to Orthodox Judaism after his bar mitzvah, aware of his father's atheism and his mother keeping kosher; his memory of Italian-American kids beating up Jewish-American kids in his neighborhood; his discovery of the richness of having a Jewish identity and an American identity, and being comfortable with both; his pleasure in sharing a love of, and knowledge of, Yiddish, with Arlene Kramer, his wife-to-be; his return to New York City after his psychiatric/psychoanalytic internship and residency and joining a synagogue, where he engaged the congregation in discussing Yiddish literature and poetry; his involvement through YIVO in the klezmer music revival; his fundraising for the movie about Polish Jews, "Image Before My Eyes." He points out that "Yiddish is a very emotional language, the language contains a very large cultural context." And, most particularly, in response to Ms. Israel's exploratory questioning, he delineated the intersection of his interest in psychiatry and Jewish culture. Tellingly, at one point, he said, "I'm interested in lost causes." Fortunately, because of the work of Dr. Richards and others, neither psychiatry/psychoanalysis nor Yiddish language and culture are lost causes!

I found four questions that Ms. Israel asked, and the answers Dr. Richards provided, particularly enthralling.

She asked, "What motivates you to promote Yiddish and to work with YIVO?" He answered, "It's part of my neshome (my soul) from my childhood…." "Yiddish redt zikh", "Yiddish speaks itself."

She asked, "What do you think is the importance of Israel or the place of Israel in Jewish life now, or to American Jews?" He answered, "I think it's central, I really do." And he repeated the story of his mother criticizing the work of YIVO, when she said, "It would have been better to save the people, not the paper," "Besser men hot geratevet di menshn, nisht di papir."

She asked, "Do you have a favorite story that you remember?" He answered, "Kvass – Motl Peyse dem khasns, Motl Peyse the cantor's son, who said, Ikh bin a yosim, I am an orphan." He cited a bumper sticker: "Rescue the books."

She asked, "Do you have a favorite Yiddish word or phrase or song that you come back to?"

He answered with a song: "Vi hot gedangen mayne yunger yorn? Zey hobn zikh oysgeshpilt vi kortn." "Where did my young years go? They got played out like cards."

I gasped when I read this. I heard Theodor Bikel sing a version of this song in the 1950's, when I was young and lived in Brooklyn, "Vi zenen meyne yingeh yoren?"

I cherish this interview conducted by Sara Israel....

Dr. Richards himself is a capable, sensitive interviewer. He interviewed Dr, Charles Fisher, who is a member of the New York Psychoanalytic Institute and Society, conducting the Oral History Project.

Very much like Dr. Richards, Dr. Fisher, examining his motivation for becoming a psychoanalyst, considers his infancy and childhood, and explored his ambiguity regarding having a "Jewish" name. Dr. Fisher's family changed their obviously Jewish surname, Cohen, to Fisher. Without a traditional Jewish surname, are they Jewish? Or not? The interview focuses on a major traumatic event in Dr. Fisher's childhood, the suicide of his mother. Dr. Fisher's father told the traumatized child that the child's mother had a bad dream, which led to her action, and Dr. Fisher concluded that dreams were the royal road to suicide! Remembering his grief, the physical manifestation of crying, he learned that memory became the basis of an intervention. "I always ask patients where they feel their depression." He remembers his grief was located in his belly. During the interview, Dr. Richards, with care and sensitivity, asks useful questions.

A compelling article co-written by Dr. Richards and Janet Lee Bachant, "Finding Integration in a Splintered World," considers contemporary psychoanalytic thought applied to clinical work. They note that practitioners can feel overwhelmed by the many theories they encounter, the range of choices. They note that people consult psychoanalysts because they are suffering. They recognize that conflict theory applied to clinical work may help analysands better understand themselves. With the evolving model of psychoanalysis, the body of knowledge that most clinicians use indeed has overlapping areas. Yet pluralism also may lead to fragmenting rather than integrating our work.

Still, there may not be a significant paradigm shift. They cite Daniel Benveniste, 2024, who emphasizes the value of using different lenses at different times, due to changes in an analysand's needs and growth. They offer the notion of interactive variables rather than dichotomies.

Perhaps we can hear an echo of Dr. Richards's review of *Gray Matter* when he and Dr. Bachant acknowledge neuropsychoanalysis, the benefit of integrating neurological concepts, saying, "body and mind are not separate domains but different expressions of a unified process."

In a paper about technique, focusing on the theories of Heinz Kohut, Dr. Richards begins, "Our fundamental thesis is that a psychoanalytic theoretician develops a theory of technique to counter his or her own anti-psychoanalytic proclivities." Hint hint—this is not going to be a benign reading of Kohut's contributions. Dr. Richards provides an overview of other significant psychoanalysts and their theories, beginning by citing Ludwig Fleck, "development of scientific ideas is influenced by historical, sociological, cultural, and psychoanalytic factors." He then considers the contributions regarding technique that address a foundation of abstinence, focusing on affect, interpersonal considerations, waiting for evidence before making interpretations, considering parameters, and softening the superego. From there, Dr. Richards ponders the fact that while Kohut emphasized empathy and authenticity, a number of Kohut's colleagues said Kohut was narcissistic, and not empathic. Yet, Kohut's analysands found him empathic.

Dr. Richards then passes the proverbial "talking stick" to Arlene Kramer Richards, who writes about the intersection of theory and personality in the work of Melanie Klein, focusing on disorganizing aggression aroused by the loss of a mother, or other maternal deprivation or intrusiveness. Her contribution is followed by Arnold Lynch discussing the work of Karen Horney, whom he describes as courageous. He points out that Horney recognized misogyny as a cultural theme, disagreed with the concept of penis envy, and emphasized pregnancy and childbirth, proposed a "primary femininity," to counteract misogyny in Freud's thinking.

And further, Dr. Richards includes a 2003 article by Jay Greenberg, who comments as a discussant about a paper, "A Plea for a Measure of Humility," by Dr. Richards, who had invited his discussants to comment. Humility is quite a concept to apply to the cultural ambience of psychoanalysis and psychoanalysts! Dr. Greenberg considers preconceptions, and Freud's tenacity. He promotes the work he and Dr. Mitchell contributed in *Object Relations in Psychoanalytic Theory*, and finds fault with Dr. Richards's critique of their concepts. He asserts that Dr. Richards's reliance on conflict theory mires him in his own preconceptions.

I find myself amused by the playfulness of Dr. Richards's title, "A Plea for a Measure of Humility," evoking the 1993 book, *A Plea for a Measure of Abnormality* by Joyce McDougall. Perhaps accepting the need for humility helps us recognize and accept that some colleagues might find our ideas aberrant, even abnormal.

To what extent can we, must we, hold onto our values, our ideas, our beliefs, in the context of humility? Dr. Richards humbly publishes Dr. Greenberg's article, which aggressively disagrees with Dr. Richards's ideas in the article Dr. Greenberg is discussing. Humbly? Rather, I should say confidently. Dr. Richards has so much to be proud of, and allows for a measure of humility because he can confidently be confident.

Without undue humility, I will state that is an honor to contribute the Introduction to *Conversations: Selected Papers of Arnold D. Richards Volume 6.*

CHAPTER 1

Arnold Richards, interviewed by Moises Lemlij in *Face to Face: Interviews with Leo Rangell, Arnold D. Richards, and Estella Welldon*

ML: *How did you become an analyst? What happened in your life that put you on this particular path?*

ADR: Believe it or not, my earliest lexical memory I can date to age five. It was reading or being read *The Forward*, the Yiddish newspaper. There was a picture of Sigmund Freud and the headline was "Famous Jewish Psychiatrist Dies" so it was September 1939. Actually, a few years ago I looked up a copy of the paper from that date and there was the picture of Freud and the headline. The bearded man may have reminded me of an older orthodox man who was the landlord of our building (by the way, I have had the same kind of beard for many years). Was this transference? I was a precocious kid. I read a lot. I could read Yiddish and English at an early age. I am not sure whether this was a screen memory or a retrospective falsification. In elementary school I read Aldous Huxley, *Point Counter Point*, Pearl S. Buck's novel about China, *The Good Earth*, and Flanders Dunbar's text on psychosomatic medicine, *Emotions and Bodily Changes.*

ML: *I know the book well because Flanders Dunbar was the analyst of my first psychiatric teacher, Carlos Alberto Seguín, who trained at Columbia.*

ADR: I was interested in reading the book because I had hay fever, a severe case. I got the message from that book that understanding of the unconscious and conflicts could help me cure it. When I was sixteen I read Freud's *Introductory Lectures* and it was then that I decided I would become a psychoanalyst. I also read the A.A. Brill translation of *The Interpretation of Dreams*. Both books, it turned out, determined my future. Growing up, I went to public school and Yiddish after-school. I connected with a bearded, orthodox Rabbi, and believe it or not, I can hardly believe it myself, not only did I get Bar Mitzvahed, I also became orthodox: praying two times a day, putting on *tefillin.*

ML: *Why?*

ADR: That is a good question; I am not sure I know the answer. Perhaps it was a way to deal with pubertal pressures. At the same time, I was engaged in orthodox Jewish ritualistic obsessive practices, in high school, in Brooklyn, Erasmus Hall (four of my classmates there became analysts, Bennett Simon, Stanley Palombo, Martin Willick, and my wife, Arlene Kramer Richards). I was reading Henry Miller, James Joyce, Kenneth Patchen and many other *avant-garde* writers. I applied to many colleges including Harvard and I was accepted at all of them, but I could not afford to go to any of them. I started at Brooklyn College, which was free. It was there when one day a letter came in the mail from the University of

Chicago offering me a full scholarship. Of course, I accepted, I met my wife there, and the rest is history.

ML: *You were a New Yorker originally?*

ADR: When I started at the University of Chicago it was the end of the Robert Maynard Hutchins Era. I arrived in October of 1951. Hutchins had left the previous spring. The first person I met on campus was Ernie Hartmann, the son of Heinz Hartmann. I remember him because he seemed to look to the side and mumble. Many years later when I saw Heinz Hartmann at meetings of the New York Psychoanalytic Society, he also looked to the side and mumbled.

ML: *Perhaps some people who read this might not know about the University of Chicago program.*

ADR: The University of Chicago College had a program based on the great books. All the readings were from original sources. The emphasis was on the philosophy of knowledge. Richard McKeon and Mortimer Adler were the originators and gurus. The final course in the curriculum was called Organizational Methods and Principals of Knowledge (OMP). The idea was to learn how to think rather than to acquire particular specific knowledge, which you might use in a profession. The program has been watered down since I was there, but the University of Chicago is still an exciting place. We had the motto, "The University of Chicago: where fun goes to die". And it is of interest that the university's ranking has increased from ninth to fifth this year. They have a system where you take exams for all the courses, and only have to take those that you don't place in. I placed in everything, but I had to take four courses; I got my degree in a year. In retrospect, I think that was unfortunate, because I missed a lot.

But getting back to my religious orthodoxy, Arlene told me that she had heard about the student who would wrap leather around his arm. Maybe it was a turn-on for her. Anyway, we met, we went out to our first date in January 1952, we went to a Polynesian restaurant, I ate shrimp for the first time in my life, and my orthodoxy was over. But I still had becoming a psychoanalyst in mind.

ML: *Or a rabbi?*

ADR: Or a rabbi. Actually, at the University of Chicago I considered going into mathematics instead of medicine, and in Medical School I became interested in internal medicine and neuroanatomy. The wish to become a psychoanalyst moved to the background. I also got interested in forensic psychiatry. By the way, our son is a criminal lawyer. But there remained the wish to become a psychoanalyst. I was part of a cohort of individuals like myself, Jewish intellectuals, who perhaps today would go into finance, but then went into medicine and psychoanalysis. Psychoanalysis was a way to combine an interest in science, and an interest in humanities, as Freud did.

ML: *But you say someone like you today would go into finance?*`

ADR: Right! They are less likely to become physicians or academics. Most of the children of our group did not become psychoanalysts. The fifties were the halcyon days of psychoanalysis. For many of us it was the ticket to ride. It was an interesting, intellectually stimulating activity and I think many of us read Freud in high school. In one of the exams, they used a paper on Freud and we had to answer questions about his thinking and his theory. Freud was a part of the culture in the fifties and sixties. The psychoanalyst was often portrayed in the movies. Psychoanalysis then was very different from what it was when someone like Charlie Brenner was going into psychoanalysis in the nineteen thirties. At that time, only mavericks pursued that esoteric occupation.

I had a summer clerkship between my second and third year in medical school at the Marine Hospital in Staten Island. Larry Deutsch, who was a candidate at the Downstate Institute, now New York University (NYU), and in analysis with Melitta Sperling, was my mentor. Sperling was interested in psychosomatic medicine. She was so convinced that she would cure psychosomatic illness with psychoanalytic interpretations that she would visit a patient in the hospital and remove the IV from the patient's arm saying "You know what you are doing? You are ingesting your mother and turning her into shit". This interpretation was supposed to cure the patient of their ulcerative colitis. Larry Deutsch had this incredible belief and enthusiasm in the power of psychoanalysis and some of his enthusiasm influenced me.

After Medical School, I interned in Baltimore, Maryland, at a public health service hospital. Our next-door neighbors were the Polands, Warren and Janice. He, at that time, was a psychiatric first-year resident at the University of Maryland. Jake Feinsinger was the chair. He [Warren Poland] had the same enthusiasm about psychoanalysis, which he conveyed to me in a very personal way. On the first day of my internship and his first of day as a resident, he told his wife who was pregnant (I hope he doesn't mind me saying this) "Whatever you do, you know when I am in session I can't be interrupted."

ML: *He had his priorities right!*

ADR: When I got home his wife was about to give birth. I was called to assist. I had an OB clerkship in medical school and sort of knew what to do, but the birth was spontaneous. I only had to catch the baby and I tied the umbilical cord with a string from her skirt. The Polands remain our closest friends.

The positive psychoanalytic ambiance at the University of Maryland was important. At that time many of the chairs of departments of psychiatry were psychoanalysts. If you wanted to get ahead in psychiatry you needed to have analytic training. After my internship, my interest in psychoanalysis did not waver. But first, I had to become a psychiatrist.

I applied to the Albert Einstein College of Medicine and I think I was most interested in it because several of my friends went there. It had a very psychoanalytically oriented program. Milton Rosenbaum was the chair. Herbert Weiner and José Barchelon were on the faculty. Many of the residents were in analysis with training analysts from the New York Psychoanalytic Society and Institute (NYPSI). I was interviewed and accepted but decided that with a wife and two children I couldn't afford to go, given the salary which was provided. I didn't really want us to live in a basement in the Bronx during my residency. I didn't think that that would be a great life for my family. I decided to go to the Menninger School of Psychiatry in Topeka instead. I liked their brochure. I didn't go there for an interview. I still remember the sinking feeling that I had as I drove down from Kansas Avenue. I said to myself, "What am I doing here?"

ML: *What the fuck am I doing here?*

ADR: Yes, what the fuck am I doing here in the middle of nowhere? What's a nice Jewish boy from Brooklyn doing in Kansas? Well, there we were and the next thing I know I get a call from Harvey Bezahler. He's an analyst and again one of my good friends. He was a third-year resident at the time. He trained at Downstate and is now one of my best friends. His job was to orient the new residents. I quickly came to feel at home and comfortable in Topeka. I think I did make the right choice. In retrospect,

I think it was better for me than the *"echt"* psychoanalytic cookie-cutter model of Albert Einstein. Even though I did my training at the NYPSI, I was able to preserve a certain degree of independence in thinking because of my Menninger training. The fifties and sixties were also halcyon times in Topeka. Many of the greats had left: David Rapaport, Roy Schafer, Robert Knight, Merton Gill. But others were still there when I arrived: Howie Shevrin, Herb Schlesinger, Sybille Escalona, the Wallersteins, the Tichos, the Murphys. Some psychologists became training analysts because of Karl Menninger's clout in the American Psychoanalytic Association (APsaA). Menninger Clinic was a terrific analytically oriented residency, but it was also a wonderful place for another reason. I mean also culturally, believe it or not.

ML: *In Topeka, Kansas?*

ADR: Yes, culture in Kansas. They had a program of visiting professorships sponsored by Alfred P. Sloan from General Motors. He gave money to get visiting intellectuals to spend a month in Topeka. Konrad Lorenz, Ludwig von Bertelanffy, S.I. Hayakawa, Margaret Mead, Max Gittleson, Chuck Fisher, Peter Kuiper, etc. gave lectures to the residents. I have the list somewhere. It was a remarkable experience. Instead of the rather narrow rigid training at Einstein, I had a training which was eclectic and open to the wider world of ideas.

Karl Menninger wrote *The Human Mind* in the thirties, and it became the bestselling psychoanalytic book for the lay public ever written. He was a very interesting person. I'll tell you about how Menninger got started. C. F. Menninger, the father, wanted to emulate the Mayo brothers. He wanted his two sons, Karl and Will, to become physicians and work in his clinic. They went to Harvard. They got interested in psychiatry and when they came back to Topeka they started the psychiatric clinic, the Menninger

Clinic. Their father ended up doing physicals on their psychiatric patients. Will probably did more for the development of American psychoanalysis than anyone else. He was in charge of recruitment for the Army during World War II. He made all these mostly Jewish doctors psychiatrists. They treated the war wounded and shell-shocked with hypnosis. When they left the Army in 1946-1947 many of them decided to become psychoanalysts and many decided to get analytic training in Topeka. There must have been 150 applicants for their training program in one year in Topeka. Will and Karl really didn't get along, siblings often don't. Will spent most of his time on the road raising money and Karl spent his time running the Menninger Clinic

We had Saturday morning sessions in which Karl interviewed patients; he was writing his book at the time *The Vital Balance*. We read it chapter by chapter.

Karl had his own take on psychiatry, he didn't believe in nosology. He believed in the vital balance; he believed in understanding people as individuals and not as diagnostic labels. He was also very much interested in the larger world. And that helped me specifically, because he established a program with James Bennett for the Federal Bureau of Prisons, and as a resident I was on active duty in the public health service. You were paid as an officer and then you had to work in a prison for two years. This was a pretty good deal for me because it was two years rather than four years as in the Berry plan.

Karl, as you know, was the first graduate of the Chicago Institute. His analyst was Franz Alexander. He took the train from Topeka to Chicago and had four sessions in two days each week to become a psychoanalyst. Will also trained in Chicago. In some ways Karl Menninger, a Presbyterian who grew up in Pennsylvania, was more Freudian than Freud. He was one of the few American psychoanalysts who believed in the death instinct. His book *Love against Hate* had to do with Eros and Thanatos. He communicated to us his enthusiasm for psychoanalysis and for understanding people. He and Alexander, his analyst, went off to see Freud and the story goes that Alexander left him in the waiting room. Alexander told Freud that he shouldn't pay much attention to Menninger. Of course, Menninger was very hurt by this. I don't know exactly what was going on between the two of them and there were some complicated aspects. I think it was Karen Horney who analyzed his [Menninger's] wife who left him. That's the usual kind of stuff that went on in those times.

ML: *And today?*

ADR: But I'll tell you what I meant about culture. Since there was no culture in Topeka, we had to bring it to Kansas. I became the chair of the Menninger School of Psychiatry Film Society (I followed Leon Levin and Otto Kernberg followed me). We showed *Hiroshima Mon Amour* and screened *The Threepenny Opera* before it played anywhere in the United States. We rented the best foreign films. There was also a Chamber Music Society run by Philip Holtzman and Herbert Schlesinger.

ML: *How long did you stay in Topeka?*

ADR: Three years. Karl wanted all the residents to return but somehow, he let me go. He would get angry if you didn't return and work in the Menninger Foundation. I am not sure why that wasn't an issue in my case. Perhaps it was because I went to Petersburg, Virginia where I became the Chief Medical Officer and Chief Psychiatrist of the Federal Reformatory, so I was in charge of the medical treatment of all the inmates and of the staff. My main treatment modality was group therapy to help the staff understand psychological forces at work in their daily encounters. I also did presentencing evaluations for the court. I was in Petersburg from

1962 to 1964. Those were very exciting times in the South. The civil rights movement was in full swing and Petersburg was very much on the front line. In fact, they closed the schools to avoid integration and set up whites only private schools. We sent our kids to the Bollingbrook Day School and I was elected president of the parents' association. Not sure why, I think it had something to do with the fact that I was Jewish and a psychiatrist. I was encouraged to stay in Petersburg after I finished my tour of duty and start a private practice. They were aware that segregation had discouraged professionals from settling there.

ML: *How did that connect with psychoanalysis?*

ADR: That's a good question because to me one of the problems with psychoanalysis is its disconnection with academic communities and the cultural surroundings. I think you are an exception.

ML: *The connection between psychoanalysis and social issues was natural for me because I was interested in politics, since I was a teenager. I think it was also the case of Otto Fenichel and people like him in the United States.*

ADR: The members of the Freudian left you know: Otto Fenichel, Henry Lowenfeld, Edith Jacobson, Barbara Schneider-Lantos, Francis Deri, George Gerö, Lilo Gerö-Heyman and Annie Reich. They had been politically involved in Vienna. Russell Jacoby said, "When they came to the United Stated they dropped their politics in the Atlantic Ocean." They became democrats. They loved Franklin Delano Roosevelt, even his dog Fala was an icon. As they became successful and made money they moved away from social consciousness and socialism. Edith Jacobson and Wilhelm Reich were communists. Jacobson belonged to the German anti-Hitler group the New Beginning. She was arrested by the Gestapo for refusing to give information about her leftist patients. Lilo Gerö-Heyman was able to get her out of jail by telling the authorities that she had to be in the hospital because of diabetes. She was able to escape to Prague after that.

ML: *Were they afraid? Wilhelm Reich did go to prison in the United States because of his orgone accumulator. He was a bit crazy, as well... I wonder if it was not fear that made them move away from their beliefs.*

ADR: They were afraid in the forties and the fifties. This is the time of McCarthy. They were very grateful to the United States. They knew they were lucky to be alive. As analysts they carried the mantel of Freud and this gave them a certain cache at analytic institutes in the United States. In New York it was the Europeans who really took over from the Americans. They were in a very good position in the institutes, which meant lots of patients and lots of money. They rapidly rose to the top of the psychoanalytic economic ladder.

ML: *So, they dropped their ideals in the Atlantic?*

ADR: The story of the role of the Emergency Committee on Relief and Immigration of the American Psychoanalytic Association, chaired by Lawrence Kubie and Bettina Warburg, in facilitating the immigration of European analysts before WWII started, is worth retelling. All but two, Kurt Landauer, who died of starvation in a concentration camp, although his daughter survived, and one other. All the members of the Viennese Psychoanalytic Society were rescued but not all of the candidates. Do you know why? Because there was no roster of candidates, so graduation was a matter of life and death.

On the other hand, American psychoanalysts of the same era, like Jack Arlow, Charlie Brenner, Eleanor Gallenson, Milton Jacoby, or Larry

Roos made money in a capitalist system but that did not preclude them from leftist convictions. There was a communist cell at NYU in the early forties, the list of psychoanalysts who belonged or who were sympathetic is long. They had grown up in the depression and had a strong aversion to inequality and championed social justice. They raised money for the Lincoln Brigade and two analysts, Aaron Hilcovich and William Pike, went to Spain. The Europeans, with the exception of Wilhelm Reich and Edith Jacobson, had an aversion to communism based on their firsthand experience. Do you know Shelley Orgel?

ML: *No.*

ADR: He was the Chairman of the Board of Professional Standards (BoPS). His father was Dean of Students at Lincoln High School where he was a student. He joined the Communist party in college. He was part of a cohort of American Jews who became psychoanalysts after joining the party in the thirties and forties. I think Jack Arlow was the last to leave, having maintained his allegiance through the purge trials and the Ribbentrop-Molotov pact. He was William Z. Foster's personal physician. Jack would not leave the country because he was concerned they would not let him return. My wife was in analysis with him. She once visited my father in the hospital and the next session spoke about how she could not understand that anyone should be so stupid as to remain a communist after the thirties! Jack left the Communist party after the Duclos letter, which had to do with the refusal of Earl Browder to knuckle under to communism. "Browder is our leader and we shall not be moved" was the song then.

Some leftist psychoanalysts replaced communism with Zionism as an ideology. I think some of them brought to psychoanalysis the same sense of certainty that was manifested in their politics.

ML: *They needed a complementary ideology, to be an analyst was not enough.*

ADR: For some of us, yes. That was true. It was certainly true in Red Vienna where psychoanalysts were socially conscious. They set up clinics for low cost treatments and every analyst was expected to participate and donate some time. The sense of social consciousness there was strong. Elizabeth Danto wrote about this time in her book *Freud's Free Clinics*. The Viennese (and Berlin and Budapest analysts) entered training with their left political commitments. My generation in the US was less politically active. They spent 8 to 10 hours every day in their offices seeing patients and making money (also teaching and supervising) and did not have much time for social activism although they did see low fee analysands as part of their training. Senior analysts were not expected to see low-fee, non-candidate, private patients as in Vienna, Berlin and Budapest, but there were some individual exceptions, Kurt Eissler was one. He also expected others to do the same. He would refer me patients for low or no fee and I usually accommodated them. Several years ago, one of those patients left me $1000 in her will, which I received after she died.

On the other hand, a group of psychoanalysts organized by Charlie Brenner and Buddy Myer—more than 100—took out a full-page ad in the New York Times during the Vietnam war protesting the Gulf of Tonkin Resolution. I think many psychoanalysts marched and protested. When we were in Petersburg, Virginia, Arlene went to the Civil Rights March on Washington. She got up at 4 a.m. and went to the Ebenezer Baptist church where she joined Wyatt T. Walker, the minister. She and the Jewish Chaplin from the Fort Lee Army Base were the only two white people on the bus. I was very frightened on that trip. I think my generation was very activist and socially conscious during the Vietnam war. The communist-socialist divide had passed.

ML: *Was any analyst that you knew in the Lincoln brigade?*

ADR: No, but besides Aaron Hilcovich from Chicago and William Pike from New York whom I already mentioned, twenty-five percent of the members of the Lincoln Brigade were Jewish, most of them from New York and more from Brooklyn than the Bronx, Queens or Manhattan, I don't know why.

ML: *Those were the children and grandchildren of the first Jewish immigration, lots of them were socialists.*

ADR: That's right. You know my parents are from Europe as were Jack Arlow's parents, and Charlie Brenner's as well. They certainly didn't talk about their left political commitments.

ML: *Why? Did they abandon them? Were they afraid?*

ADR: Psychoanalysts were not supposed to talk about their personal life or their politics, because that would impact on the transference. I don't know how much that generation knew about each other's politics.

At the NYPSI there were two groups, the ins and the outs. The ins ran the place. The ins were mostly Europeans like Otto Isakower, Ruth Eisler, Kurt Eissler, Lillian Malcove, Nick Stein, Robby Bak… I'll tell you a joke. When Bak was Chairman of the Education Committee he said, "I never took a majority vote lying down". When Otto Isakower was the chair, there were seven women on the committee, Phyllis Greenacre, Ruth Eisler, Annie Reich, Bettina Warburg, Lillian Malcove, Ruth Loveland and Mary O'Neil Hawkins. Someone asked: "Dr. Isakower, what is like to be Chairman of the Education Committee with seven women?", Otto—who was very short—replied: "It's like seven Snow Whites and one dwarf." Otto was a very interesting man; he published 29 pages and became a phenomenon. He went from Berlin to Liverpool, England, before he came to the United States. I always wondered whether his Liverpool connection was why he loved The Beatles.

The politics of the NYPSI was divided between the Europeans and their supporters. Martin Stein and Phyllis Greenacre were not European, but they came out of the tripartite Berlin model, the training analysis was central. The structures were authoritarian, fundamentally anti-democratic and self-perpetuating. On the other side were Jack Arlow, Victor Rosen, Charles Brenner, David Beres, Martin Wangh... the Americans who were not part of the in group. People are amazed when I tell them that Jack Arlow was never on the Education Committee nor was Charlie Brenner. Since they couldn't make it at NYPSI they invested their political energy in the American Psychoanalytic. Jack Arlow was never President of the American, but he did serve as chair of BoPS. There was also a consequence for the politics of the International Psychoanalytical Association (IPA) in 1969. Do you remember who became President of the IPA in 1969?

ML: Leo Rangell?

ADR: Yes. And do you know who wanted to become president? There wasn't an election in those days.

ML: *No, no, it was a sort of consensus.*

ADR: And do you know who decided? Anna Freud decided who would be the president. Heinz Kohut very much wanted to become President and he thought it was a done deal. He had selected his Secretary, Francis Hannett, Gittleson's wife.

ML: *Kohut was from Vienna. He told everyone that he went to the train station when Freud was leaving Vienna and that Freud tipped his hat to him. Freud went to London and Kohut went to Chicago.*

ADR: I think August Aichhorn was his analyst in Vienna and Ruth Eissler in Chicago.

ML: *He developed his own ideas ...*

ADR: Yes, but this was in 1969, before he wrote *The Analysis of the Self*, which was published in 1972. Leo Rangell insisted that Kohut became a self-psychologist because he experienced not becoming President of the IPA as a narcissistic blow. But the fact is that Kohut developed those ideas before 1969. I know the real story. I was able to read the correspondence between Marianne Kris, Ruth Eissler, and Miss Freud about the Kohut matter. Kohut's dream was to become President of the IPA and he was ready to have that dream fulfilled when he was told by Anna Freud "You have to withdraw in favor of Leo Rangell because the Europeans don't want you and we are afraid that Arlow will run against you and be elected." In one letter, Rangell was referred to as the "lesser of two evils"; the greater evil was Arlow-Brenner.

By the way, Jack assured me he had no intention of running for president of the IPA. As I mentioned before, he was afraid to leave the United States because he was afraid he would not be allowed to return because of his Communist Party connection but I don't think that was an issue in 1969. Jack told me he remembered having a meeting with Martin Wangh, David Beres and Charlie Brenner about whether he should run and they all advised him not to run, apparently Ruth Eissler was not aware of that. Her fear was that Jack would run and win and that the IPA would give the Arlow-Brenner group more political clout and that would affect the balance of power at the NYPSI.

ML: *So local politics were more important than the rest of the world.*

ADR: Of course, that is if there was a "rest of the world." Did you know Phyllis Greenacre was against APsaA publishing a roster because people would think that everyone on the roster were real psychoanalysts? For her, the only real psychoanalysts were the psychoanalysts at the NYPSI. This reminds me of the story about Winnicott. He was giving a paper and he put a revolver on the lectern. He said: "That's for the person that says I am not a psychoanalyst."

ML: *Because his last paper was the one on the use of the object.*

ADR: Yeah. It's a long story. He came from London, landed at the airport in the rain and no one came to pick him up. He got pneumonia and had to be hospitalized. Milton Malev, a member of NYPSI paid his hospital bill. He died soon after that. What killed him, the criticism or the pneumonia?

But to return to the 1969 IPA election, Anna Freud didn't like Arlow also because he was for Board Certification for psychoanalysis and not sympathetic to lay analysis or child analysis. Why was Anna Freud so influenced by Ruth Eissler and by Marianne Kris? Miss Freud needed money for the Anna Freud Center. Marilyn Monroe was in analysis with Marianne Kris and was encouraged by her other analyst, Ralph Greenson, to give money to the center. Doug Kirsner has written about these relationships. Not psychoanalysis's finest hour. Royalties from Monroe's estate were a major source of the Anna Freud Centre's income.

ML: *You're referring to a period in which the power that psychoanalysts had in the psychiatry departments in the United States began to peter out. Were they so involved in fighting each other they didn't see what was going on?*

ADR: That's a very good question. To what extent was it our own doing and to what extent did it have to do with factors beyond our control: pharmacology and managed care? The fifties and the sixties were the halcyon days of psychoanalysis. It was what I called the "psychoanalysis a plenty", plenty of patients, plenty of candidates, plenty of prestige and plenty of money for psychoanalysts. Leo Rangell practiced in Los Angeles and treated Hollywood stars who could afford high fees. But, in Los Angeles there was an effort to destroy the Kleinians. It was led by Ralph Greenson and Milton Wexler and Leo to some extent. The internecine warfare diminished our ability to present a united front to the world at large. In the fifties and sixties, we promised more than we could deliver. People expected to be magically altered by psychoanalysis and were disappointed.

ML: *When it was believed that an interpretation could actually cure colitis.*

ADR: That was one issue, the other was arrogance. Dick Simons, who was President of APsaA during the lawsuit, wrote in the *Journal of the American Psychoanalytic Association (JAPA)* that APsaA was not guilty of antitrust violations, it was guilty of arrogance. The arrogance was institutionalized with the reorganization of APsaA in 1948, and the establishment of the BoPS, a self-perpetuating body who would decide who was a good analyst. This was not an attitude that is consistent with the development of a science and a profession.

ML: *Those were who came after the socialists. I mean, those arrogant people who actually perpetuated themselves in power positions.*

ADR: They were not the socialists. Who were they? Was it the Berlin Eitingon model, which had its firm stamp on psychoanalysis? They functioned more like the Communist party in terms of democratic centralism.

ML: *I think it was the model.*

ADR: The Certification Committee is the membership committee of BoPS. They decide who is eligible to become a training analyst. Only training analysts can become fellows of BoPS and elect the BoPS chairs who in turn appoint the Certification Committee that determines who can become a fellow and elect the chairs and so on and so on. It wasn't always that way. Before 1948 there was a Committee of Psychoanalytic Education whose decisions had to be supported unanimously by the institutes. It changed because Sander Rado had left NYPSI and established a new institute at Columbia. There was a concern that Rado would have a three-times-a-week training standard. There was also a concern that William Allison White would want to join APsaA with people who were not physicians. If you review the minutes of the BoPS and the APsaA —for decades— the mantra is the same: it is not "What can we do to advance psychoanalysis?" It is "What can we do to keep people out? What can we do to make rules? What can we do to set standards? How rigid can we be? My major effort as a psychoanalyst and a psychoanalytical political activist has been to try to change that system.

ML: *In the beginning political ideology participated in the development of psychoanalysis and then suddenly it did not.*

ADR: It drops out.

ML: *And then it was as if you're an analyst you should be only an analyst and withdraw from hospitals, from universities and other public and private venues. Psychoanalysis constructed an ivory tower for itself. We are paying a heavy price for that even now. I don't know if you agree with that.*

ADR: Yes. I'll give you some specific examples. When Charlie Brenner wrote a letter to the New York Times about the Vietnam war he was attacked by the members of NYPSI because they said his action would disturb transference. Analysts shouldn't be doing that. There were analysts who were also working in hospitals that couldn't become training analysts because they weren't committed enough to the private practice of psychoanalysis. One of my classmates was Herbert Pardes; he probably is now one of the most important psychiatrists in New York if not in the United States. In fact, the Psychiatric Institute at Columbia University has been named after him. When he graduated, he couldn't become a member of APsaA because he did not want to apply for certification. That didn't make any sense to him. He resigned from NYPSI and APsaA and went on to become one the most important psychiatrists in the United States.

ML: *In a sense, people who run the APsaA, and I think it is the same in different parts of the world, became psychoanalytic fascists. I am not sure if it is the right word .... There was a change of ideology.*

ADR: It all began in 1948 with the establishment of BoPS, which became more exclusive as time went on. When I applied for certification I sent in my cases and got a letter back saying I was certified, this was in 1972. As time went on the procedure became more onerous and they added interviews. Some say it is more like a fraternity hazing than a collegial process: 50% fail the first time but 95% pass with persistence. So, what is the point? Is the test a valid and reliable test of psychoanalytic competence? What? A ritual with no objective criteria for making assessments?

ML: *It was just to keep people out. Then little by little, drugs appeared in the sixties and so forth. Were they fighting the wrong enemy?*

ADR: That's right. I don't know how we can understand the psychology of the people who move the organization and maintain the organization in that kind of hierarchical authoritarian direction.

After the Institute for Psychoanalytic Training and Research (IPTAR) joined the IPA and IPTAR members could become members of the IPA and APsaA, my wife, Arlene Kramer Richards, became a member of APsaA. That pleased me a lot because it had always been my ambition that Arlene could become a member of every organization that I belonged to. I almost made it with the exception of the NYPSI because they have a requirement that you can't become a member even if you are member of the IPA unless you've been trained at an APsaA Institute. Andre Green couldn't become a member of the NYPSI, nor Moisés Lemlij, even if you moved to New York. I fought for decades to get them to agree to train social workers. They finally agreed last year.

But getting back to Arlene, after she became a member of the APsaA I told her "Why don't you get certified? We are actively encouraging members of IPTAR and the Freudian Society to join the APsaA and we wanted to show that all their procedures were fair." She flew to Toronto to be interviewed by the Certification Committee. The member of the committee to whom she presented her cases made no eye-contact. At the end of the meeting, he said "Now, I have what I need." She thought that meant that she had been accepted. No, she was rejected. Keep in mind that at that time Arlene was a training analyst at two institutes and several of her analysands became training analysts themselves. But the committee decided that she was not a competent analyst.

I felt badly that I had put her through this. I was editor of *JAPA* at that time, so I started a discussion about the certification procedure. I began the discussion with a quote from Bob Michels paper, "A Psychoanalytic Case Study", in which he said that the purposes of the Certification Committee and the purposes of the Committee on Scientific Activities are mutually incompatible. He was saying that certification is not scientific. At the time of that discussion if you weren't certified you could be a member, but you couldn't vote, and you couldn't hold office and you couldn't be a training analyst. So, it was a very active discussion back and forth and finally a bylaw amendment was passed. The first delinkage allowed uncertified graduates to become members; the second delinkage allowed all members to vote for everything and run for office. This was a very important change. More recently we submitted a bylaw (Institute Choice) that would allow institutes to appoint members who were not certified. But I remember Sandy Abend, who was from New York and someone I've known quite a long time, said to me "Arnie, I will never forgive you for what you did." "What did I do?" I asked. "You provided a voice, a platform for the people who should not be talking about education."

ML: *What exactly did he mean?*

ADR: He meant that the members list was a platform where ordinary folk, the uncertified, those who were not training analysts, the unwashed and the unanointed, those not part of the educational establishment, could talk about the pros and cons of certification. For some, APsaA is divided into alumni and faculty. The members are from the alumni association and the training analysts are faculty. Another friend, Leon Hoffman, said he will also never forgive me because I destroyed psychoanalytic education.

ML: *That was democratic centralism, which is of course the least democratic of all systems because it perpetuates the Stalinian elite until it dies.*

ADR: The Coordinating Committee of BoPS is composed by the chairs of BoPS and the chairs of the BoPS Committees. The committee chairs are appointed by the chairs of BoPS and the Coordinating Committee meet four times every year. This small group decides BoPS policies, which are then approved by the full Board that meets twice a year. They think they are protecting psychoanalysis from the barbarians—me, Judy Schachter, Paul Mosher, and others. We are the bad guys who are intent on destroying psychoanalysis. By the way, someone who was elected BoPS chair was thrown out of APsaA for boundary violations, Ralph Engle. And one of the recent BoPS chairs said that an uncertified member would become a training analyst over her dead body.

ML: *Do they believe that if psychoanalysis is not kept "pure" it will be destroyed?*

ADR: I really think that mostly it has to do with power and being in charge. They just want to stay in charge. I think it has more to do with power than with principles. I don't know to what extent this is a conviction and to what extent this is a rationalization. They are convinced if they are not in charge that it would be bad for psychoanalysis. When change is imminent, they threaten to leave the organization. They're gonna take their marbles and run. But they don't have a place to go and they won't leave.

ML: *They want to keep things as they were in 1948 in 2010.*

ADR: It's 60 years, it's amazing.

ML: *What amazes me is that most analysts have tolerated this situation for decades.*

ADR: Well, part of it is that if you knock your head against the wall long enough enthusiasm is replaced with apathy and you leave. Nothing can change, so why bother? They are very well organized. They have a machine. They talk to each other. They tell people how to vote, who to vote for or who to vote against. It is like the Daley machine in Chicago. I know first-hand because I was once part of the in-group at NYPSI. They have telephone trees. Their incentive is that their livelihood is based on the training analyst system. Their patients are candidates. And once in power, people are reluctant to stand up against them because the fear is that you won't get faculty appointments or referrals. Real or imagined, actual or magical, fear keeps the system in place. I was able to become an activist in APsaA when I became editor of *JAPA*. Some said I was improperly using my position to give credibility to the opposition who were posting on the members list, but I saw it as my position enabling me to act against the "compact majority." I thought I was doing it for principle. In the end, Marx was right.

ML: *Money.*

ADR: Yes. Don't underestimate how money drives people.

ML: *It looks as if it was, for you, a crucial moment when you became editor of* JAPA.

ADR: I think you are absolutely right. How did I become editor of *JAPA*? First of all, I owe a lot to Homer Curtis. Homer Curtis made me the Editor of the [APsaA] Newsletter. It had no name when I took over. Helen Fisher came up with the name: *The American Psychoanalyst.* Most people felt I did a wonderful job for three years.

ML: *How come? I mean, how did he choose you?*

ADR: Why did he choose me? At that time, I was part of the establishment. I think Shelley Orgel recommended me. I was not known for being political. I trained at NYPSI and was involved in Downstate/NYU, as well. I didn't have a track record as a writer or editor. I was a new achiever. Also, around that time Ed Weinshel was supposed to write a paper for the *Psychoanalytic Quarterly* on the future of psychoanalysis.

ML: *He was the treasurer of the IPA.*

ADR: Yes. Ed Weinshel was a very good friend of Shelley Orgel and he got sick and I wrote the paper "The Future of Psychoanalysis" for the *Quarterly* instead of Ed. It was well received. Charlie Brenner liked it; Jack Arlow liked it. I was a good writer and I had good ideas. I had the right friends in high places.

As I said, I did a good job as editor of *The American Psychoanalyst.* The first issue was dedicated to the 50th Anniversary of the death of Sigmund Freud. I did a lot of historical stuff during the three years I was editor. It became a very engaging newsletter. Lots of interviews and other substantive stuff I didn't want it to be just a house organ. So, then the question of becoming editor of *JAPA....*

ML: *Who was the editor then?*

ADR: The editor was Ted Shapiro.

ML: *Why did you apply?*

Why did I apply? I was encouraged by Jack Arlow and Charlie Brenner. I always had an interest in writing and publishing. I applied for the position. Ed Weinshel was the Chair of the Search Committee, but he got sick and Jack Arlow took his place. Now some people maintain that I got the job because Jack Arlow was Arlene's analyst. The committee included Otto Kernberg, Arnold Goldberg, Herb Schlessinger, Phyllis Tyson and Harry Trosman. In the running were Bob Michels, Ethel Person, Warren Poland, and Bennett Simon. Poland and Bennett Simon sort of dropped out. Ethel Person wanted it very much. Fortunately, Otto, who favored Ethel couldn't make it to the meeting in which I was interviewed. Otto and I had a big falling out because of the IPA election. I supported Hanly who was running against Otto—which is another story. We knew Otto and Paulina when they first came to Topeka. Paulina was a resident with me at Topeka, so I would probably have known Otto longer than anyone else in the APsaA. Arnold Goldberg voted for me even though I had written some very critical papers about self-psychology. In any case, I made a terrific presentation to the Search Committee. I told them things about the journal that they didn't know themselves. Everyone there was positive, and they voted for me. I was told it was unanimous in the end. I was appointed editor in 1993.

That gave me standing in the sense that I was not beholden to anybody. Through self-publishing I increased the revenues of the APsaA by about $900,000. Not chump change as they say. Circulation increased as well as revenues. When I took it over we increased circulation to 4000 from International University Press (IUP), the publisher. At our high point we reached 5,200. When I became editor a lot of the increase of subscribers was from outside of APsaA, from people I knew from IPTAR and the Freudian Society and William Allison White. My approach was to break down walls and become more inclusive. I gave a paper about the politics of exclusion (The Brill Lecture at NYPSI). My thesis was that the shadow of the founder falls over an organization. APsaA's founder was A.A. Brill who was adamantly against lay analysis. APsaA was exclusive in regard to other matters as well. I was determined to be inclusive.

ML: *Becoming editor gave you political power because you could publish and give a voice to whoever you thought fit.*

ADR: I felt secure enough in my psychoanalytic professional position that I could afford to take controversial stands that wouldn't be approved by everybody.

ML: *You increased revenues and subscriptions but then things went back again. This must say something about you and something about the organization. They were not able to maintain what you created or maybe your time was the exception and the real self of The American Psychoanalyst was the one before and the one after you.*

ADR: I have a reputation for being open and inclusive. The original plan for the PEP CD-ROM was to include five journals: *JAPA*, The *Psychoanalytic Quarterly*, The *Psychoanalytic Study of the Child*, The *International Journal of Psychoanalysis* and the *International Review of Psychoanalysis*. Owen Renik and I said we need to include *Contemporary Psychoanalysis*, which is the journal of the William Allison White Society. David Tuckett, the editor of *The International Journal of Psychoanalysis* said that he never heard of *Contemporary Psychoanalysis*, or the William Allison White Society. We said that from the point of scholarship and subscribers more journals would be better. (Now most psychoanalytic journals are included).

I wrote, in my introduction to the first Symposium of the PEP CD-ROMS, that the search engines would bring us together. The symposiums were very successful because they were eclectic and inclusive. We had Kleinians, Relationalists, Self-Psychologists, Freudians, Jungians, and others. Our symposia were much more successful than the programs for mental health professionals run by APsaA. My view was there was a larger world out there and we had to invite presenters from other groups and from other orientations. Freudian contributors outside APsaA were reluctant to submit their papers to *JAPA* because they thought they would not be accepted. My first year as editor I published five papers by members of IPTAR. The rate of acceptance of the papers by IPTAR was higher than for any other group. I think circulation increased because of the expanded authorship.

ML: When did you begin to relate to the wider psychoanalytical world?

ADR: That's a very good question. If I look at my own background, I had to go back to my father who was a Bolshevik. He was a librarian for a unit of Trotsky's army.

ML: *My father was a Bolshevik, as well.*

ADR: In Trotsky's army?

ML: *No, no.*

ADR: My father deserted the Red Army in 1920. He got typhus and was hospitalized in Odessa. He met some Jewish doctors who encouraged him to go to medical school in the Soviet Union. He would be one of the new Soviet men. He went back to his hometown to tell his father of his plans.

His father told him he needed to leave Russia because the Bolsheviks were just as anti-Semitic as the Czarists. My grandfather was a very wise man. He told my father that he hoped someday he would be able to help his two sisters to leave, as well. He deserted the Army and crossed into Rumania in the middle of the night in a small boat with his gun on his lap. In Rumania he joined a Zionist youth group and went to Palestine. He was in Nahalal (Moshe Dayan's *moshav*), worked draining the swamps, got malaria and left in 1924 for the United States. I don't really consider myself a red diaper baby because my father was not politically active, but I was sympathetic to the left as most Jews of my generation were. I was always concerned with social justice. I don't do well with exclusion. I'm big on my civil rights activism, in Petersberg, Virginia, as I have already told you about. I've always felt connected to the larger world. I didn't want to just have an office, treat patients and be oblivious of what's going on in the society around me.

ML: *What about the morals, the moral stand for American psychoanalysts, the idea that if you were working in a hospital you could not be a training analyst?*

ADR: Exactly, right! Their justification was you wouldn't have enough time to see enough patients. It took Ed Shapiro a long time to become a training analyst because he was working in a hospital.

ML: *How did this sort of international background of yours translate into psychoanalysis?*

ADR: I guess you know I'm very involved with Yiddish. I was Chairman of the Board and Director of YIVO Institute for Jewish Research. Many say that the only reason I got involved in the certification discussion was because of my wife's experience. To some extent, that's true, but I don't know if I would have the drive and the commitment without my own imperatives. I have the sense that the American Psychoanalytic Association was given a precious gift by Freud and that we have squandered that legacy because of our arrogance, lack of humility, authoritarian structures, and the politics of exclusion. Whether that accounts for the fact that there are institutes who don't have any candidates and candidates who don't have any patients is not clear. Was it the rigidity of the theory in the hands of some or the fact that the training was not patient centered? The patient has to come four times a week to meet the institute requirement. The patient had to fit the Procrustean bed. Irwin Hoffman told his patient she had to lie on the couch because he wanted to graduate. There is a whole system of conformity and compliance. In the end the patient loses out.

ML: *And all of this because of the shadow of Brill...*

ADR: Psychoanalysis was mostly a medical discipline in the United States because of Abraham [Arden] Brill, who was a poor boy from a *shehtl* in Poland. He came to the United States at age 13 with two dollars in his pocket. Becoming a physician and a psychiatrist was his way of making it in the New World. And he did. Medicine was his ticket to ride. He established the medical identification of psychoanalysis in the United States. The NYPSI and APsaA excluded non-physicians, some of whom might have been more fertilizing. A problem now is that psychiatrists for the most part are not interested in psychoanalysis and the ones who are interested are rather dull. They don't have a humanistic approach. To be a good psychoanalyst you have to be a *gebildet Mensch*. Freud's *Bildung*, his interest in archaeology, history, literature, and the wide span of human culture contributed to making him the psychoanalyst he became. Also, his Judaism. Not ritual and observance, but the ethical system and its roots in the Enlightenment, in the *Haskalah*. Brill had none of that. You can make a case that Brill and APsaA adopted the medical model out of insecurity. Was the board certification model of medicine adopted by APsaA for that reason? It is an interesting question. Did they feel they had to have standards because they were insecure about what they were doing? Freud was insecure in a different way. He felt his theory was at risk from dissidents and heretics like Jung, Adler, Stekel, and others.

ML: Do you believe that this was what allowed psychoanalysis to hold such an important place in society in the United States?

ADR: Well, right now psychoanalysis is more part of the culture in Argentina.

ML: Of the culture, but not of the power structure.

ADR: And in France it's also part of the culture more than in the United States.

ML: But it isn't part of the French establishment.

ADR: Which establishments are you talking about?

ML: Universities and public health institutions.

ADR: There is no question that it became part of that establishment in the United States until the sixties.

ML: And then arrogance and hubris

...

ADR: They could afford to do this exclusion because they were pretty much sitting pretty again. There was a psychoanalysis of plenty and they were very secure, and they wanted power and they wanted to maintain their power. Theodor Reik was at the NYPSI but they wouldn't let him become a full member, so he left and started the National Psychological Association for Psychoanalysis (NPAP). After a while he was referring patients to members of the NYPSI.

ML: *Now let's go back to your story. You finished Topeka?*

ADR: Right, I finished Topeka and as I said it was a very important part of my psychiatric and psychoanalytic development, and to my relationship to non-medical analysis. It was a very good clinical residency. Then I went to Petersburg, Virginia, where I was the Psychiatrist and Chief Medical Officer at the Federal Reformatory. A psychiatrist in a prison is not the model of a psychiatrist in a private office. My effort was to have an impact on the prison environment. I worked more with the staff than with the inmates. I did decide to apply for analytic training either in Washington or in New York. I applied to the Washington Psychoanalytic Institute, and to the Columbia and New York Psychoanalytic institutes. I did not apply to Downstate in Brooklyn because I went to medical school at Downstate. My teachers in psychiatry were from the Downstate Institute: Shelly Orgel, Sam Abrams, Leonard Shengold, Austin Silber… They were *gung-ho* about psychoanalysis.

ML: *The fire?*

ADR: The fire, yes. Some of it came from them. So, I didn't apply to the Downstate institute because I was from Brooklyn. I guess I didn't want to go home again. I wanted to live in Manhattan. I didn't want to commute.

My interview at the Washington Institute was an interesting experience. The committee was Dan Jaffe, Edith Weigert, and Harold Searles. Harold Searles said: "I see you are working in a prison. Is that because your childhood was a prison?" Edith Weigert came to my defense. I had three interviews at New York. My first was with Bernard Fine. Each interviewer saw the applicant three times. The second was Andrew Peto, he was Hungarian. A lovely man. I told him I had a dream the previous night. In the dream someone said to me "That's fine."

Lili Bussell was last. At the end of the third interview, she said: "Dr. Richards, now I understand your case." That, of course, meant that I had passed. She had determined that I was analyzable and therefore was acceptable for the training. The year I applied there were 40 applicants and they accepted 13. My class was 12 men and 1 woman: 12 psychiatrists, 1 psychologist. The psychologist was from the NYU Center for Research in Mental Health. He had to sign a statement that he wasn't going to practice. We had terrific instructors like Rudolph Lowenstein, Otto Isakower, Bert Lewin, Edith Jacobson, Margaret Mahler, Nick Young, Chuck Fisher and Charles Brenner. Those four years were great. I did very well—you know I'm good at doing well in school. I also started my analysis. My analyst was Henry Lowenfeld. He was part of the Freudian left. He was in the Weimar Government in the twenties. He was very smart. He left Berlin in the early thirties anticipating Hitler. He went to Czechoslovakia. He had the foresight to leave early. I had the occasion to talk to his son because someone from Europe wanted to do his father's biography. His son asked me: "Oh, when were you in analysis with my father? Did you help pay for my college education?" He told me a story about when he was 2 years old leaving Berlin. His father found a sign for the car which said *"Judden sind unger unglück*" (Jews are our misfortune). He thought that was why they were able to proceed without being stopped. My analyst was quite *Kosher*. I wonder if there was some way he conveyed to me his own involvement in the left.

ML: *Was he German?*

ADR: Yes, German. He was very different from the usual American analyst in terms of his political background.

ML: *He knew what it was like.*

ADR: And I'm sure something got conveyed to me. Analysts responses can encourage some views and discourage others. I began my training in 1964 and graduated in 1969. Five years, not too bad.

ML: *... but exceptional!*

ADR: Very exceptional. My first supervisor was David Beres. My first case was a person who had hypochondriacal delusions. Analysis went well. My second supervisor was Theodore Lipin. He moved to Sweden and died there. He was analyzed by Lillian Malcove. She said: "even I didn't understand him". Many found his writings totally incomprehensible. Of the 12 people he supervised only two survived: myself and my friend Lester Schwartz.

ML: *Why did you choose him?*

ADR: He was assigned. At NYPSI you don't choose your supervisors.

ML: *That's so un-analytical. In most countries you choose your supervisor.*

ADR: In fact, I didn't choose Henry Lowenfeld. I was assigned to Ruth Loveland. Do you remember her?

ML: *And what happened?*

ADR: She said we would start and then she said that she couldn't because a patient who she thought was terminating didn't. Perhaps it was alphabetical—Loveland, Lowenfeld. My third supervisor, George Gerö, was a wonderful European, different from Lipin and Beres. Lipin attended to the minute by minute process, Gerö was more on to the big picture: the organizing unconscious fantasy and so forth.

ADR: After I graduated, I attended the affiliated staff conferences. The usual thing was for the Europeans to say that the patient was severely disturbed and un-analyzable. The Americans, like Charlie Brenner and Jack Arlow, thought differently. Every patient had conflicts, which you could try to understand, whether it would help or not. That was 1965–1966. I then continued my postanalytic education at the Madison Delicatessen on 86th Street and 3rd Avenue where we had lunch once a week, Charlie Brenner, Bernie Brodsky, Sandy Abend, Mervin Peskin, Arlene and me. We would discuss psychoanalysis. Now I remember it must have been around 1972 that Charlie said to me, "You know this fellow Heinz Kohut? He has written a new book. Read it and let me know what you think".

ML: *You mentioned Otto Kernberg in your days at Topeka. He has developed very influential ideas. I don't know if one can call them a school but certainly he must be one of the most familiar names of American psychoanalysis today.*

ADR: Yes, Kohut and Kernberg had two different approaches to narcissism and narcissistic disorders…

ML: *That was in the seventies, but your disagreement with Otto was not theoretical but political.*

ADR: With Otto my political disagreement was not until the Hanly Election. What year was Otto elected president? [Otto Kernberg was President of the IPA 1997–2001]

ML: *Around 1993 or 1994.*

ADR: Yes, because it was after I became editor of *JAPA*. I had a very good relationship with Otto until that time. Paulina called up Arlene and said: "Are you voting for Otto?" and Arlene told her she was going to vote for Charles Hanly because he did a lot to help IPTAR. Otto and Paulina got very upset with us because we supported Hanly.

ML: *Did you support Hanly because of Arlene?*

ADR: Yes.

ML: *That's a different chapter.*

ADR: I was on Otto's side because, in my view, unlike Kohut I felt conflict was more important than deficit. I titled the *Festschrift,* I edited for Charlie, *Psychoanalysis: The Science of Mental Conflict.*

ML: *You are not that convinced about that…*

ADR: I believe that conflict and deficit are interactive variables. Conflict leads to deficit and deficit impacts on the way conflict is experienced. I have a problem with dichotomies. That was my problem with Stephen Mitchell and Jay Greenberg, their drive vs relational dichotomy. I think the reason Freud has survived as well as he has is because he never came down on one or the other side of a dichotomy. It was always nature and nurture, conflict and deficit. He had a complex view of human mental functioning. Otto had referred me patients. We were close to the Kernbergs socially and we sold them our first house in Maine. But I guess it was Arlene's falling out that became the problem between us.

ML: *I participated a lot at the IPA when he was president. He made important modifications. He eliminated the House of Representatives that Horacio Etchegoyen established and organized the current Board of Representatives, which is elected regionally. While it appears to be democratic, I don't think it is. I think the House of Delegates allowed a better representation for societies and their memberships. But that's a different story.*

ADR: I tend to agree with you because I do sense right now a distance between the IPA and most members of the APsaA.

ML: *But the APsaA has never been too close to the IPA. Something that comes to my mind is that because of the regional rotation the current president is a Canadian, not an American, and the previous president from North America was Otto who is really marginal to the Americans in many ways. He was not an American mainstream representative. So, I think for the last 20–30 years there have been no real representatives of the American. I think there might be something important about this because maybe half of Latin American psychoanalysts vote in the elections but only 10% to 15% of American psychoanalysts vote.*

49

ADR: And mostly from the non-IPAs institutes in the USA, correct? There is a long history. Look what happened in the thirties with the International Training Committee. NYPSI said they were not going to let the IPA tell them how to train and who to train and took a very strong stand against lay analysis, which was enshrined in the Maresfield Garden agreement. APsaA was not going to subordinate themselves to any organization including the IPA. APsaA and BoPS would be a law unto themselves. There was very serious consideration of having a Board of Psychoanalysis. Jack Arlow and Charlie Brenner were in favor, but it got sunk because of the fear that if they had become part of the American Psychiatric Association as a medical specialty board, they would become subservient to them. No one was going to tell them who to train, and how to train. Everyone outside their circle was excluded, a small number of people ran the show. Those not in power become apathetic or dropped out so the majority of the ruling class increased. The opposition got marginalized or melted away. Psychoanalysis paid a heavy price for this.

ML: *Where is the APsaA right now?*

ADR: I think the APsaA has a problem. They are talking about having one national meeting rather than two, membership is declining, members are getting older, the dues base is going down, the number of candidates is decreasing. They're fighting over a system to allow psychoanalysts who haven't been trained in the APsaA to become members. They are trying to define functional equivalence, but BoPS is the naysayer in this effort. If we won't take people from the outside and we have fewer new members from the inside (our own graduates) our prospects are not very good.

ML: *So, the big enemy of American psychoanalysis is the BoPS.*

ADR: The big enemy in the APsaA in my opinion is the small number of people who control the BoPS. I have a friend who died last year who said to me "You know, Arnie, we've had a good ride. Who cares about what happens next?" They would rather maintain the purity and the power of their position than do things that would benefit the organization as a whole. I am not sure I understand what motivates those people. But one thing is sure, I am certainly *persona non grata* among those folks. I have been called a loose cannon and a gadfly. One member of the NYPSI said: "Arnie we need you to be a gadfly, but we don't want you to drink hemlock". I see myself differently. I feel I'm trying to save them from themselves. I like the quote from *The Leopard:* "If you want things to stay the same, they have to change". I did convince the NYPSI to train those with a Masters of Social Work.

It took 15 years during which I was considered a loose cannon clinically, maybe politically... I mean, I tried very hard and finally I've succeeded in getting them to train them, but it's been about 20 years. BoPS adopted a new certification procedure, which was an improvement but not enough. There's no transparency.

ML: *What is the current make-up of the APsaA membership?*

ADR: Probably the largest consumers of psychoanalytic treatment and training and practitioners are social workers. That's the trend in the United States in my opinion. So even among psychologists it's becoming less the thing. There is an upside, from what I've seen among some of the candidates. Since psychoanalysis is not a very lucrative profession with a lot of prestige, we are beginning to now see people going into training who are committed to the endeavor as they're not motivated by these other things that motivated people in the past. There are some people that are really attracted by the intellectual challenge of psychoanalysis: to understand how the mind works.

This may be because of one's own experience in analysis, and there are some analytic enterprises that are very exciting. *Philoctetes* sponsors meetings and round tables with psychoanalysts, academics, poets, neuroscientists. My point is that the profession is not as attractive as it has been in the past but there remains an inherent excitement in plumbing the depths of the human psyche. I wrote in my paper on "The Future of Psychoanalysis" that psychoanalysis will provide concepts for the neuroscientist to discover rather than neuroscientists just finding ways to validate our concepts.

ML: *I think that's great. Have you been in touch with neuroscientists?*

ADR: I just read them. And I have a lot of stuff on my website www. internationalpsychoanalsyis.net which talks about these connections. Unfortunately, I don't go to the neuroscience meeting because it's on Saturday, we're up in the country on Saturday.

ML: *Can you explain to me a little bit more about the fact that we, as analysts, think or conceptualize something and then neuroscientist might find it interesting?*

ADR: For example, the psychoanalytic concept of defense. We should have some neurophysiological correlates. Charles Fisher was a pioneer psychoanalytic neuroscientist. He had some ideas about dreams and REM sleep. He went into the laboratory and discovered the penile erectile cycle. There are some studies that have demonstrated a connection between loss and panic disorder, which should have neurophysiological correlates. Our clinical experience is that early loss has a profound impact on development.

Donald Klein, among others, has been looking into the neurophysiology and neuropharmacology of loss. Trauma has important developmental sequelae. My point is that psychoanalytic concepts derived from clinical experience can provide fodder for neuroscientific studies.

ML: *You were saying, in a way, that we analysts may make interesting contributions to neurological sciences, but this does not necessarily mean that we are going to profit from what they discover. So, in a sense it is the other way around. Because some people may think that neurophysiological discoveries may be beneficial for us analysts, but you are saying that it is the other way around.*

ADR: At the moment I'm taking that position. That's my point. But we may benefit from the interaction with people in other sciences. For decades we kept aloof from other disciplines and we paid a price. It impacted on our prestige and we got fewer patients that way because when we connect with academics and show them we understand something, they may end up becoming our patients, as well.

ML: *What do you see in APsaA's future?*

ADR: There are things that concern me a lot. For example, the NYU institute has disconnected from the NYU Department of Psychiatry. The Department is interested mostly in money and grants. I am not sure how long the Columbia Institute will stay connected to the Columbia Department of Psychiatry after Herb Pardes leaves. NYPI has a loose connection with Mt. Sinai but it is essentially free standing. At Columbia the main source of candidates are psychiatric residents. They go into training for a low-cost analysis and many drop out before they finish classes.

ML: *But it is as if you feel more hopeful about the non-APsaA societies.*

ADR: Yes, IPTAR is doing quite well because they have a program of respecialization. They take people who are not physicians or psychologists, give them clinical experience under supervision, and make them into psychoanalysts. Some are from overseas and come with student visas. I hear that they are a lively group: smart, interested, and committed. In the 1930s, things were different in the United States. Psychoanalysis didn't have status in the culture. Those who went into analysis for treatment or training were interested and committed and now.... It's very hard to predict the future. I like to quote the young girl that Selma Fraiberg treated who said, "Dr. Fraiberg, you are very good in backwards fortune-telling".

ML: *Prophets of the past.*

ADR: So, the question you raised is how can we develop a more vibrant profession when there's more that's interesting, attractive, and exciting to people who have ability, intellectual interests, and clinical skills?

ML: *Obviously, you are interested in publications. You increased the readership but somehow you were not able to teach your successor how to do that part of the job.*

ADR: Let me talk about what I did that was successful in *JAPA*. First of all, I redesigned the cover: new logo, new graphics. I feel very pleased that my successor has kept my design. We had a different color for each season so if you looked on your shelf you could identify the recurrent issues—Summer, Fall, Winter, Spring. I was also trying to make a statement that *JAPA* was changing. My aim as editor was to give the journal a voice. I wanted to forge a relationship between myself as editor and the readership. I liked to do thematic issues: papers from different authors talked to each other. I ran *JAPA* as a collective. I like collectives. My associate editors were Glenn Gabbard, Phyllis Tyson, Larry Friedman, Harry Smith, Bonnie Litowitz. All were actively involved. Every paper was read and responded to within three months, four months max. That's not what is happening now, I am told. I rarely, if ever, overruled the judgments of my three readers. Some journal editors do just that. I would always try to mediate the differences of opinions. Some papers would go through three or four revisions before they would be accepted. I had a file of dozens of letters sent to me by rejected authors telling me how much they appreciated the critique. I also liked doing supplements, theme issues, and anniversary issues. I published plenary addresses with commentaries. I developed an internal interactive format to engage the readers. I was trying to forge a connection with the readers. If readers feel that the journal has an identity, they are more likely to maintain their subscription. A journal should be more than a series of papers. The current editor has several other jobs including Director of the Institute, and the Head of the Department of Psychiatry.

ML: *You mean an editor has to be an editor and that's it.*

ADR: Correct. Other editors told me they spent five hours a week on the job. For me it was a 24/7 job. I was involved in every detail including production and marketing.

ML: *How much were you paid?*

ADR: $25,000. Do you know that story? They had removed the stipend and I was ready to start with no stipend. There was a meeting with the Executive Council and Ted Shapiro came and said: "This is ridiculous, you have to pay the editor." and then someone from the Executive Council said "This is ridiculous! *JAPA* will be on your bookshelves long after you're gone." The Council voted to restore the stipend even though I would have worked for no money.

ML: *What happens now?*

ADR: *JAPA* is now much more medically oriented. More research papers are published although I'm very underwhelmed by some of them.

ML: *I think part of the reason why a lot of people voted for Charles Hanly is because he is a non-research person. However, he raised the budget for research, so in a way he has disappointed a lot of people and now there is a lot of money each year given to two things: the school of Peter Fonagy, where people are trained for research, and to people who actually do research. More than half of all the money in the IPA goes there while for instance cultural endeavors only get $20,000 a year.*

ADR: I always thought that is what happened when Otto Kernberg was running against Charles. Otto promised Bob [Wallerstein] he would give him money for research if he supported him. I think for the first year Bob did get $150,000 for research. Is that correct?

ML: *It might be. I don't know the amount, but I know that in a way, he was in charge of that budget. There was a committee to assess projects but basically, he was the chair.*

ADR: Is there any effort to evaluate the cost-effectiveness of these projects in terms of psychoanalysis?

ML: *When I was the Treasurer, I did write exactly that. I suppose that was one of the reasons why Otto was so strong against me on several occasions. Peter has been asked to justify and he did edit a publication, which has 300 copies, with a review of some of the research but basically there has never been a review of the research projects that have been subsidized with millions of dollars.*

ADR: It's my feeling that we should spend money on cultural programs to connect with real people and give them some sense of what psychoanalysis is about. Some may seek training or become patients. I'm always interested in doing things that bring organizations into the community and connect them with people. That's what psychoanalysis needs right now. Otherwise, it will become a dinosaur, a relic.

ML: *I don't understand why Charles has continued that policy.*

ADR: I had the sense that somehow, he was taken by David Tuckett and Peter Fonagy. How did that happen?

ML: *I don't know.*

ADR: When Charles wanted me to be on his committee for the website, he let me know that he wanted Tuckett, as well. I think he views him as an expert. But I never did get on the committee.

ML: *Anyway… I wonder how you would describe your own psychoanalytic ideas.*

ADR: In terms of theory, my approach is patient centered. You follow the patient rather than the patient following you. Theodor Reik wrote about listening with the third ear, I would add listening with the fourth ear. Listening, being mindful of everything you know about different theoretical approaches to the patients' pathology. The fourth ear includes not only different psychoanalytic psychological ideas but also neurophysiological concepts. And it is not enough to be right, you also have to be helpful. You always try to understand what has caused the patients' difficulty. The patient who gains understanding is different. The patient has changed. Brenner is more specific about what constitutes change. Charlie has a much more specific idea about what you are trying to do, namely, help the patient have more pleasure, less anxiety, less guilt and better adaptation. Another broad framework.

ML: *You know how to achieve that.*

ADR: You ask yourself "Have I achieved that"? You have an idea about what you are looking for. But there is not only one way. In every instance; with every patient you need to determine why the patient is unable to have pleasure, why he/she has too much anxiety, has too much guilt and not enough adaptation.

ML: *If you try to understand that with your patients perhaps even the process of trying produces an improvement.*

ADR: That's my conviction and you need to have conviction to do this work. Einstein said that if you don't have a sense that it is possible to figure out how the universe works, why bother? You can't have a totally relativistic approach to your patients. You have to have a sense that you know something and that what you know can be conveyed to the patient and will be helpful. But also figuring out why a certain understanding doesn't lead to change can also be helpful. I think I have changed along with my patients. I see patients now in a much less rigid, open fashion. Why do they say the patients now are less neurotic?

ML: *They say you find more depressive and more borderline patients now. That they are different from the classic neurotic ones.*

ADR: All I can tell you is that when I was in training the patients were just as borderline then as they are now and just as depressed then as they are now. As for the widening scope, the patients haven't changed. Who we are willing to treat has changed. I've seen patients who supposedly were psychotic, *meshuggah,* until you get to know them as individuals. Patients are hungry. They need a connection with someone who is dedicated to trying to understand them and help them rather than use them or misuse them.

ML: *You use meshuggah as a broad clinical definition. That brings me to your connection with the Jewish mind, to Yiddish as different from Jewish in general. I mean, you were talking about your Bolshevik ancestors, about the centrality of being a Jew.*

ADR: The fact is psychoanalysis is a quintessential Galitzianer enterprise. The first fourteen analysts in Freud's group were from Galicia themselves or their parents were from Galicia. Now how do you account for that? And Freud's whole life and work was played out, in my opinion, in the context of his *shtetl* origins and has a relation to anti-Semitism. That's where psychoanalysis began.

ML: *The relation with anti-Semitism. Explain what you have in mind.*

ADR: Anti-Semitism was very much part of Freud's life and experiences from 1880 on. Freud joined the B'nai B'rith where he presented some of his work. He wanted to be part of the Gentile establishment, part of academia, but that was impossible because of anti-Semitism. When I was a candidate we had classes on Yom Kippur. I was one of those who insisted that we shouldn't have classes on Yom Kippur. They were all trying to be assimilated rather than recognize their own identity. How does that impact on an analysis? Kohut denied that he was Jewish. After he died, one of his analysands told me he felt betrayed because Kohut would not acknowledge that he was Jewish and when he died his analysands and his colleagues found out.

ML: *He was supposed to have left Vienna...*

ADR: So? But he got Bar Mitzvah and wouldn't tell his colleagues that he was Jewish. He would make a point of going into a Kosher restaurant and ordering a ham sandwich as if he didn't know. He was a deceiver. He would not acknowledge that he was the analysand, Mr. Z. I think this is important. Psychoanalysis was created by a Jew and its first hearings were Jewish. Now these Jews were mostly secular Jews (Freud did write *The Interpretation of Dreams* in *Shul*). Being a Jew had to do with a commitment to humanistic values, the Enlightenment. Humanism and the intellect were the central aspects of Freud's Jewish identity. When he left Vienna and disbanded the Vienna Psychoanalytic Society, he said he was reminded of what the Jews did after the destruction of the Second Temple. Rabbi Johanan ben Zakkai went to Yavna and founded an academy, which is interesting because of what they studied at that academy. Of course, they studied the Tanakh at that academy. So here is Freud, the godless Jew, celebrating Johanan ben Zakkai, who was anything but a godless Jew. But I think the importance of how psychoanalysis developed a relation to humanistic values and the value of the intellect is a very important part and should be a part of the identity of an analyst. This is a part of my identity as a psychoanalyst.

ML: *Were you involved in the Jewish thinking? I mean, you were going to Yiddish schools from your childhood.*

ADR: I was a secular Jew. My father was an atheist who went to the movies on Yom Kippur so he could drive my mother crazy because she was from an orthodox family. Then, of course, I became orthodox myself, maybe that involved some kind of connection in the relationship to my mother. But in college it changed dramatically. I went to Quaker meetings and worked for the United Farm Service Committee and disconnected myself from being Jewish. In medical school I was too busy for religion. In Topeka we sent out our children to Sunday school at the local congregation. We wanted to invite Harry Golden, editor of the *Carolina Israelite to* speak about integration. The rabbi was not very happy about it. He thought the local folk would say "Oh yes, do you wanna bring all your n****r friends?" It was only when I came back to New York that I joined the Synagogue so our son could get Bar Mitzvah. Then I got involved in YIVO.

ML: *That was central for you.*

ADR: Yes, that became central for me. I organized a conference on anti-Semitism: "Old Demons New Debates: Anti-Semitism in the West", and one on the Jewish World of Sigmund Freud at YIVO. We were responsible for the Yiddish revival in New York. I organized the first New York Yiddish Film Festival in 1972 and the second one in 1973. I brought together several institutions: YIVO, the Jewish Museum, the American Jewish Congress, the Workmen Circle, the 92nd Street Y. That, in itself, was an accomplishment.

I learned a lot from bringing groups together, which I also did at the PEP CDROM symposiums. YIVO was responsible for the *klezmer* revival. The people that worked for us mined our extensive collection of *klezmer* sheet music.

ML: *What about anti-Semitism? I think there is a revival again.*

ADR: Of course, there is. When Freud's father told him about the hat in the gutter incident, he was eleven years old. The incident happened before Freud was born. It was a more anti-Semitic time. The decade of 1860 was a much better time for the Jews, his father in telling the story about the hat knocked off his head was saying how much better things are now for Jews. For Freud it meant his father was a coward.

In the 1870s there was a big bank failure just as happened in the United States recently. A lot of banks failed because of the cheap imports from the United States and a housing bubble. Of course, the Jews were blamed. Around this time, the pogroms in Eastern Europe began—in 1880s. Anti-semitism was really on the rise. Lueger, an anti-Semite, was elected mayor of Vienna. Jews became less hopeful about becoming part of society. It wasn't going to work. How did this impact on Freud? James Cuddihy wrote a book, *The Ordeal of Civility*. His thesis is that one of the things that Freud was doing by talking about the unconscious as universal, was affirming that the Gentiles are just as *shmutsik* as us. Freud's generation had a problem with their identification and connection with their fathers and their wish to become part of a society and part of the Enlightenment. What they did, in my opinion, was to become introspective and more self-aware about what was going on. I think that this is part of the whole ethos of psychoanalysis. During this period in the Habsburg empire there were two sciences that were established by Jews, one was psychoanalysis and the other was sociology. The people who started sociology were all or almost all Hapsburg Jews. I think the idea is the same. Sociology is an effort to understand oneself and how this has an impact on the culture.

ML: *Why did you get interested in YIVO?*

ADR: I am very interested in history. Interest in YIVO, in Yiddish, and in Judaism, connect with my interest in history. I've also been interested in and written about the history of the American Psychoanalytic Association. I comment that it seemed strange that we as psychoanalysts are so interested in the history of our patients but have little interest in the history of our own institutions. How do we account for that?

ML: *You tell me.*

ADR: Denial, avoidance, repression. A need not to know. It's easier to think about the history of our own patients than to think about our own history.

ML: *But for psychoanalysis that sounds dramatic. I was reading a paper by Ricardo Steiner on how terrible Ernest Jones, and even Freud, behaved with religion, with Vienna and Berlin societies.*

ADR: On what specifically?

ML: *Actually, they were negotiating with Goring.*

ADR: Oh, yes, yes.

ML: *And accepting the exclusion of Jews by those societies.*

ADR: The one who was admirable in that regard was Richard Sterba, who wasn't Jewish. He said if the Jews go, he would leave as well. He is Bob Michels' father-in-law.

ML: *No!*

ADR: You didn't know that?

ML: *No. no, no… I think there are so many things that we don't like to know about our origins as analysts that actually somehow have chosen our behavior, but there are some exceptions in New York psychoanalytic wars.*

ADR: That was written by Doug Kirsner in his book *Unfree Associations*. He got a lot of it from me. But this connects with the more general principle about psychoanalysis and the attitude of the elite. The idea that patients certainly shouldn't know about bad stuff in relation to Freud or anyone else because that would disturb the transference and would affect the treatment. I think there is something about hiding bad things and hiding secrets from yourself and the community and the patient…

ML: *And they are rationalizing. I'm not telling you the truth because you can be damaged …*

ADR: Exactly, exactly. As if they are protecting psychoanalysis, right? But they are protecting their own position, their own standing, their own posture in the field, rather than really protecting psychoanalysis. If we are going to have any standing in the scientific and academic arena, we have to tell the truth. We can't have secrets. One of the big complaints about how institutes run is the lack of transparency, so people can't say what they think because maybe a candidate may hear what they're saying, and this would affect the analysis. I think they believe that, but I think that comes out of insecurity and fear.

ML: *But we are talking about anti-Semitism being a big sword of Damocles hanging over every Jew, and that's how secure you feel. Suddenly, you might feel Vienna: half of the physicians were Jews and the lawyers were Jews. What can happen to you? And then it does. This is a big era of anti-Semitism, again. Something that nobody thought might occur again and then it happened.*

ADR: Let me get back to what was happening in Vienna. At that time the Jews were very successful. Freud himself and other Jews thought that the cause of anti-Semitism was the unwashed, *unkempt shtetl* Jews who came from the *shtetl* and were very much present in Vienna. That is what was causing anti-Semitism. I think that was a rationalization. I think it was the Gentile envy of the success of the Jews. It was the successful Jews that generated anti-Semitism rather than feelings about the poor Jews. I am convinced that Freud was very embarrassed, ashamed of his *shtetl* Galician origins. He made the point that his parents or grandparents came originally from Western Germany, Hamburg. He had a family romance about his origins. He didn't want to locate his family in Galicia. That's what he said. There was an article in Haaretz in the late '30s by someone named Grinberg. He traveled to Vienna from Buchach and gave a paper about a play "Yochanan The Prophet, a *shtetl* Jew" where he quotes Freud saying, "I would rather be the Jew in the tuxedo than the Jew in the koftin". I think Freud was very sensitive and embarrassed about his *shtetl* origins, when it impeded his efforts to assimilate. On the other hand, he was very proud of being a Jew in his own terms. He said, "I used to be a German, my language was German, my culture was German, but because of anti-Semitism, I am a Jew." I think now, Jews say it's really not because of us but because of the Israelis. They do not recognize that anti-Semitism comes not from Israel, but from the same roots that anti-Semitism has come from for two thousand years.

ML: *Which are? I've just read* My Unwritten Books *by George Steiner. He is a secular Jew…*

ADR: I've heard about it.

ML: *He says the main cause of anti-Semitism is that we have killed God. But, first, how can you kill God? And second, if we had killed God that is why Christianity exists. So, they hate us not because we have killed God but because we had given them a God.*

ADR: That's exactly the point. The problem is that Christianity and Islam are derivatives of Judaism and Abrahamaic traditions that came from Judaism. That's why Christians have to kill us. That is why the Muslims have to get rid of us as well.

ML: *There is an extra bit for your excitement. Steiner says that we have given them such a terrible God that they are right to hate that God. The problem is that instead of hating God and denying it, they accept that God and they hate the people who have given them that God.*

ADR: That's all about the same thing.

ML: *But what sort of a hate. I'm thinking in the Venezuelan president Chavez and his association with the Iranians. I think there is a real risk that I feel.*

ADR: Of course! But what happened to Castro? He must've had some sort of connection with Jews who came early from Europe in his earlier life. All of a sudden, he was saying nice things about Israel.

ML: *About Jews, but he is also now changing his mind about homosexuality because in the beginning they persecuted homosexuals.*

ADR: And now he's not?

ML: *Now he says that it was a mistake... You were saying that an important part of your involvement with Jewish issues derives from your interest in history...*

ADR: It is also my connection to my parents, to my family who came from Eastern Europe and my father who came from Podolia. I wrote an article for the *YIVO Encyclopedia* on psychoanalysis in Eastern Europe, an article about Jews in American Psychoanalysis, which is in the *Encyclopedia of American Jews* and an article in *Encyclopedia Britannica*—the health and science issue—which is entitled "Psychoanalysis Burgeoning and Beleaguered." It was written in the '80s. My wife tells me that when I go to a dinner party the first things I ask are, "Where are you from? Where were your parents from? Where were your grandparents from?" The idea that Moses was an Egyptian was Freud's origination myth for the Jewish people. The myth is that he really wasn't originally Jewish, but he was Egyptian. It is part of his family romance as a Jew in Habsburg Vienna.

ML: *And a prince, because he was not a humble Jew, he was really a prince.*

ADR: Right. He wanted to be the son of Hannibal and his father would not be who he was.

ML: *Yes, and the Jewish general Napoleon who was not Jewish, but he thought he was.*

ADR He thought he was. You know why Freud's father left Freiburg?

ML: *I think he didn't do well there.*

ADR: Yes, but do you know why the business failed? Because the train did not stop anymore at Freiburg. They changed the station. What if they hadn't changed the station and he had stayed in Freiburg? What would Freud have become?
A wool manufacturer? A factory manager?

ML: *Or if he had emigrated with his relatives to England and become a very rich man. What about his grandson? He is one of the top painters in the world.*

ADR: Incredible.

ML: *18 to 19 million dollars per picture.*

ADR: But he has a lot of problems. He's a gambler apparently but he buys a lot of houses.

ML: *What about being married to an analyst? What about Arlene's process?*

ADR: That's a very important question. We got married when I was finishing college on the first day in spring, March 21, 1954. Then I started medical school. Arlene, who was also a graduate of the University of Chicago, worked to support us for the four years in medical school and all she had was a BA. She gave up pursuing a career at that time. I always had the wish that somehow Arlene would also have a successful career, and when she did, I had the wish that she should belong to every organization I belonged to. That was why I became involved in the lawsuit, which is a whole other story. When I was in medical school, she taught at a public school. During my stint in Petersburg, she taught Remedial Reading at Richard Bland College. She began treating children and adolescents with learning disabilities. When we moved to New York for my analytic training, she started an Ed.D. at Teachers College. She took mostly statistics courses because in clinical or theoretical psychology courses she was identified as the wife of a Freudian. Her instructors would ask her, "What would Freud say about that?". Her thesis was on language acquisition in 6-year-olds (our youngest daughter was 6 years old). She got her Ed.D. and she applied to the NYPSI as a research candidate. She brought all her research data to the interview. I'm sure David Kairys and John McDevitt had no idea what it was about; they asked her if she was interested in practice. She said, "Yes" and wasn't accepted. Arlene has never gone to an Institute. She has had no formal training. It is like being home-schooled. You know that?

ML: *No.*

ADR: She is an autodidact. She couldn't get into an institute, so she decided to train on her own. She went into analysis with Jack Arlow, she paid for supervision, she got a group of people who met with George Gross, read all of Freud, and took other courses. She was in supervision with Donald Kaplan who was running for president at the Freudian Society against Emily Anne Gargiulo. He said, "Do me a favor, join the Freudian Society, and vote for me". She joined the Freudian Society and after she became a member, she became involved in the lawsuit and I did, as well. When the lawsuit was settled, she became a member of the IPA, IPTAR and APsaA. That is how she became an *echt* psychoanalyst. We have always shared offices. We practice together where we live. Her *hegira* is an interesting story. I think she has been much better for not having formal institute training.

ML: *So, she must have been one of the very few cases of an analyst who has become an analyst through alternative routes.*

ADR: Correct. I don't think there are that many but clearly she was a very determined person and I was determined.

ML: *And how did you feel in those days? You were a member of NYPSI when she was not accepted.*

ADR: Well, I wasn't very happy about it. I thought that it was totally stupid.

ML: *How active was she in the lawsuit and you as well?*

ADR: There was a meeting of Division 39 in Puerto Rico to organize the lawsuit. I remember the group: Arlene, Ernie Lawrence, Rita Frankiel, Nat Stockhammer. Someone turns to me and says, "What are you doing here? Aren't you a member of The American Psychoanalytic Association?" "Of course," I said. And then they said: "Are you a spy for Herb Schlessinger?" Herb was a member of the American and not that sympathetic with the lawsuit. We gave a lot of money to the lawsuit. Money made the difference.

How did it come about? It was clear to the psychologists that the whole thing was unfair. There were several motivations. Some had misgivings about winning the lawsuit because they wondered what impact this would have on their own institutes. APsaA was preventing their members from teaching and supervising in non-medical institutes. That could be construed as restraint of trade. Some felt that they should pursue the suit with the hope that it would bankrupt APsaA. So, there were three different attitudes: some felt they shouldn't sue, some felt they should sue because it would open up training, and some had a 'burn the house down' attitude. They got Bryant Welch. He was a psychoanalyst and a lawyer.

There were four people in the suit: Arnie Schneider, Bryant Welch, Helen Desmond and Toni Bernay. There was a meeting with Ed Joseph, President of the APsaA in Washington to work out a settlement. After the meeting Joseph sent Division 39 a bill for his dry cleaning. The plaintiffs thought this was the ultimate arrogance. Joseph said it was a mistake. Then Dick Simons became president. Dick was terrific. The smoking gun was that Ed Joseph said in some public meeting that this really was a pocketbook issue. We can't let you win because it would affect our livelihood. The lawyer from Paul Weiss argued our request for summary judgment and lost. Jack Arlow and I felt that we were very poorly represented. The lawyer that APsaA used was the lawyer NYPSI used. I got a call from Fred Pine, who said that they were going to file an anti-trust action. I told this to Helen Fisher who told this to Dick Simons and they agreed that they needed another lawyer. Dick Simon had met Joel Klein at a meeting at the American Psychiatric Association. He hired Joe Klein. That made all the difference because Joel Klein was determined to settle the lawsuit. Kaplan, the lawyer from Paul Weiss, said we could win but Klein said no way. Dick thought we shouldn't win and, in the end, losing the lawsuit saved the APsaA.

ML: *What did you feel at the time?*

ADR: I was all for settling the lawsuit. My only reservation was we should train psychologists but shouldn't be forced to do it. But the fact is that if they hadn't had a lawsuit, we would still be deliberating.

ML: *What about living with a psychoanalyst or being a psychoanalytic couple?*

ADR: I feel incredibly lucky, fortunate to have this kind of relationship. There's so much that we can do together and share. I joined the Freudian Society, I belong to the American Psychological Association, I belong to Division 39, both of us belong to all those organizations together. You know she doesn't belong to the NYPSI or TPI or NYU but we both belong to the Psychoanalytic Association of New York (PANY). We go to meetings together so that gives us many opportunities for a certain kind of connection. Arlene writes her things and I write my things, but we also collaborate. We've written things together. We wrote a very interesting paper about gambling and three Las Vegas movies: *Leaving Las Vegas, Bugsy,* and *Casino.* It was published several years ago. We wrote a paper together on the relationship between psychoanalytic theory and psychoanalytic technique. We used a case of Arlene's. We had responses from Self psychologists, Kleinians, Relationalists, and others. They responded and then we responded to the responses. It's a very good paper. It is published in the journal of the NYPSI, which is now defunct. We are going to present the paper in Mexico City [IPA Congress 2011] and respond to candidates' presentations from three institutes.

ML: *What comes to my mind is that actually all of the 39, the lawsuit and everything else was also a fight of Arlene to join you.*

ADR: That's correct. You're absolutely correct.

ML: *In a way she wanted to be legitimate, to become your true wife, your mate, not a sort of professional mistress. She wanted to be your professional wife.*

ADR: That's right because this gives us a kind of equal footing and equal status. We both see patients, we both practice very similarly, we go to meetings together, we write together. What more can we want from a relationship? Not many people have that advantage, have that luxury, which it certainly is. Socially I am more involved with her friends, I'm more connected with her groups than I am with my own.

ML: *Why? How come?*

ADR: Because most of the people that I know belong to the Freudian Society and IPTAR. I'm not that socially involved with the people at the NYPSI because they see me as the maverick, the loose cannon or whatever. I used to belong to CAPS, The Center for Advanced Psychoanalytic Studies in Princeton. It is another organization that perpetuates the elitism of the APsaA. I wanted to present the Mexico paper at CAPS with Arlene, but they refused because she wasn't a member of the group. I ended up resigning from the group. I think on some level there was a certain amount of hostility toward Arlene, perhaps because of the lawsuit.

ML: *Did they see you as a traitor?*

ADR: You know what? My friends excuse it by saying, "Well you were just doing it for your wife. So that wasn't so bad. You really didn't believe it, but you are doing it for your wife". Do you follow that?

ML: *Yes, yes.*

ADR: And the same thing with the certification thing. Some said: "The only reason you're doing this is because of your wife". The group does not tolerate dissidence. They have a fixed point of view and dismiss or deny contradictions.

ML: *Is APsaA now accepting psychologists?*

ADR: They certainly accept psychologists and I don't think there's any discrimination at all but it's curious because some of the non-medical people are becoming even more conservative and supportive of the BoPS exclusionary principles. Perhaps it is identification with the aggressor.

ML: *It is because they have become part of the elite.*

ADR: Right, I won't mention names but there are people I can think of along those lines.

ML: *What about your children in terms of having a mother and father who are psychoanalysts?*

ADR: I think children of psychoanalysts are very wary about psychoanalysis. I think all of our children have been in treatment of one kind or another and have their own issues. I was just having a conversation with our daughter today about the trip to Mexico and I was very pleased that she was interested.
I'm very reluctant to tell the kids about what I'm doing.

ML: *How many kids do you have?*

ADR: We have three children, two grandchildren.

ML: *What do they do?*

ADR: Rebecca was a labor and delivery nurse. She divorced and then became a nurse educator. She is in San Francisco. Steven was a public defender in Chicago, he worked for the County and did death penalty defense. It's very interesting because he wrote the brief that Governor Ryan used to commute the sentences of 188 prisoners on death row. I said to Steven, "I haven't saved 188 people in my life". He wanted to become the head of the whole Public Defender Department, but he didn't get the job. The person who got the job fired him, which is not unusual, right? So, he went into private practice. He is doing very well. Last week he won his first jury trial and he is doing phenomenally financially.

ML: *A blessing in disguise.*

ADR: A blessing in disguise. He went to the University of Chicago. He has an interesting career. He went to graduate school in history at the University of Rochester to work with Eugene Genevese, but Genevese had left for London so he spent a year working for Christopher Lasch and then left Graduate School. He worked for three years as a waiter in a Chinese restaurant, taught himself Chinese and read all of Freud. Then he went to law school, Brooklyn Law. After he finished law school, he decided he didn't want to work for a law firm. He applied to 104 programs for teaching Legal Writing and Legal Reasoning. He got one job, at Kent IT in Chicago. Steven is an incredibly inner-directed person, not like anyone I have ever known. After that he clerked for [William G.] Clark, Chief Justice of the Illinois Supreme Court. Then he became a public defender. He has had visible cases, including the Brown's Chicken massacre. All of our kids are interested in doing good.

ML: *Don't you feel disappointed that none of them has followed you?*

75

ADR: I am not sure. They have their own life and their own interests. I'm very impressed with the good stuff they do. Our other daughter, she and her husband are in a way very important people in psychoanalysis. They manage many of the analytic meetings in NYC. They run my book publishing company, and they run the blog. Frankly, I couldn't do what I do without them. Do you have an assistant?

ML: *Yes, Dana, and without her I certainly wouldn't be able to do anything... I have two children, a daughter and a son. My son works with computers, my daughter is an architect. As there aren't psychoanalysts in my family, I decided to give my 40 years collection of psychiatric and psychoanalytic journals to a university in Lima, some thousand psychiatric books to the Peruvian Psychiatric Association and all my child stuff to the Peruvian Children Psychotherapy Association. I kept the books I use, but all the rest I have already distributed.*

ADR: We sent ours to China because there's nobody in New York I could give that stuff to.

ML: *I decided to do that, but I think if one of my children would be an analyst, obviously I would give it all to them.*

ADR: I don't know any three individuals like my children who have as good a sibling relationship with each other. Tamar and [her husband] Larry spend one day of the week at a soup kitchen for the homeless, they volunteer. I would say there is something *lamid vodnik* about them. Do you know the term?

ML: *No.*

ADR: *Lamid vodnik* means "stands for 36". There were 36 good people in the world. *The Last of the Just* by Andre Schwarz-Bart?

ML: *Yes.*

ADR: That's a *lamid vodnik*. It's an especially good person. So, I've just made up a new word, it's an adjective. That's a good word, it talks about someone who has a genuine feeling of humanity for other people.

ML: *That was after or before your choice of profession?*

ADR: Much, much, after. It's very complicated. My father was murdered.

ML: *How come?*

ADR: Well, he was in business, he had a painting and decorating company. Someone at his work knew he had the payroll. It was the day before the Fourth of July: "Your money or your life". He was stabbed and died. My father was the kind of person who would fight. He told me that when he was in Palestine, he would walk across the Galilee even though he knew it was dangerous. He had a brother, David, my middle name, who was two years younger and wanted to join the Army as well. My father told his father it was too dangerous. They came to his town looking for him and they found this brother apparently wearing his hat and they killed him. I'm sure my father had a profound sense of guilt so when he wanted to stay in Russia his father told him he should leave and try to get his family out of Russia. He came to the United States, he worked very hard, he got a visa and money for his sister to come. But just as he had the money, they closed immigration. His sister couldn't come. He sent the money and the visa to his cousin who came as his sister to Canada. She was a Yiddish reader. She had two children, one died. The other is a physician. There's an annual lecture in Montreal in her honor. My father's sisters were killed in the Holocaust, his brother went to Brazil. The other brother stayed, was in the Russian Army and we learned recently that he was a General and was killed in the Battle for Berlin. The only thing that puzzles me is how could a Jew from the cohort of the '20s survive the Stalin purges in 1936. But apparently, he was still alive in 1945. Moises, every Jew has a story.

ML: *That's why so many Jews are novelists.*

ADR: hat's right.

ML: *And others are psychoanalysts. . . But your father was killed . . . In 1976.* He was murdered.
What a waste! And you think it was because he wanted to fight.

ADR: I think so. But to what extent he was influenced by the guilt about his brother's death?

ML: *How did that affect you?*

ADR: It was very traumatic.

ML: *Because, of course, it was a death that in a way was avoidable.*

ADR: To me it was a terrible thing. They found the person who did it, they convicted him, they put him in Rikers Island prison and he escaped. He went to Florida, got married, started a family and a new life for a while. The detectives in Borough Park, who are very protective of the community, finally tracked him down in Florida. He was brought back to New York.

A film maker, Barbara Kopple, who did "Harlan County" wanted to do a documentary about his rehabilitation. I felt this would be terribly traumatic for my mother. We threatened to sue, and she dropped the project.

ML: *He went back to prison?*

ADR: Yes. And she didn't make a movie about him.

ML: *You have terrible stories about your family. The eldest sister of my mother, there were six, came to New York. She was a dressmaker and her husband worked in a laundry. They had a daughter who is still alive. She did send money to bring her siblings, but immigration was closed by then. That's why my mother and two other sisters and brother went to Peru.*

ADR: So, you have family in the United States.

ML: *I have first cousins and quite a lot of Malamuds (my mother's last name). My father's immigration was earlier, so I have family in the USA and Argentina as you have in Brazil. Something that interests me is how much of a Jew I am, but also how much of a Peruvian I am, how much a typical representative of a Latin-American Jew I am.*

ADR: I think I am unlike a lot of colleagues, because I enjoy connecting with people all over the world on the basis of my being Jewish and on the basis of Yiddish and family. I think that's unusual.

ML: *What about the other American psychoanalytic Jews?*

ADR: I know very few colleagues who are quite like me. Selma Duckler, from the American Psychoanalytic Foundation, was at a meeting at Sandy Abend's. His wife Carol said to her, "You're gonna meet Arnie Richards, he's probably the most Jewish psychoanalyst there is".

ML: *As a compliment?*

ADR: I don't know. I'm often faulted. I mean, some people fault the blog because it is too Jewish.

ML: *What do you understand they mean by that?*

ADR: I think it has to do with their wish to be more disconnected from being Jewish and to insist that this is not very important to them. I think very few people have the same Yiddish background as I do. Sometimes I make a joke, "I'm involved in lost causes, psychoanalysis and Yiddish".

ML: *When you finished your job as editor of* JAPA *you remained with the taste for editing and applied for editor of the* International Journal of Psychoanalysis. *I think it might have been a blessing in disguise that you didn't get the job and started your website.*

ADR: I have to admit that I was ambivalent about becoming editor of the *International Journal of Psychoanalysis.*, but I really thought I could make a difference in terms of the internet and so forth, it certainly seemed to me to be a challenge. I probably understood that I wouldn't get the job.

ML: *They wanted another editor, an American editor to claim that the International Journal is international, but it is not international.*

ADR: I think the relationship between the Executive Council of the British Society and the Journal is very different from the relationship between APsaA Executive Council and *JAPA*. At *JAPA* I felt I had total control, I didn't have to account to anybody, really nobody told me what I couldn't do or couldn't print. I had total autonomy and independence and I value that very much.

ML: *How do you organize your blog? How does it function?*

ADR: What I can tell you is that I find everything for the blog. Every morning, I search the web and find things that are related to psychoanalysis, Freud, or whatever and I send it to Lawrence Schwartz Partners and they post it. I get great contributions: original novels, original plays, ideas. I have a very large editorial board from all over the world but essentially, Moises, it is just me. When I was editor of *JAPA* I felt I had an audience, I have a need to communicate with—if not the world—with the psychoanalytic world. I probably post more on websites than anybody else. Maybe it's some kind of social need I have; I want to engage people in a dialogue to raise their cultural and intellectual awareness. That's what it's about. I think to me it is a wonderful opportunity to connect people. And I think technology is the future. Journals are not the future. It's to make stuff accessible for everybody.

ML: *What about peer review? Some people are very much against it, others think it's essential.*

ADR: You put something on the web and the peer review becomes everybody. All can comment and propose changes. The web has unlimited space. In a journal, space is limited; you can only publish papers of a certain size, with a certain number of words. The web provides for the rapid dissemination of information.

ML: *Let's talk about who influenced your thinking.*

ADR: For the last ten years, or so, I've been influenced by a Polish immunologist and philosopher of science, Ludwig Fleck, who in 1936 wrote a book on the origin and development of scientific knowledge. Fleck believes that science is influenced by personal, psychological, cultural, social, and historical factors. He developed the idea of the Denk [thought] collective, and the 'thought style' – people with similar ideas formed groups. In APsaA, BoPS is one "thought collective" and the ordinary members is another. He called it "the sociology of scientific knowledge". I proposed "the sociology of psychoanalytic knowledge". You cannot understand a person's psychoanalytic position without understanding the facts that impact on its development, as is true for all sciences.

ML: *What about American psychoanalytic thinking?*

ADR: There are different collectives and sub-collectives. I certainly was influenced by Charlie Brenner and Jack Arlow. The centrality of conflict and unconscious fantasy were foundational to them, but they also had their differences. Brenner, as I anticipated early on in my introduction to his Festschrift that I edited with Marty Willick, held views that were in step with the anti-metapsychology developed in response to David Rapaport by George Klein, and Merton Gill and Roy Schafer. They were against the concept of reified agencies Id, Ego, and Superego. Charlie didn't appreciate my telling him his ideas were like Roy's and Roy didn't like the idea that his idea was like Charlie's. Jack Arlow didn't go as far as Charlie, but he said that the Id, the Ego, and Superego only existed in psychoanalytic textbooks, not in a person's mind. I was interested in the anti-nosological approach, which was central to Karl Menninger and the anti-metapsychological approach also had its roots in Topeka.

My supervisors were also important influences. Ted Lipin, who no one could understand (like Lacan perhaps), was important. He stressed looking to the moment to moment variations in the patient's productions. First you pay attention to slips, elisions, contradictions, double meanings, metaphors (like Lacan) and then step back to formulate the overriding organizing of unconscious fantasy. In the paper that Arlene and I wrote about theory and technique, we came to the conclusion that people that were closest to us (because of the centrality of conflict in unconscious fantasy) were the Arlow-Brennarians and the Kleinians.

Then there is the Richards and Richards theory of psychoanalytic technique. This is a joint project. Our theory is that a theoretician develops a theory of technique to counter his or her own anti-therapeutic proclivities. For example, Sigmund Freud was a busy body and activist. He was always intrusive on his patients' lives. He told them to get married and so he stressed abstinence. Otto Fenichel was an incredibly obsessional human being. He kept the record of every postcard and every playbill. His stress was on affect. Heinz Kohut, who is probably one of the most narcissistic human beings, stressed empathy. Kurt Eissler, was an activist who would call his patients in the middle of the night because he forgot to tell them something, writes about parameters. Paul Gray, who many experienced as an authoritarian person, writes about the superego. Jack Arlow is very intuitive, he can listen to one session or half a session and formulate the operative unconscious fantasy, stresses waiting for the evidence. Charles Brenner is one of the most thoughtful, kind and generous people I know. He's always the first to offer condolences, but he writes, when there is a death in your patient's family don't say you are sorry.

ML: *And you?*

ADR: I also am an activist and a revolutionary, so I stress analytic restraint. Todd Essig, a relationalist, told me that relational psychoanalysts are those who had trouble getting dates in high school.

ML: *I think in general lots of analysts I know are or were very bad at dating.*

ADR: So, is there anything we can say about Winnicott according to my theory? What was his central therapeutic idea? The holding environment?

ML: *Yes, the holding environment. He was a transgressor.*

ADR: Yes. What about Bion?

ML: *What do you think about that sort of British School that in a sense had produced a very peculiar theory?*

ADR: I think my problem with them is they generate acolytes rather than serious conversation as far as I can tell. I think the British tend to be quite unaccepting of difference and I was told that before you can publish a paper you had to get an imprimatur from Betty Joseph or Hanna Segal. Is that really so?

ML: *It used to be. While I was training there, if you were from one group— hat was my case—one supervisor had to be from my group, but I could choose a supervisor from another group, which was my case, and my second supervisor was Nina Coltart. But the Kleinians were the group that had to be supervised by Kleinians only.*

ADR: I may give the Kleinians more credit than they deserve. I'm sympathetic to their centrality of conflicts and unconscious fantasy, but I think they talk a lot in the session and impose their view on the patient ... They talk too much.

ML: *Do you know the story about the difference between the Kleinians and Freudians? In a Freudian analysis the analyst might die, and the patient will barely know and in a Kleinian analysis the patient might die, and the analyst won't know.*

ADR: Oh, that's wonderful! I value precision in language. I don't like what people say in ten sentences what they could say in one. People complain about me, they say my communications are too cryptic. I think I probably talk more in a conversation than when I write.

ML: *What about French psychoanalysis? Does it interest you?*

ADR: We are publishing the complete work of Jean Laplanche in English translated from the French. Look, I don't speak French, I don't understand French and I think, probably in that sense, I am pretty narrow in regard to my focus on American Psychoanalysis, self-psychology, object relations, relational psychoanalysis. I am not as knowledgeable about either the Brits or the French.

ML: *With whom do you feel you are speaking with the same voice?*

ADR: Warren Poland, he's one of my closest friends. Another very close friend is Arnie Wilson, who is a psychologist. I used to be very close to Bill Grossman before he died. Obviously, I've been close to Jack and to Charlie.

Then, I am close to people that are not members of the APsaA, Shelly Bach, Steve Ellman, and my co-authors, Art Lynch and Janet Bachant.

ML: *Steve Ellman is very much into research.*

ADR: His research is physiological research, but he is interested in psycho-analytic theory. Have you seen his book?

ML: *Yes.*

ADR: It's about this thing.

ML: *But at the beginning...*

ADR: That was in a different kind of research. It has dealt with dreams, it was neurophysiological research, it is not the kind of research that is really analytic, in my opinion. I think one of the problems with research is that it is under a committee. It's an opportunity to give up money.

ML: *You become a paid....*

ADR: I always felt that some people want to become president so they can reward their friends and punish their enemies. That's one thing I tried not to do as editor of *JAPA*. The other thing I didn't do is, which some other editors have done, insisting that every paper that gets published has you as a reference. If you look at one issue of the *Quarterly,* every paper had Harry Smith (aka Henry Smith) as a reference, we went through them all.

ML: *What is the destiny of publications?*

ADR: That's a good question. I'm supposed to write an article as the former editor of *JAPA*. The Division 39 Journal edited by Joe Reppen was a good journal; he was succeeded by Elliot Jurist and it's not nearly as good now. I have published several papers in the *Psychoanalytic Review*. I think Harry Smith overall did a pretty good job at the *Quarterly*, except for his not rejecting papers. I think there is an issue with print journal publication because unless they're subsidized by the organization, the publisher makes money now, by selling individual papers online. They may charge $30 for the PDF of a single paper. I am not sure that APsaA is benefiting from this. The publisher can get as much from selling three papers than from a single subscription and there is no postage or printing cost. That's a new model!

What is more of concern is book publishing because psychoanalytic book publishing is becoming a disaster. You're lucky if you can get five hundred books published and make money. It is a big problem, and that's why I started IPBooks.

ML: *How many copies do you usually print? A thousand copies?*

ADR: A very few books sell a thousand copies now.

ML: *Is it because people don't read? Is it because there are less people interested?*

ADR: First of all, you know that many publishers are no longer publishing psychoanalytic books anymore. Several analytic presses are out of the business because they feel they can't make a living.

ML: *Karnac is the only one.*

ADR: Yes, Karnac is OK. The internet is also a factor. People read stuff. Maybe Kindle will help. *Freud Jewish World* [Full title: *The Jewish World of Sigmund Freud: Essays on Cultural Roots and the Problems of Religious Identity*] is on Kindle now. We sent 50 copies to Mexico and sold them all. But that's a crossover book that appeals to analysts and Jews. Once upon a time, Charlie Brenner's elementary textbook sold a million copies over the years.

ML: *Some Lacanians do sell a lot.*

ADR: Yes, that's true. That's a whole other phenomenon.

ML: *Do you have an opinion on that?*

ADR: On what?

ML: *On Lacanians.*

ADR: Do you know the joke when you meet a Lacanian?

ML: *No.*

ADR: He makes you an offer you can't understand.

ML: *But they're really successful.*

ADR: Yes, and are getting more successful.

ML: *They have cornered the academic market in many European countries.*

ADR: Right. And what about Argentina?

ML: *What has happened in Argentina is that the societies have incorporated Lacanians. The only thing is that they should keep more or less the time schedules and give full sessions. Some Lacanians have accepted that. There is a very strong Lacanian influence on some of the Argentinean Societies.*

ADR: Lacanians understand that life is theatre and people like to go to the theatre.

ML: *Perhaps we should learn something from them.*

ADR: Yes, but you have to be willing to put yourself out there and try to connect. I've always thought a lot of Foucault.

ML: *He was a good friend of psychoanalysis.*

ADR: I like Foucault, and I can understand him, I understand what he wrote. The problem is that Lacanians are less understandable.

ML: *What do you feel is ahead of you?*

ADR: My practice, I have to spend half my time in clinical work. That's bread and butter, the day to day stimulation and challenge of helping people.

ML: *How many sessions a week?*

ADR: About 25 a week. I have some patients four times a week, three times a week, two times a week, one time a week.

ML: *You were saying that they are the same type of patients you've always had.*

ADR: People have interpersonal problems, marital problems, depression and anxiety, and so forth.

Returning to the blog, I have the blog but what I do hope is that this publishing venture can serve a very real need for the psychoanalytic community and that I can publish books and get them distributed. I think that will be a real contribution.

ML: *Are you still involved in your society?*

ADR: I am currently involved in the APsaA because we are doing a letter in support of a by-law amendment, but I'm not very involved in my own society at all. My latest project was that they wanted to fire the person who runs the bookstore, Richard, so they could save money and give more money to the administrator. They came to me to see if I can help because they felt the bookstore was very important, so I got my friend Silvia Brody to contribute with some 7000 dollars for his salary in return for them naming the bookstore, the Sylvia Brody Bookstore and putting a plaque on the outside of the building. They were very reluctant to do it but as you know or may not know, I got someone to give a million dollars to establish the Bernard Pacella Parent Child Center of NYPSI. There is a plaque on the outside of the building for them. This came through a patient of Bernard Pacella who wanted to give this money for something connected with children. I came up with that idea. A million dollars is a lot of money, so I was very pleased about doing that.

ML: *You have been involved in the Sigourney Prize also.*

ADR: From the very beginning.

International Journal of Psychoanalysis. *It is the most important psychoanalytic prize.*

ADR: Absolutely. But they should rethink who should be getting it. Should it be going to younger people to use, to build their careers, and to tell people to recognize their careers? I don't know.

ML: *That is a good question... Well, it has been a pleasure having this long talk with you.*
Thank you very much.

Arnold Richards's Afterword

I see the almost full decade that has elapsed since the interviews with Moises Lemlij as a time of consolidation of my professional, clinical, and pedagogic identity. Since the interviews were conducted, I have remained very active professionally in CFS and AIP. I have taught at both institutes, and am a TA in AIP. The opportunity to connect with candidates, who are our future, is very important to me.

I have also written and published many psychoanalytic papers and reviews over the past decade. I have contributed to many journals. And I have also published new work in the volumes of my selected papers. Of these selected papers, volumes I and II have already been published and translated into Chinese. Volume III is in production and Volume IV is in preparation. All four volumes are edited by Arthur Lynch, and have introductions also written by him. I think there will be enough contributions for a fifth volume within the next two years.

Eight years ago, Arlene Kramer Richards and I started a psychoanalytic psychotherapy training program in Wuhan, China. We have already completed two three-year sessions, with more than 200 students meeting twice per year. In 2020 we will conclude the third course, four sessions in three years. The institute includes faculty from China, France, Greece, Turkey, Argentina, and Israel, under the leadership of Dr. Tong, a Chinese psychologist who is now an IPA training analyst. Many of the faculty were recruited by Arlene and me. All the faculty give lectures to all the students and there is often a daily three-hour supervisory meeting with a smaller group (20 to 30 attendees). In addition to meeting in person in Wuhan, many of the faculty also conduct supervisory and didactic sessions on the internet.

I completed last year a course on 50 essential papers in psychoanalysis, attended by more than three hundred mental health professionals. I also offered a single online supervision exercise via Skype for Chinese speakers worldwide that was attended by 38,000.

A recent personal and professional consolidation of mine has been my work as a book publisher. IPBooks was established in 2007. Since then, it has published more than 140 books. In addition to books on psychoanalysis and psychoanalytic literary and film criticism, IPBooks has published works of fiction, poetry, humor, children's books and memoirs. Our books are widely distributed. They are available on Amazon and are sold at major psychoanalytic meetings.

Many IPBooks have been reviewed in prestigious journals, including *The Journal of the American Psychoanalytic Association,* and *Psychoanalytic Quarterly. The Interwoven Lives of Sigmund, Anna and W. Ernest Freud* by Daniel Benveniste was reviewed by *the Times Literary Supplement,* probably the most important English language book review publication. Of course, without the IPBooks staff, including especially Larry Schwartz and Tamar Schwartz, I would not have been able to accomplish much.

Finally, there is a larger context for my professional life. A central figure for me is the philosopher of science who formulated the concept of the thought collective, Ludwik Fleck. His insights have contributed to my work of offering critiques to help us all remain true to our core values and save us from ourselves. In addition to the psychoanalytic thought collective, I see myself as belonging to a Jewish left intellectual thought collective concerned with progressive values. With all my experience in China over the past decade, I now also have a more global perspective. And I will always be grateful to the colleagues and students I've met and worked with there for their generosity.

CHAPTER 2

National Yiddish Book Center Interview by Sara Israel with Arnold Richards, conducted 2012

SARA ISRAEL: So, this is Sara Israel and today is June 1st, 2012. I'm here at the National Yiddish Book Center in Amherst, Massachusetts with Arnold Richards and we're going to record an interview as part of the Yiddish Book Center's Wexler Oral History Project. Arnold, do I have your permission to record this interview?

ARNOLD RICHARDS: Yes, you do.

SI: Thank you very much! So, to start out, can you tell me briefly what you know about your family background?

AR: Yes. It was a mixed marriage. My father was from Podolia. My father was a Bolshevik. He was very much interested in Russian and the family was more Russian. But, of course, he did know Yiddish. My mother was from Galicia. She was from—little town called Uziran in Yiddish. I think it's [Jezierzany?] in Polish, near Lanovits, not too far from Skała. And her parents were Orthodox and her father was—taught a lot of the children in the shtetl [small town in Eastern European with a Jewish community]. We have a relative named Izzy Metzker who wrote "Dos bintel brief." He wrote a novel, a roman, in Yiddish, called "Oyf zeydns felder [In grandfather's fields]," which got translated into English. And if you look at the cover of the English translation, there's a little girl on the cover and that's my mother. So, that's the family background. I lived wit —my grandmother lived with us and she only spoke Yiddish and I learned Yiddish from her. And she died when I was probably about six years old. So, I grew up bilingually in Yiddish and English. But what's interesting: although my father was from Podolia and my mother was from Galicia, the distance was probably about sixty kilometers. So, their Yiddish was essentially the same. That was my family background. And my mother was lucky because her family came to the United States in the '20s. My father wasn't as lucky. Well, a brother came to Brazil. Another brother stayed and ended up in the Red Army. And two sisters and two nieces were murdered by the Nazis outside this town of Nova Ushytsya. A cousin escaped. She was eighteen years old. I saw her in Petersburg at the Hermitage. She came to see me and she said-—when they took them out to the field, she said, "I hid behind a rock and my parents didn't look back." So, she ended up surviving. She went to Siberia and she went to Chernivtsi. My father worked—well, he deserted the Red Army so that—his father said, "You need to leave. The Bolsheviks are just as anti-Semitic as the czarists and maybe you'll rescue your sisters." He did get money for—and a passport to bring his one sister, Itte, in 1928 or '29. But they closed immigration to the United States from Russia. He had a niece by the name of Itte, Yetta, and she came as his sister. She then lived in Montréal and became a very well-known Yiddish lezerin [reader]. And there's an annual Yetta Feldman lecture in Montréal in her memory.

SI: That's wonderful. And so, you grew up in Brooklyn, New York.

AR: Yes.

SI: How did your family come to be in Brooklyn?

AR: I mean, at first they started out, as they did, in Brownsville. And then, when things got a little better, Borough Park was a better place than Pennsylvania Avenue and Livonia Avenue. That's how they got to Brooklyn. Of course, now in Brooklyn—in Borough Park, everyone speaks Yiddish. When I grew up, that was not the case. It was a mixed Jewish and Italian neighborhood. And I could speak and read Yiddish by the time I was, I think, three or four. In fact, my earliest lexical memory is reading in "The Forward" and the title was "Barimter [Famous]"—I don't know, "psikiater geshtorben [psychiatrist dies]." It was when Freud had died. And I went to YIVO and found that original copy of "The Forward" and there was this picture of Freud. So, then I went to elementary school and I went to Yiddish shule [Yiddish secular school], to the Arbeter Ring. And it was a very important experience for me, those after-school Yiddish—I'm sure you know about the Arbeter Ring and the Workmen's Circle and so forth. And so, we read—by the way, at home, we had a complete set of Sholem Aleichem, you know the—and also one of Yud Lamed Peretz and other Yiddish books, which then, when my mother died, I brought to my house and then I gave to the National Yiddish Book Center. And Yiddish shule, school—so, I was there, I guess, from, what? From '41 to '46, through the Holocaust. So, the reason I say that: I think the Holocaust was very much part of my childhood experience. Unlike, I would say, the experience of many other Jews, because we read the Yiddish newspaper, we had some sense of what was going on. I remember a poem that I learned. And the poem went, "Mir veln kayn veyts un kayn korn nisht hobn, di felder zey zaynen mit griber far grobn [We will not have wheat, nor any rye, the fields are sown with graves]." So, you imagine that for a six, seven, eight-year-old boy. We had singing on Saturday. Kholile [God forbid] you shouldn't go to shul, right, because the Workmen's Circle was a secular organization. And our singing teacher was Sholom Secunda. And I remember when he came one Saturday morning and taught us a song that he had just written. It was "Dona, dona, dona, dona." It was really quite remarkable.

SI: That's pretty incredible.

AR: And the other thing I remembered about Yiddish shule was it was my thespian debut. We put on a play at PS 134. It was a large auditorium with lots and lots of people. And the play was Sholem Aleichem's "Dos meserl [The pocketknife]," and I was the little boy with the knife.

SI: So, were most of your friends when you were growing up Jewish and Yiddish-speaking?

AR: No. None. I mean, the only ones that were Yiddish-speaking were the ones that I met in Arbeter Ring shule. And so, I didn't have many—no, I was—and my sister was not particularly interested in Yiddish. And so, actually, now that you ask, I did not grow up in a Yiddish community or culture at all. And certainly in elementary school —no, this was very separate and just mine. And when I finished shule, there was—should I go to mitlshul [high school] and so forth, but I didn't. And then, I was—kind of a turn because I had to get bar mitzvah. So, my mother sent me to— found a rabbi and a shtibl [small Hasidic house of prayer] who taught me the haftorah and so forth. And believe it or not, I then became Orthodox, which surprises me to this day. And I went to high school and then, when I went to college, I took my tfiln-zekl [small bag for carrying and protecting phylacteries] with me. And I did, for the first semester at the University of Chicago, daven twice a day. And my wife said, oh, yes, she heard about this freshman at the University of Chicago who wrapped leather around his arms. (laughs) I don't know, that must have intrigued her. Now, my wife, Yiddish was her first language 'cause she grew up with her grandparents. She lived with her grandparents 'cause her mother worked and her father worked. And she learned English when she went to kindergarten, yes. So, obviously, we have that in common. We are both—that Yiddish is our original language. And some of the stuff that I will tell you about had to do with some joint projects.

SI: So, you were saying that you turned Orthodox after your bar mitzvah. What kind of a religious environment were you raised in? What did your parents do and —

AR: I had an uncle who was religious and I used to go over there and—my mother just kept kosher. She was Orthodox. On the other hand, my father was an atheist. And, in fact, he liked to go to the movies on Yom Kippur to drive his in-laws crazy. So, my father was certainly a secular atheist. But my mother was Orthodox. Orthodox how? Oh, at the same time that I was going to Yiddish shule, I was also going to Hebrew school, to Machzikei Talmud Torah. So, I mean, the thing is that I got sent to every school imaginable.

SI: Was that your mother's decision?

AR: That was my mother's doing. My father was more interested in teaching me Russian but didn't get very far with that. That's a whole other story because, you see, I also remember—it must have been in 1939, it was a Wednesday night and I was listening to the radio and Gabriel Heatter, who you may not know about, he would say, "Ah, yes, there's good news tonight." It was Wednesday at nine o'clock. And he said, "Ah, yes, there's bad news tonight. Hitler and Stalin are marching together." So, that was the signing of the Molotov-Ribbentrop Pact. And my mother said to my father, "See? I was right! Stalin is no good!"

And that was a big blow, which, though, he recovered from after the Nazis invaded the Soviet Union. But certainly, he was very much concerned about what was going on in Russia because his family was still there.

SI: What kind of awareness of the war did you have when you were growing up?

AR: Awareness?

SI: Of the war and the Holocaust?

AR: Well, it was very much part of my awareness. I mean, I think I knew a lot about it before other people knew it because I had the Yiddish newspaper, I had Yiddish school and the concern about the family. So, it was certainly very much part of my awareness.

SI: Was it something that your family talked about a lot?

AR: I don't think so. I think my father —he certainly was very worried. Well, I mean, they were just aware of what was going on and concerned and trying to figure out what they could do. But my mother was fortunate because, I think, all—she had no relatives left in Poland. And that was quite remarkable for—that they all had left Galicia.

SI: Yeah. So, I'm curious about your neighborhood. You were telling me that you grew up in sort of a mixed Jewish and Italian neighborhood.

AR: Right.

SI: How did people interact with each other and what—can you just close your eyes and sort of describe it for me?

AR: Well, the Italian kids beat up the Jewish kids, right? (laughs) And we played stickball and punchball in the street. And that was the way it was. And I went to elementary school and there was—certainly, my going to Yiddish school had no—was not part of the dialogue. It was just—there was 13th Avenue, which has transformed. And it was a Jewish lower- to middle-class neighborhood, and Italians. And then, of course, my mother, who lived in that same apartment all her life, had the experience that her childhood life was reconstituted around her because it became a Hasidic neighborhood, with mostly—I guess most of them were survivors. And the street on which Alan Dershowitz—and who else? It was, I think, Sid Gordon lived on 48th Street —became Satmar Way or whatever it's called now, right? Yeah, that's how it changed.

SI: So, how do you think your American identity interacted with your Jewish identity when you were growing up?

AR: I mean, I had a Jewish-Yiddish identity, which was quite strong. And I had an American identity. And I didn't see that they were either contradictory or had an impact one on the other. And I would say I was very comfortable with both. But I returned to Yiddish and involvement with Yiddish later on. I mean, specifically, I went to college, University of Chicago, and I had no really Jewish—I guess what I would say is that in college and through medical school and internship and residency I dropped connection with the Yiddish community. Then, after, when we came back to New York, we joined synagogue B'nai Jeshurun. I don't know

101

if you know B'nai Jeshurun. It's a very, very large synagogue in New York. And we left because the rabbi said that Vietnam was good for the Jews. So, we left that and went to the SAJ, the Society for the Advancement of Judaism, established by Mordecai Kaplan, who left the Jewish Center because he wanted to have bat mitzvah for his daughters, okay? So, we joined the SAJ and the rabbi there was Alan Miller. And it must have been in the late '60s, the rabbi asked Arlene and I to do a martyrology service in Yiddish. So, Arlene wrote a service using Yiddish poetry: Glatstein and Sutzkever and "Mayn kind [My child]" and so forth. And the congregation was very taken by that and said they were interested in more Yiddish. So, we started a Yiddish program at the SAJ and we invited—we had Chaim Grade, we had Singer, we had Sutzkever. We had Buloff. I mean, people came. They even came and there was a play, something about Columbus. And so, that was one way we got back into Yiddish. At the same time, we got involved through—first of all, Leib Trepper was the head of the Red Orchestra, this spy network run out of an umbrella store in Brussels. And Trepper was responsible for sending information to the British that resulted in several German divisions being defeated. He was in prison in Russia and they wouldn't let him leave. And so, his son came and chained himself to the UN. So, we tried to help that. At the same time, we were told about Ida Kaminska. Ida Kaminska was coming to New York, right? And she wasn't well off. And so, I arranged —I got ten people to give each a hundred dollars and have Ida Kaminska do a performance at the SAJ, right? And she did. And so, I think that was the impetus for this interest in Yiddish at the SAJ. We also began to show some Yiddish films, which we got from Sharon Rivo in the Brandeis film -—and so, that was the beginning of this Yiddish revival at the SAJ. Then, Jim Hoberman wrote an article in the "Village Voice" about Yiddish films. It's a wonderful article. I don't know if you know who Jim Hoberman is, but he curated a series of Yiddish films at MoMA. So, Arlene said, "Well, why don't we get to see these films?" So, I organized the first New York Yiddish Film Festival in 1972. And it was sponsored by the SAJ, YIVO, the Jewish Museum, the American Jewish Congress, the Brandeis film thing and the Workmen's Circle. And it was the first New York Yiddish Film Festival in '72 and the second in '73. The Yiddish program at —it was supported and I was encouraged by the Workmen's Circle. Yosl Mlotek, right, was very much interested in having Yiddish programs. And so, we owe a lot to him for this whole effort. So, both Yiddish Film Festivals were an incredible success. I will never forget it because Arlene's cousin is married to Hillel Halkin. You know who Hillel Halkin is, right? And Hillel Halkin had just made aliyah—and we knew him —to Israel and he came back. And I told him what we were doing. He said, "What are you doing? There'll probably be ten old men," right? And the fact is, we filled the auditorium. Was it the—I forget. Kaplan Auditorium at the 92nd Street Y. Nine hundred people came to see these films. It was really quite remarkable. And I always thought it was interesting because in the Sholem Aleichem movie, one of the talking heads is Hillel Halkin, who has subsequently made a career of translating Yiddish. But I can tell you he didn't always have that view. However, he wrote a wonderful piece in "Commentary" called "Yiddish As She Is Spoke." And what the article said was that even though, in Israel, Yiddish was the language of the galut, right, the language of the Diaspora — it said that it returned in the syntax. In other words, the expression in Hebrew "shachor b'enayim [Hebrew: dark in the eyes]" is the equivalent of "finster in di oygn [to faint, lit. "dark in the eyes"]," you see? So, the syntax, it was the return of the denied. So, because of that connection to YIVO specifically, I was asked to join the board of YIVO. And that, of course, has been a major, major commitment to Yiddish and Yiddish culture, as you can imagine. And so, I was chairman of the board of YIVO for several —no, I was a member of the board of YIVO for several years and then I became chairman of the board of YIVO for several years. And then, what I did was I got Bruce Slovin to succeed me. And, of course, the rest is history. Now, when Sam Norich was the director, we thought that it would be nice to have a center of Jewish history. At that point, the Gimbels building at 86th and Lexington was up for sale and we tried to get —to raise ten million dollars to do it but it fell through. Then, another member of the board of directors of YIVO, Joe [Greenberg?] and I decided to pursue this effort. And we had a meeting with Leo Baeck. It was in Wilbur Daniels— who was the head of the—with the heads of Jewish organizations, about the possibility of YIVO and Leo Baeck collaborating on a center of Jewish history. And I will never forget that meeting because one of the directors of Leo Baeck got up and said, "We are no longer yekes [German Jews]." What he was referring to was the fact that children of German Jews don't identify as German Jews but children of Eastern European Jews do. And so, that began the connection and it ended up with the Center for Jewish History, which includes YIVO, Leo Baeck, the Yeshiva University Museum, the American Jewish Historical Society, and the Sephardi House. And I must say, this has been an incredible achievement for the Jewish community and I'm very proud of my contribution to that. I think it was a great idea.

SI: So, what were some of your responsibilities as chairman of the board at YIVO?

AR: Well, I was the chairman of the board (laughs) and—

SI: It's a big responsibility. (laughs)

AR:—I can tell you something about it. I was told when—the board of YIVO has always been famous for its contentiousness. They're Jews! They fight with each other. And some of us spoke Yiddish and not and so—I mean, we have a very distinguished history. Sigmund Freud was originally a trustee of YIVO and then, many, many very important Yiddishists. And I was told that when I was chairman of the board, there were very few fights. Of course, I'm a psychiatrist. People were afraid to do—the main thing I did—do programs, Yiddish programs for YIVO, and involved in the administration and selecting a series of directors after Norich left. And we had others, some better, some worse, and now we have Jonathan Brent and we are doing some very, very, very interesting stuff. Oh, one of my responsibilities was fundraising. And I don't know if you know Helen Nash, the Nashes, they're very important philanthropists. The Nashes and us co-chaired the first YIVO benefit. I think we'd had something for "Yentl" with Barbra Streisand and then we had another one. And we had a dinner at YIVO, which was at 86th and Fifth. And I think we ended up raising sixty-seven thousand dollars. And then, we went on and I think at the high point, we raised, I think, a million-six in the—I think last year, I think we only raised about nine hundred thousand. So, that was one of the things I did. And we had some very good honorees. I just learned, because — we did a cabaret for Joseph Papp and apparently it was Joseph Papp who invited Mandy Patinkin to be on that program, right? And Patinkin said, "I don't know any Yiddish! How can I sing any Yiddish songs?" So, Joseph Papp sent him the song, "Yosele," 'cause it's Yosl Papp, and he learned that. And now, as you know, he has a very large repertoire of Yiddish songs. So, that was one of our contributions. But, look, YIVO, I think—the klezmer music revival started at YIVO. Lorin Sklamberg worked for us, right? Alicia Svigals worked for us. It was the sheet music at YIVO that was the stuff for the klezmer revival. And I think that was a very significant development.

SI: Yeah. Is there a particular cultural event or something that was particularly memorable that you remember organizing—

AR: Well, I remember—who do I remember? Stella Adler was one of our honorees at a benefit. We had good honorees and not so good honorees. Stella Adler—because she came, she must have been in her nineties, and she was incredible. I mean, she looked—I will never—Philip Roth and he says, "What am I doing here? I'm not interested in Yiddish." Of course, we had Robert Maxwell but he died before he arrived. So, we had ups and downs. Oh, well, two things, when you $7.61first of all, I was involved and raised money for the Waletzky movie, "Image Before My Eyes." And I hope you've seen it. It's a wonderful movie. So, we produced that. And then, a group of us from YIVO went to Poland to Jagiellonian University, where they had an exhibit from "Image Before My Eyes," because that had been an image of YIVO. So, I will never forget that because the people there looked at it as if it was an archaeological exhibit. And then, we drove from Kraków to Warsaw. And I remember going through these shtetls and seeing the holes on the doorposts where the mezuzahs had been. And I have a paper in a book about the power of witnessing about the Holocaust. And my paper has to do with the destruction of Yiddish culture in the Holocaust. And the doorpost, the holes, is the kind of image that I tried to create. And what I did was, in this article, I said there was a group of Yiddish writers who had an audience before the Holocaust. There was a group that survived the Holocaust, like Singer and Sutzkever and so forth, who had a reputation after that. But there were those who were killed during the Holocaust. And my paper is a kind of kaddish for these people and I list all the people with some descriptions of the ones who did not survive. So, I'm very proud of that paper 'cause I think it's a very important service to remember these people. 'Cause when you think about it, it's not only that $7.61of the amount of Yiddish culture that they would have produced. I also wrote the article in the YIVO Encyclopedia of Eastern Europe, which I think is the thing that we've done that I am the most proud of, and I have an article in it about psychoanalysis in Eastern Europe. I also have an article in an encyclopedia about Jewish psychiatrists. There's an encyclopedia about Jews in the United States. And so, I've written about that.

SI: It's interesting that your interests in psychiatry and in Jewish culture intersect in that way.

AR: Well, to be facetious, I've sometimes said I'm—see, I'm interested in lost causes: Yiddish and psychoanalysis. (laughter) Well, of course they intersect because in Freud's original group, all of them—I think the first eighteen or maybe it was thirteen—they or their parents were from Galicia, right? And one of the foundational texts in psychoanalysis is the joke book and the jokes are Yiddish jokes, right? So, that was very important to Freud on the one hand. On the other hand, he denied that he knew Yiddish, even though his mother only spoke Yiddish and he went to visit her every Sunday morning. So, that's a whole other story. And I've written a paper about this, about Freud's Jewish identity and Freud's need not to believe. And my thesis is the reason that he denied that he had this attitude towards Jewish ritual and Jewish language, essentially was because of shame. He was in Vienna, he wanted to make it in Viennese society, and he was embarrassed about the scruffy Galician Jews who had come to Vienna. I found an article in "Haaretz" written by someone named Grinberg in the '30s—no, maybe it was '42—who said that thirty years earlier, he had come to Vienna and presented a paper about Yochanan the Prophet. So, Yochanan was this Orthodox Jew with a kaftn [long overcoat traditionally worn by observant Jewish men] and so forth. And he gave this paper and Freud said, "I'd rather be the Jew in the tuxedo than the Jew in the kaftn." And Grinberg says, "See how far from his heritage Freud has wandered." So, the whole question of Yiddish, and the psychoanalysis and Yiddish, you cannot escape it. And, of course, right now, my latest project is to look at American, mostly Jewish psychoanalysts who belonged to the Communist

Party, which very few people know about. I gave this paper on Jews of the Left and the far Left, which you can—it was videotaped and you can find it on my blog, InternationalPsychoanalysis.net and on the YIVO archive. And we just had a very successful conference at YIVO on Jews and the Left. And that's of interest to me and it relates to psychoanalysis as well as just the larger political issues that we face.

SI: So, I'm really interested, also, in what you were saying earlier. You were saying the klezmer revival got started at YIVO, the archives of YIVO have been very important. So, what do you think is the role of YIVO in American Jewish life today?

AR: Well, see, I think it's a very important role but I would say we have two groups. How can I put it? We have the farbrenter [zealous] Yiddishists for whom our Yiddish tradition is the main thing, but also I think YIVO has to relate to the larger Jewish community and to be concerned with whatever concerns Jews. And that's why I think the conference on Freud and the Left is very, very important. I mean, my hope is that YIVO will be a place for particularly Jewish young people that will find out about our culture, our heritage, the genealogy project, and there's more interest in it. But it just occurs to me: many psychoanalysts, if you ask them where their parents have come from, most of them came from the Ukraine, right? Some of them, the ones from Vilna went to South Africa and that's one group of psychoanalysts, and the others came from Galicia and the Ukraine. But certainly, there's a disproportionate number of psychoanalysts with that background. And there's interest in their roots. See, Yiddish is a very emotional language. I mean, it's not just the language. Its life is with people. I mean, that's the language. The language contains a very large cultural content, which is very important and which has been very important in the United States. I mean, you can go from the Yiddish film to Hollywood, right? And, of course, every time you pick up the newspaper, you read about another Yiddish word, right, that's now an American English word. But I think --

SI: Do you see people being aware of that?

AR: What?

SI: Do you think people are aware of that?

AR: I think so. I think so. But I think YIVO's main mission, and maybe we haven't succeeded in that as much as we can, is to promote scholarship on Eastern —yeah. So, our mission is different from your mission. I remember Aaron, when, in the first building, when he first opened the Center, and it was a long time ago. And I think some of us at YIVO are rather envious of your success in terms of your being able to relate to a very large audience, right? But in some ways, we haven't been as successful. I think one of the problems has been that there's a tradition in YIVO of kind of looking down on the people whose Yiddish isn't good enough, right? Yeah, that was that whole idea that it has to be proper Yiddish, the Yiddish according to YIVO, right? And I'm not sure that's so good. (laughs) Yeah.

SI: Why do you think that is, the high standard of—

AR: Well, I don't know. I mean, Weinreich was a world-class linguist, right? His books on the history of the Yiddish language—is unequaled. And I guess we had a certain aspiration to be at the top of the intellectual—I mean, YIVO was founded to bring the best scholarship to linguistics and philosophy and culture and everything. That was the approach that Weinreich had. But I think if we could have more of that, that would be good. But, on the other hand, I think KlezKamp started at YIVO. I think Henry Sapoznik started KlezKamp 'cause he worked for YIVO, right? That was another—and there were some very wonderful people. I don't know if you knew Adrienne Cooper-Gordon who died recently. She was very, very important at YIVO and a really wonderful person. (pauses) So, look, we're doing okay, YIVO, but one of the reasons that we've been getting money and legacies—we just got one from, what, the partner of—who did "All in the Family." So, people who we had no contact with, but they're leaving us money. But this is not going to last forever. So, by the way, I have a book publishing company called IPBooks and we've just published a book with YIVO which was originally called "Ir betokh ir —A City Within a City." And it's the diary of someone from the Warsaw Ghetto. And it's very good and it's a joint YIVO-IPBooks publication. We also published a book —we had a conference, which I was very much involved in, on anti-Semitism. It was called "Old Demons, New Debates," and that was published as a book. And that was also a very important—and we've had some very, very good programs at YIVO. And it's amazing: they are very, very well-attended. I mean, even programs in the middle of the afternoon on Russian attitudes toward Jewish conscription in the army or something and people come. And certainly the audience is older, but not exclusively.

SI: So, what motivates you to dedicate your time so much to promoting Yiddish culture and working with YIVO and that?

AR: Well, that's a good question. I mean, look, simply it's part of my neshome [soul] from my childhood. I think that's very important. If you don't get it at as a child—you know what they say about Yiddish? "Yiddish redt zikh," right? Yiddish speaks itself. And I think my interest in Yiddish speaks, it comes out itself. And it intersects with many other interests, right, in terms of organizational interests, community interests, intellectual interests. So, it's very natural. And my wife has always been involved in all these projects. I'm sure there are many things that we've done that I haven't mentioned. I can't remember them all. But it's been many, many years of stuff.

SI: Have there been particular memorable individuals or mentors that you've had that have pushed you and made you think more about Yiddish culture or—

AR: Well, I think Yosl Mlotek was very, very important. He sort of enlisted 0me in this whole enterprise. So, he was important. And then, there was Sam Norich, who was the director and the person who was the head of the "Forward" corporation who was on the board of directors. And there were some wonderful people on the YIVO board: Shloyme Krystal, right, Hannah Fryshdorf, who was Shloyme Krystal's sister, I think, and she was very much important for YIVO and had a whole feeling about Poland and so forth because there's always been a tension in the board about what we should or shouldn't accept from Germany and so forth and our relationship to the Holocaust. There were discussions about the Heritage Museum having a connection with YIVO and we certainly do not want us to be identified as a Holocaust—but the fact is our archives—we have an incredible archive of French Holocaust material, I think. Someone came from the French government to look at some of the stuff. Oh, the other—I mentioned "Image Before My Eyes" but I didn't mention the "Partisans of Vilna." Aviva Kempner did both movies and we were involved in that as well. And I just put on IP Books that you can buy a series of DVDs from Eric Goldman, Yiddish films. A couple of nights ago, I saw a movie called "Brussels Transit," which is in Yiddish. It's a wonderful movie and you can get it from Ergo Films. You really should watch it. It's an incredible movie done by—it's in Yiddish and the narrator is his mother and has to do with family that goes from Lwów to Brussels. It's an incredible depiction of what it's like to be a refugee.

SI: So, how does your personal connection to Yiddish and Eastern European heritage fit into your broader Jewish identity?

AR: Well, one of the things that occurs to me is that people in my profession and my friends—I've been faulted for being too Jewish (laughs) because— well, if you go on my website, InternationalPsychoanalysis.net, I have Yiddish on it. I have a Glatstein poem in Yiddish and in English. I have the videos of the fellow who goes to China, have you seen those? About the khinezer [Chinese person]? Oh, yeah, you should look—go on my site and put Yiddish in the search engine and there's this—I forgot his name. He interviews people. He went to Kaifeng where there used to be a Jewish community and he asked people, "Do you know what's Yiddish?" and so forth. So, it's very interesting. And so, whenever I have an opportunity to convey to others something about Yiddish, the language, the culture—and actually, most of my friends have some connection through their parents and they have some interest in that. But, of course, there's a sadness at what could have been and what might have been and what isn't, which is why I think the Center, your Center, is such a wonderful place, because it provides a physical presence for the culture. And even if not everyone reads the books in Yiddish, it's still an incredible achievement, and, I mean, more than what we've done at YIVO in terms of its impact on the community. And I'm sure you recognize that, that this is not—how important it is.

SI: So, I'm curious: you go to the SAJ and you interact with other parts of the Jewish community in New York. What's your sense of how people relate to Yiddish?

AR: Well, (laughs) I try to make it interesting for them. And they relate to me and so—but I think that there's a very positive aspect to it. Yeah, I don't have a sense that this is problematic for people. Yeah, of course, there's the whole issue, which—in terms of Israel and Zionism and so forth. And unfortunately—I mean, I have some friends who I think use their Yiddish connection to avoid a—Israel connection. And I don't think—I don't approve of that, yeah. Or to use the Yiddish secular connection to avoid any kind of involvement with Judaism and synagogues and so forth. But, we try to counter that.

SI: What do you think is—I mean, this is a broad question but—(laughs)

AR: Yes.

SI:—you were saying that they try to avoid a connection with Israel. What do you think is the importance of Israel or the place of Israel in Jewish life now or to American Jews?

AR: I mean, I think it's central, I really do. It's central. And, of course, I think there has been somewhat of a Yiddish revival, yeah, in Israel. Do you know Chava Alberstein? Wonderful, wonderful singer and she collected all these Yiddish poems from Yiddish writers and—yeah, do you know the song "Mayn shvester khaye, mit [My sister Chaya, with]" --

SI: Di grine oygn [The green eyes] --

AR:—"mit di bloye oygn un di goldene tsep [with the blue eyes and the golden braids]." I think it's one of the saddest songs I've ever heard. Yeah, you know that song. Yeah, she's a wonderful, wonderful performer. Yeah, she comes to the 92nd Street Y and she has a large audience, yeah.

SI: So, with your own kids, what has been important for you to transmit to them about Jewish identity?

AR: Well, unfortunately, they really don't know Yiddish and they grew up in another era and another time and another time of my life when I really wasn't involved in Yiddish. But my son is—well, they keep kosher. He's more Jewish and he has two children. And one wants to be a filmmaker and the other's a lawyer, going to be a lawyer. But they relate to the family and the background and the grandparents and so forth. In fact, my grandson found out more stuff about my father than I knew about, right? And so, they know who we are and what we are connected with. I think had I been more involved when they were younger, they would have had a different connection to Yiddish than they do because we—I had this long Hegira [Arabic: the journey of Muhammad and his followers from Mecca to Yathrib] from Orthodoxy to God knows what until I returned to New York and Topeka, Kansas and Petersburg, Virginia and these are real, rather un-Jewish communities. But I think kids imbibe, interject stuff through example.

SI: What was it that—I mean, it's interesting that you were talking about moving around from place to place and your own sort of journey from Yiddish to Orthodoxy, something else, back to Yiddish. Do you think that place was important to your Yiddish identity?

AR: Place.

SI: Like being in New York City, for example, or --

AR: I think being in New York City and being—certainly getting involved with YIVO—I mean, it hadn't occurred to me, but that was a very, very important thing. I think if—if I hadn't gotten involved in YIVO, I don't think I would be sitting here today. I don't think so.

SI: So, you think your involvement with YIVO came before the revival of interest in Yiddish, almost?

AR: No, well, it was revived at the SAJ, then the connection with YIVO, and then there was all the stuff that I've been doing, quite intensively. I mean, as chairman of the board, as a member of the board in terms of recruiting people for the board and raising money and so forth and projects and programs—and it goes—and there's always something going on in that regard. And books and papers and so forth. But the book, "The Power of Witnessing," I have a paper in it and Arlene has a paper in it called "Blood." And it's about Yiddish Holocaust poetry or—well, not only Yiddish, Celan and—yeah, but it's about—including a poem of her own about the Holocaust, yeah. The men in her—she had relatives in Paris and the men all ended up in Drancy, the women were hidden in the south of France. So, that's a connection that she has. We had a launching of this book in Washington couple of weeks ago and 350 people came. And I think it's a very, very powerful book and I'm particularly proud about the chapter about Yiddish culture and—because it has autobiographical stuff, some of the stuff I've told you about, about how I came to Yiddish and the trip to Poland and so forth.

SI: So, you were talking before also about your children growing up in a different era. How do you think younger generations of Jews differ from yours in their identity today?

AR: Now?

SI: Um-hm.

AR: I think they're very different because there is this disconnect between the grandparents and the children. And they didn't have that connection like I did. Now, whether or not that can be rekindled and reconnected --- but you know, children always sort of skip a generation. They become interested in not what their parents are interested but in the—so, I have more—I have some hope for our grandchildren to look into their roots and try to reclaim that part of their heritage. But it's important that there be Jewish institutions which will provide them with the opportunity to do just that, right? And if you can have lectures and concerts and so forth, it's very, very important. But look, and as you know, the Yiddish literature is an incredible literature that was produced during those years. And of course, I was lucky 'cause that was part of my childhood. I grew up on that, on—I mean, the names come back to me. Not only Sholem Aleichem, Yud Lamed Peretz and Mani Leib and, I mean, the poets and all that stuff. But I feel privileged to have had that experience and that connection. And I think it's you guys who have to somehow maintain it and communicate it, yeah, 'cause there's some very, very interesting stuff. I remember you did—there was an issue of the "Pakn Treger" which had to do with the—well, it was the Sholem Asch play, "Di got fun nekome [God of vengeance]," you know that, right? Yes, and wasn't that about a prostitute? Yeah, yeah, yeah, yeah. Pretty—see, that's the other thing that I sort of mention in this article is that many of the Yiddish writers were avant-garde and the poets. And they were very much—there was a connection between these Yiddish writers and modernist, avant-garde writers in Europe, right? So, Yiddish was an evolving civilization during those years, which, of course, makes it even more tragic about what was lost.

SI: So, despite sort of a recent resurgence in Yiddish and interest in Yiddish, I guess, a lot of people still say that Yiddish is dead or dying. Do you think that's true?

AR: What did Singer say about that? Didn't he have a favorite famous quote about the obituary's been right—no, I don't think so. I don't think so. I don't think so in the same way that Shakespeare is still around. I mean, things from the past that have substance and interest and quality just do not go away. There are a lot of—I mean, aren't there more Yiddish programs in universities recently? Right, so how do you account for that? I mean, and people—and, of course, there's some non-Jews—who is—I mean, several people. Shane Baker, there are a whole group of people who have gotten involved in Yiddish and on a scholarly level. Of course, it's very important linguistically, right? There's a story about a very famous—was it Schmeruk? Famous Yiddish linguist who went to Harvard and they told him the place to go was the University of Iowa if you want to be a linguist. And so, he got a call from them and they said—he said, "Do you know Finnish?" Because Finnish is very important linguistically. And he thought they said, "Do you know Yiddish?" (laughs) So, he came there and, of course, he didn't know Finnish. But, of course, he was a—became a world-class linguist. Yeah, well, we had—I remember we had Sutzkever at the SAJ. And we took him out for lunch and I was telling my friend, "This is Sutzkever, the greatest poet in any language." And I think I said to him, "Do I have to translate that?" He said, "No, you don't have to translate that." (laughs) And in some ways, he was. And, of course, Glatstein was an incredible poet. Now, whether these people will survive—well, my hope is people will start writing PhD dissertations and studying this culture, and there's a lot to study.

SI: I'm curious, what was Sutzkever like?

AR: Sutzkever thought he was the greatest, that's what he was like. (laughs) And nobody could tell him otherwise. But, well, he certainly was an incredible person. And you know the whole story of the Vilna—and the papir brigade [paper brigade]. In the article, when we discovered the rest of our archives in this book repository in Vilna, I told my mother about how wonderful it was. And she said, "Beser men hot geratevet di mentshn, nisht di papir [It would have been better to save the people, not the paper]," which is true but it was really an incredible—but that's remarkable. You know we have most of our archives here with the stuff that was on a siding in Frankfurt that someone sent there—well, the Germans sent there and this American officer found it. And then, we found the rest in Vilna. I mean, that's a miracle. A lot has—some, not everything—I mean, there's stuff that was buried and never recovered, but a lot that was.

SI: So, what do you think is the place of Yiddish in today's world?

AR: Well, I think people need to become aware of how this culture has impacted on many aspects of their life and culture and that will help them understand things better. I mean, I don't think you can understand the American film industry and its comic aspects without understanding—it's just like Yiddish as (UNCLEAR) spoken Hebrew, right, so that all the stuff by these people—I mean, they grew up in a Yiddish environment and they didn't sort of trumpet their Yiddish but it was part of their life. So, it's important for people to be aware of how this impacts—I mean, I think the Halkin example is very, very telling, is that things don't just disappear.

SI: So, what would be your ideal image for the future of Yiddish?

AR: Well, I would certainly like to, obviously like to see YIVO survive, and our Yiddish summer program survive and grow and more people get involved. And every person who gets involved can influence others. And I would think—my hope is that little by little, there is a beginning of an upward trajectory in terms of the language, the culture, and the interest. And I think there are opportunities. It's hard work. We're going to Chicago for the American Psychoanalytical Association. The YIVO—we have a branch in Skokie in Chicago and a friend of mine, Aliza Shevrin, who is probably the most important 0translator of Sholem Aleichem, is giving a program there for Father's Day and they said, "Return to your fathers." And Aliza Shevrin on—do you know? She's translated a lot of Sholem Aleichem, yeah. Very wonderful translator and I'm sure you have some of her books. And there will be people there. Obviously, it's Skokie that has a survivor community. And, of course, there's a whole generation of—at my level that went to all the Yiddish camps. Hemshekh has a Facebook page, did you know that? Yes, and Hemshekh and Boiberik and Kinderland and Kinderwelt and Kinder Ring, right? I mean, it was—yeah, and we have a house in Garrison, which was a Yiddish socialist bungalow colony. And so, there there were people who spoke Yiddish. So, that's a whole other— people have had that experience and they have children and, of course, they talk about their own childhood. And some kids are interested in their parents' childhood and other kids are not. But I guess really the key is community. How can you develop a community? How can you sustain a community? How can you enlarge its horizons and its interests? Not easy. Certainly not easy. And I'm not sure that the Orthodox who speak Yiddish are going to do it for us.

SI: So, we're coming to the end of our time here, but do you have any other stories or memories you'd like to share?

AR: I'm sure a lot will come back to me. But, look, I'm very grateful for this opportunity to talk about this part of my life because it's going to be on the website, right? And so, I can have all my friends and all my children watch it. And maybe they'll learn something about me that they did not know. And that will be nice. And, of course, it's here forever. This is a wonderful—I mean, I've watched some of the interviews. I'm very pleased that I was invited to do it, as well.

SI: Well, we're very glad to have you.

AR: Good.

SI: Do you have a favorite Yiddish word or phrase or song that you come back to?

AR: A song just came back to me and it's, "Vi hot gegangen mayne yunger yorn? Zey hobn zikh oysgeshpilt vi kortn—Where did my young years go? They got played out like cards." It comes from a movie, a short, called "Chicken Soup," which is set in New Jersey. And this couple, she makes a chicken soup for her husband and puts in the soup and greens and all that stuff. And then, she serves it to her husband and then she sings this song. Sad, but it somehow came back to me. And maybe it's because I'm talking about my life. Did you know that song?

SI: I'd never heard of it.

AR: You never heard that song?

SI: It's really wonderful.

AR: Yes.

SI: It's a beautiful line.

AR: Yeah, yeah, I should see if anyone has recorded it. But the music, the song, well, look, that is a very important part of my childhood—is the music. "Reyzele, geyn mir in gesele [Reyzele, we walk together down the street]" and the line "Fayf nisht. Fayfn iz nisht yidish. [Don't whistle. It's not a Jewish thing, whistling]," isn't it Yiddish? "Kum, kum, kum [Come, come, come]." I mean, the songs that we sang in Yiddish school have a certain kind of resonance in one's mind that it can't—is very, very, very, very important, yeah. And so, the music is essential and the Yiddish folksong is—yeah, but I'm very privileged. I met Joseph Buloff and we had him. I mean, he was an incredible actor. And Miriam Kressyn. There's an incredible number of people who were part of this world and gave a lot to us, yeah, and it was a great legacy. Yes, what's the song about—I'm not sure I remember. And I remember the books, the stories that we read.

SI: Do you have a favorite story that you remember?

AR: What was the one about kvass—you know what kvass is? Kvass is a drink. It's a drink and there's something about someone who's selling kvass. It'll come back to me. Actually, it's a poem story. Something-something kvass.

SI: I don't—

AR: Yeah, well, what I remember—I mean, I remember "Motl peyse dem khasns [Motl Peyse the cantor's son]"—"Ikh bin a yosim [I am an orphan]," right? I mean that's—I remember that as a kid, reading that, right? So, yeah. And also, some of the poems of protest, of oremkayt, oremkayt [poverty, poverty] about the husband who—and "Motel the Operator," you know those, right? So, well, obviously, I mean, I have this repertoire in my head which is part of, again, my neshome. But I don't know how many other people have that. I mean, I think if you went to Hemshekh, if you went to Arbeter Ring, if you went to shule, you got some of that. And that, I think, has more impact on one than learning the grammar. That's what you remember, 'cause that—it's affect, it's the emotional connection that really makes the difference. So, that's what you guys have to work on. Tall order.

SI: (laughs) Do you have any advice for future generations of Yiddish scholars or people interested in Yiddish?

AR: Advice? I mean, I think the scholars have to try to achieve the highest level of scholarship. You see, I mean, look, there is a—in Yiddish, like in the teater [theater]—by the way, I will never forget Zvee Scooler. Have you ever heard him? "The Forward" Grammeister [Master of rhymes]? Do you have his records from "The Forward"? Check it out. Well, I grew up on "The Forward Hour" and Zvee Scooler in Yiddish. I listened to Yiddish. See, there's this thing in Yiddish, the differentiation between shund [art deemed to be of inferior quality] and the opposite, right? Like the theater, shund was the low-class and the other was the high-class. And I think both deserve attention, right, and recognition. I think that's one of the great things that BKG, Barbara Kirshenblatt-Gimblett is doing is that everything should be part of our interest and our study, right? And you just can't— you have to avoid the rarified. And, of course, YIVO's idea, they see—the zamlers [collectors], they went, they collected stuff from the people and what—the folklore, the music, that's what needs to be preserved. And that's wonderful. So, I think we have to continue in that vein and increase the material and increase the legacy and—the legacy and the record. And "ratevet bikher [rescue books]." Do you still have that bumper sticker?

SI: I haven't seen it around but --

AR: Do you remember it?

SI: I'd heard of it, yeah.

AR: You heard of it.

SI: Yeah. (laughs) My mom was—(laughs)

AR: What?

SI: I think my mom had one.

AR: "Ratevet di bikher [Rescue the books]." You have to bring that back! Yeah, right. We had a t-shirt of the first New York Yiddish Film Festival, right? That was fun, right. Okay.

SI: Okay, well, thank you very much. It was a pleasure to --

AR: Okay.

[END OF INTERVIEW]

CHAPTER 3

Interview with Dr. Charles Fisher, New York Psychoanalytic Institute and Society Oral History Project by Arnold D. Richards

CF: Some 20 years ago, Margaret Brenman sent out an announcement through the American that she was specifically interested in what analysts had learned from their own analyses about their motivations for becoming analysts. Not things like a way to make a living, interest in helping people, etc., but the more irrational aspects of their motivation. I'll try to deal with my own case later . First, in this respect I have to tell you a little bit about myself in chronological order. I'm the younger of two brothers. I'm ten months younger than my brother. He is now dead. This means that I was a "preemie", a precipitate baby, born on a staircase. My father tells my birth story sort of like that of Moses in the bullrushes. My mother plays no role in it. My mother is always absent. Very early in my postnatal life, my father came to the hospital in Los Angeles where I was born, and there I was in a basket. This was before the days of incubators, and he said I was lying in the basket and I was dying, so he said, so he took me home and he nursed me, not my mother. My mother had a 10 and 1/2-month-old baby, my brother, to take care of.

AR: How did he know you were dying?

CF: I don't know. That was my father's diagnosis. He picked me up and he took me home and he prepared the bottle and he nursed me. And there was never anything said about my mother.
So, I grew up in Los Angeles.

AR: Had your family been in Los Angeles for a long time?

CF: Not a long time. My parents were both immigrants. My father was born and raised in Romania. He had a very hard childhood. His mother died when he was nine and he had a wicked stepmother. All I know about him was when he was nine he was apprenticed to a tinsmith, and in those days you were sent to a distant village to be apprenticed. He was sent away and he never saw his parents. He came to the United States. I don't know much about his life before that. It was about 1900.

AR: They went on foot across...?

CF: Irving Howe told me how in Romania large masses of Jews marched to the Hamburg ports to attempt to come to the United States, where they all thought they would become wealthy. It must have been about 1880 – 1900. He came around the turn of the century, maybe earlier, because he came before my brother and I were born. My mother came from Odessa and I never knew until much later just when.

AR: A mixed marriage.

CF: A mixed marriage. My mother came at 13. They met in night school and lived on the Lower East Side like everybody else. They obviously had a very unhappy marriage.

There was a set of fraternal twins born before my brother and I were born. My brother was born in 1907, I was born in 1908. The twins were born a few years before that and they both died early. Somewhere in that interval my father left my mother, whether he actually deserted her or whether it was to go to California to see if he could make a living and send for her, it was never clear. I know he was at the St. Louis Fair, the St. Louis Exposition, in 1904, and my father had a passion for expositions.

AR: He was certainly adventurous.

CF: Yes. He was a tinsmith. In those days they were like peddlers. He was not a traveling businessman, but he was a traveler. When he left Romania, he stayed in Hamburg for a while. He was an uneducated man but he spoke about five or six languages. He spoke Roumanian, Yiddish, English, some Russian.

AR: Many Russians came originally from Germany.

CF: Yes. But he had a passion for world fairs because he could pick up prostitutes, at least that was my private opinion; I have some evidence for that. Anyway, he landed in San Francisco. He was in the San Francisco earthquake, which was in 1906. He woke up one morning and the city was shaking, plaster was falling off the walls, and everyone ran to the bank to get their money. That's the last I heard of the earthquake. The next thing I know he was in Los Angeles and he evidently sent for my mother. By this time the twins were dead. They died very young.

AR: Of what, do you know?

CF: I don't know what they died of. I have a picture of my mother holding one of these twins—it looked like it had marasmus. That's the only picture I have of my mother. So, they settled in Los Angeles and my brother was born and less than 10 months later I was born. My father was a Jewish anti-Semite. His real name was Cohen. He had some Romanian name. He got to Ellis Island so on his naturalization certificate he was Herman Cohen, but he had a lot of trouble with that name because wherever he went he would be the object of anti-Semitic comments, because of the name Cohen. My father did not look Jewish. A lot of Romanians don't have Semitic names. He would get into fights and he once got into a fight with a man and hit him over the head with a wheel and almost killed him, so after that he decided to change his name. So, he picked the name Fisher. Why did he pick the name Fisher? Because half the Fishers were Jews and the other half were not.

AR: There was a proper degree of ambiguity.

CF: Yes, that's right. On my birth certificate I was named Charles Cohen. Many years later I had it changed, but from the time I was born he was already Fisher. My father would not live in the Jewish section of Los Angeles, an area called Boyle Heights. We lived in a section of Los Angeles, lower-middle-class. Now it is close to the center of town but then it was kind of far west, and it was a Gentile neighborhood. We had an Irish family on one side and a family called Best on the other. My father was 40 when I was born, my mother 32. My father kind of retired early. He had social inhibitions. He was very shy and self-conscious and somewhat withdrawn. He bought a house and he was a skilled workman, and he built a shop in the back of the house.

He made a fairly good living. In 1916 he bought a Model-T Ford, a Victrola—"His Master's Voice." He bought us toys. You notice I don't say much about my mother. As far as I know, she was always depressed, she may have had a postpartum depression, and I have very few memories of her. My mother committed suicide when I was eight by taking poison. In those days there weren't any barbiturates around but there were poisons, a stuff called bluing, bichloride of mercury.

They would bleach clothes with it and it came in little bottles with a skull and bones. It wasn't a liquid; it was pills which you dissolved. Now, she got up early one morning, locked herself in the bathroom—about four or five in the morning—and I think my brother heard her in there and heard her vomiting and must have awakened my father, and by this time, my memory is that I was standing outside the door (describes the layout of the house) .

AR: You were in the bathroom and the kitchen?

CF: Here's the kitchen, the bathroom was here, and I was over here somewhere, standing against the wall very coolly watching the following scene. My father broke down the door and I got a glimpse of a glass half full with the blue liquid. Then I recovered the following memory in analysis, and I'm not sure if it was a memory or a fantasy. I see him carrying my mother out over his shoulder, and in the kitchen she starts to vomit and he drops her. She's lying on the floor in a pool of reddish vomit, and that scene ends.

I remember now my father calling the doctor, who told him to give her a raw egg, and the next thing I know an ambulance came and took her away. She lived for four days.

She died on April 1, 1916. A few things are relevant to my future history. I asked my father, whom I was very fond of, I admired him—I was eight—what made my mother do that.

He gave me a very strange answer. He said, "She did it because she had a bad dream." What a thing to tell a child!

AR: When did you ask him this?

CF: When I was eight. Within a day or two after that.

AR: Dreams are very powerful.

CF: I had no difficulty understanding that dreams were the royal road to suicide, the royal road to the unconscious. I had no trouble with that, but it was very puzzling. She had a bad dream. You understand, I spent my life with dreams, I dealt extensively with nightmares, and that little statement may have determined my career. That's associated with another scene. My brother and I and my father are sitting together and my father has a bottle of pills and he is calmly counting them, and he announced that my mother took enough to kill an army—16 pills—I learned to have a cool and detached attitude.

AR: An experimental attitude.

CF: Yes, that's right. But my father was not a scientist, he was a very emotional, passionate man. He was very unhappy with my mother, partly, I had reason to believe, because they had a very poor sex life. I have some memories—this was a little house with two bedrooms, and there was a wall separating my parents' room from my brother's and my room. I don't know how many experiences you telescope into a single memory, as Anna Freud suggested about memory, but at least on one occasion I knew that my father made sexual advances to my mother and she was pushing him away. That may have happened many nights because the amount of amnesia I have of my mother is extensive.

AR: Was this retrospective amnesia, after the suicide?

CF: This is what Greenacre talks about in her paper on girls, latency girls, who had some traumatic experience which served as screen memories, repressing everything that went before, but I have as much memory of the first years of my life as most people. It's just that I have lots of memories of my father and only a few of my mother. I thought my mother didn't speak English and I don't remember her speaking. She was silent, she had a white face, sort of blank, depressed, and I didn't think she could speak English because I don't remember her speaking it. I found out later, when I was in my forties, that she came over when she was 13. That's still on a borderline where it's possible to learn to speak English well without too much of an accent, so my mother may have spoken it very well. Furthermore, she may have been more educated than my father. My mother could write Yiddish. I think that was an unusual accomplishment for a woman at that time, wouldn't you say?

AR: Well, there were women who learned to write it.

CF: If she could write Yiddish at 13, she certainly could speak English. One of the reasons my mother was depressed was that they had no friends; she had family in New York, two brothers and a sister. She used to write to them and she used to write in Yiddish, but she had no Jewish connections in Los Angeles, and they were friendless because my father had reclusive tendencies and maybe my mother did, too. But all my memories of her are silence, she was a silent person . She hardly spoke, so I thought she didn't know how to speak English. That was a big distortion. She was so depressed she didn't speak.

AR: You don't remember her speaking to you in English?

CF: I have no memory of her speaking to me at all. The few memories I have of her were her washing my hair. My most pleasant memory I have of her has a sort of glow around it. She must have given me a bath. I remember she was carrying me out of the bathroom to bed and had put a towel around me, and that's the most intimate memory I have of her. Now when they'd go places—my father had a lust for living, he could never get satisfied. He would take us to vaudeville shows, take us to the beach in the summer. My mother never seemed to get involved in these things. My mother would take me shopping. Whenever the family divided-up, I would go with my mother because I was the youngest; my brother would go with my father. My mother used to spit in her handkerchief and wipe my face, which I hated. We were very well taken care of as children. We were very well dressed when we were kids. My mother's suicide occurred when she took the poison. It was a terrible death. She died of uremic poisoning.

AR: Yes, it attacks the kidneys.

CF: My eighth birthday was on the 26th of March and she took the poison on the 28th or 29th, and she had made a birth day party, she had made a cake, and one thing I could never understand or be able to forgive her for is—--how could she have done this so close to my birthday?

AR: It was her bad dream.

CF: Her depression was connected with childbirth. And I learned many years later, I was told by her sister that she hated my father, that my father had killed her and was responsible for her death. She was always pregnant; he was always knocking her up.

AR: She only had three pregnancies.

CF: That's true, but I remember she may have had a miscarriage of some kind when I was little, but they said she was pregnant all the time. My brother never enters into these considerations at all. I was so smart, and I had just skipped a grade, in February, I skipped a half year, then another half year. Then I caught up with my brother and so I was in the same grade as my brother, and my brother didn't like that. Teachers in those days didn't know anything about psychology and they were always making comparisons between him and me. In those days I was always the smartest one in the class. Anyway, to come back to what all this has to do with becoming a psychoanalyst—my father was my first patient. He would confide in me and I learned to listen to him. I never told my father my troubles. He began to tell me things when I was five, six, seven years old about my mother and he said he was going to get me a new stepmother, even though at other times he'd tell me that stepmothers are terrible people.

He would also tell me some sexual things.

AR: When you were six and seven?

CF: Yes. All this is between four and eight, so I learned how to listen. I was obviously his favorite. He wasn't a bad father. He only hit me once that I can remember. He slapped me when I once said the word fuck to him. But I never figured my father really meant it. I must have been about 13 when I told him that I masturbated and he pretended to show some disapproval of that. My father was a very sensual man, very frustrated. I lost my mother when I was eight and my poor father was dying to marry someone else.

He was by this time 48, and he was a very attractive, very handsome man, so he hired a housekeeper.

AR: Your mother was 40 when she died?

CF: Yes, 40. I was eight and my brother was nine. So, my father tried to keep us and he hired a housekeeper, a very masochistic little woman who had a little six-year-old girl. She only lasted a couple of months or so. Somehow the child got drunk on beer. There were some big scenes and she disappeared, and shortly after that my father found a foster home for us with a Mrs. Goldberg, and we stayed with her it must have been a year, because my mother died in April 1916, and in July 1917, my brother and I were put in an orphanage where I remained until I was almost 18. We lived in a Jewish orphan home in Southern California. All I've been telling you I've told at least three analysts and a lot of other people, and every time I tell it I get upset.

AR: What do you make of that?

CF: There are certain trauma you just never get over. I've had a number of abreactions, of an odd kind.

AR: It must have been an incredibly puzzling experience for you.

CF: I never thought of it in those terms. It was certainly baffling. I'll tell you about an abreaction, a particularly bad one of some significance. My mother was in the hospital for four days before she died and we were never taken to see her. A uremic death is not a pleasant one. I recently saw one. I had become very close to Margaret Mahler and she died rather quickly over a week's time, although she seemed to be doing very well before that. They operated on her because they thought she had an obstruction, but she didn't.

She was an 88-year-old woman with cardiac and respiratory trouble. First she had cardiac failure, then respiratory failure, and then kidney failure, so what carried her away was a uremia, and I saw her and she was already in an uremic coma, and they had put a white sheet over her and she was all blown up. You can get urinary retention with uremia.

And it was a very shocking experience because when my mother died, we were taken to the funeral home and somewhere, I was in the car with my brother, and the car stops and a man comes to us and says, "Would you like to see your mother?" and my brother said, "No," and I, being brave, said, "Yes." So, I go in and all I see is my mother in an open coffin with a white face and a white gown, all blown up, and I was very calm and detached, so when I saw Mahler, this was the only other person I saw like that, it was a very shocking, very upsetting experience.

AR: Did your father cry? Do you remember him crying?

CF: I didn't see him cry. We used to wait for him on the front lawn of our house. We knew he had gone to the hospital. We'd wait for him to come home and give us a report. Finally, the fourth day came and we knew that she had died. So, we went into the living room and he told us that she was dead and then he began to cry, and at that moment I threw myself on the floor and I started to cry and I checked myself. I said to myself, "What are you crying for? You didn't love her and she didn't love you," or something like that. The scene ends then. I remember my brother crying, not my father. Then years later, I was in California and my brother and I went to the cemetery to both my mother's and father's graves. We talked. We talked about the day when our mother committed suicide. He remembered things that I didn't and I remembered things that he didn't. One of the things that he remembered that I didn't was that our father cried, he wailed a long, long time. You could hear him a block away. I repressed that. It was a massive repression.

AR: So, you stopped your own crying.

CF: I stopped my own crying . Years later, after I went into analysis with Edith Jacobson, not too long after I started with her, there was something about it and a lot of time was spent around the few days around my mother's suicide, and suddenly I began to wail. This wail was coming out of me. I was detached and listening to it, and it went on for the whole hour, I couldn't stop. It went on and on and on, and it was my father's wail. I did that in two sessions. And that was a very important therapeutic experience. I always ask patients where they feel their depression and some people say in the head, some say in the belly, but I had the distinct impression that mine was in my belly. I used to outline it.

It was over on this side, it was an introjected lump, and after that experience, the lump disappeared, it palpably shrank. My father made a number of attempts to get remarried, but after he put us in the orphan home, he told us that in a short time he was going to get a new mother for us, but he never did. From then on he was a broken man and I guess guilt-ridden, and he just went downhill. He continued to work at his trade. He would come every Sunday to the orphanage and visit. We were not allowed to go out or to go home either. There were three modern cottage-type orphanages in the United States (Jewish)—the first was in Pleasantville, New York, the second in San Francisco, and the third one in Los Angeles, built maybe around 1912. I went there in 1917. It was beautiful. There were big stucco buildings, there were cottages, a ten-acre paradise, full of fruit orchards, orange groves, and there were cows and chickens, and the plant was beautiful and we were not treated badly, we were well taken care of—it was a Jewish charity. By the way, this was before modern social work. There were no social workers, the superintendents tended to be rabbis. We had an old man rabbi; he was about 65 and he knew nothing about children. His wife, who was some kind of bitch, ran the place, and they had ignorant, untrained female matrons. There were about 100 kids. It was a small institution and we had everything there but love, unless you could eke some out from somebody in some way.

AR: Were there counselors?

CF: There was a housemother, either widows or old maids, who had had nothing to do with children. Some of them were witches, some were very nice, none of them were lovable, except one, and I was already grown up by then.

AR: And you went to school from there?

CF: Yes, we went to public school. The public school adjoined the ten-acre plot so all the kids at school knew who the orphan kids were. One of the worst things about being in an orphan home was that you knew you were inferior and there was a stigma attached to it. And you know that they closed up the orphan homes. There were Jewish, Catholic, and Protestant homes, and the Jewish charities were always far in advance ideologically of the Catholic and Protestant ones, but it was finally around 1940 concluded that orphan homes were not as good as foster homes, a dubious proposition, because a good orphan home is better than the majority of foster homes because it has a certain stability and you have friends, other kids, and you make close relationships. There were things that weren't too bad about it, being in an orphan home, but it was bad enough. You spent your whole life waiting. You were supposed to leave when you were 16. There were no social workers. They kept me there until 1926, a year longer than most of the kids. I was the first kid there who went to college. When I came there, everyone agreed that I would be. ...

AR: The group decided that you were somehow special, from the very beginning?

CF: The authorities did. Everyone said I would be the first one to go to college. It was true, I was.

AR: You knew when you were nine.

CF: Yes. I would bring home report cards, all A's. So how I would go to college or what would become of me, that wasn't clear.

Arnold Richards's Interview with Charles Fisher Part III: From LA to Chicago to DC to NYC

... thing to do. There were cops, bulls, and they would shoot at you. I was pulled off the train twice, once in Cheyenne and another time in Grand Island, Nebraska. A big guy stuck a gun in my ribs. What they do is put you in a jail, which is filthy. They kept you overnight and gave you a bowl of mush and said leave town and don't come back again. By the time I got to Chicago I wired Betty and she wired me $10 and with that I got to New York and we began to live together, and we have been living together ever since for 60 years.

AR: In 1925—you met in 1925?

CF: We met in 1926.

AR: Sixty years.

CF: So, Betty really saved me, not just my life, my sanity. She was a very maternal woman, along with her other assets. So, what we did then, I still hadn't decided what to do with my life. I knew the only thing to do was to go to school. So, I looked up my relatives. They were still alive. The brother of my mother and her sister. I went to see her sister and husband, and they fell on my neck. They wanted me to come to stay with them. There was another uncle named Isadore. He was rich. He was a building contractor. I was living with Betty in the Village. We weren't married. We were very advanced for that time. We lived together for three years. It was in the early Depression years.

AR: There is one area from our discussion last time that I have a personal curiosity about. You told us that you spent these years in an orphanage which was essentially a Jewish institution, and I was wondering about that aspect of your development—your Jewish education, Jewish Identity.

CF: Yes, there were some difficulties about that. My Jewish identity was marred long before I got to this institution. My father was an anti-Semitic Jew. I told you that he was a sheet metal worker. He came here around the turn of the century, and most of the places where he worked he worked with Gentiles. The name he was given by Ellis Island was Herman Cohen, and Cohen got him into a lot of trouble.. He used to get in fights because of anti-Semitic taunts and once almost killed a man. He therefore decided to get his named changed, and he changed it to Fisher because half the Fishers were Jewish and half the Fishers were non-Jewish, and this assuaged his conscience, and he changed the Herman to Henry. On my birth certificate I was named Charles Cohen; the name was changed. My brother, unfortunately, was called Isadore and he had a lot of trouble because Izzy, Ikie, and Abie were names everyone knew were Jewish. It's very ironic that Isadore is a Sephardic-Spanish name, but I have not known any Jew in a long time who named his child Isadore. So, we never went to synagogue, we didn't celebrate the holidays, we never lit candles. And my father got so he could eat ham, but he couldn't get himself to eat pork. His conscience couldn't let him do that. So, I had no religious upbringing until I was eight years old. Before my eighth year, although we always were aware that we were Jews and my father was a very Jew-conscious person. What my mother was I have no idea. I told you that my mother could write Yiddish, and I remember her writing to relatives in New York, and I was very impressed that she could write Yiddish, which I don't think my father could. So, there was no religious upbringing until we got in the orphan home. The orphan home was Jewish. The superintendent of the orphan home was a rabbi in his sixties, named Sigmund Frey. He knew nothing about children. His wife was the superintendent. There was on these beautiful grounds a building that had a little synagogue in it, and so we had Friday services and we had Saturday services and we were taught to read Hebrew and I got so I could read Hebrew very well, but we were not taught what the hell it meant.

AR: You just learned it to pray.

CF: Yes. Later on, when I was about 15, when I was at the temporary institution between leaving the old one and going to a new institution, I used to be asked to conduct services, so I was something of a substitute rabbi. I think I told you that the orphan home decided to build a fancier place. I told you about that and why we moved to this more orphanlike tenement closer to the center of Los Angeles. We went to the B'nai Brith Synagogue, which was one of the principal Jewish synagogues in Los Angeles. There was a terrible rabbi there, named Rabbi Magnin, who became rather famous in Los Angeles because he built a beautiful synagogue on Wilshire Boulevard, and I guess all the rich Jews in Los Angeles were in it. Anyway, when he was a young man and I was still an orphan attending this synagogue, when I was still at the orphan home, I was about 15, he approached me once and asked me if I wanted to be a rabbi.

He would see to it that I was sent to Hebrew Union College.

AR: This was in Cincinnati?

CF: In Cincinnati. I hated this guy. I couldn't stand him. I knew he was a hypocrite. So instead of being flattered by his asking me that, I was angry and I told him very clearly that I didn't want to be a rabbi, which was stupid. I could have been sent to Hebrew Union College. They have a first-rate education, I understand, and I didn't have to be a rabbi if I didn't want to. But I had no one to guide me in these matters, so I refused him, in fact, was insulted, because being a rabbi to me—I was just a little kid— meant being like this son of a bitch, and I didn't want to be him. So, I was confirmed—in those days reform Jews had a confirmation.

AR: At 13?

CF: At 15. Boys and girls together. There was no Bas Mitzvah. All those were post- World War II developments, when reform Jews went back to Bar Mitzvahs. There is no such thing as confirmation any more. So, I remember it as—there was practically no preparation, very little Jewish education. I don't even remember that we had any classes. I think we went to services there, but neither in the orphan home or later on in the synagogue were we given any Jewish education of any kind. But I always recognized myself as a Jew and was rather proud of it and I never in my life experienced any personal anti-Semitism. Occasionally my brother did because of his name, but very little.

AR: Maybe we can get into this theme later on. Maybe we should return to where we left off last time, which I think was some time in college.

CF: We left off when I got to New York.

AR: You had returned from Wyoming.

CF: I bummed across the country, and Betty and I began to live together. So, we were only in New York for no more than about six weeks. I got in contact with my relatives, my Aunt Fanny and her husband, Max, and Rubin and Moe, my cousins, and they got on my neck and wanted to take care of me and come and live with them and they'd send me to school. And again, I turned them down. I hated what they were. In those days-- this was in the mid-twenties—I wasn't a political radical. There were no radical movements at that time, the Communist Party wasn't around yet.

AR: What about the anarchists?

CF: There was the IWW, International Workers of the World, they were beginning; there was the Socialist Party of Eugene Debs, that was around, that didn't have very much power. The intellectuals were against the system—people like H.L. Mencken, Upton Sinclair, Sinclair Lewis,

Sherwood Anderson, Ben Hecht, Lincoln Steffens, all those early writers. So that was the kind of intellectual atmosphere. You were against the capitalist system, which at that time was presumably at the height of its prosperity, although there were weaknesses, for sure. I was in New York in 1927 and I couldn't get a job, so I had contempt for these relatives of mine. It was also based on other things. They told me some things about my parents and they hated my father.

AR: Were they your mother's relatives?

CF: They were my mother's relatives. My father had a brother who died many years before. My mother had two brothers and a sister. There was my Uncle Isadore, but I think he was dead by that time. He had become very wealthy, according to some standards. He lived in Flatbush. So, my poor relatives didn't know what to do with me and they knew I was living with this little whore in Greenwich Village and were very shocked, and I didn't know what to do with myself. I couldn't get a job. Betty had a job but she'd lost it and we were practically out of money. Anyway, my aunt and uncle decided to send me back to California where I came from. So, they said they'd get me a ticket, so they got me a ticket and Betty and I decided we would stop in Chicago, where she was born and where she had one brother and one sister who still lived there, and also I got the idea from I don't know where that I'd like to go to the University of Chicago, but I don't know how I knew anything about it. So, you must understand that in those days one could afford to be daring because you didn't have any alternatives.

AR: This was around 1925, 1926?

CF: This was already 1927. 1 was 19 and Betty was a couple of years older, and we were just on our own. We had broken off with our families.

AR: Did they give you two tickets or just one?

CF: I think they just gave us one because they weren't interested in her. I think she must have had a little money left and she had some friends. All I know is we got the train and got off in Chicago and turned the ticket in. We had $75, and we started off life with $75. So, since I had decided I wanted to go to the University of Chicago, I got a job. First we found a room near the university on East 61st Street, it's across the Midway.

AR: Yes. 61st and where?

CF: Woodlawn.

AR: Where Burton Judson is now—the dormitory of the University of Chicago, it's right there. Yes, 61st, because the el is on 63rd. Was the el on 63rd then?

CF: Yes. So, I forget how but I got a job as a stenographer for a little company called the Stahmer Coal Company. I was Mr. Stahmer's secretary.

AR: Ah, your stenographic background.

CF: That's right. I got $30 a week or something, which was a lot of money. So, I worked there for a month and I was going mad because I thought if I have to do this for the rest of my life, I'd die. I was certain I was made for better things. Betty got a job and I decided I'd go to the university and I would get a part-time job. So, I quit Mr. Stahmer and I sent away for my transcript and there was no trouble getting into the University of Chicago in those days. Besides, I had a very good record from the University of California. No one seemed to have any trouble getting in, but the University of Chicago was a very select place and the undergraduate school was always very small. It must have been even smaller then. Anyway, my story is that I was admitted to the University of Chicago and graduated without ever having seen the Dean or an advisor or anybody. I don't know if that was so unusual, maybe it still happens these days. So, whatever I did, I did it on my own. I never had any advice, but unfortunately I sort of knew what I wanted to do. But first I had to get a job, so I went to the employment office and I was about to reach—I was standing in line and there was this fat man in front of me and I heard him tell the girl that he was looking for a male stenographer, so I thought this was a gift from heaven, so I tugged at his coat and I said, "I'm a male stenographer," so he looked me over and he said, "Come to my home tomorrow at 2:00." So, I went. He didn't ask me any questions, and he turned out to be Samuel Harper. Do you know who Samuel Harper was?

AR: I know who William Rainey Harper was.

CF: Samuel Harper was his son. He lived in a big mansion right off Woodlawn. He was an old bachelor who lived with his mother. William Rainey had two sons. One was psychotic and was in an institution. Samuel was a big, fat, unattractive man without much grace or charm, who was professor of Russian language and history. He became that because—the story used to go around campus—old William didn't know what the hell to do with him so he placed him a field where there was no competition and besides it wouldn't be a bad idea to have a Russian department. So, he hired me for 50 cents an hour and I worked for him for about four years.

Besides what Betty made I brought in a little money myself.

AR: So those were the four years you had in Chicago in college?

145

CF: No, I entered there as a junior. I had two and a half years at the University of California but I lost a half year when I transferred; I don't know why. I had a liberal arts course, political science, economics, etc. I took Spanish, which was a terrible mistake and which made trouble for me later on. Everyone took Spanish there.

AR: Where, in California?

CF: Yes. So, I signed up in the psychology department. The University of Chicago at that time was a great, free institution. William Rainey had hijacked many of the better Eastern universities for famous professors because of a heavy endowment from the first John D. Rockefeller. There were splendid professors in every department.

AR: This was before Hutchins arrived?

CF: I graduated in the summer of 1929. Hutchins was there then. I was in his second graduation class. You could take pretty much what you wanted, there were often no special prerequisites. I was only taking things I liked, a course in the French Revolution, a course in paleontology and geography.

I entered as an undergraduate in the summer of 1927. By the spring of 1928 I was taking premedical courses and in two years I finished all the four years of chemistry—general chemistry, qualitative and quantitative analysis, organic—which were very hard for me. At the University of Chicago, you were up against students who were superior to the ones at the University of California. I didn't do too well. I got B's and C's. By the time I got through and graduated I had completed a minimum of premedical courses. Three months after I graduated, the crash came. I think I may have started to apply to medical school then. But it was already difficult to get in. In the first place, my grades weren't good enough and I had a lot of courses in social sciences and psychology, which tended to be held against you. So, I couldn't get in. I don't know how many medical schools I applied to. What happened was that very shortly after the Depression kids couldn't get work. Medical tuition was $200–$300 a year. If one could live at home and pay the relatively modest tuition, it was possible to go to medical school. As a consequence, the medical and all the professionals schools were flooded with applicants, making it difficult to gain admission. All the schools had Jewish quotas, just like Czarist Russia. But I just happened to be in the one medical school on the planet Earth where they didn't have a Jewish quota.

AR: You were a psychology major as an undergraduate?

CF: Yes, I was a psychology major. At the time the University of Chicago, that had once had a -magnificent psychology department—el and John Watson taught there and for some period Lashley. I was there when the department had deteriorated, in a period when there was Harvey Carr and Bills—they were second-raters. I took a lot of courses but I was not excited about them, except for several courses in abnormal psychology. I read a lot of Janet. There were no inspiring psychology teachers. But I read things by Morton Prince. I was always interested in dissociative states and hypnosis. I don't remember that I particularly read Freud at that time. I remember there was a guy in the psychology department, a student, who sat in the library all day long and everybody said, "He's reading Freud from beginning to end," and everyone made fun of him, and I had a sort of contempt for him, too. And my developing ambition was that I wanted to be a psychiatrist and that included being an analyst, but I don't know if the passion for analysis started then—how early that started.

AR: When you say analyst—a Freudian analyst?

CF: Yes, a Freudian analyst. There weren't any other kind around.

AR: But you weren't reading Freud?

CF: I don't know how much Freud I read. I don't think very much—excerpts.

AR: What made you interested in dissociative states? Do you know where that came from?

CF: Yes. it came from dreams, from my father's statement that my mother committed suicide because she had a bad dream and she must have done something in a dissociated state.

AR: Ah, I see. So, the dissociative state was the waking part of. . . .

CF: The waking part of something unconscious. I struggled with the idea of an unconscious mechanism, some compulsion, propulsion. . . .

AR: Some action that is out of control.

CF: That's the way I explained it. It hadn't been proved. So, I very early read Morton Prince on multiple personality. Those things were what interested me.

I was taking all the science courses and it was very difficult. But I persisted with this crazy notion to be an analyst, that some miracle would happen and I would be able to get into medical school. By the end of my first graduate year, I was at my rope's end. However, after I left Los Angeles periodically I wrote to the superintendent of the orphanage where I was raised, whose name was Joseph Bonaparte, like Napoleon's brother. He was a cut above the average superintendent. He had a master's degree in social work. That was unusual. Things were picking up in the Jewish charities. So, he was more educated—a rather cold man but nice, and he took a kind of interest in me. I left the orphanage without any financial support. I got a job as a secretary to the registrar of the university in Los Angeles and I was able to support myself. I would write to Bonaparte periodically, and I wrote to him that I really wanted to go to medical school and he wrote me a letter that suggested he thought I was kind of presuming above my position, but he said he would try to help me. He got some money for me that would support me through a year of graduate school in psychology. I don't know how much money I was making or Betty was making, but I took a year of graduate work in psychology. I started a dissertation. The dissertation was interesting. There was a friend of mine named Daniel Flanagan, a charming Irishman, who did a rather clever experiment that was far ahead of his time. It had to do with perceptual defenses. He may have been the first one to really do this. He would take paired nonsense syllables, one of which was neutral and the other like "FUK" or "COK," taboo words. Flanagan was able to demonstrate an inhibition in perception of the taboo words. That's the sort of thing the leading psychologists were doing in the 50s. Erikson, Lazarus, Bruner. They got hung up on the idea that in order to be able to not see something, you had to see it first. This led to the idea of a homunculus that scanned the unconscious and recognized the dirty words. I was very impressed with Flanagan; I understood the significance of the unconscious aspects of his experiment toward which I had no resistance. Poor Daniel Flanagan. He was thrown out of school because he had to take a French examination to get his degree and they caught him cheating. I took a French examination, which I'll tell you about in a little while. I tried to devise something equivalent to Flanagan's experiment using pictures, but I never got a decent thing going. All I remember is a dermatology textbook with a lot of pictures of disgusting diseases, syphilis of the skin, of the nose, leprosy, but I never really got the thing set up. My advisor was a man named Bills. At any rate, that quarter ended and I was disgusted. I was sick of the field. I didn't want to go on. This takes me to the summer of 1931. I had one year in which I just took courses. During that time, I had a lot of jobs. I was a night watchman in a garage. I worked as a night x-ray technician. It was in Pullman, Illinois. Do you remember the famous Pullman porter strike? Betty and I had a little room above a veterinarian whose place was full of barking dogs who kept us awake all night. It was filthy. I worked as a waiter in a fraternity house and did all kinds of shit. So that was the summer of 1931. I was desperately depressed. I didn't know what I was going to do. I didn't want to go on in psychology, so I thought I would make one more attempt to go to medical school. The University of Chicago was an extraordinary place. They had extraordinary rules, some of which were probably illegal. They would let you take your first year of medicine, and if you did well, they'd accept you. I don't know of anyone else but me who really accomplished this.

AR: They would take anyone?

CF: I don't know if they would take anyone but they took me. However, they would predate your admission but they'd only predate it to the time you took your language exam. Most medical schools required French or German, and of course I took Spanish. I didn't know any French or any German. So, one day--this was the most important decision in my life—I found out that the next French exam was ten days off so I said to myself, maybe I can learn enough French in ten days to pass the exam. I reasoned thusly. I had had a Romance language, Spanish. The exam was a translating exam. They gave you a page and you could bring a dictionary, so I got myself a French grammar, and I went through it, and I got myself a French dictionary, and the dictionary also had the principal parts of the verb forms. I tried to read some scientific French. It didn't go too badly. Most of the technical words were the same as English. All I had to do was learn the little words in between. So, I reasoned, if I had to learn the little words in between, why read scientific French, why not read literary French? So, I got out a couple of volumes of de Mau- passant, short stories. I was always quite well-read. So, I sat down and I began to read, De Maupassant's stories were short and interesting, sexy, and easy to read, with a nice pure French, so I tried it and I could see that I could read it and make sense. So, what I did for the test is I sat and read de Maupassant for ten days. At the end of the ten days, I could read de Maupassant. And this was my preparation for taking the exam. So, when the day came, I appeared, with 15 others, and we were handed a sheet with five paragraphs on it. You had to translate four of them. And I said to myself, if you don't quite understand, at least write a clear English sentence, but I did understand, I did very well. I translated all five paragraphs. I had to wait for about three weeks and after three weeks they posted the results on the bulletin board and there were three names of those who passed and I was one of them.

AR: Three out of 15?

CF: Three out of 15. You must understand, all these other people had at least two or three years of French, and they couldn't translate, evidently.

AR: You were good at decoding.

CF: I have no gift for languages, no ear, I can't talk, but I'm very good at decoding.

So now I said, all you have to do is go to medical school. I signed up for gross anatomy.

For the first time since Betty and I were together, I was able to devote full time to my studies. She was working for a man she didn't know was a bootlegger, connected with Al Capone. He had a mineral water sign in the window as a cover. But he was smuggling scotch. Betty worked as a secretary. She was making about $50 a week, which was a big salary in 1931.

AR: On the South Side was the Al Capone headquarters. 63rd Street was the center of his gang.

CF: I was taking laboratory courses, especially anatomy. I didn't have time to work; named Butch Harvey, an Englishman. He taught the anatomy course. In the summer of 1931, it was ghastly hot. I was given the cadaver of an 80-year-old woman. The student next to me had a huge, muscular Negro with burn marks on his wrists and ankles. He had been electrocuted. Electrocuted convicts ended up in a medical school anatomy lab, often men with great physiques, prized in anatomy classes. My 80-year-old woman was not so prized. I had some terrible corpses. However, I was very good at things like anatomy, and so I worked hard, and once a week we had a recitation, a lecture, and Butch Harvey, the Dean, was there, so I plunked myself down right in front of him. This was a terribly hot summer; nobody else was very much interested in anatomy at the time, so I sat in front of him and he would ask questions and I would raise my hand. I wanted to call his attention to me so he would remember me, and so I did that, I made myself very much in evidence. At the end of the year—I liked neuro-anatomy—and I got an A in it, H, Honors, and an H in gross anatomy.

AR: Do you remember the neuro-anatomy textbook?

CF: It was Ranson.

AR: Right, that's the same one.

CF: That book was very important to me because it was Ranson for whom I went to work (I later got a fellowship at Ranson's Institute of Neurology at Northwestern).

AR: I knew there was a reason I asked the question.

CF: I was impressed with the textbook and I was impressed with certain experiments that Ranson had done on peripheral nerves, cranial nerves, and I found that I was full of admiration for certain things on esthetic grounds because they were done beautifully, which was the beginning of my interest in research.

AR: That textbook became Ranson and Clark.

CF: That's right. Clark was a graduate student when I was there.

I got through the first trimester; the second trimester I signed up for head and neck, for histology, and something else. The head and neck course is the important thing. I was a whiz at the cranium and the cranial nerves. However, at the time the professor of anatomy and the one who was actually dissecting was a man who was named Professor Swift, a tall man, about 6' 8". So, I ingratiated myself with him, and he saw that I was very good and one day it came up—I probably insidiously brought it up—that I wasn't in medical school, and he said, "How come you're not in medical school?" So, I said very resentfully, "They won't let me in." He was indignant. He said, "How come?" I said, "I don't know," and he said, "I'll see about that. I'll go to see the Dean." So, I guess he did go to see the Dean. It was nearly the end of the trimester and I got another H, some more H's, and he had gone to see the Dean and I was admitted into the medical school and I was predated back to that French exam. So that's how I got into medical school. It was a chance in a million, the combination of being in the right place at the right time, being lucky and daring and scared.

AR: This was Billings?

CR: No, the way it was then, you could take your first two years on the campus and then you could take your second two years at Billings or at Rush, downtown, so the end of that year when I was firmly in medical school and I could see that if things went well I could come back....

AR: So, you went to medical school then with some background and interest in psychology and neuro-anatomy.

CF: That's right, and in psychiatry, psychopathology. I was interested in that.

AR: Were you the only Jew in your medical school?

CF: No, there were lots of Jews. I didn't really have a class. I don't remember any Jews in that particular class. I don't remember knowing anybody, I can't remember a soul. I had other friends who were Jews and other non-Jews. In fact, when I first got to the university I met some nice people. There was a daily paper that was called The Maroon.

AR: *The Chicago Maroon*?

CF: *The Chicago Maroon.*

AR: It still exists.

CF: The first year I was there I wrote a book review and there was a famous book called *Companionate Marriage* by Judge Lindsey, who was recommending doing what Betty and I were doing.

AR: So, you were still not married at that point?

CF: No, not yet. We didn't get married until 1930. So, I wrote a review, a favorable review, for *The Maroon*. Through that review I met a number of campus radicals, interesting people, and so I began to make some friends that way. That was 1927–1928. This was the summer of 1932. I had run out of money. I had heard that Ranson had a fellowship so I went up to see him and he said, "Oh, you're just the person I was looking for," with a year of medicine, some training in psychology. I never liked Ranson. He was a sort of cold fish, a Yankee, he had a peptic ulcer, he was cold and ambitious. Anyway, Ranson is the man who had been working on peripheral nerves, and he was the one who discovered the nerves that carry pain. So, he got the idea that he wanted to try to correlate the portions of unmyelinated nerve fibers with the sensory spots of the skin; there were different sorts of spots (pain, touch, temperature, etc.), so he wondered if there was a correlation; so, what he wanted me for was to map out these spots on the skin. I died at the idea of doing that because it was tedious, an uncertain thing to do.

AR: Was it the staining of the myelin?

CF: No, first you had to examine people and map out these spots, and he would make—say you found certain areas were innervated by the radial nerve—you would get the branch of that radial nerve and you could count the number of unmyelinated and myelinated fibers to see if the proportions correlated with the number of spots. It was crazy, impossible, so I dreaded doing it, but I looked up the literature and I saw that the crazy Germans, systematic, obsessional Germans, had already done this. They had gone all over the body for touch, warmth, cold, pain, and everything, but the literature was all in German and I didn't know any German. So, I thought, "German ain't French," but maybe I could pull the trick again. I'd seen Ranson early in the summer and since he had hired me I was supposed to go to work in the fall and start his crazy experiment, so instead I spent the summer with a German dictionary. I didn't know any German at all. I was reading these articles by men named Strughold and Frey, crazy guys who had done all this, and so I painfully translated these half-dozen articles and they were not bad translations. I had to learn to teach myself some German so I had my own ways of doing that. I read literary works. I got so I could read Thomas Mann's short stories. His early stories were sentimental. I read other writings by Schnitzler, Reigen, for instance.

AR: Schnitzler? Schnitzler always shows up in psychoanalysis, doesn't he?

CF: Yeah. I read the *Christian Science Herald* because it was English on one side and German on the other, and that was what I was doing, learning to translate. So, when fall came I brought all these translations and he, Ranson, was so delighted he said I wouldn't have to do the work myself. But that first year I didn't do much of anything.

Now there was a very fine group of researchers, the principal one being Magoun. And then there was a guy named Ingram. They were all full-time researchers. This was in the days when a research person—I was earning $600 a year. There was some research money around for principal investigators. Ranson by this time had a research institute of his own and quite a reputation, so I had done a little research in Chicago in anatomy. One semester when I had a little free time I went to Dr. Bartelmez and said, "Do you have some work I can do?" So, he put me to work and I did a little experiment and wrote it up. Anyway, Ranson put me to doing something which I was not interested in.

AR: That was your first paper, then?

CF: No, my first paper was written in 1933. I came to Ranson in 1932. In 1933 I wrote this paper on the sympathetic cells in the spinal ganglia. Around that time, the end of 1931, beginning of 1932, what had happened was that Ranson had picked up a so-called Horsley-Clark machine. It's an instrument you put over a head—a monkey's head, not a human one. You can put electrodes into any part of the brain so you can explore the interior of the brain. The Horsley-Clark machine was invented by Sir Victor Horsley, an Englishman, in 1908, and Clark, who was an engineer. It looked like a cap. It has a metal frame which has movable electrodes that you can move in any direction and you had to do the preliminary work to work out a series of coordinates to guide you in placing the lesion. The thing wasn't used because it was too hard to do the pre liminary work, but two important pieces of work were done in English, including one by Wilson on the basal ganglia. But the thing wasn't used. Three of these apparatuses landed in the United States. One was at Yale, one was at St. Louis, and someplace else, but it wasn't used at all. Ranson picked the one up that was at Washington University in St. Louis, brought it to Northwestern, and he and a young man I worked with named Ingram spent a couple of years perfecting the instrument, and just when I got there, it could be used, and it was a gold mine. Imagine. You could stimulate and make a lesion any place in the interior of the brain you wanted. So, I had never been lucky much at anything. I was always lucky in my career, by accident. So, one day Ingram came to me and he handed me a big black box of slides and said, "Go through these and see what you can make of them." They happened to be a series of slides, stained lesions in the hypothalmus; they peppered it with lesions, both laterally and in the midline. The only behavioral or other observations they made were that they collected the urine of these animals and they found that a certain number of them were pissing their heads off and they found they had diabetes insipidus, so I went through the slides. I was never very good looking through a microscope, I could never see anything, but if I was looking for something I could see it. Anyway, I put together the lesions that cause diabetes insipidus. It is a rare disease, and the whole thing was important because I worked out the pathophysiology of the disease and the connections between the posterior Pituitary gland and the hypothalamus.

AR: The neurohormonal relationships?

CF: That's right. The relationship between the pituitary and the supraoptical-hypophyseal tract, and I did a lot of work from 1932 to 1939.

AR: You had finished medical school at this point?

CF: No, I just had one year. My struggle to become a doctor never ceased.

AR: You couldn't continue medical school? You went to work. . . .

CF: I couldn't, but I did. For two years I stayed out of medical school and during the second I got involved in the hypothalmic work. By 1933, I was making $1500 a year. You could live on that. Anyway, in 1934 I got my Ph.D. Magoun and I got our Ph.D.s together.

AR: Magoun? He hadn't got a Ph.D. before?

CF: He was a young man. Ranson had an eye for talent.

AR: So, in a way you were the first of the M.D.-Ph.D. people.

CF: I was one of the few. Then my troubles began with Ranson. We really had a gold mine. He never let anybody work for their M.D., so when I got my Ph.D. in 1934, I told him I wanted to go back to medical school and could I work part-time? He said absolutely not. However, I always had something hot going, so he let me work there part-time and I could go to medical school. I was taking part-time medical courses and doing research, so from then on I worked for him a year part-time and I went to medical school part-time, from 1934 to 1939.

AR: That was another five years.

CF: Altogether it took me eight years to get my M.D. and my Ph.D. It was well worth the time.

AR: So, during this time your interest in dissociative states and psychopathology was on the back burner, so to speak.

CF: It was on the back burner. With all that I was doing, I did a lot of work that became very well known, but by 1937 Ranson got some money and asked me to publish a monograph on diabetes insipidus. One of the important areas that the work on diabetes insipidus led to was the demonstration of the hypothalamic-hypophyseal control of pregnancy, labor, and sexual behavior. The latter processes were controlled by the same areas of the hypothalamus as was water metabolism. We observed that our cats and guinea pigs with anterior lesions in the hypothalamus did not mate or become pregnant, while those that were already pregnant had very prolonged and difficult labors and some of them died in convulsions. We had found that the hypothalamic lesions producing diabetes insipidus resulted in atrophy of the posterior lobe of the pituitary gland and demonstrated that the latter had a total deficiency of Pitocin. Pitocin was known to be a powerful uterine contracting substance and its deficiency probably had something to do with the difficulty our lesioned animals had in delivering their young.

The same anterior hypothalamic lesions destroyed neural pathways having to do with mating behavior and neurohormonal pathways to the anterior pituitary having to do with ovulation. We had serendipitously localized the areas in the hypothalamus that controlled sexual behavior, and it was not until a decade later that the accuracy of our localization was confirmed. Without knowing it, the effects that we produced undoubtedly involved the destruction of the hypothalamic-pituitary areas having to do with the so-called releasing hormones.

By that time, I was earning $2000 a year and all I had to do was write this monograph, but I continued to do other work. Ranson protested every year when I wanted to go back to medical school, but every year he let me go back. Not that he had any special fondness for me—I never became really friendly with him.

AR: Can you think of anyone else, just offhand, who was well known?

CF: I finally wrote this monograph—they were all working on different things.

I had about 20 papers and this monograph, which became something of a classic. So, I left an extremely promising career in neurophysiology. Sometimes I regret it.

AR: Yes, as Freud did, as Charlie Brenner did.

CF: But it was a very exciting period. Those were the Depression years. During the worst part of the Depression, from 1931 to 1939, I was able to get my degree, Ph.D., stayed married, and some other things. Betty worked. She stopped working in 1936. We had a little boy who lived to five and a half, who had an accident and was killed. It was a terrible, terrible business, but it is dubious whether I would have been able to accomplish all this if it wasn't for Betty. From 1936 on I was self-supporting. Betty didn't work then. We got married in 1930. I graduated from medical school in 1939. In 1936 we had our little boy and I had to get an internship, so I applied for an internship with the United States government, in St. Elizabeth's Hospital.

AR: The Public Health Service?

CF: Yes. So, we moved to Washington. It was a terrible internship, no teaching, no supervision, psychotic patients. My whole education was somewhat sporadic, in and out of medical schools. The State Boards which I took at Hopkins, I had a 90% average, which wasn't bad. Anyway, it was a miserable internship. In 1940 I became a student in the Washington-Baltimore Psychoanalytic Institute and I was in analysis with Edith Weigert. At the time, Leslie Farber, who was also at St. .Elizabeth's, and I became very good friends. Now at that time the Washington-Baltimore Society was still ostensibly Freudian.

AR: Sullivanian?

CF: This was before Sullivan. Sullivan was not on the scene. There was Frieda Fromm-Reichmann. She was rebellious in some way against classical Freud, although she was not enough of a theoretician to know what to do and always attached herself to some man who influenced her, for example, Groddeck, Fromm, and finally to Sullivan.

AR: What about a psychiatric residency?

CF: It was a two-year internship; it counted as a residency.

AR: In psychiatry?

CF: I didn't have a real residency. In 1942 the war came and I got into the Public Health Service and was stationed on Ellis Island for three and a half years, where they had a neuropsychiatric service, and that took the place of a good residency.

AR: So, you were just starting the Washington-Baltimore Psychoanalytic Institute, you and Leslie Farber? Did you both start?

CF: Yes. He started his analysis a little before me. He started in January 1940. Edith was a classical analyst. She was very nice to me. Leslie and I were both going to her. There was some rivalry.

AR: Sibling rivalry.

CF: I did my first piece of research with Leslie. He had begun to do some hypnosis, and he taught me how to hypnotize, and we decided to do an experiment together in giving people suggestions to dream, and then we added another thing. We would give dreams to some subjects that had been dreamed by other subjects and ask them to interpret them, which some of them were successful in doing. We published a paper on this work in The Psychoanalytic Quarterly in 1943.

AR: Was that your first analytic publication?

CF: Yes, it was my first analytic publication. It was entitled "Suggested Dreams under Hypnosis." It was superior compared with other things in the literature, such as a paper by Schroetter in 1912. Schroetter was awfully crude. For instance, he gave a suggestion to a female subject to dream about a homosexual relationship. She dreamed of carrying a bag on which was written, "For women only." We didn't do anything that crude. Leslie was a very good hypnotist and I became a very good hypnotist, too. For example, we would say to a subject, "I am going to remind you of something that once happened to you. You were walking along the street and saw a woman sitting on a stoop nursing a baby." She was then told, "You're going to have a dream. When you wake up you will tell me about it." The subject reported, "I was taking a streetcar up to Mt. Pleasant and I went into a store and bought a lot of apples, fruit, and candy." We asked the girl to draw the mountain. She drew a breast, but she was not aware that she was doing it. The experiment was very successful. We published it and it's part of the classical literature on the subject.

AR: So, it's interesting in a way that your career recapitulates Freud's professional development, neuro-anatomy, hypnosis, and dreams. Do you remember much about your training at the Washington-Baltimore Institute? Who were your teachers and supervisors?

CF: I'll tell you about my non-training at Washington-Baltimore Institute. About this time my son was killed in an accident. He fell off a cliff in Rock Creek Park in Washington and fractured his skull. That day my analyst got ill and was away for eight months. About a year later, after the war started, I was drafted into the Public Health Service.

AR: On Ellis Island?

CF: Yes. They gave me a choice of location. I chose the Marine Hospital on Ellis Island so I could be in New York. It was a marvelous service. In Washington there was very poor training, poor supervision. In 1939 the psychoanalytic field was quite well developed, but it wasn't too difficult to be admitted to an institute. I talked to Fromm-Reichmann and she said I had to go into treatment right away. My first supervision was with Frieda. I also had supervision with William Silverberg, the homosexual, at Flower Fifth. I shared an office at that time with Leslie Farber. We were in private practice and both got jobs at Chestnut Lodge as psychotherapists. It was an ideal time to start our careers and was very exciting. You know Chestnut Lodge, it's a famous place (*I Never Promised You a Rose Garden*). Frieda Fromm-Reichmann was a national figure. Did you ever see her? She was a little Germanic woman and overly sweet in manner and voice. She got famous at a 1940 meeting at the Richmond annual meeting of the American when she gave a paper called "Transference in Schizophrenia," in which she demonstrated that some kind of transference goes on. It was a very touching, moving paper which everyone applauded when she told how she would go and sit on a cold, damp cement floor with a mute schizophrenic for eight hours until the patient talked. At Chestnut Lodge they had real acutely ill schizophrenics. It was a very noble enterprise to attempt to treat them with some kind of modified psychoanalysis.

AR: Who was it, Rosen? What was that fellow's name?

CF: That's a different story.

AR: Not Victor, the other Rosen.

CF: I knew him very well. I've known a lot of the people of historical significance since 1939.

AR: Good, that's good for the purposes of this project.

CF: The other Rosen is, I'll think of his name. It was John. Well, Farber and I were sort of Frieda's favorites at Chestnut Lodge. When you came there, they assigned you a couple of patients. I had two patients, a paranoid doctor and an extremely disoriented and hallucinating schizophrenic woman of about 36, named Cunningham. You were told to go and take care of her but they didn't tell you how to take care of her. Frieda would just give you one instruction—just go in and listen—so I don't think anyone there, including Frieda, knew very much about schizophrenia, and no one had any theoretical framework.

AR: Burnham?

CF: No, there was me, Leslie Farber, the Cohens, and there was Stanton.

AR: Of Stanton and Schwartz?

CF: Yes, of Stanton and Schwartz. He was the most original.

AR: Was Bob Morris there?

CF: Yes, Bob Morris was there. He was a very minor talent.

AR: Bob Morris came from Topeka. He trained at Topeka. He trained with Leo Stone at Topeka. I wasn't there then but I knew of him. But I applied to the Washington Institute and I was interviewed by a committee, and the committee included Edith Weigert, Bob Morris, Dan Jaffe, and Howard Searles. Searles gave me a terrible time, but Edith sort of stood up for me.

She was very nice, and Searles was horrid. Jaffe and Morris didn't say much of anything.

CF: Edith was nice. She did me some good. She favored me over Farber.

AR: Which helped.

CF: And she recognized that he was a son of a bitch.

AR: You were telling me about Frieda.

CF: I liked Frieda to begin with. I liked anyone who seemed to like me. I had two patients at Chestnut Lodge. I had a schizophrenic woman who was not in contact at all, and I would take her for a walk every day. They did a lot of things like that. They were experimental. Their whole effort was admirable. They had the sickest schizophrenics you could imagine. Periodically I'd be able to establish contact with the woman.

AR: Did Frieda learn this from Simmel? Was she part of that—Simmel's hospital?

CF: Yes, she had been at Simmel's hospital. I forget the name of it.

AR: In Berlin?

CF: Yes. She had been influenced by Simmel. I was having a hard time with this schizophrenic woman, but she seemed to be getting somewhat better. In the end I thought I'd helped her a lot, but I forget what I did. Frieda said to me one day, "Your patient has a real Oedipus complex," and I said, "Doesn't everyone?" And she said, "No. Not everyone, just some people!"

By this time, I was sufficiently psychoanalytic that it wasn't pleasant to hear her judgments. Also, Farber and I had gone into private practice. We were seeing patients for $5.00 an hour. That (Frieda's comment about the Oedipus complex) made me raise my eyebrows. What really turned me off of her was that we'd have conferences and Frieda would say things that supposedly I had reported to her during supervision that didn't go on, things that I didn't say. She would say things she wanted to hear. So, I became suspicious of her. I always said what I thought was the truth, tell the truth no matter what. That supervision was a disappointment. Chestnut Lodge was the most disturbed place. Patients who couldn't commit suicide in any other way would take a needle and stick it in their chest. They did have an arrangement to try to split the transference which was introduced by Stanton.

AR: Having a treating doctor and an administrative doctor?

CF: Yes. There was this paranoid doctor, he was a killer. I was in the library with him one day and there was no guard around. He accused me of not letting him see his wife. He threatened me with a cigarette, poked at my eyes with it, blew smoke in my face, yelling at me. Then he said to lie down, so I lay down on the floor. He talked all this mumbo-jumbo. I was shaking so much and he was scattering ashes on me. He put a vase of flowers on my chest, going through some burial ritual. That's all I remember. I don't remember how it ended. It scared me to death. There were only two patients I tried to treat. All in all, I was there for a year, from September 1941 to September 1942. Then the war came and we were all drafted. I saw patients during that year, trying out my skills, such as they were.

AR: So, you had good clinical exposure but not much in the way of good clinical teaching or training.

CF: No clinical teaching. There were courses. Very poor training program. In Baltimore there was Lewis Hill. He was smart and quite orthodox. I just remember going to Baltimore once in all that time. Harry Stack Sullivan came the last year I was there. He had been at St. Elizabeth's before. He had a curious history. There is a marvelous article by Farber that appeared in the *London Times Literary Supplement.*

AR: I read his biography. You know that was published not too long ago?

CF: He was crazy. He had a weird charisma. He didn't have it for me. I was never taken in by him. He had a crazy way of talking—convoluted sentences, more heat than light. But he had a tremendous influence on psychiatry.

AR: Even our friend Merton Gill has recently become enamored of Sullivan. He sees himself as an interpersonalist. Sullivan cornered the market on that.

When we left off last, we left you at Ellis Island in 1942.

CF: I came there in December 1942, and I was very happy that I got there. First I didn't want to be in the army, and then I was turned down by the navy. I was accepted by the army but then I heard the Public Health Service was looking for people. So, I rushed there, and they grabbed me because they were very impressed with my background and my research, and they gave me my choice where I wanted to go, so I said I'd like to go to New York, so they sent me to Ellis Island—that's how I got there. Anyway, it was a very interesting place. I was there for three and a half years. I spent the whole war years there, from 1942 to March or April of 1946.

AR: Do you remember your rank?

CF: Yes, I went in as a P.A. Surgeon and I left a P.A. Surgeon, with two stripes. They never promoted anyone. We were Reserve. We weren't Regular. Anyway, the thing that was interesting about it was they had a wide variety of cases, but mostly they had some genuine combat neuroses, war neuroses, in the merchant seamen and later on amongst the Coast Guard. The merchant seaman were—did you ever treat a merchant seaman?

AR: Certainly. Do you know the Greek merchant seaman's disease? It was abdominal pain masquerading as appendicitis...

Part IV: Charles Fisher Interviewed by Arnold Richards

AR: Certainly. Do you know the Greek merchant seaman's disease? It was abdominal pain masquerading as appendicitis.... and you had a normal abdomen. It was good for the merchant seaman because they got off the ship. The Greeks ships were terrible.

CF: We didn't see anything like that. What we saw was, beginning in 1942, that's when Lend Lease was on with the Soviet Union, and these guys were the unsung heroes of World War II.

They went on the Murmansk run. Did you deal with anyone on that? You were after the war. You didn't see these guys. These merchant seamen were only happy when they were in a boat and, hey were miserable on land, and so it was easy to keep them on these ships, which were living coffins. The Murmansk run would start out with a convoy of 60 ships, and about eight would arrive at Murmansk. They'd be bombed from the air, they'd be torpedoed, they'd be bombed when they got into port. They went through all the most terrible forms of death you can imagine; they would be sunk at sea and they would be boiled to death in engine rooms and jump into seas of fire. Some of them would get into lifeboats and they would float around for days, and most of them were never recovered. They would die of thirst and hunger. It was miserable. Anyway, I saw a number of very good war neuroses. I wrote a paper called "Hypnosis and the Treatment of War and Other Neuroses," in War Medicine. You remember there was a journal called *War Medicine?* And in it I reported a case of hysterical blindness that I treated, a case of hysterical paralysis that I treated, a couple of fugue cases.

AR: All with hypnosis?

CF: All with hypnosis.

AR: They weren't using Amytol in those days?

CF: We didn't use Amytol at all. We used hypnosis. I used it because I was a very successful hypnotist during the war, but not after. So, this was published in *War Medicine.* Then, during the wartime is when you see amnesias of all sorts; you don't see them in civilian life, but the motivation to develop a fugue-state is extremely great during wartime. You see complex fugue-states, like fugue with loss of personal identity, fugue with change of personal identity, fugue with retrograde amnesia. This was my classification. So, I saw and reported on more fugue cases than anyone in history.

AR: Since Charcot?

CF: Charcot never reported on fugue-states. Janet talked about them and Schilder wrote a paper on fugue-states while he was at Bellevue. At any rate, Rapaport was interested in them, and the people at Menninger's—

Geleerd, Hacker, and Rapaport wrote a very nice paper on them. It was around the time I got in touch with Rapaport.

AR: He had already come from Osteotomy to Topeka.

CF: No, he had already gotten to—when did they get to Austen Riggs?

AR: That was much later.

CF: Much later.

AR: Early 50s.

CF: I forgot when I got in touch with Rapaport. It was later. Geleerd I knew. She came to Ellis Island once. She was engaged to Rudy Loewenstein. Geleerd was a very beautiful woman back in those days. She kind of changed afterward, but she came to Ellis Island, and I showed her one of my fugue-states and I was very taken with her. She married Rudy and she had a very disastrous end, as you know. I know lots of gossip about all this stuff but I won't—I could interest you in the gossip but that's not what this is for. I tend to wander too much anyway. So, I wrote a paper on fugue-states.

The first thing I did when I got here was I went back into analysis with Carl Harold, whom no one has ever heard of, and I was with him a year, and he got tuberculosis. I was a person who had had significant deaths in his family, my first two analysts got sick on me. Just as an aside, a friend of mine brought a friend of hers over to the house the other night. He was a Pole. He was about 40 years old, a musician, a composer, and he lives in Washington, and somehow he made friends with a group of analysts there who were interested in creativity, and were interested in how he composed. Amongst the young, not so young, analysts who were interested in him was Wolf Weigert. Wolf Weigert was the 45-year-old son of Edith Weigert. I remember he was either a baby, yes, he was a baby when I was there. I never saw him but I think I would hear him cry at times; it was a curious experience, 45 years later, to be reminded. I was in analysis with Carl Harold. I liked him very much. He helped me a good deal, but then he got TB and quit, which may be one of the reasons I waited--it took me up to 1947 before I got into analysis again with Edith Jacobson.

I don't know how it came about but I got invited to give my paper on fugues to the New York Psychoanalytic, when I was not a member. I don't know who engineered it or how. It was before 82nd Street, it was an interim period. The original Institute was on 86th Street on the West Side. They used to meet in one of the smaller rooms at the Academy of Medicine. I appeared there one night in uniform. It was very good to be in uniform in those days in the presence of people who weren't. By that time, I'd already had dealings with Gregory Zilboorg. I can't even remember how it came about. I got to know Kubie, who was interested in hypnosis. I got to know Zilboorg, who also took an interest in me. They both took an interest in me.

AR: Kubie wasn't in the service?

CF: No, Kubie never got into the service. He, of all people, felt guilty about it.

AR: So, he stayed in New York and practiced during the war?

CF: That's right. He practiced, and he offered to supervise me, free of charge. I said okay, and I used to go to see him once a week for a while. It was terrible supervision.

AR: Was this in his office?

CF: It was in his office at 7 East 81st or 82nd. He lived in a marvelous little house there, and Kubie was a very kind of aristocratic man, at least pretentious. He studied in England for a while, and he came back with a kind of British accent, and he was an elegant man. I don't think he really knew how to analyze, frankly. Anyway, he'd drag himself up in the morning, come out in his bathrobe. I was sent two patients by Sam Atkins for analysis. one of these I supervised with Kubie.

AR: How had you met Sam?

CF: I met him through his wife, Edith. I knew Edith in Chicago. I've known Edith for over 50 years. I knew her and her first husband, and I got to know Sam when I got here; it's a long story. The first patient was a young Italian boy who had the delusion that people were looking at the right side of his nose, and he was convinced that there was an inequality in the two sides of his nose.

AR: Would you believe that I'm treating a man with a very similar symptom? He had had a nose job.

CF: This one didn't have a nose job.

AR: He spends his time--he thinks there's a line right here and he looks in the mirror and he's convinced that's the reason women don't like him, because of his nose.

CF: This kid was about 21.

AR: My patient was about 23

CF: An infantile kid with polymorphous perverse inclinations. He was a voyeur, exhibitionist. He used to look through the telephone book and call up girls, and he would talk to them in a girl's falsetto voice, and he was extremely subtle, clever. He would get them to talk about their sexual experiences. They would think they were talking to another girl, and then he might get them to masturbate, and he had these wild experiences over the telephone, but it shows the possibilities if one is ingenious enough. I think he only once arranged to meet anybody.

For some reason my first impression of Edith Jacobson was not so good, but I used to go to the Institute meetings when I wasn't a member and I heard Edith a few times, and I finally became obsessed with the idea that she was the person for me because she had a marvelous, warm voice. Did you know her?

AR: Sure.

CF: And I knew that her special field of interest was depression, and I was getting very anxious and depressed for one reason or another, and I finally decided I had to go back into treatment. I went to see Edith, and she really didn't have time to take me. Then she suggested I go to see Kronold. I saw Kronold. It was the best interview I ever had with anybody. I thought he was the most perceptive person, and I liked him. I thought he was really sharp—not that Edith wasn't. So other things being equal, I would have gone to him, but other things weren't equal. I was determined to go to Edith because I thought, for whatever reason, she was the person I needed. I hounded her a little, and she finally took me. My analysis lasted from 1947 to, I guess, 1955, about eight years—which I consider short.

AR: That was short for Edith, too, wasn't it? Didn't she tend to see people for a long period of time?

CF: Well, she never hesitated to let you come back, and I have such a practice myself, never being very confident that I've finished with anyone and never thinking that anyone really does get finished. I am as of now seeing my star patient--I've seen him many times. He's in his 40th year, with long gaps. He's been back about two years. I've had a number of patients I've followed for many years, which is fascinating because things happen which you could never predict. There are improvements that go on, there are changes that go on which you would never have predicted. I've followed the patient from 24 to 64, and he's in trouble now, but you follow people through various phases of what Erikson called the life cycle, and there are many crisis periods. I have a half-dozen people who come back to me. It's not that anyone really exploits the transference, but they come back when they're in trouble. I saw Edith over a period of 40 years actually, whenever I needed her. It should be done more often. We exaggerate our results. In the first place, we don't measure them. We don't know how good or bad they are.

Granted, it's an impossible task. But that's another story.

Up to this point in my history I'm almost 40 years old. I'd not had either any supervision or any course work that I considered had great validity.

AR: Of course, you'd read a lot.

CF: Yes, I'd read a lot and I'd listened to patients a lot by that time. So, I told you I was with Edith about a year, and she sort of urged me to get into the Institute, a process which she fostered, and I said, well maybe I can do a little supervision, and in 1947 or 1948, our standards weren't too high, but I always thought that I was sick enough that under rigid standards, I wouldn't be admitted to an institute. But I was admitted to Washington without trouble, and after a half- dozen meetings with Annie Reich, I was labeled a mature analyst, which I didn't feel I was, and I was admitted.

AR: As a member of the Society?

CF: Yes, and now this gets us to the end of the war, which was 1946. I went into practice. In those days it was easy to build up a purely analytic practice, starting at $10 or $15 an hour, but in the spring of 1946 I got on the Mount Sinai staff. For eight years I was in full-time practice aside from spending six hours a week at Mount Sinai.

AR: Moe Kaufman was the head?

CF: Yes. That was a wonderful experience because Moe collected around him a marvelous bunch of men, all of us just out of the service. Vic Rosen was there, Paul Brower, Lou Linn, a lot of them had been in the army. You know that wars make psychiatry, but wars especially make psychoanalysis. The First World War helped psychoanalysis. By the time of the Second World War, the United States psychoanalytic movement was already well developed, and this was before the Europeans came over, and then a great thing happened. Bill Menninger was made Surgeon-General of the Army, and the first psychiatrist ever to be made a general. In World War I no one got above a colonel, so he had tremendous power, and he appointed a lot of very good analysts to the more important psychiatric jobs in the army. Moe Kaufman was in the Pacific, and a bunch of young analysts, men who had just started in analysis, like Vic Rosen, Lou Linn, all kinds of other people, a lot of people who became professors of psychiatry.

AR: Like John Romano.

CF: John Romano, and a couple dozen of them: Maurice Levine, Milt Rosenbaum, all the guys who became heads of departments of the principal medical schools in the United States. You were just a kiddie at the time, but you don't know what it was like after the war for psychoanalysts. We were real heroes. Why did we become such heroes? The reason for it is analysts, psychiatrists in general, but especially analysts, played a big role during the war, and since they showed more understanding and sympathy for war neurotics and managed to get them medical discharges more readily than other doctors, our reputation spread. Also, during wartime millions of people and their families became aware that the perfectly normal American boy next door can break down in what was called shell shock in the First War and combat fatigue was another euphemism in the Second World War, so that by war's end, we were real heroes, not only amongst the population but amongst the medical profession. The attitude toward us at Mount Sinai was simply astounding. We were looked upon with considerable awe. It didn't take many years before everyone become disillusioned with us. It didn't last. Anyway, Moe established the first inpatient psychiatric ward in a general hospital. I think Massachusetts General had started one earlier, maybe about the same time, but Moe was one of the pioneers in inpatient care in a general hospital, which then gradually spread all over the United States and in every city the principal hospitals gradually had inpatient services. It took the load off the state hospitals and also kept many people from ending in the state hospitals. And then things like liaison services, psychiatrists on every service. We were supposed to perform miracles.

AR: George Engel I guess must have been-there.

CF: George Engel, Mirsky.

AR: Yes, the cure of ulcerative colitis.

CF: Mount Sinai was the place. We had this ward with mostly psychosomatic patients, because Mount Sinai collected a lot of psychosomatic cases, especially a lot of ulcerative colitis cases. The delusion was then present that you could treat psychosomatic diseases with psychoanalysis--asthmatics, hypertensics, etc. First the field was dominated by Alexander's psychosomatic profile; Alexander really started it, and there was a definite kind of profile for each disease, e.g., the ulcer profile; that was a man denying his dependency reactions.

AR: Was Flanders Dunbar at Sinai?

CF: No, she wasn't. She may have been at Sinai for a while but not in my time, but she was very important, she wrote a big book, and things were very exciting. We were going to cure these things. Well, gradually we began to notice that the ulcerative colitis patients would die like flies, and no one seemed to be getting better, and then Sidney Margolin—do you know that history?

AR: No.

CF: Do you know who he was? He was an analyst, Kubie's favorite man, and very important at Mount Sinai and a kind of flawed genius, very conceptualizing mind. It was just that he was grandiose. It wasn't quite clear if he was psychopathic or delusional. Ordinarily when you do an experiment, you do the experiment and you collect your data and you go through it and you come to conclusions, the Baconian method. Well, Sidney Margolin did it differently. He formulated some ideas and then he tailored the data to fit the conclusions.

AR: Was he a member of the New York Society?

CF: Yes, he was a member of the New York Society. And he thought that he was going to inherit Moe Kaufman's position, although Moe had many years left—I shouldn't bother you with this story. It's just the history of psychosomatic medicine that's important. He had a case like Beaumont's—a woman with a stomach fistula, a black woman, and he set up a famous experiment, a joint venture between the physiology department, the GI department, and Margolin would analyze the woman and the GI experts would take the secretions, measure acidity, motility, and vascularity of her stomach mucosa, and they would correlate the changes with the psychological changes. Now this was a chance to do a marvelous experiment. Do you remember? This was at the height of Sidney Margolin's fame, so after some time he gave a paper at the New York Institute, a wonderful paper. I forget the title.

AR: What was the paper?

CF: It was on this case. It was a very impressive paper, in which he claimed that there were certain correlations that could be made 100 percent of the time-—-he used the word 100 percent--between what was going on psychologically and what was going on in the stomach. There might be certain dissociations but you could always predict what those would be, that is, the vascularity or the acidity or the motility would change. At any rate, Sidney was a great man for theory-making, he was very impressive in the formulations he made, very articulate. He said that, one way or another, when drive was active you would get, let's say, more motility, more vascularity, less acidity or something, but when defensive processes were more in evidence, you would get the opposite or some other pattern, and it was a very impressive thing, and he said you could make these predictions 100 percent of the time, and Kubie discussed the paper, called him a new Beaumont, and he was hailed as a conquering hero.

AR: He put analysis on the physiological map, so to speak.

CF: That's right. The article was published in the *Quarterly* and something unusual, Kubie's discussion was added to it. Discussions are never given with the paper—the one which hailed him as a new Beaumont. So, some time passed and the experiment was continued, and I was very suspicious of this, knowing that to get something as complex as this 100 percent of the time, that doesn't happen. After all, if science demands that you get something at the .05 level significance, it permits you about five percent error in the so-called null hypothesis, but with Sidney it was 100 percent of the time. So, I knew that he was faking and I knew enough about him from my own judgment of him that I said to him one day, "Sidney, did you really get those changes 100 percent of the time?" and he said, "Absolutely." I had something to do with Sidney Margolin's downfall. He was at the peak. He was considered throughout the country one of the leading psychosomatic theoreticians, and this brought him a lot of notoriety. So, one day—in those days Moe Kaufman was very accessible—we could always go in and bullshit with him—one day I went in and we were talking about this experiment, and I said, "Moe, is it really true that you got these correlations 100 percent of the time?" He said, "Who said that?" and I said, "You know, this paper that Sidney Margolin gave, he said he got these correlations 100 percent of the time." He turned white, he ran to the bookcase and pulled out the volume that had the article and he looked through it, and I showed him where he said these things. He said, "Well, nothing of this sort ever happened." What used to happen was that Margolin and Moe and others who were working on the psychological aspects of things, making predictions, would meet with the physiologists who were giving their reports on physiology, so Moe said, "Nothing of this sort ever happened, we could hardly ever make a correlation." I said, "Well, didn't you ever read the paper or hear it?" Now, Moe was a kind of a son-of-a-bitch in many ways, he never read the fuckin' article. Furthermore, it turned out that the physiologists were very pissed off at Margolin because he gave this article on his own, and he was the only author. He may have mentioned the physiologists but obviously they never read the paper or they wouldn't have let it go through.

Moe was in an uproar about it. Within a couple of weeks Margolin was let go.

AR: Really? He was fired from Sinai?

CF: I don't know if he was exactly fired, but he began to disappear and look for another job elsewhere, and he would tell me he had been asked to come to many, many places. He ended up in Denver, the University of Colorado, and nothing ever happened to him any more. He got an extensive psychophysiological laboratory with all kinds of apparatus. He never published any more on this stuff. He did some anthropological work studying aggression in a tribe of Indians out in that area, and since then he was just a ruined man.

AR: Is he still alive?

CF: Yeah, he's still alive, he's a man about my age, very impressive, a great big man, football player, and nothing ever happened to him. After that they got another case at Mount Sinai. Aaron Stein did the study. I don't know what happened to that but they didn't come to the same results, and some apology was written for the Margolin paper. From then on (it may have been retracted from the *Quarterly* in the second paper, I don't remember whether the second paper was published), but around that time, Sidney Margolin had also developed a new theory of treatment, a regressive treatment.

These were the kinds of ideas he'd get into his head. He'd regress people back to a stage, an oral stage, before the presumed conflicts—who the hell knew what the conflicts were? —but before the presumed conflicts that caused the ulcerative colitis or whatever.

AR: People did that in Topeka when I was a resident. Ethel Baum, who then went to Denver. I remember we would take these sick people and feed them and baby them.

CF: Really? Margolin was giving them a bottle or something.

AR: Right, exactly. I didn't do that but they were doing it.

CF: Did it work?

AR: No.

CF: It didn't work. Well, then one day a famous gastrointestinal surgeon whose name begins with a G asked Moe to call a special meeting of the psychiatry department, he wanted to give a lecture on ulcerative colitis. He was a very handsome and charismatic man and a great surgeon. He begins by showing us some pathological slides of what the gut looks like in an advanced state of ulcerative colitis and he was treating advanced cases of ulcerative colitis, and he said you can't ever reverse these changes. Once they go this far all you're doing is making patients worse. What he was advocating at the time was total colectomy. He then brought up on the stage three or four of his patients whom he had treated with total colectomy. They happened to be a couple of handsome men and rather beautiful women, whose guts he had cut out, but they just looked marvelous. They had gained weight and they were well, and he had a special erotic relationship with all of them. He'd hug them and pat their behinds, he was very seductive with them, which probably didn't interfere with their getting well, and it was a very impressive demonstration and also an admonition to us that we were barking up the wrong tree. He said there may be some cases of ulcerative colitis early that you can do something with.

AR: The same thing happened in Brooklyn with Melitta Sperling.

CF: Yeah, they were doing the same thing, but with an advanced case it's much too late.

*****

CF: Isakower wanted me to give a course in early ego functions. I hardly knew anything about mature ego functions, let alone early ones, so I consented to give it, but I wouldn't give it on early ego functions because I didn't know what the hell to talk about. Anyway, he sort of liked me. It was during the time I was working on my subliminal experiments, and I was giving a paper at the Institute. Do you want to hear this?

AR: Absolutely, fine. I have no objections.

CF: This will give you also something about the atmosphere of the Institute and about some of the leading characters. So, I asked him if he would discuss my paper. This was a paper on sub- and supraliminal influences on dreams. And he said, yes, he would. He had never discussed anybody's paper—after he gave the Mudler paper—for 25 years. I gave him my paper to read, and the night arrived. Robie Bak was President of the Society at the time. My paper was a really good paper—it was well received.

Isakower got up, and he had a kind of elegant way of talking, sometimes circumstantially. He went on talking, and I could see that he was getting more and more critical and hostile, and finally he said things that were really rather psychotic. What in effect he said was that I was showing a slide tachistoscopically of a snake and a vase with a swastika on it. These are powerful stimuli. I'd made one supraliminal and the other subliminal, and I'd alternate them, although at this time I had only shown the subliminal snake and the supraliminal vase with the swastika. Now the subjects had some interesting fusions between the snake and the vase. The subjects produced dreams of a homosexual nature, as if they were being orally attacked by the snake. One of the purposes of the experiment was to see if the dream handled the subliminal stimulus differently from the supraliminal stimulus, and I had evidence that it did. The subliminal stimulus was much more connected to primary process, the deeper wish fulfillment aspects of the dream, whereas the supraliminal stimulus, which was also represented in the dream, had to do with the swastika and would produce associations of concentration camps and Hitler, Nazis and things like that were perfectly rational secondary process associations. The snake had to do with id stuff. The dream also showed certain defensive processes in the subject and attempts to deal with the anxiety about and desire to be homosexually attacked. Isakower said these are not dreams at all. He said these are dreams from "above," not dreams from "below." These were all dreams from above, and he said they weren't even dreams. He said the subjects had a right to protest because they were being homosexually attacked. What in effect he was saying, he was mistaking the symbol for the thing symbolized, you understand? I didn't quite gather all that he said until I thought about it afterward, and I told him. He didn't pay any attention to me and never talked to me again after that; he was such a crazy character. He acted as if I was actually putting a penis in their mouth—as if this was a real event. I said I was just showing them a picture of a harmless snake. The rest was a dream, the unconscious did all this. I wasn't attacking them, but this was a "psychoanalytic" interpretation on his part, and it was weird. It tells you something about him which fits in with everything you know about him. It was a disastrous evening because he hadn't been up on that podium for a long, long time. He went on talking and talking for about 40 minutes, and he and Robie Bak didn't get along at all, and Robie Bak never took any nonsense from him, and he hinted that he was going past his time. It's late, there are other discussants. There was a good deal of discussion that night, as a matter of fact, and Bak finally simply told him he had to stop. Isakower never appeared again, and he never talked to me again. If I passed him he would ignore me, as if I had done something bad to him, that's how nutty he was.

AR: But he stayed on and taught his course for many years after that.

CF: Yeah.

AR: I presume he was a training analyst, and he analyzed and he supervised.

CF; Yes, he did. Some people thought he was quite wonderful, although I asked a lot of students, what did you really learn from him? And everyone always had trouble telling me just exactly what. But he did have a kind of subtle mind, and his three papers have some interesting things in them. However, a paper I wrote much later after he was dead and so he couldn't read it was on "The Spoken Word in Dreams." He never gave a single example of such a dream in his paper on the subject in 1948. He gave examples of psychotic productions, he gave some examples of things that Freud reported somewhere, I think in his book on aphasia. Several times Freud was threatened with death. He heard out loud some thoughts like "Your time has come," something like that, but it was out loud, and he gave that as an example. He gave a few other things, but in the one example dream he gave there were some spoken words but not in the dream, but after the dream. Isakower was interested in a certain kind of spoken word, ominous, portentous, the voice of the superego, speaking in its most punitive, harsh terms, the kind of dreams that don't occur very often but they have occurred with him or he was very acutely aware of them because they probably represented the kind of superego he had, harsh, portentous, ominous, whiplash, like the way he'd treat students. He'd make a fool of you, destroy you. Well, that was my adventure with Isakower. My relationship with analysts was more in connection with their pathology, these notable people.

AR: Well, there was a very special group at New York connected with the dream, and Isakower was one, Bert Lewin in a sense, Nick Young, and yourself.

CF: Bert Lewin I had troubles with, too, although Bert I admired. He was really something special, but I never had much confidence in his dream screen. It was only a kind of metaphor, although he treated it as if it were real. And Nick Young, that monster. There is today a world industry in REM sleep, and it's an accepted phenomenon, but he still doesn't believe it's real.

But you knew that.

AR: Yes, I had him for the dream course. Didn't you give a special thing on REM sleep that was added because Nick wouldn't talk about it?

CF: For about five years, I gave a course on the psychophysiology of sleep and dreaming.

AR: Exactly. That was to make up for the aspect of the subject that Young wouldn't talk about.

CF: That's right, and nobody else has talked about it either. I think Bill Grossman talked about it a little, but I've seen the bibliography that's given out in the dream course.

AR: I've taught it in my course at NYU in my course on Chapter 7.

CF: Yes, but you're not New York. Although the students used to like the course.

AR: It's an excellent course. It's a wonderful bibliography. I used it in my course on Chapter 7.

CF: You know, I've made some revisions to Chapter 7, which have never been incorporated into the teaching at the Institute.

AR: They've never been published?

CF: Oh, sure. In 1957.

AR: Oh, yes, of course, I've read that, I know it well.

CF: I made some much-needed corrections in the Picket model and that's another story, I'll come to that.

AR: We'll get to that later. You gave your paper at New York, you came in uniform, you were clearly invited, you had no connection, and the next paper you gave you were already a training analyst, so there's a gap that has to be filled between those two presentations.

CF: I gave my first paper as a member at New York in 1953.

AR: Was that the paper on fugue-state hypnosis?

CF: No. I have a period to fill in. Fugue-states and hypnosis was in 1944. I wrote three papers on fugue states, one with Ed Joseph in 1948. The first paper I gave at the New York Institute was in 1953.

AR: The current New York Institute.

CF: Yes.

AR: But the first one was given to the Society, I thought, the one on fugue-states in 1944.

CF: Yes, that was given to the Society in 1944.

AR: So that was the first paper.

CF: That was the first paper, yes. Anyway, to come back to Ellis Island. We saw a lot of stuff there, a lot of neurological stuff. Sam, Wortis used to come over once a month, and we saw a lot of psychiatric cases of one kind or another. One of the most interesting things we had to deal with was that Hitler was sending over some of the flotsam and jetsam out of the concentration camps. There was a certain amount—we had captured a number of German submarines in the war, and some of them were imprisoned in Texas or somewhere. The State Department arranged a trade of some of these prisoners for some of the Americans who were in concentration camps but who had married German women or vice versa, and some of them had kids and periodically a couple would be sent back. And we had about six or eight doctors there at Ellis Island, all of them Jews, and a couple of them became members of the Institute, like Dave Kairys. Herb Kupper, who is out in Los Angeles, was there.

CF: Anyway, we had a very good time. I worked eight hours; we were on duty one night a week; you could live in New York and have a practice. During that period, we had our two kids, one of them born on Staten Island in the Marine Hospital. Well, that's enough about Ellis Island. I published three papers on fugue-states, which have become....

AR: One in *War Medicine*. Where are the other two published?

CF: There's a long article in the *Quarterly*, two articles in the *Quarterly*, one with Ed Joseph in 1948;.those have become kind of classics, those papers. I provided the first classification of fugue-states and very little was written on the subject. Analysts don't see them. During these years my analysis with Harold came to an end and I was still trying to make up my mind where I belonged professionally, whether I wanted to get into the New York Institute, and for a few years I didn't do anything. In 1946 I went into practice. I had a little office in my apartment. In 1949 I got an office outside the apartment. It was in the Croydon Hotel and it was an office that I shared with Clara Thompson.

AR: Really?

CF: Yeah, and so I was there from 1946 to 1949. Now during that period, I still had contact with the Washington people. There was formed the

Eastern Branch of the so-called Washington School of Psychiatry, which later became the William Alanson White. You know the history.

Thompson, Eric Fromm, a bunch of people defected from the New York Institute—Horney and Silverberg in 1946. Horney was a dictatorial woman and the Institute remained medical, you know, and so there was a problem about Eric Fromm. Finally, later Eric Fromm, Clara Thompson, and Silverberg and others, Janet Ribah, split off. Silverberg, by the way, went to Flower Fifth Medical School and formed his own group, which is still around, and that was really the first medical school that analysts got connected with, I think.

That was a time I had a chance to read a lot of Freud and analytic literature, and the Washington School of Psychiatry was for a little while giving courses and sometime around there-—was I still at Ellis Island?—I took a course with Eric Fromm and I had a very bad impression of him. I noticed that he would always quote Freud incorrectly and I always had a pathological bias toward truth. I would be finished with someone as soon as I noticed—like I was with Fromm-Reichmann--as soon as I noticed that they didn't tell the truth because I thought that we were in a field where we dealt with so much fantasy and had so much trouble knowing what the factual basis of our work was, that if people were telling lies, we were sunk, so it isn't accidental that I preferred to deal with experimental data, where it's much more clear what a datum is than what we ordinarily think of. Anyway, then I had some dealings with Sullivan.

Sullivan was connected with that so-called Eastern Branch of the Washington.

AR: Sullivan was in New York?

CF: He had come back to New York. He went to Washington; he was with the Washington Society for a while. This was long after Shepherd Pratt.

This was long after his famous experiment with schizophrenics. You know about his experiment with schizophrenics?

AR: No.

CF: He and Silverberg, way back around 1924, supported by the authorities at Shepherd Pratt (Sullivan had already acquired a reputation for being able to treat schizophrenics) had a special ward to treat young schizophrenics' first attack at 18 years old or so. He wanted to choose the personnel, that is, the attendants, who took care of them, so he chose male nurses, I guess homosexual males, and what he actually did--it became kind of a scandal, although it's never really been written up--he permitted or encouraged the male nurses to have homosexual relations with these newborn schizophrenics. The idea was to gratify their unconscious homosexual wishes which were making them psychotic. How that was supposed to cure them never became clear. This was at Shepherd Pratt. He did this with Silverberg. I had heard about it—now Silverberg once—and my memory is so faulty—I don't know whether this was after I got to New York or how I got in contact with him. He once gave me some of the notes, ward notes, nursing notes that were kept about these cases. No one had ever seen this stuff. Neither Silverberg nor anybody else had ever.. published them. Shepherd Pratt might have had some government money to do this. Anyway, the funds were withdrawn and they hushed it up and it never became public; it never got published.

AR: Nobody got sued?

CF: Nobody got sued. Sullivan had some kind of idea—one of his things was that if a boy doesn't have a chum, you have to have a chum period, early adolescent or preadolescent, if you're incapable of having a chum, that is a dire predictive factor for schizophrenia.

AR: He had a chum, a Dr. Sullivan, who was very important in his adolescent period, as I remember from the book.

CF: Well, he thought you needed a chum when you're a kid, it takes place when you're seven or eight years old, that's when you're supposed to have a chum. He didn't have a chum. He was raised somewhere in isolation.

AR: Yes, upstate New York.

CF: Upstate somewhere. I must send you that thing that Farber wrote about him. It's a brilliant piece.

AR: So, you took a course with Fromm, you were unimpressed with him.

CR: Yes, I was unimpressed with that. And then I was once invited by Clara to present my material on fugue-states to a group and Sullivan would be there, so I did, and Sullivan foamed at the mouth. He completely dismissed it because I talked about the unconscious and all that stuff and my formulations were all Freudian, and then I got some impressions of him which finished him off for me. He boasted he never read anything Freud wrote after 1921, as if that was something that deserved some accolades. And Sullivan was a bitchy fag and full of contempt, so after that I wrote Sullivan off, too. I had read a lot of his works and never thought much of them. I thought they were pretty empty; he didn't have much to say. The more I saw these people, the more admiration I had for Freud. Also, I was analyzing the best I could in those days and my own experience was pro-Freud. This was from my own personal analysis because Harold was a Freudian and Edith Weigert was still a classical Freudian and conducted classical analyses. So, of all these people of considerable talents, even originality, what I was most impressed with was their defective characters, and yet a man like Sullivan could gather a following, he had a very charismatic quality, was a cruel, cruel person, vicious. So, in 1947—when I first came to New York, Edith Weigert had given me three names, all Berlin analysts. one was Edith Jacobson, one was Carl Harold, so I went to see Edith first, but I kind of had the idea that I wanted to go to a man, so I went to see Harold and I liked him and began analysis with him in 1943.

AR: The last time, when we left off we had gotten you to New York and hooked up with the New York Psychoanalytic Institute and even gotten you to become a member.

CF: Had I become a member? I guess I told you how I was inducted into the Society by Edith Jacobson and Annie Reich. I had no idea of becoming a member at the time. As a matter of fact, I didn't even think about it. I was absorbed in my own analysis and struggling toward mental health, that distant galaxy which I never hoped to reach. I never thought of becoming a member. I never asked to apply. Edith once said to me, "Don't you think it's about time you became a member?" So, I thought I would have to take some more courses.

AR: What year was that?

CF: 1947. I stopped my analysis with Carl Harold I guess in 1944, so from 1944 to 1947 I was adrift. I purposefully wanted to be adrift because I was breaking away from those Washington people and seeing a few patients on my own and trying to make up my own mind where I belonged and where I increasingly thought I belonged was with Freud. During those years I did a great deal of reading and the more I read, the more Freudian I became. Carl Harold was Freudian and that influenced me and, of course, Jacobson. But I was not much interested in those things at the time. I was just mostly looking for someone who would analyze me, because I was in very dire need, so by about 1947 I was already at Mount Sinai, the war had ended, and I volunteered to work at Mount Sinai six hours a week and that was a great experience. I came there in 1946 and in a few months it will be 40 years since I've been there, and there was a remarkable bunch of very talented people.

AR: Moe Kaufman was the chairman?

CF: Moe Kaufman was the chairman and he set up a very gemutlich atmosphere, everyone called one another by their first name. He was a war veteran and half the others were war veterans, and that kind of produced a feeling of camaraderie. It also was that glorious time when Kaufman had established an inpatient ward at Mount Sinai, full of psychosomatic cases, and the first great wave of optimism was that psychoanalysis was going to solve the psychosomatic problem. There had already been a lot of writing then, like Flanders Dunbar and Sidney Margolin, and a lot of other people were writing, and it was believed that psychoanalysis had something to offer and also that we would provide a therapy.

So, I established my private practice. In those days it wasn't difficult to get patients, because beginning about 1946, after the war, there were floods of patients and I think I was making $10 to $15 an hour, that was the going rate, so I stayed in private practice for eight years and just saw patients. I became progressively dissatisfied with that because, frankly, I didn't like the loneliness of it, I didn't like the idea of not having anyone to talk to. I did have one association which was an influence on me. I had my office in the Croydon Hotel, I shared it with Clara Thompson.

Sidney Tarachow had his office there at the Croydon Hotel. By the time we had both moved in, we had become friends and every day we'd have lunch together and we'd go for a walk. Sidney was in analysis with Heinz Hartmann, so Sidney would tell me about the wonders of being in analysis with Heinz Hartmann. What I had had absolutely no training in or understanding much of was the analysis of the transference, so Sidney used to tell me all about the subtle things that got analyzed in the transference, so I considered that one of my first and greatest teachers was Sidney Tarachow, he really had a great influence on me.

AR: He was a great teacher for a great many other people as well.

CF: Yes, he was a good teacher. Did you know him?

AR: A little bit, because I was at Downstate.

CF: He was a great teacher and a great wit, a great storyteller, a very lovely human being. He was very helpful to me. Those years are kind of dim. We had our two children then; Carla was born in 1943 and Barbsie was born in 1946. I'm talking about after 1946 when I was in practice. I didn't have any affiliation at the time. I started my analysis with Jacobson in 1947 and I was going to Sinai and became a liaison psychiatrist, but interestingly enough I was always looking for something to research, that is, I had a yen for doing experimental work, I had a yen for experimenting with anything psychoanalytic that I could lay my hands on. Not that I was interested in confirming psychoanalytic propositions; I was interested in the experimental exploration of psychoanalytic propositions. They might or might not confirm Freud but they might produce some new knowledge. I was interested in a new discovery because the fun of research was always to feel that you're going to make a new discovery.

AR: Yes, that you're on the frontier.

CF: Yes, that's what I enjoyed. Anyway, one of the influences on me was Rapaport's book on the organization of pathology and thought, which came out in 1951. Did you ever read it?

AR: Yes, early in my career.

CF: I read that avidly because it had a lot of things in it that interested me.

AR: It's organized like the Talmud, like the Bible, with commentaries on the back—the same format.

CF: You know that Rapaport—I just flipped through the book lately—there's a little bio of text and then pages and pages of his commentary. Rapaport was a funny guy. He hardly ever wrote anything that was original. He systematized Freud and he systematized Erikson, and *The Organization of Pathology and Thought* was not original but the footnotes were original, full of original criticism and original ideas, but he was a man of tremendous ambition, who was inhibited in writing anything himself—there are people like that—but he could write these critical things about other people. If you gave him a paper to read, he was famous for this, if you gave him a six page paper to read, he would write a six-page critique of it, single-spaced, take endless time, but he obviously had some block about writing himself. He wrote a book called *Emotions. and Memory,* which was as close as he ever came to writing a book, and then one article which he thought of as his most original article, a short article on activity and passivity—do you know what he did with it? It was published in an obscure Spanish journal in Spanish and it was only accidentally discovered.

AR: Didn't George Klein pick up on it?

CF: George Klein picked up on it. I think I picked up on it. I found it somewhere. Anyway, it got back here and was translated. So, he didn't have a big output, but his influence was on others and he could be a very hard taskmaster.

AR: He was an influence on his counterinfluence.

CF: That's right. So, Klein and Holt and Irving Paul and Schafer and I think Fred Pine and Spence and Luborsky, that whole crowd, fell heavily under Rapaport's influence and he was a real slavedriver. There are others who came later. Anyway, in *The Organization of Pathology and Thought* there was frequent mention of Poetzl but he mentioned him in such a way that I never quite caught on to what Poetzl had done; he'd talk about he did something about apperception within perception, or apperception and perception. I didn't know what the hell that meant. Anyway, I'd done this one research with Leslie Farber on experimental dreams. However, I did do something quite independent on my own in 1952–53, I wrote two papers on the nature of suggestion. I did mention them to you.

AR: Yes, they're in the *Quarterly.*

CF: No, they're in the *Journal of the American, JAPA.* Did I tell you the story? They were picked to be the lead article in the first edition of the *Journal of the American Psychoanalytic Association.*

AR: There were a lot of very illustrious people in that edition.

CF: I thought it was great—the lead article is always—I thought that was a great honor. I was terrified at even handing it in because I thought I'd be excommunicated for doing what I did. I would stop patients in the middle of their hour and say, "Tonight you're going to have a dream about your father and you'll remember it in the morning and write it down and bring it to me the next day." Now, that's interference. At any rate, I wrote those two papers, which were interesting and really said something about the nature of suggestion. It was accepted and then I called it back as not ready to publish, I had left something out. I had left out a certain control which both Merton Gill and Sidney Margolin had pointed out to me I should have done. Agreeing with them and being conscientious, I said, "I don't want you to print it now. I'll rewrite it and send it," so six months later they were published. I've never heard from then since. I only know one person who ever seems to have read them and that's Leon Chertok in France. The editorial board must have thought something of them and wanted to publish them. Anyway, I mention those papers because they have something to do with Poetzl. I bumped into Lou Linn one day and he was carrying a book. He said, "Have you ever read Poetzl?" I said, "No, but I've always wanted to." He said, "Well, it's very interesting. You want to take it?" So, I said, "Yes." It was in German. I took it home and sat down with a dictionary and ploughed through this terrible German, which I have described as "the most turgid German that ever flowed from the pen of man." I was able to figure out what he had done and what the Poetzl experiment amounted to, and I got very excited. You understand, these articles were written in 1917. This was 35 years later, and no one had ever bothered to repeat them, although Freud devoted a long paragraph to them in *The Interpretation of Dreams*. He said this was the most interesting dream experiment that anyone has done; they stand apart and they have implications not only for the psychology of dreams, but they go way beyond what concerns analysis. Now Poetzl had been a member of the Vienna Psychoanalytic Society for three or four years, and he was a neurologist who belonged to the Vienna Neurological Society. He became interested in analysis and wrote a long monograph on what came to be known as the Poetzl phenomenon, which shows the influence of Freud. He dropped out of the Vienna Society. Certain people remained interested in his experiments. Schilder mentioned them from time to time. He influenced Schilder, and a couple of Americans named Malamud repeated the work. They did an interesting experiment. They used patients in a mental institution. They exposed pictures, not tachistoscopically but for 30 seconds, and were able to show the same phenomenon, that is, even looking at a picture for 30 seconds, part of it may be repressed, denied, or not looked at, and that part that is not apperceived at the moment, that constitutes a fleeting day residue and gets into subsequent dreams. The Malamuds were really the first ones to repeat the experiment, not as it was done. The real experiment, which was the most interesting, involved the pictures being exposed for 1/100 of a second, so you couldn't see anything. At that time, I was 45 years old, a boring period of my creative life, so I got very excited about the Poetzl experiment and I decided to repeat it, all on my own. So, I got a slide projector and a lens off of a camera, and I had a primitive tachistoscope about like the one Poetzl had used. It doesn't take complex apparatus and I began to repeat the experiment.

AR: You were doing this at Sinai?

CF: Yes. I had a little room off Ward A where I could work. I did a number of experiments and they came out pretty classy and I put them together and published them, and the *Journal of the American* was excited about them and they gave it the lead article of that issue and that article caused a big stir. This was called "Dreams and Perceptions," and I got hundreds of requests for reprints, had little notes from everybody, from Karl

Menninger, complimenting me for doing this marvelous experiment. of course, it all had the prestige of—I introduced the article by quoting Freud, you can't go wrong if you quote Freud. I don't know if I quoted Rapaport, yes, I quoted him about other things, and I wrote a 50 page article and I included drawings of dreams and pictures, and when I presented it in 1954. I brought my tachistoscope and flashed some pictures on the screen, which impressed everybody. I did my experiment right in front of them. This was at the New York Society. By that time, I was sufficiently over my phobia for speaking that I was able to perform. That was the first time I had given a paper in the Society aside from the one back in 1944 which I gave in my uniform. This one I gave without my uniform. It always helps if you know you have a good thing and I knew that I had written an important paper, which would excite some interest, which it did.

AR: Who were the discussants, do you know?

CF: I think Kris was a discussant. He was very friendly What did he say? I can't remember the discussion. He wanted to do something together with me on memory. Kris was interested in memory. I don't know what he had in mind. Anyway, that was a great success and then in 1956 I published a second paper called "Dreams, Images, and Perception." By that time, I had heard of the Foundation's Fund for Research in Psychiatry at Yale, they were giving out money, they had just started, so it was suggested to me that I apply. At that time, it had a marvelous board. It had Sybil Escalona, the guy who became Dean of the medical school at Yale, Fritz Redlich, and many others in research who had influence. This was the beginning of a revolution in psychiatric research.

NIH had begun back in the 40s—it used to be when you were a principal investigator in a medical school on a project, you didn't get paid. The Foundation's Fund for Research in Psychiatry was willing to pay the senior researcher, who was also an analyst in private practice, a certain sum of money for giving up some of his time for research. They gave me $7500 for 15 hours of work. It wasn't much money but a principle was established. Around the same time, the National Institute of Health was doing the same thing. I don't know who started it first.

AR: That's when they started the career investigator.

CF: It was a little later than that that they started the career investigator, but that changed the whole complexion of research. otherwise, if you were in private practice and wanted to do a project, they wouldn't pay you. If you had enough money and you got a big grant and you had some assistants, they'd pay the assistants. Anyway, that changed the climate of research in this country. They continued to give me grants from 1954 to 1959, so in 1956 I published a second paper on "Dreams, Images, and Perception." In 1957 I published another one on "Construction of Dreams and Images," and altogether from 1954 to 1960 I published about nine papers. They were always thick papers. I was always longwinded, and I had pictures and diagrams, about 50-page papers. Anyway, I need not go into the details of the work.

AR: Have you thought of having them collected?

CF: Yes, people have been asking me for years to collect them and publish a monograph or a book. The Foundation's Fund wanted to do it, the *Journal of the American* has a monograph series, Basic Books, I think. We had about three offers but I just never bothered to put them together.

AR: You got three offers?

CF: I just never did anything; I wasn't ready to do it yet. In a sense I was correct, I wasn't ready. I was always somehow dissatisfied with whatever I did, it had to be better. Not that I'm the most perfectionistic researcher in the world—I'm not. I do something even though I know it's defective or faulty. I'm perfectly willing to publish and I always feel if there are any mistakes in it, as long as the basic stuff is okay, someone else will correct them or I'll correct them. I didn't have to have perfection. I wasn't that way. Anyway, at that time I got dozens of requests for reprints and invitations to talk all over, and I understand many institutes were having seminars going over these papers of mine. For a period of 13 years, in the early 60s to the mid-70s, my secretary saved all the invitations I would get. I have a big folder, it has 80 invitations, from practically every institute in the country and lots of other places; to lecture, write papers and monographs. It all created a big stir. It also got into my next phase when I got into the REM stuff.

AR: I don't know of any other psychoanalyst who created such a stir in quite that way.

CF: No, I don't think so. It lasted a long time, for a period of 12 or 13 years. I was getting six invitations a year that I had rejected. I'd just write that I didn't have time, and I'd select some. For a while I gave papers to half the institutes in the country and then I couldn't do any more; all these honors detract from your work. I was offered at least three professorships, which I turned down.

AR: Really? Where?

CF: Some good ones, I've forgotten. You know, once you make some kind of reputation there's a concerted effort to keep you from working any more, so what you have to do is to refuse honors. I was asked to run for President of the American three times. Like Caesar I rejected them.

AR: Is that a corollary of the Peter Principle? The principle that people get to a certain level and then they deteriorate. There's some administrative principle which says that people are pushed higher and higher to a point where their talents—it's a reflection of how inefficiently organizations are run in that regard.

CF: If that's the Peter Principle, I resisted the Peter Principle. The reason I've been able to work as long as I have and still be somewhat productive is that I refused these honors. First, I didn't want to be President of the American, as nice as that would have been. My narcissism is great enough, but it's like being president of a large labor union and you have to devote a lot of time, and I was not sufficiently interested in politics. I had no great ambitions to change the course of psychoanalysis in this world, nor did I notice that anybody else was doing it, and I just simply refused. I was offered to be the President of the Institute. I finally did accept to be the President of the Society. I did that because it didn't take any work. You'd go to meetings, you'd wear a tux, you didn't have to do any preparation, and you had a secretary who did what little work there was to do.

AR: You were the President when I became a member.

CF: You remember my being the President?

AR: You must have signed the certificate.

CF: I must have. Anyway, I enjoyed being the President. I was there from 1965 to 1967. There wasn't much to do. I always enjoyed going to the meetings. Also, you notice, particularly on the part of your German and European colleagues, who have a quite different attitude toward authority than Americans, suddenly you were treated as if—not even Heinz Hartmann, Kris, all of them. Termination—suddenly you're the President. It doesn't make any difference to the Americans. The Europeans with their authoritarian souls really treat you differently and you notice that. Anyway, I enjoyed being President for a couple of years. You didn't have to do anything. I put in my dues at the Institute for a number of years, although I did manage to preserve my practice in the afternoon and I did my research in the morning, and I managed to preserve my time so I could continue to do some work and also make a living, but I committed myself to be on a good many committees. There were periods when I was at meetings three days a week. I was on the Education Committee for six years, at a nice time, in the 60s. Things were rather peaceful. What authority there was reigned supreme. It was not a time of friction. Hartmann was on, Loewenstein was on, Bak was Chairman, and he was a very good Chairman. He was a real politician, a manipulator. He was the one I said never took a majority vote lying down. But he was very good in those days, he was liberal. When issues came up, he was on the liberal side, and everyone was friendly.

AR: That was before the Victor Rosen-Robie Bak confrontation.

CF: That was at the end of my time. Do you know that whole story?

AR: No. I would be interested in it.

CF: I won't take up this time. I know the whole story, I was inside it, and I'll tell it to you. But during those years Margaret Mahler was on the Education Committee, Edith Jacobson, Annie Reich, Rudy Loewenstein, and a few minor characters like me. I. was intimidated. Nothing much happened, just normal business went on, and there were no crises at the time; it was a rather peaceful period. The Institute was at its peak of prestige and power in the 60s. Patients were still available. There was money coming in and it was a nice time. That was the Golden Age. Then I got honors. I got the first Menninger Award for the best research of the year. I gave the Brill Lecture in 1965 and the Freud Lecture in 1969. I got the Hartmann Award.

AR: Then you must have been the second Hartmann Award person?

CF: Actually, the Hartmann Award was supposed to be for young researchers. When I got it in 1957, or 1967, I was nearly 60 years old. It was supposed to be for young investigators. What happened is that all the older analysts got it. Greenacre got it when she was about 90, Bert Lewin got it, even Anna Freud.

AR: There were two awards, the junior and the senior.

CF: There wasn't at that time. That was a wise move to do that—they gave one to Anna Freud, to Greenacre, and Bert Lewin got one, and then about that time I represented the youth, about 1960 I got it. So, in 1956 I was made a training analyst. Again, it was conferred on me. I made no application. I was just told one day. Annie Reich called me up and said, "You've been made a training analyst." I said, "That's fine," and the next thing I was told they wanted me to teach a course.

AR: By the way, you were probably one of the first Americans to be made a training analyst at the Institute. How many of them were there before you, who weren't from Europe? I think just Jack Arlow and Charlie Brenner.

CF: We were made training analysts around the same time. Arlow said I was made one before him. I think there may have been some others before me, I'm not sure. I'm quite sure there were. It's worth looking up. The *Archives of Psychiatry,* is it called? The *Journal of the American Medical Association*—is it the *Archives of Neurology and Psychiatry* or just the *Archives of Psychiatry?* They took a poll once of the most popular analysts or something. It started out with Hartmann and Erikson and went down a list, I wasn't quite at the bottom of it but I was the only one who was a full American, the only American on the list, the rest were European.

Anyway, I'm getting off the track. I wanted to tell you something. In all this I never felt that I was an adequately trained analyst because I had not had the advantages of good courses or supervision. I was kind of self-made. I had my own analysts to imitate, as one tends to do. I didn't imitate in any kind of slavish way. I didn't take on my own analyst's research interests, which I readily could, since my primary preoccupation was with depression, and you understand what led me into my own interests were deeply involved with depression as I knew it, and actually altered states of consciousness in which people do crazy things, dreams, fugue-states, where people commit murder, sleepwalking, primitive ideas of a little boy, not so primitive, but I understood somehow the power of the forces inside that could not be controlled and they could do crazy things like commit suicide. This formed the core of my basic passion for exploration, I think, and I was always interested in depression and always thought that Freud's paper on "Mourning and Melancholia" was—one of his great, great masterpieces as well as a great literary masterpiece, and I read a lot of the literature on depression. It was not anything I wanted to explore except in myself. I haven't gotten through with my own career. I have had several careers.

I learned a lot from George Klein, Bob Holt and Irving Paul, Wolitsky, and that whole group. I learned how to do an adequate experiment.

AR: Is that in relation to the dream as wish and so forth? I've used your material in teaching a course on just chapter 7 at NYU.

CF: The dream as wish I still cling to, with modifications.

AR: Well, the purpose is the preservation of sleep.

CF: I modified that, that the dream does not act to preserve sleep, because you can do away with dreams by suppressing them with drugs or the so-called waking method, and sleep continues. Freud said that the dream work fails in its function when anxiety is produced so that one awakens from the REM dream. If the dream work is successful, let's say in binding anxiety, then REM sleep is preserved, but not sleep in general. People can sleep quite well during the night, even if REM sleep is suppressed altogether. Nonanxious dreaming thus preserves REM sleep.

AR: Yes, you don't need dreaming to preserve sleep. You need dreaming to preserve REM sleep.

CF: That's right. And then I made modifications in the Picket model, which I think are important, and I made it way back in 1957. And it's a model now that the cognitive psychologists, using different terms, have picked up. Theirs is not as good as a model as I made.

AR: What was your model?

CF: You remember the Picket model? Freud made one mistake, one inconsistency; although he said that all mental life begins in the unconscious and some of it ends in consciousness, he equated perceptual with conscious. The greater part of what psychologists would call perceptual processing or information processing goes on in the unconscious and in a final phase some of it reaches consciousness. In his model, Freud equated perception with consciousness, e.g., if you look at something you're conscious of it at the moment of perception. All the work that's been done since Poetzl shows that conscious perception is preceded by a phase outside of consciousness. Shevrin and others have shown that between the instant of registration and the arrival of a percept it into consciousness takes about a half-second, and that's quite a long time. These findings have important implications for the theory of perception and the theory of dream interpretation.

AR: That was an exciting new field.

CF: This goes back to 1917. This is what Poetzl said: With a dream, he said, that parts of the percept that aren't seen nevertheless register. It's a very weak stimulus which becomes a memory trace, and in the middle of the night there's a second activation of that preconscious memory trace, and it gets into dream consciousness as a delayed delivery. The same is true for images, for hallucinations, and for dreams.

AR: Isn't that like Palombo's ideas about dreaming as a system for the sorting of memories?

CF: Palombo? I haven't read Palombo lately. He is a believer in information processing, and I think he's coming closer to combining it with psychoanalysis. I have been in touch with some information processors, and conscious perception and dreaming can be put in information processing terms. They are now making diagrams, quite like the diagram I made 35 years ago, although mine is more complicated because it shows how the dream is formed. What I would call a precocious schema, they would call short-term memory, and they equate long-term memory with the unconscious. They now agree that these first two phases of perception and the dream process take place outside of consciousness.

Erdelyi has written a book on *Psychoanalysis: Freud's Cognitive Psychology,* and he puts it in information processing terms, but he's read a good deal about psychoanalysis and he understands it, so he's been translating these things into information processing and attempting to reconcile them. I have no objection to it. What I'm trying to do is put together the old subliminal discoveries of the '50s and make some kind of synthesis with the recent work of the cognitive psychologists. They've shown something that Poetzl was on to long ago, a thing called blind sight. Have you heard of blind sight? A man is blind, he can't see.

AR: But yet there's some awareness of where things are.

CF: You tell him there's something out there that he can't see but he should try to reach for it. Marcel, an Englishman, takes pictures of these blind men reaching for a glass, everything he does, the movements he goes through, reaching for it; he found that they made the motions that a person who can see would be making, and not just random. It's as if he can see without knowing that he can see. What that means is that his vision is perfect but he can't see. He has a cortical blindness. If you have cortical damage, the pathway that registers percepts and interacts with memory traces is intact and can inform one there is a glass out there, but the path way from there to consciousness is damaged so that the person can't have any awareness of it. However, he has registered it so that in some way he "sees." It's just the final step of getting into consciousness that is missing. There remains a preconscious knowledge of the glass.

AR: They've done these studies with the split brain.

CF: The split brain stuff has something to do with this. Anyway, it's just that there is an interruption of the complete visual pathway, but there is enough of the pathway that registers and makes a memory trace. There is a memory trace there without visual recognition. Dream formation involves related processes. Poetzl put all this together, this kind of blind sight, because he was essentially a neurologist. He put together blind sight, eidetic imagery, hallucinations, the normal dream, and normal perception.

AR: The definition of geniuses, right?

CF: He was a crazy genius.

AR: He'd seen things before everyone else. Freud had it.

CF: Freud had some of it. Freud kind of lost sight of it. I didn't have it, but I had enough of it so that as soon as I read Poetzl, I had a profound conviction that this was true, and I said this is the way the brain and the mind work, must work.

CF: At that time, I had become closely collaborated with George Klein, Bob Holt—Hartvig Dahl claims he was influenced by me to go into research many, many years ago. The group around George Klein at the Research Center for Mental Health was Irving Paul, Leo Goldberger, Wolitsky, Spence, and Klein, and they all became research students at the New York Psychoanalytic Institute. I was Chairman of the Research Students' Committee.

AR: By the way, you know that in the early 1960s Howard Shevrin was doing research based on your work in Topeka?

CF: Yes, that's how Howie and I became friends. In 1953 I gave my paper before the Institute, which was the first replication of the Poetzl experiment. In 1954 it was published. They were just preparing to repeat Poetzl themselves. Actually, Rapaport had tried to repeat it but Rapaport was a theoretician, he wouldn't know how to set up an experiment. I'm not attempting to criticize him, but. . . . So, George and Holt never repeated it. Aside from Poetzl there were a couple of Germans in 1922 named Allers and Teller who did an imagery experiment, that is, they'd flash a slide tachistoscopically and then have a person close his eyes and see an image— it was more complicated. They'd have a first image and then have a word association test and were able to show that the unseen portions of the picture emerged into consciousness. I repeated their experiment myself and modified it and made it simpler to do--that became a thing that the psychologists took up and, in fact, the actual Poetzl dream experiment was hardly replicated, which is in many ways more important, though the imagery experiment was also important.

AR: You know the work of Shevrin and Stross?

CF: Oh, yes. Then Howie in 1956 got in touch with me and they were fooling around with hypnosis.

AR: Right.

CF: And then they read my paper. They were elated and so they repeated these things themselves in a very nice way, and then they went on; they were psychologists who had ways of doing things that were foreign to me. They wanted to quantify it, score it, and scale it, and they did their famous Rebus experiment. Do you know about that?

AR: You know who the subject for that experiment was.

CF: You?

AR: No, Arlene. You know the tiny rebus dream that was Arlene.

CF: Is that right? Isn't that cute?

AR: Yes, in Topeka, in 1960. She could not understand how after she woke up and they asked her to tell a story, she said she began talking about this tiny, teeny town. A picture of a tie and a knee were presented, and they unconsciously fused to make the rebus of tiny, these tiny, teeny, people, and kept on in that vein.

CF: That was a marvelous experiment. They wouldn't always get the Rebus effect but they would get the associations to tie or knee, especially with people who had a looser unconscious.

AR: Arlene was a great hypnotic subject.

CF: They were the ones who would condense and make rebuses. So, in 1963, I went out to Topeka and spent a month with Howie.

AR: Were you a Sloan Professor?

CF: Yes, I was a Sloan Professor. I was squeezed in between Margaret Mead and Aldous Huxley, I think. Were you there when I was a professor?

AR: Yes.

CF: Do you remember me?

AR: I really don't—yes and no—I remember some lectures.

CF: I gave a couple of lectures and I gave a seminar. I put in a month's work there, because Howie and I did an experiment.

AR: We had Huxley over for Passover, and Margaret Mead (she was not that involved with the residents) but I was there then. Huxley came for Passover, that must have been about April, and I think Mead came just as he was leaving, and that was in June. You were probably there in May.

CF: No, I went the day Mead left. She had a party and I went to the party. It was in June, and then she left. I had a very bad impression of her. She never stopped talking and the yield was about 30 percent. She talked and talked and a lot of it was just nonsense.

AR: I had just finished my residency and we left, because we took our leave at the end of the year, at the end of the residency.

CF: They had some very great people. I was flattered that I was asked.

AR: Lorenz came.

CF: Yeah, Konrad. Well, I was included in that whole gang. About 1960 the subliminal stuff was blowing up in smoke. The academic psychologists attacked their own work viciously. They were doing something they called perceptual defense. Some people were doing subliminal advertising, which gave subliminal perceptual research a bad name. I was running out of ideas. I didn't know quite where to go, and then we were under attack from the psychologists, who repudiated their own work on perceptual defense. Now 25 years later it's coming back amongst the cognitive psychologists. In 1955 Bill Dement wrote me a letter and asked me for a reprint and then he sent me his thesis.

AR: He was in Chicago then?

CF: He was in Chicago, so I read that, and that was like another revelation. I said, "Jesus Christ, what a thing." There was a built-in neurobiological cycle in the brain, in the central nervous system, in the neurochemical system of the brain, which—it seems that there is a cycle that every 90 minutes develops into a REM period, and is there every night from birth to old age with some variations, and it's during that time that you dream. You dream two hours a night, and whoever knew that—we all thought that dreaming, and Freud thought it, too, was a fleeting experience that occurred once in a while, although Freud in his omniscience had expressed the idea from time to time in *The Interpretation of Dreams* that we may dream all night long. The REM cycle was discovered by Kleitman and a graduate student named Aserinsky in 1953. It was a serendipitous finding, and they didn't know how important it was. Aserinsky was given his Ph.D. very reluctantly, on the basis of his work, and he ran away to Pittsburgh and he wasn't heard from for 10 years. After 10 years he emerged and discovered that a whole revolution had taken place in sleep research. He came to the annual meeting of the sleep researchers in the early 60s and was greeted as a conquering hero, and he didn't know all this stuff was going on. Dement picked up the work after Aserinsky quit. He worked for five years, and he understood the significance of what was going on. I began to communicate with him in 1955 and we got friendly. He had his Ph.D. and his M.D. but he never had an internship. This work was so little known at the time, in the 50s, it had no particular prestige. He wanted to take an internship. So, I said, "Why don't you come to Mount Sinai and we can do some work together?" So that's what he did. He came to Mount Sinai in 1958, took an internship. In 1959 we got a joint grant from the National Institute of Health. My grant from the Research Foundation at Yale had come to an end. Dement took an internship there, and, after he was through, we established a little laboratory and we began to do some work together. I was 20 years older than Dement, and we began to have trouble from the very beginning. He was bringing his sleep research to me and he had done a lot of work, and by collaborating with me, he was afraid I would get the credit for it. The first thing we were both interested in was to learn more about the REM cycle that beats away every night. When you want to know what something is for, you suppress it, e.g., you cut out an organ to see what happens.

AR: Or you make a lesion in the brain.

CF: That's right. So, we thought of ways of suppressing REM by giving drugs or using hypnosis. Dement had noticed that if he suppressed a REM period, the next one came in sooner, so he got the idea that there was a push to get REM sleep. He developed the following method: Every time the eyes began to move he would wake the subject, keep him awake for a while, and then let him go back to sleep. If he did that the first night, the subject's eyes would begin to move seven times and he would be wakened seven times. If we'd keep doing it, the second night it would be 10 times, the third night 16 times, and the fourth night 20 times, the fifth night 40 times. And so, pressure builds to get REM sleep, and if you get REM sleep you get dreams. So, this was a remarkable psychobiological finding. That's what set off the whole worldwide industry of dream research. Now, we were afraid to do this suppression, and I was afraid because Freud said a man deprived of his dreaming would undoubtedly go mad, and that the dream is the normal psychosis. I coined a phrase which is often quoted. W. H. Auden put it in his book of quotations that he published—he'd keep little things that he found, and he once quoted me as stating, "Dreaming permits each and every one of us to be quietly and safely insane every night of our lives." We were afraid that suppressing REM sleep would cause dreaming during the day or psychosis. Dement stayed up 250 nights the first year. I would see the subjects every morning and go over them and talk to them and make sure they were not going nuts. We did detect certain things. A couple of guys went into a state of depersonalization, a lot of them showed a certain amount of hostility and anxiety. We only suppressed at the most five days, on one person for a week and one person for 15 nights. This was a joint experiment. It was my laboratory. He had come to work for me, and I did a lot of work. I watched these subjects to make sure we weren't doing them any harm, and Dement needed me. He wasn't a psychiatrist. But I began to see, he began to get more and more secretive and wanted to do experiments by himself and not let me know about it. So, he came to me one day and wanted to publish some preliminary results, and he said couldn't he publish these preliminary results under his own name? Because it was the first original thing he had done and he wanted to get the credit for it so I thought about it. I was the senior person, I helped him set up the lab, and we collaborated. I said, "You can publish these original physiological results, but we'll write a second, joint paper on the psychological results," that is, the observations I had made. He agreed to that, but then he never acted on it. He wrote his paper and didn't even give me a footnote. He's always gotten credit for the work, and for years it was kept rather secret that I collaborated with him. I regretted that I had not insisted on a joint publication. Our relationship went from bad to worse. He became paranoid. Arguably, he became paranoid because of chronic sleep loss, which can make one paranoid. He wasn't getting enough sleep, and then he did other nasty things. He would go off and give a lecture without telling me he was going and people told me he would never mention me at the lectures, or invite me to come along, so his fear was that I would absorb his reputation—and I used to say to him, "Look, Bill, this is your work, you began it long before you ever came here and you are going to get very famous for your work, quite independent of me." And I tried to reassure him that I would not displace him. After two and a half years, I said, "Bill, you don't belong here. There's no future for you. This is a hospital." It wasn't a medical school yet. I said, "You need to get into an academic department," and so he agreed finally. David Hamburg quickly became interested in Dement and he became full Professor of Psychiatry at Stanford, and he and his laboratory are famous.

This was a time when they were beginning to give the title of professor of psychiatry to people who were not psychiatrists. It started with Seymour Kety, who went to Hopkins, and he was made professor of psychiatry, but he only stayed a little while. He said he felt uncomfortable being called professor of psychiatry when he didn't know any psychiatry. But that didn't interfere with Bill. Anyway, Bill probably has the biggest sleep laboratory in the world. He made a big success out of it at Stanford, and his laboratory has produced extremely important work. But I had a lousy time with him.

I was left with the sleep laboratory by that time—this was 1962. I was the sole director of the sleep laboratory, which I have remained all these years (until 1985), and I proceeded to do important work on my own. As an investigator, I didn't need a Bill Dement, although he was a first-rate one, very imaginative. The first thing I did was begin to work on nightmares, which I was interested in, and night terrors. Before that I demonstrated the REM erection cycle. I had heard that Aserinsky had mentioned that some Germans named Ohlmeyer et al., back in 1943, had done a curious experiment, which I always suspected was done in concentration camps, because they were always doing sexual experiments. However, this was a harmless experiment and a very good one. They hooked up males with some sort of gadget, some sort of ring which could expand, and if you got an erection it could end up in a tracing on a smoked drum. That's how primitive it was. They published a tracing showing just when these erections occurred during the night. Aserinsky, I think, had noticed that the erections seemed to occur every 90 minutes and he got the idea that they may have been occurring synchronously with the REM periods, so that idea was around. Several people tried to repeat it. One was a very good English psychiatrist named Ian Oswald, a very sardonic but bright guy. He and a man named Berger tried to repeat the experiment. Oswald wrote a little book on sleep in which he said they tried to repeat the experiment but they couldn't get the apparatus right and they couldn't make it. work. And then he went on, nastily and ironically, to say. that this is grist for the mill for psychoanalysts, but they probably don't read the right journals. Ohlmeyer, Hilsprung, and somebody else published two papers in *Pfluegers Archive*, an old, old German journal. So, I hastened to go and get that article. I could read enough German in those days. I became excited after reading the article by the German workers and was convinced that the periods of erection could be correlated with the REM periods and felt that this was an important psycho-biological finding which had implications for psychoanalytic sexual and drive theory and important for understanding the neurophysiological basis of dreaming. I was determined to repeat the Ohlmeyer experiment, and, with the assistance of an ingenious resident named Joseph Gross, succeeded in constructing what we called our "plethysmographic bagel," a doughnut shaped plastic device that enabled us to place it over the penis which when it erected at night exerted pressure on the walls of the bagel, forcing water in it through a tube hung on the wall by which we could get a manometric reading of the extent of the rise in the tube, thus obtaining a quantitative measure of the degree of the nocturnal erection. With this device plus the use of several other methods including direct observation we obtained very good results. We found that 95% of

REM periods were associated with nocturnal erections, that they began and terminated in close temporal relationship to the beginning and end of the REM periods, that two thirds of them were maximum, that they were present from birth to extreme old age, that nocturnal emissions occurred during them, etc. Nocturnal penile erections are associated with nearly every REM period and are present from early infancy to old age, though diminished in the 80s and 90s. Somewhat later on, I and my competitor simultaneously discovered nocturnal erections could be used as a test for impotence.

AR: Who was your competitor?

CF: A guy named Ismet Karacan, he's out at Baylor. What we demonstrated was that in psychogenic impotence these erections may remain intact. In organic they are partially or wholly impaired. However, it turned out to be not that simple, and the test has to be used cautiously because there are intermediate formations where it's partially organic and partially psychogenic. A high percentage of organic impotence is due to diabetes, but there is no reason why a man with diabetic impotence can't have a lot of psychogenic factors also. Anyway, it's a long story. My name is mentioned more in the urological literature than in psychoanalytic. Urologists are doing a lot of work with the NPT method. When used cautiously and with other means, it is a useful method. It's one of the practical results that grew out of sleep research, one more thing that I did—my final piece of research. The question kept arising, is there anything in the female that corresponds to nocturnal erection in the male? I was convinced that there was; there just had to be some way of getting at it. The logical place to look was to see whether there was clitoral tumescence during early sexual arousal. I explored that possibility and couldn't get any consistent results, and then someone produced a gadget, an intravaginal gadget, by which you could get a recording. The essence of sexual arousal in male and female is vascular engorgement. When the penis engorges, erection occurs. In women there is increased pelvic engorgement. There is a lot more erectile tissue in the female than one would suspect. The vestibular bulbs which surround the distal aspect of the vagina are highly vascular, resembling erectile tissue. The clitoris is composed of erectile tissue but it isn't very big; the so-called crura of the clitoris are rather large and probably are composed of erectile tissue. There are large veinous complexes surrounding the vaginal walls which engorge with sexual arousal. The clitoris also erects. The clitoris is a kind of trigger; the easiest way to arouse a woman is to stimulate her clitoris. I think that's the method universally followed by the male, and with that she will also engorge. The first thing that happens in sexual arousal in the female is increased secretion associated with increased vascularity and tumescence. The last paper I published, in 1983, is called "Sexual Arousal in the Female, Diurnal and Nocturnal Sexual Arousal in the Female." It was published in the *Archives of Sexual Behavior*. If you want to read it I'll send you a copy. All these studies were long and arduous.

AR: What did that show, the last study?

CF: It showed that women engorge in 95 percent of their REM periods. However, there is not as much engorgement as there is in the male. There are some differences. I have some records that I published. One record is of a woman who had an orgasm during sleep, and I have some records showing graphs of two women who masturbated in the laboratory. In a laboratory you can get men and women to do most anything for science. They masturbated to orgasm; these are unique demonstrations. Then I found out that vascular is not infinite, it reaches a certain point. The engorgement that occurs at night without orgasm is as great as the engorgement that occurs when a woman masturbates, the same as in the male. A male gets a hard erection during the night, and they are as hard as any erections you get, and that's erection without ejaculation. I have one recording of a wet dream in a male. The psychological purpose and function of all this is obscure. What do we need all that erection for? It's clear that when you have a wet dream, it occurs in a REM period, but why do we need 20 percent of the night in a state of full erection? It's a good question. I haven't been able to answer it. That's the last of my research.

AR:, By the way, what about Stanley Friedman?

CF: Yes, I forgot to mention Stanley. I collaborated with several people who have been very helpful. Irving Paul and I did a study trying to make the method of subliminal perception more objective. Irving Paul is a very clever experimenter. We did a couple of very good papers together. Stanley and I did a couple of papers together also. The idea was around that the REM cycle beats away during the day. Oral cycles and even the erections have been shown to go on during the day, but hidden by the waking state. Stanley did an experiment which I didn't think would work but it did, in which he had people in an isolated room, gave them food ad lib, and just kept a record when they ate, over an eight-hour period. They seemed to eat in a cycle, a 180 minute cycle. This has been confirmed. Oswald, who was always making fun of analysts, got very impressed with the fact that I demonstrated the erection cycle, which he wasn't able to do. Then he got even more impressed with the fact that Stanley and I demonstrated there was an oral cycle. He then repeated the experiment himself and, to his surprise, found that we were right. Oswald respected me, but he hates psychoanalysts. I always had a special position amongst these sleep researchers. They knew I was an analyst but also that I had done a lot of work in neurophysiology years ago, and my old work and reputation helped me a lot. But none of this tells you anything about my role as an analyst. One thing was certain. What I did was very hard to do, to do this kind of hard-nosed physiological work is antithetical to the kinds of intuitive talents required to be an analyst.

What I had from Tarachow was the equivalent of a good course in the nature of the transference and in supervision in general. And that's really the best supervision I ever had. Later on, when I was admitted to the New York Institute and was told I ought to have a little supervision, I had six hours with Annie Reich. Annie Reich was a great woman, but she hardly said anything to me during those six hours. After six hours she said I was a mature psychoanalyst, which I never believed, and I wasn't a mature psychoanalyst. I really needed a lot of help. I was very uncertain of myself and, however, I reported to her precisely what went on with me and the patient and what I said and what the patient said, and she seemed sufficiently impressed. The only thing I ever remember that she brought to my attention, which was then a new idea to me, was about the pregenital defense against oedipal material, that is, there was a regression to pregenitality, as you know, against talking about oedipal things. And I hadn't heard of that, no one had ever spoken about that in Washington, and I hadn't read enough, so I didn't know about that kind of thing. But as I remember, that's the only thing she said to me that struck me in my six hours with her. There was a misunderstanding. She had kind of believed that I was going on with the supervision, but I thought I was supposed to stop at the end of the six sessions when I was admitted to the Institute. I should have gone on with her. She was a very good, brilliant analyst, and she also wrote some interesting things.

AR: I think Tarachow had a profound influence on the Downstate NYU Institute. People had been analyzed by him, and he was really very much a role model and an ego ideal.

CF: Yeah. Kanzer is also brilliant, but he is a very peculiar gent. I know him fairly well. He's a real schizy person. He is now very depressed. He had a son who committed suicide. Do you want to know these details? He had a son who committed suicide, and his other son won't talk to him. His wife either died or left him. He's a lonely person, and he speaks about himself freely and says that all he has is his work. He recently gave the Freud Lecture. Were you there?

AR: No, I missed that. He's also very bitter about many analytic organizations—ours and NYU.

CF: Maybe. I think he was President of Downstate. I think some of their leading members were bitter that they did not get the recognition they thought they deserved from the New York Institute. They all were talented, but I think they either made some enemies or were disapproved of because it was felt they were too neurotic.

AR: What about Maury Friend?

CF: I knew Maury Friend. As a matter of fact, we followed one another across the country, but I didn't know him.

He went to the University of California, Southern Branch, around the time I did. He was in Chicago when I was, also in Washington, and I got to know him some here, but we were never particularly good friends. We had some patients, I mean families, in common, and I know he did a very good job on a real paranoid kid. He had the son of a patient of mine, and he was a decent guy, and I think somewhat competent, no ball of fire.: You know the Communist Party had learned that a small, organized nucleus who worked together, if there were just four or six people, could enter a factory and organize it and take it out on strike. Amongst psychoanalysts in New York, small groups played a rather important role. The first group was the most important and the most prestigious, which was the Arlow-Brenner-Wangh-Bores group. Those four used to meet together and they were very influential. Three of them became President of the American. They decided to-—don't .know if it was a decision—put their efforts into holding office at the level of the American. In doing so they neglected their politics at the New York. However, I think all of them have been—I don't think Arlow has ever been President of the Society or the Institute. Now Brenner has been President of both.

AR: None of those were ever head of the EC or the head of the faculty.

CF: No, they were never. They were all on the EC at one time or another, but they never had real power, and they thought they deserved power. They were very arrogant, knew their value. They said that they had new ideas but they never had a chance to put them into practice.

AR: In regard to training, they were against starting at the beginning, from what I have been told, reading all of Freud. They wanted to stress Freud post 1925.

CF: Really? I never heard any of these ideas expressed, and they certainly never had a chance as a group to put them into effect. But Brenner, in later years, managed to carry a majority of the Institute but he missed a two-thirds vote by about eight votes, and his power ended there. He really organized all the malcontents, the malcontents being those who lived in the suburbs, those who were disappointed because they weren't made training analysts, those who thought our Institute was too big to give everyone a function. And a lot of people thought that they had nothing to do. The Institute didn't mean anything to them, and it was too remote an organization.

AR: In a sense that's being repeated now as well, without Brenner. The current group that controls, the Board of Trustees, is also an alliance—I'm talking about George Gross, who is taking the same political posture that Brenner took.

CF: Things have a tendency to repeat themselves.

AR: It seems that way, yes.

CF: And once a group gets in power, the group that was on the outs, when it gets in power it begins to behave like the group that they replaced. That seems to be the way things work. Anyway, they never did attain the power that they wanted. Jack Arlow for some years sort of boycotted the Institute. He had been asked to run for, I know, the EC. He's been asked a number of times but has refused on the grounds that he doesn't get his way. I think he openly says that and I'm sure they've wanted to run him for President of the Society, which, of course, he deserves more than anybody for his scientific contributions, but he's not been. I don't know whether he's refused that or what. He's gone around and done a lot of lecturing, maybe in defiance, to lay groups. At the time it was disapproved of, so I wonder if there wasn't some rebellious thing in that.

AR: Well, you know—did you know much about the episode that caused the great problem? That was the Waldhorn problem.

CF: I told you I was instrumental in getting Waldhorn finally made a training analyst. Did I tell you that?

AR: I think so—but what did you do?

CF: He had been turned down 11 times. I was on the Faculty Advisory Committee a few times.

The last time I was on, Dora Hartmann was on, she was chairman, and I think there was Donadeo and Lily Busell. Anyway, Dora Hartmann was a very nice human being. I think she was not any ball of fire but she was a decent person. So, she insisted that we investigate these people more thoroughly than they were investigated in the past and the whole thing was often very perfunctory. And I brought up—why was Waldhorn rejected 11 times, what did they actually have against him? The only same year or a year apart, and I may have been the first, although no one ever said that. I know Edith Jacobson and Annie Reich had a lot to do with seeing to it that I was made a training analyst, a post for which I did not at all feel qualified. I didn't seek it or welcome it or want it, and I was very anxious when I was given it. And I have my anxiety problems about such things and a lot of self-depreciation. I never thought I was good enough, but in fact I wasn't good enough in my own estimation. And then what they asked me to do—they asked me to teach a course. And I guess it must have been Dr. Jacobson's doing because she had an overestimation of me, so it seems. She had a lot of countertransference, which she controlled very well, but I knew that she cared a lot about me, which was a corrective emotional experience much needed. So, she promoted me.

AR: They asked you to teach a course.

CF: Yes, the course was a reading course. The students had to read four papers, *The Problem of Anxiety,* the book, which, by the way, had never been taught until then. It's impossible to imagine why that happened, so I had to teach that, the paper on the "Unconscious" (the 1915 paper),

"Mourning and Melancholia," and a paper by Bibring on the instincts-all those four papers. I was not a good teacher. one of the things I must say about the Institute—there's been some correction since—in those days a person might be appointed a training analyst and be permitted to teach without any inquiry whatsoever as to whether he was able to teach, whether he wanted to teach, whether he had any experience in teaching, whether he had a talent for teaching, as if teaching was something anybody could do. Teaching is not something that anybody can do.

AR: That continues to this day.

CF: I wouldn't be surprised.

AR: I was appointed training analyst last year and then I get a call from the Curriculum Committee telling me that I'm going to be teaching a course on obsessive-compulsive neurosis next year, which is something I think I can do, but it seems to me it would have been more appropriate for someone to ask me.

CF: Do you want to, are you interested in teaching it?

AR: Yes, there's always been the attitude that what they have to offer is very desirable and they just make the decisions.

CF: It's nonsense. There are geniuses who make terrible teachers. There are especially a lot of research men who have no gift whatsoever for teaching.

AR: And some of the great analysts, the great theoreticians and writers as teachers.

CF: And some of the great teachers are not creative people, but they're good teachers. They know how to teach what is known. So here I was confronted with—what I had to do was keep a step ahead—my first class was with six very bright students.

AR: What year was this?

CF: 1956.

AR: What class?

CF: It was a first-year course. That may have been the time I had Manny Purer, Horowitz, Bill Grossman, I'm not sure. I may have got them mixed up, but I had all these people, some of the brightest students we've ever had—Joan Erle, who was extremely brilliant at the time. She's no dummy, Joan; I don't like her. Then there was another woman who died, who I think was a student, who I thought was just the most brilliant thing we had—I forget her name, she died of some disease. Anyway, I had students of that caliber who were as bright as I was, and all I had to do was keep a little bit ahead of them, and I never felt comfortable teaching. Then a little later on when Isakower became Chairman of the Curriculum Committee and, you know, the arrogance of the New York Institute carried over into things like, we boasted that we had the most superb curriculum of any institute in the country. I don't know what the proof of that was—probably it was—but it was something we seemed to be especially proud of, although I didn't see that there was anything so terribly great about it. What was so great about it, the greatest thing about it, was that there were some great teachers, and it was supposed to be a perfect curriculum, presumably imitated by many other institutes, which is probably true. But Isakower, who at that time had an interest in me, and this was long before—1958 or 1959—when he discussed a paper I gave at the Institute and never spoke to me again after that, as if I had done some harm to him—he was such a crazy human being. Anyway, he wanted me to teach a course in early ego development. I didn't even know anything about later ego development, and I also told him that we don't know much about early ego development, I didn't know what to teach. So, what I did was—he insisted that I go ahead and do what I could—so while I was doing my subliminal perception work, I spent a good deal of time talking about my own work, which had to do with perception and memory and at least certain ego functions of that kind. And as I remember, the students used to give reports on their teachers. I got some fairly good reports. They used to complain that I had a monotonous voice, sometimes sounded very tired, and the part they seemed to enjoy most was my own work, when I talked about perception, when I must have come to life, and I showed some slides and things of that sort. So, I stumbled through that course, and I taught it for a number of years.

AR: Were there students who stood out at this moment?

CF: Oh, yeah. The students who stood out were Manny Furer, Bill Grossman, who I was always very impressed with, Horowitz, Joan Erle, I told you-. And then for about five years I taught a course on sleep and dreaming, "Recent Research in Sleep and Dreaming-" That was very successful. I knew that it was all new. The students were especially enthusiastic during the early years. Then everyone seemed to get tired of it.

AR: Was Howie Roffberg in your class?

CF: No. I know that Howie Roffberg was a student for a while, but they let him go. You know one of the reasons they let him go? He was interested in dreams, you know, but he never could remember a dream of his own.

They figured he was very tightly defended, but I don't know what the real story is. It was probably a mistake to have let him go. He was a very bright person, and I think had a lot of problems. But he had a real brilliance as a researcher and was humble enough to want to have analytic training. Why did they let this talented, original man go and take in a lot of hacks? We have a couple of papers together. There was one paper on the ontogenesis of dreaming from infancy to old age. He did the essential work. It was done under me, and then he did the best paper ever done on the relationship of eye movements to dream content. There's still a controversy over the problem.

AR: Yes, the dream where someone is going upstairs? (associated with a series of vertical eye movements).

CF: Yes, and the eyes would go up. I had suggested this experiment to Dement in 1955. He had done some preliminary work on a man looking up, at an airplane or someone climbing a ladder or watching a couple playing tennis, where you get back and forth eye movement. There's no doubt there's some relationship, but it isn't a one-to-one relationship. The whole trouble with the attempt to relate the events in a dream to the occurrences in a dream, that is, the direction and motion and so forth of events in a dream to the physiological concomitants has been fraught with particular difficulties. It isn't as simple as anyone thought it would be, and there's a correlation of low significance when it's not a one-to-one relationship.

AR: How did your course end, after five years?

CF: I wanted to end it but I remember there was a meeting of the Curriculum Committee on which I was then serving. At that time the committee was in charge of these various students—Aaron Esman was one of the students, too, whom I was impressed with. There were a lot of them, all that group that's now in power. I remember I wanted to give up the course. The reports on the course were getting more critical than they had been, and I was getting tired of giving it. Anyway, and so I told them I didn't want to give it any more. Maybe I'd give it again later. So, I remember that Horowitz and Esman and all those people leapt on the idea that I was going to stop giving it, and the implication was that I would be asked to give it again later on. But I never was asked; and I think they wanted the slot for some other course. The interest in the psychopathology of sleep and dreams made very little impact. People would ask, "Well, does it alter the way we interpret dreams?" I would assure them that it really has nothing much to do with the way you interpret dreams. You can go on interpreting dreams the way you always have. Everyone would give a sigh of relief and then dismiss the whole matter from their heads. And no one seemed to be interested in the theoretical implications. All the problems that this remarkable psychobiological cycle built into the central nervous system and neurochemically regulated, what the hell it was doing there, why it was there, what its function was, and the many, many problems that it raises.

AR: Did you have any discussions with Nick Young about this?

CF: Nick Young, yes. When Dement and I first gave the paper at the Institute—that was in 1960—Dement and I presented the first findings on REM deprivation, which I think we got Rapaport to discuss, he came and discussed it favorably. Ostow got up and denied that the whole thing had any validity. He insisted that dreaming occurred in stage four, all with that booming, rabbinical, self-assured voice of his, and Nick Young, who never said anything at meetings, he was afraid to get up and discuss a paper because he had such murderous ambitions and aggression toward everybody. He probably quivers in his boots. He has never given a paper, written one, but he's been a tremendous force for evil in that institute of ours, if you want my private opinion. Well, he from the very first scorned. the whole dream research business. He thinks that Freud said the last word about dreams, and there isn't any more to be said about it. And to this day, I think that he thinks the whole business of all these major discoveries—which have created a whole new look at the way the central nervous systems works and its relation to sleep and waking and to dreams and all kinds of phenomena, it's spread all over the world and the basic findings are as certain as anything in science—this son of a bitch seems to deny that it exists, and he doesn't mention it in his dream course.

It was on account of Nick Young that Steve Ellman got into a fight. It was just when he. was about to graduate and I think he wanted to provoke a fight and wanted to get some excuse to resign, out of his own peculiar motives. Anyway, they got into a fight over me. They began talking about REM sleep, and Nick Young made some disparaging remarks, and Steve, who respects me and my work a lot, began to defend REM sleep. I don't know the details, although he told me. They got into a bitter fight, and Steve then resigned from the Institute. There was some attempt to make him stay in which Arlow was active. Arlow thought highly of him, enough so that he defended him, but he insisted on resigning.

Sidney was in analysis with Hartmann, and he used to tell me about his analysis. What I had absolutely no supervision in was transference. I knew it was around but in the very poor supervision I had—Kubie, for instance, never mentioned transference once and no one in Washington mentioned transference either, so I didn't know anything about analyzing transference, and to this day I think I'm deficient in picking up the subtleties of transference. It's like I have some sort of block about it, but Sidney used to tell me about the kind of things—if the patient came late, Hartmann would indicate that it had to be analyzed, or if he entered the room in a certain way or he took a certain position on the couch—he went into lots of details. Sidney was a good teacher, as you can tell from the book. So, I had a long course with Sidney.

AR: What was the point of talking about Sidney under supervision? What was the point you were trying to make?

CF: The point was that that was the only good supervision I ever had, aside from the sessions with Annie Reich. Somewhere I told you that Annie Reich never said much. She made the interpretation about preoedipal defenses and oedipal memories.

AR: We've done that. So, you were a training analyst for 20 years.

CF: Yes. I was a training analyst for 20 years, and during this period I only really analyzed three students. What that represented was an average analysis of about six to seven years. I told you about the first patient I analyzed, who turned out to be a psychopath and the Admissions Committee passed on him, except for Nick Young, who had an extremely astute eye for paranoid psychopaths. And it was alleged that when he first began supervision and was on the Admissions Committee, the first 12 students he saw, he made the diagnosis of paranoid psychopathy, and they were all rejected. So that if he made the diagnosis often enough, he was bound to hit on one. The one I got really turned out to be a psychopath. He was a physician. The Admissions Committee, as I said, approved of him, all except Nick Young, who made a very good case against him, but nobody paid any attention because by this time his credibility had been exhausted. But in his first session with me, he confessed to all kinds of terrible things he had done as a doctor, like performing an abortion on his wife and engaging in a lot of dishonest things involving money. And so, I kept him on in analysis, trying to give him a chance to change himself, but at the end of two years, I concluded that I wouldn't be able to analyze him. I reported to the Admissions Committee that I thought he ought to be given a chance with another analyst to see what he could do. So, he was turned over to Arnold Pfeffer, who kept him for another year and ultimately concluded the same things I did, that he was unanalyzable and a psychopath.

AR: Were you at that point a reporting analyst—how did you handle that issue?

CF: At that time, we used to write rather lengthy reports.

AR: Everyone did.

CF: I think so. It was Robie Bak, when he was Chairman of the EC, who kind of pressed for secrecy, to the point where we were finally given the option that we could write one line, like "the analysis is progressing." You didn't even have to say backwards or forwards, or you didn't have to record anything at all. But what went on all the time is the nonverbal kinds of communication that were passed on by training analysts to other analysts and to one another in committee meetings and other places, by a tone of voice, an expression of disgust on their faces, or other ways. And there was always a debate about "how should we do this?" There was a considerable amount of gossip, betrayal of confidence, and all kinds of things. I don't know that the matter was ever successfully resolved to this day. Somehow with some cases you feel there ought to be some reporting and with other cases that are going on successfully and you think the guy is going to make it—you might not have to say much, but it's a very thorny matter and one of those unresolvable things.

AR: Who was aligned on the other side from Robie Bak?

CF: I don't know. I don't remember that there were divisions in the matter. I think in general people were rather reasonable but no one really knew quite what to do, as I remember. I don't remember any desperate battles about it.

AR: I think the people who left to form Downstate tended to take the reporting ethos with them.

CF: Really? Well, anyway, what ended up with us was a sort of mishmash. Some people would report, some would not report anything, some people were lazy and didn't care to report. And there were different motivations for it, and I'm sure you know more about how it is now. But it's not resolved, there's no good way to do it. So that was my first case. Now there's a gap of some years there because I only had him for about two years, then I had another patient for six or seven years who was of dubious quality, but his supervisors finally thought enough of him to recommend him, and it was a difficult analysis, but he was made a member and he has found a niche for himself. Shall I name names? I won't name names. He had some special training that gave him a special position and he's done all right. I didn't make a mistake with him. The third one was a man who had a severely pathogenic history with a psychotic mother but with a good father who served as mother, who never remarried. His mother was hospitalized when he was five and he never saw her after 13, but he had a father who was both mother and father to him. The one good object seemed to have saved him, and after a long analysis, he did okay. For a long time, he would lie rigidly on the couch and not move a muscle. I remember I considered it a great analytic triumph when he finally raised an arm off the couch and his affect in general loosened up, and he was a sensitive guy with a certain amount of talent and a very decent human being. And in spite of his background, he was approved for graduation and it has turned out very well, very nice. So those are my three cases. Since I was doing research and had only a part-time practice, I didn't think I could take more than one student, partly for financial reasons. All the years I did research, I did this at a considerable financial sacrifice. I always did some supervision, which I liked to do, but I used to take one case—for a long time I think I took two cases, even, which was about average—but in later years I took one case, but I supervised up until relatively recent years. I enjoy supervision. But as I say, I did it all at a financial sacrifice. What I got paid—people had some delusions about how much money I made doing research. I never made much for half-time, 20 hours a week—that was just what I gave in the laboratory. I didn't count all the times I gave nights and staying in touch with the laboratory or all the time I spent weekends and all the days and nights I spent writing, because I was tremendously productive in those years. So, the most I ever made was $20,000 a year, whereas in private practice I would have made three times that for an equivalent amount of time. So that's the kind of sacrifice I made. At the same time, I was giving a lot of time to the Institute, but I was not one of these giving three or four times a week at the Institute. I held a lot of offices, and also was for years Chairman of the Research Students' Committee, which represents a certain amount of work, a lot of work, and you had to write reports and have admissions interviews. The Research Committee had the role of the Intake Committee, Students Committee, Graduation Committee. But finally, when the waiver for a full training was adopted, it was decided it was too risky to have the Research Committee take that responsibility, that the EC had to do it. So, the EC took it over and changed the rules on them, causing a tremendous amount of resentment because the research students were only required to supervise two cases, and by this time the research students were having a hell of a time getting any cases. Practice began to get bad, and they couldn't get good cases, and they weren't all gung-ho for doing more supervision. Many of our regular students in those days couldn't get enough supervision. They would not only do their three, they would do four or five, and keep supervising for years, and in the end—this is a story worth telling. The chief research students were six from the Research Center for Mental Health and George Klein was the first, Bob Holt was always believed to have been a research student, but he never was, he never applied. The six were George, Spence, Pine, Irving Paul, Wolitsky, Leo Goldberger. These were six very talented men who had all produced some creditable research but for the most part they did not enjoy their training. They were all full-time students. They were all engaged in research. They finally had to supervise cases, had classes three times a week and five times a week analysis, which ate into their research time. And, as you know, they have all ended up not doing hard-nosed experimental research—but, like Fred Pine at Einstein, Wolitsky and Leo Goldberger at NYU, are important in clinical psychology departments around New York. Irving Paul at City College, Spence at Rutgers. Spence has done a little and he has recently gone back to doing a little subliminal research. He was in many ways the most original and talented of those people, but they were all very talented. The theory was that they would do the hard-nosed psychoanalytic research which we were unable to do. Their interests all stemmed from Rapaport, and George Klein during those years in the fifties; all of them were engaged, including Klein, Wolitsky, and Spence, in doing subliminal research of one kind or another. Rapaport was interested in memory and perception and in ego functions and in the thought process, primary and secondary process, and he influenced all of them. He was interested in how secondary process grew out of primary process, an unresolved question to this day. And all kinds of questions of this sort. So, several of them told me, "We probably went into analysis because we were becoming rather disillusioned with the research we were doing and didn't exactly know what our own goals were and where we were going."

So, you see how they ended up. They ended up doing something very valuable. The protocol for being a research student emphasizes not only research but teaching, so all these people were teaching and supervising theses in various places and writing books on psychotherapy, and whatever deviations they have—George Klein had a lot of differences and all of them have a lot of differences... but they are in some ways basically Freudian.

AR: They enriched psychoanalysis, I think.

CF: With some of their writings, some of them have. I think George Klein wrote some interesting things, which I don't think anyone pays much attention to. One of his best papers is a paper on consciousness, which is something that is practically ignored. One of Freud's allegedly great papers was supposed to be on consciousness, which I think maybe it's been discovered since....

AR: No, it was a paper on hysteria.

CF: But amongst those metapsychological papers there were about five more which never....

AR: That was one of the missing papers.

CF: But he never wrote the one on consciousness, but George Klein wrote a very good paper distinguishing the functions of consciousness and preconscious and unconscious, and George was a very bright man and an influence on me. I don't know if I told you that story but I'll get around to it.

To come back to the research students. They felt like second-class citizens as against the medical ones and they had the reputation of not being as clinically savvy as the medical ones but having better theoretical minds, which is about true. They could handle theory better because they were more critical, more methodologically oriented, and that kind of thing. So, when George Klein was the first one to get ready to graduate, he put up a fuss. He said he would not accept graduation unless they changed the rules, and the rules were that they be graduated and given full membership, that they be allowed to teach, and that they be allowed to practice. At the time they had to take a pledge that they would not practice and they were not allowed to teach, and also that they would have the right to vote, they wanted full rights. And so, I remember Sam Atkins and I and some other people supported them, and we managed to push it through the EC. And I don't know if it ever came to a vote by the membership, but finally they were granted full rights. However, they then changed the rules on them. They said they would have to have three supervisions. They had come in with the idea that they only had to have two. So, I remember we had a meeting and I chaired the meeting, and they protested violently. They said they had trouble getting patients and, by the way, none of them had much of a practice.

AR: But three supervisions was the requirement for everyone else.

CF: Yes, but they were never told they had to have three supervisions to begin with and they resented, one, because the rules were changed, and secondly because they had such trouble getting suitable cases. So, if you look at the roster of membership, you see the only ones who are members are, I think, Spence and Fred Pine. Fred Pine is and Rogaw is, you remember Rogaw is a political scientist. He was not with this group at all, but on his own.

AR: From this group, Spence and Pine became members. Wolitsky could have become a member but he either decided not to or resigned. Paul never did it nor did Leo Goldberger. George Klein died.

CF: That's right, George Klein died. But I think he was posthumously made a member because he died about that time. And Wolitsky supervised with me. He'd gone to Nick Young. Nick Young just had contempt for him and wouldn't say much of anything. And the guy had little experience, even doing psychotherapy, and what he needed was instruction about how to go about doing therapy, which he had never really had. So, I supervised him, and he turned out to have quite a bit of talent. He did very well with a somewhat difficult patient he had, and I think he had three supervisions. I don't know why he never became a member.

AR: I think he decided he didn't want to be a member.

CF: Maybe. There was something funny about it. But I was friends with all of these people, and I liked them, especially I liked George, and I had a lot to do with Bob Holt. So, on the whole I had come to the conclusion that having research students was a problematical thing and I questioned whether we should continue to do so. We didn't seem to do them much of a favor. They were all full-time academics with their own research careers and doing very well. They got waylaid for six or seven years by the demands—by this time they were in their early thirties and when they ended they were 40 years old. There was no way they could make a change and furthermore they were dedicated psychologists and had their own careers, and, by this time I guess, a lot of them had tenure and stuff. Whatever problems were in the imaginations of the people who thought up the idea of having research students were never resolved.

AR: How do you feel about full clinical training for people without M.D. degrees?

CF: I'm not opposed to full clinical training. I have a bias toward medical training, but it's perfectly obvious that there are nonmedical people who can make perfectly fine analysts, and some of our best analysts have been lay, right? I also have a bias against the trivialization of therapy to the extent that's going on because in my day we used to believe, or certainly I believed, that you couldn't get enough training. I approached this treating of human beings with a certain amount of trepidation and awe, and I never thought I could know enough, whether neurology, neurophysiology. All the training I had I thought was valuable. I just thought I never had good enough psychoanalytic training to satisfy my standards. But I always thought that if provisions could be made for lay people to get decent training, I would have no objection to it. And, of course, Freud was all in favor of it, and it's done in Europe without causing any great revolution. And half the London Society were lay, weren't they? Although it seems to me that the London Society always had a lot of first-rate women analysts, like Brierley and Payne.

AR: And Segel.

CF: No, Segel was Kleinian. These brilliant women, most of them were M.D.s, not all of them. One of the best of them was Ella Freeman Sharpe. as she an M.D. or a Ph.D.? But her little book on dream interpretation is one of the most superb things that anyone has ever written and has a lot of original things. She taught that symbolism was not the only indirect mode of representation. She was a literary person, and you remember she introduced the idea of other forms of indirect expression.

AR: *Metaphor and Dreams?*

CF: No, the book is called *Psychoanalysis of Dreams or Dreaming*, but the whole first section is on metaphor, simile, synecdoche, part for whole, and all of the mechanisms, literary mechanisms, such as plays on words, punning, and all those things. She wrote a couple of beautiful chapters on that stuff, and she gave examples of how she analyzed. It's a beautiful little book, there's nothing better, and she talked about names and how a name like hers, Sharpe, appeared in disguised form, and I thought it was superb. I don't know if it's read very much or thought of very much. Anyway, how did I get onto that?

AR: Essentially, the question of lay analysis, full clinical training for lay people.

CF: I don't know what happened to the experiment that Bob Wallerstein started out in San Francisco.

AR: There were some administrative and political problems.

CF: It seemed to be a good idea. Did it work out?

AR: It did not work out.

CF: They were going to give a quasi-medical thing.

AR: The point is, they were going to train these people, but then these people couldn't get the right licensing and so forth. There were a lot of administrative problems in California and so forth, and therefore the program didn't work.

CF: So, I've never been opposed to that, although I say my own bias—I have a biological bias and my work tends to be connected with psychophysiological matters and the mind/body problem, and I'm pretty well rooted in the brain and body and my old neurophysiological training has always been influential. And there's a continuity between me.... Did you read Mort Reiser's book on mind-brain-body?

AR: I haven't read it yet.

CF: I believe the medical model has been neglected. There is a myth that's gone around that Freud said—Freud did say it—that we have biological roots and the biological roots lay in the somatic sources of the instincts. And Freud, as you know, in his early years was concerned with the origin of the somatic sources of drives, so his first theory was they were in the erogenous zones. Then he gave that up and he spoke vaguely about libido but he didn't know from where libido arose. But in "The Three Essays," which is one of the works of Freud's that influenced me most, which I think is one of his great creations, next to *The Interpretation of Dreams*— he makes a remark, one of those little side things that he tossed off, little sparks of genius, often in footnotes—this he said right out in the text. "The chances are the libido is generated by the action of the sex hormones on certain parts of the brain," and that's one that turned out to be true. It has now been known for a long time that the neurophysiology of drive, that is, drive in the physiological sense, not in the psychoanalytic sense, involves the feedback of the male and female sex hormones acting on the sexual areas of the hypothalmus.

CHAPTER 4

Book Review Essay: *The Selected Papers of Arnold D. Richards, Vols 1 to 5* Reviewed by Marco Conci, MD[2]

"Years of repression, exclusion, and schism have cost us dearly. It is time to face our history, grow beyond our foundations, and learn at last to deal constructively with the fact of our differences" (Richards, 2017, p. 211).

"My vision of the psychoanalytic theory of tomorrow will be realized only if we promote vigorous dialogue among the proponents of the

---

2 During his analytic training at the Milan Scuola di Psicoterapia Psicoanalitica (SPP), in 1991 Marco Conci won the Candidates Award of the International Federation of Psychoanalytic Societies (IFPS) and in 1994 he became a member of the editorial board of the IFPS journal, the International Forum of Psychoanalysis. Since 2007 he has been its coeditor-in-chief, at first with C. Sjoedin (2007-2014) and then with Grigoris Maniadakis (2014-2022), and since 2022 with Gabriele Cassullo.

In 1991 he was the editor of the Italian edition of the young Freud's letters to E. Silberstein. In 2000 he published Sullivan rivisitato, translated into German, English (as Sulivan revisited – Life and work) and Spanish; and in 2019 the volume Freud, Sullivan, Mitchell, Bion, and the multiple voices of international psychoanalysis (New York, IPBooks).

He is a training and supervising analyst of the German Psychoanalytic Society (DPG) and of the International Psychoanalytic Association (IPA), and a full member of the Italian Psychoanalytic Society (SPI).

He is also the author of more than 280 publications, and a member of the editorial board of several journals, including Psychoanalysis and History, Contemporary Psychoanalysis and The Psychoanalytic Review; the Italian journals *Psicoterapia e Scienze Umane* and Rivista di Psicoanalisi; and the Austrian journal *Texte*.

Furthermore, Marco Conci is a member of the executive committee of the International Sándor Ferenczi Network (ISFN).

He works in private practice in Munich (Germany) and Trento (Italy).

divergent theoretical view-points of today. The kind of dialogue I have in mind is premised on the belief that theoretical controversy is vitally necessary to the growth of science" (Richards, 2017, p. 51).

"Writing for me has always been activism. And I think my self-identification as an activist also goes back to my father the revolutionary. My aim has always been to make a difference in the lives of my patients and my students and in the organization of which I am a part. And this is what I have hoped to do in my own writings and in the part I have been allowed to play in bringing others together by publishing their writings" (Richards, 2021, p. 284).

A.A. Lynch ed. (2015). Controversial Conversations: Selected Papers of A.D. Richards, Volume 1. (IPBooks), 413pp., $35.

A.A. Lynch ed. (2017). Perspectives on a Thought Collective: Selected Papers of A.D. Richards, Volume 2. (IPBooks), 341 pp., $35.

A.A. Lynch ed. (2020). Psychoanalysts at Work: Selected Papers of A.D. Richards Volume 3, (IPBooks), pp., $35.

A.A. Lynch ed. (2021). The Peripatetic Psychoanalyst: Selected Papers of A.D. Richards, Volume 4(IPBooks), 304 pp., $35.

A.A. Lynch ed. (2022). The world of Psychoanalysis and Psychoanalysts: Selected Papers of A. D. Richards , Volume 5. (IPBooks), 317 pp., $35.

I do not remember any more when I approached and spoke with Arnold Richards for the first time. In July 1993 I was in Amsterdam for the first congress of the International Psychoanalytic Association (IPA) in which I participated, and then came Nice (2001) and Berlin (2007)—and I bet he was himself at all of them. Starting with Chicago in 2009, I participated—and gave papers—at all the following IPA congresses, including London (2019), that is, the congress at which we did a panel together—with him, his wife Arlene Kramer Richards and with Giovanni Foresti. As far as the congresses of the American Psychoanalytic Association (APsaA) are concerned, I started participating in them in 2007, and I was there, in New York City, every year till 2020—as he himself was. In 2015 I asked him to become the publisher of my 2019 book *Freud, Sullivan, Mitchell, Bion, and the Multiple Voices of International Psychoanalysis,* and I admire him and his work so much that I am very happy to present his *Collected Papers* to the readers of our journal. If I do not remember when I first spoke to Arnold Richards, I remember the first topic which brought us together. But before revealing this, let me declare the following, for all the readers who never met him. I never met at an IPA or APsaA congress any colleague who was there not just to listen to the papers (whose authors he would all know, and whose contents he would be able to imagine on his own), but to meet and talk and exchange ideas with all his friends—and together shape the psychoanalysis of the future. In other words, what brought us together—me, more than 20 years his junior and him, a bearded man looking like a Jewish prophet—was our common curiosity and passion for psychoanalysis. This was how, talking to each other just for the pleasure of doing it, we discovered something really significant for the both of us: in 2000 I had written a review of the biography that my German colleague Thomas Müller had written on his training analyst, the Berlin colleague Henry Loewenfeld (1900-1985). Last but not least, a few days ago, at the beginning of August 2024, Arnie turned 90 years old.

Richards's parents were Jewish immigrants from Eastern Europe, the father having sided with Trotsky during the Bolshevik revolution, and he grew up in Brooklyn (NY) in a Yiddish and English speaking household. As he reports in the first chapter, "Growing Up Orthodox" of Volume 1 of the first of the five volumes of his *Selected Papers,* his first contact with psychoanalysis must have consisted in his reading about Freud's death in the *Yiddish Forward* in September 1939, aged 5. As an adolescent he read not only about psychosomatic medicine, but also Freud's 1933

New Introductory Lectures on Psychoanalysis, whose "interlocutory style" he found "absolutely convincing," thus seeing psychoanalysis as "a lens through which I observed a whole host of intellectual, literary and scientific experience." Being able to keep such an interest alive during all the years of college (Chicago) and medical school (at Downstate), with all their intellectual seductions, Richards had what he seems to always have considered the good luck of doing his residency in psychiatry at Topeka's (Kansas) Menninger Clinic, at the time a very open and interdisciplinary institution. "I like to tell myself—Richards writes in the same chapter—that when I began analytic training at the New York Psychoanalytic Institute in 1964 I brought to that rarefied and perhaps somewhat stultifying atmosphere a sense of the large scientific landscape" (p. 14). In fact, it was the institute of Heinz Hartmann, Rudolph Loewenstein, Edith Jacobson, Annie Reich, Kurth and Ruth Eissler, and George Gero, and of younger American giants in the field such as Phyllis Greenacre, Jacob Arlow, Charles Brenner, and David Beres. In other words, "hardly a place that promoted skepticism, questioning and argument," but still a place in which he could personally validate the basic principles of psychoanalysis through his training analysis—psychic determinism, the centrality of unconscious mental functioning with all its implications, the conflicts of childhood and the centrality of the experiences with parents and siblings, and with the body, the role of transference, and, last but not least, the role of affects. It was the time of Leo Stone's "widening scope of psychoanalysis," and Richards admits to have had the good luck—at variance with the classical orientation of his training—of "analyzing patients with severe psychopathology early in my career". Such a training is—as I understand it —is what allowed him to combine so well as he does both major poles or emphases of our work, that is, on the patients' unconscious fantasies, on the one hand, and on the relationship which we create with the patients themselves, through the emotions we share with them and the interpretations we give and/

or construct with them. In other words, such a basic analytic attitude also represents the compass on which—as we will see—Richards's critical approach to a variety of alternative theories is based, that is, what he calls the perspective of a "contemporary Freudian analyst".

As such he dealt, with as much curiosity and openness as possible, with the challenges posed by the following alternative points of view emerged during his long career: the anti-metapsychology movement of George Klein, Merton Gill and Roy Schafer; the self-psychology of Heinz Kohut and John Gedo; and, last but not least, the emergence of the interpersonal, intersubjective, and relational points of view. An important role in the exercise of Richards's dialectical approach was played—as he admits it— by his familiarity and interactions with a whole series of non-medical colleagues, including his wife Arlene. "My career and my approach—he writes at the end of this same chapter—belie the claim that the American Freudian establishment is an orthodox monolith" (p.21). And: "My own commitment to Arlow's and Brenner's emphasis on conflict, compromise formation, and unconscious fantasy works well for me as a personal compromise formation, enabling me to be part of the establishment, while espousing what I see as an evolutionary, though not revolutionary, point of view" (*ibidem*). But what I find even more interesting for my own way of working and dealing with psychoanalysis as a whole is what Richards calls "the fourth ear," which he presents as follows:

"What does all the foregoing have to do with how I work? I think I have come to listen with a fourth ear. The third ear, as Theodor Reik observes, listens to the patient's unconscious. The fourth ear, I believe, tries to listen from the various vantage points of competing theoretical schools. I practice this kind of listening because it holds the promise of validating clinically competing hypotheses about how the mind works. But I also do so because a receptivity to new ideas, a willingness to consider them on their own merits, follows from the therapeutic nature of the analytic situation, which requires a pragmatic commitment to what works best for one's patients" (*ibidem*).

Exactly this is the state of mind behind the two following chapters of the first part of volume 1, by the title "Diversity and Unification", that is: chapter 2, "A.A. Brill and the Politics of Exclusion" (1999), and chapter 3, "Psychoanalytic Discourse at the Turn of Our Century: A Plea for a Measure of Humility" (2003), two of his most important and influential papers.

But, going back to his professional curriculum, let me first give to the reader the following essential information. Entering in private practice in 1964, he also became a member of the faculty of the Department of Psychiatry of the Albert Einstein School of Medicine; once finished his analytic training, he became a member of the faculty of the Psychoanalytic Institute of New York University in 1975, and of the New York Psychoanalytic Institute in 1982, where he became a training analyst in 1985. In 1980 he had become an assistant professor of psychiatry at the New York University School of Medicine, and worked a such till 2013; and in 1989, to the present, an adjunct clinical professor of psychiatry at the Mt. Sinai Department of Psychiatry. Interestingly enough, in 2011, and to the present, Richards became also a visiting professor at the Chinese Wuhan Hospital for Psychotherapy, affiliated with Tongji Medical School. But what is even more important for understanding his work are the following editorial appointments and initiatives: between 1988 and 1993, he was the editor of *The American Psychoanalyst*; and between 1994 and 2003, Richards became the editor of the *Journal of the American Psychoanalytic Association* (*JAPA*). Having at this point applied for the position of editor-in-chief of the *International Journal of Psychoanalysis*, and having been turned down, in 2004 Richards founded the blog/website *InternationalPsychoanalysis. net,* and in 2009 the publishing house International Psychoanalytic Books, through which he (helped by his daughter Tamar and by his son-in-law Lawrence L. Schwartz) has published about 150 books. Indefatigable as he is, in February 2020 he launched the online *International Journal of Controversial Discussions.*

Besides this, he has been for many years on the editorial board of leading journals such as the *Psychoanalytic Quarterly,* the *Psychoanalytic Review,* and the *American Journal of Psychoanalysis,* and was the editor of important anthologies such as the *Festschrift* books in honor of Charles Brenner (1913–2008) (1986, with M. Willick), Jacob Arlow (1912-2004) (1988, with A. Kramer Richards), Martin Bergmann (1913–2014) (1993, with A. Kramer Richards), and Horacio Etchegoyen (1919-2016) (1993, with A. Kramer Richards, J. Ahumada and J. Olagaray). To this dimension of his work belong of course also the many book reviews that Richards wrote in his long career—most of which are to be found in volume 5. A lover of poetry and photography, in 2022 Richards also published a volume with his best poems and pictures (Richards, 2022). Last but not least, among the many awards he received the most important is the Sigourney Award in 2000. Not to mention the fact that, together with his wife Arlene, they have two daughters (Tamar and Rebecca) and one son (Stephen).

At this point, before going through the single volumes of his *Selected Papers,* I would like to complete the image of Arnold Richards which I have been trying to create for the readers (especially for those who do not know him) by referring to the resonance that his life and work have had for the colleagues whom he invited to write some introductory words to them. In his introductory words to volume 1, "An Appreciation of Arnold D. Richards", his predecessor as editor of the *JAPA* (1973–983), Harold Blum (1929–2004), after having very much praised the multiple ways in which he promoted the growth of the journal of the APsaA, speaks of him as "a unique polymath who can plumb the depths and scan the horizons of our field with boundless energy." Or, let us take the famous New York colleague Lawrence Friedman, whose introductory words to volume 1 bear the title "A One-Person Thought Collective": after having praised his unusual organizational skills, and his love for history and for fairness, he affirms to see him "more interested in accomplishing his ends than in self-promotion", thus living he the concept of a "thought collective, ... even before he discovered Ludwig Fleck" (see below). His successor as editor of the *JAPA* (2014-2018) Bonnie Litowitz speaks of him in her "Introduction of Arnold Richards" of volume 2 in terms of his "dialoguing" as "his natural mode of being-in-the-world," and is very thankful for having found in him such a "generous mentor, stimulating colleague, and warm friend." I personally also feel much in tune with the following words of Janet Lee Bachant, also to be found at the beginning of volume 2: "During an era in which collaboration is very difficult to come by, Arnie's generosity of spirit and dedication to collaboration is a beacon for us all." As far as I am concerned, I can confirm the fact that once found the common wave length I talked about at the beginning, Richards was ready to accept my book proposal and to support it without hesitations. By the way, going beyond my own expectations, my 2019 book ended up receiving the 2020 Historical Book Prize of the American Board and Academy of Psychoanalysis. Very eloquent are also the words which Daniel Benveniste placed at the beginning of his detailed "Introduction" to volume 4: "His goal through the years has been to offer constructive critiques of the psychoanalytic thought collective, and, in doing so, save psychoanalysts from themselves." No wonder that Richards's life-long friend Jane Hall speaks of him—also in volume 4—as "the most impressive person I know." Of course, we have also to be very thankful to Arthur Lynch (a training analyst of the American Institute of Psychoanalysis and a close collaborator of Richards) for having edited the five volumes and provided a detailed introduction to four of them.

"Arnold Richards' psychoanalytic contributions follow the leitmotiv of 'integrative pluralism,'" Lynch writes at the beginning of his preface to volume 1, whose chapters 2 and 3 bear the titles mentioned above, and directly come after chapter 1, "Growing Up Orthodox", with which I dealt in detail. The common denominator of these two further chapters is not only Richards' "integrative pluralism," but also his special passion for and unusual awareness of the history of our field which informs many of the papers of these five volumes. In chapter 2, "A.A. Brill and the Politics of Exclusion" (1999), Richards celebrates the way in which Abraham Arden Brill (1874–1948), the first North American psychoanalyst (who had come to the Unites States from Galicia aged 14, alone and penniless, later succeeding in becoming an MD, and then in getting in touch with Freud's work in Zurich in 1907), was able to promote psychanalysis in the US, and, at the same time, sharply criticizes the way in which (contrary to Freud's sympathy for lay analysis) he made of the APsaA an exclusively medical association. Having such a monopoly been maintained by the following generations of analysts and having it come to an end only as a consequence of the lawsuit filed against the APsaA by a group of psychologists in the mid-1980s, Richards sees "the drive/relational antithesis" promoted by the psychologist and psychoanalyst Stephen Mitchell (1946-2000) "as a reaction to Brill's politics of exclusion" (p.36). Having personally known Mitchell well (see below), I agree with him, in particular regard for what Richards writes in this regard in the following chapter, "Psychoanalytic Discourse at the Turn of the Century: A Plea for a Measure of Humility," that is:

"My problem with some relational theorists is that they want not only to celebrate the relational school, but also to dismiss the entire contemporary Freudian tradition as anachronistic, and to parlay the emphasis on interaction in the relational literature into a claim that even today no one else understands its importance as they do" (p. 57).

In fact, chapters 2 and 3 are complementary with each other, being the contemporary fragmentation of analytic theory at the center of chapter 2 and the institutional history of psychoanalysis in North America at the center of chapter 3, two aspects which Richards rightly connects with each other.

In chapter 3, he even comes to speak of the "insurmountable barrier—the Berlin wall —between Freudians and Interpersonalists" (p. 58) which came into being after the renunciation of the White Institute to apply for membership in the APsaA in the early 1950s. As many of us know, the members of the New York Psychoanalytic Institute and the members of the White Institute did not talk with each other for many years. Only in 2015, the White became a member society of the ApsaA—and in 2017 of the IPA. Of course, psychoanalysis as a scientific discipline could not adequately grow in such a climate, but the measure of mutual respect and fruitful dialogue necessary for such an achievement has not yet been definitively achieved. This is why Richards' concluding words of chapter 3 still have such a relevance as to deserve to be cited in full length:

"Although I call myself a contemporary Freudian, my loyalty, as I said at the outset, is not to Freud as a human being, who for all his greatness had his share of frailties, but to psychoanalysis as a method of thinking, working and living. This method, though it originated with Freud, has been enriched by Klein, Winnicott, Sullivan, Hartmann, Kohut and all the other figures who form the tradition to which we are heir and to which we have the opportunity to contribute in our turn. In Winnicott's profound words (1971), 'in any cultural field it is not possible to be original except on the basis of tradition' (p. 99). Psychoanalysis is a coat of many colors. Let us cease fighting over our inheritance and resolve instead to share it and to wear it with both humility and pride as we enter the twenty-first century" (p. 59).

How much work and what a long time it took for Richards himself to come to such a constructive conclusion is what we can see in the second of the six sections of volume 1, "Self Psychology and the Work of Heinz Kohut", with its three further chapters. In fact, he wrote chapter 4 "Self Theory, Conflict Theory, and the Problem of Hypochondriasis" (1981) to show how nonpsychoanalytic Heinz Kohut's theory of the self was, given how it "severely neglects the importance of the role of unconscious conflict in mental life" (p. 63). He wrote chapter 5, "The Superordinate Self in Psychoanalytic Theory and in Self Psychology" (1982) "to argue against the use of the self as a superordinate concept in psychoanalytic theory" (p. 94). And he wrote chapter 6, "Extenders, Modifiers, Heretics" (1994) to critically revisit Kohut's self psychology in the light of such categories, and introduced by Martin Bergmann in 1993, proposing to quality it as "a separate"—and therefore heretic—research tradition (p. 107).

In the third section of volume 1, "The Hermeneutic Science of Merton N. Gill and Irwin Z. Hoffman", we find a much more sympathetic, but not less critical evaluative approach. This is what emerges from the title itself of chapter 7, "Transference Analysis: Means or End?" (1984), in which Richards sharply criticizes what he considers as being Merton Gill's (1914–1994) one-sided insistence on the analysis of the transference. More generous is Richards with Gill in the following chapter 8, "Merton Gill: A View in his Place in the 'Freudian' Firmament" (1996), in which he talks about him in terms of "a theoretical extender," "going beyond Freud in an authentic Freudian spirit, challenging to psychoanalytic theory in a way that has helped us all" (p. 137). Different is the author's tone in his review of Irwin Hoffman's 1998 book *Ritual and Spontaneity in Psychoanalysis: A Dialectical-Constructivist View,* chapter 9 of volume 1, in which we can read the following critical acute observation: "The paradox of constructivist thinkers embracing a positivistic position about the importance of constructivism may make dialogue confusing" (p. 145). A further interesting articulation of this debate is what we find in chapter 10, "How New Is the 'New American Psychoanalysis'? The Example of Irwin Z. Hoffman" (2002), partly based on Jay Greenberg's 2001 paper "The Analyst's Participation: A New Look", and his own critique on Hoffman's work (with particular regard for his collusion with his patient Diane; see Hoffman, 1998). In as much as Richards welcomes Greenberg's critical appraisal of the transformation of the relational point of view into a movement (see pp.159–160), he can more easily recognize how Hoffman "has enriched us all by making public his often risky but always honest and compassionate labors as a clinician," and take the possibility of such a constructive exchange as "the best possible omen for the future of American psychoanalysis" (p. 176).

Such a constructive turn came only after the not easy exchanges that Richards had had with Mitchell after the critical appraisal of the latter's 1988 book *Relational Concepts in Psychoanalysis. An Integration* formulated by Richards together with Janet Lee Bachant in their 1993 book review appeared in Mitchell's own journal *Psychoanalytic Dialogues.* We encounter this review as chapter 11 of volume 1, that is, as the first of the three chapters of the fourth section, "Interpersonal and Relational Psychoanalysis.. The review is still worth reading, in as much as the dichotomy between the drive and the relational models and Mitchell's reductionist view of Freud's legacy, which Richards strongly criticizes and opposes, still represent a very interesting and debated topic in contemporary psychoanalysis—

although Greenberg had already gone beyond such a dichotomy with his 1991 book *Oedipus and Beyond: A Clinical Theory*. The following chapter, chapter 12, "Relational Models in Psychoanalytic Theory" (1995), co-authored with Bachant and Lynch, represents the product of a further phase of critical reflection upon the big and creative challenges posed by Mitchell's "revolutionary turn," as we can gather through the following considerations:

> "We contend that there is a place for both constructivistic and positivistic epistemological perspectives in psychoanalysis. They exist in a dialectical tension with each other. Rather than asking the analyst to choose between these two dimensions, this understanding requires that the analyst develop a sense of what emphasis will be most helpful at a given moment. Maintenance of evenly hovering attention to this aspect of the psychoanalytic situation guards the analyst against immersion in one neglecting the other" (p. 226).

A wholly dialogical and even conciliatory approach is what we can find in chapter 13, "Benjamin Wolstein and Us: Many Roads Lead to Rome" (2000), written by Richards with his wife Arlene, having they been invited by Jay Greenberg, then editor of *Contemporary Psychoanalysis,* to revisit his work. Born in 1922, Wolstein had been a training-analysand of Clara Thompson in the 1950s, and the author of pioneering contributions on the clinical work with transference and countertransference (see Wolstein, 1988). Centered around his work is also a very interesting interview he had with Irwin Hirsch (2000). And here are Arnie's and Arlene's appreciative words:

"We think that if Wolstein were alive today, he would find a congenial audience for his ideas among contemporary Freudians, and a place in *JAPA* for both his theoretical contributions and his wisdom.... We hope that he would have found some interest in our response here, and that it might have served as a basis for an ongoing discussion. Although clearly that is not to be, we do hope that other members of the interpersonal tradition will increasingly join in such conversations" (p. 243).

Before ending my report on volume 1 of Richards' *Selected Papers,* I find important to present the reader with some personal recollections on Stepehen Mitchell, with whom I already dealt in detail in a chapter of my above mentioned 2019 book and in the paper "Harry Stack Sullivan and Stephen Mitchell in Italy: A Historical and a Personal Account". I had had the good luck of meeting him during his first trip to Italy (together with Jay Greenberg) in Florence, in April 1988, invited as they had been by the Istituto di Psicoterapia Analitica. I was so fascinated by his creativity and generosity, and by his readiness to remain in touch with me, and develop an interesting analytic conversation, that I ended up helping him promote his work in Italy, starting with the 1993 Italian edition of his 1988 book. I learned very much from him, and I still think of him as one of the best colleagues I ever met in my life. Of course, at the time, I did not have a clear idea of the political context (of both he and Jay Greenberg not having had the option to train within the APsaA) out of which Greenberg's and Mitchell's 1983 *Object Relations in Psychoanalytic Theory* came, nor of the New York climate in which the 1983 and the 1988 books were received. Only later, I became aware of the political dimension of such books (which Peter Rudnytsky deals with at length in his interview with Mitchell of 2000), and this helped me understand how such a political dimension might have ended up weighing more than the scientific one. In other words, if on the one hand I appreciate the scientific challenge represented by a journal like *Psychoanalytic Dialogues* (1988), and a network like the International Association for Relational Psychoanalysis and Psychotherapy (IARPP) (2001), I on the other hand do think that psychoanalysis ought to survive, or can survive only as a unitary scientific discipline founded by Sigmund Freud and including his own legacy, as opposed to its developing in the direction of a particular technical stance —risking of losing touch with the main body of the discipline. Going back to Richards's reconstruction of the history of North American psychoanalysis, we could say that if Brill had some good reasons for introducing the medical monopoly of psychoanalysis, it should have been the task of his successors to rethink and change his position.

At this point, we can eventually come to section 5, the longest section of volume 1, "Contemporary Conflict Theory," with its five chapters. Chapter 14, "Introduction to *Psychoanalysis, The Science of Mental Conflict: Essays in Honor of Charles Brenner*" (1986) represents Richards' introduction to the above mentioned book. Without entering into further details, I will limit myself to reporting the author's final evaluation of Brenner as "an extender who innovates by addressing the meaning of traditional psychoanalytic concepts—drive, defense, superego, affect, transference, countertransference, and regression." with his contributions "culminat(ing) in significant reformulations that are part of a process by which Freudian thinking in psychoanalytic discourse accommodates the growth of psychoanalytic knowledge" (p. 276). Chapter 15, "Psychoanalytic Theory" (1991), is an encyclopedia article written with Jacob Arlow; chapter 16, "From Ego Psychology to Contemporary Conflict Theory: A Historical Overview" (1998), is a book chapter co-authored with Lynch; and chapter 17, "Leo Rangell: The Journey of a Developed Freudian" (2010) is an article on Rangell also co-authored with Lynch.

By the way, I remember how happy Arnie was to hear that I, as coeditor-in-chief of the *International Forum of Psychoanalysis,* had been able to have an interview with Rangell made by Beth Kalish Weiss come out in our journal in 2009—the year that I had the chance to shake hands with him at the IPA Chicago Congress, two years before he died at 97. In terms of psychoanalytic politics, Rangell had become president of the IPA at the 1969 Rome IPA Congress (the first one to ever been held in Italy), running and winning against Kohut. As I already mentioned, Brenner, Arlow and Rangell are—together with Wallerstein—the authors whom Richards felt the closest to and with whom he interacted the most, coming to formulate his own position in terms of his "modern conflict theory" - which I have repeatedly been referring to. But the aspect of his work which interests me the most is his interaction with the analytic world outside of his "Freudian home", and this is the reason why I will now turn to the following chapter of volume 5. I am referring to chapter 18, "Notes On Psychoanalytic Theory and its Consequences for Technique (Plus: "A Response To Our Respondents") (1995), written with his wife Arlene. In it we can find the following words concerning Kleinian theory, which does not seem to have ever concerned him much:

"The Kleinian mode of thought was alien to ego psychologists ion the United States for decades. Ego psychologists believed that they had nothing in common with the Kleinians. Arlow (1981) recalled Loewenstein's (1969) critique of Kleinian technique as blurring distinctions between 'past and present, reality and fantasy, between the values of genetic and dynamic interpretations and reconstructions' (p. 586).

In the past decade, interest in Klein's theories has been picking up until it is almost a vogue. Why should this happen now? One answer is that the self psychologists taught a generation of analysts to avoid aggression rather than confronting it. This left the Kleinian view to reintroduce an appropriate place for interpretations of aggressive components of the character and personality of the analysands" (p. 377).

The article centers around a constructive revisitation and critique of Robert Wallerstein's (1921-2014) concept of "common ground", the concept he had started formulating at the 1987 IPA Montreal Congress in his paper "One psychoanalysis or many?" (Wallerstein, 1988).

Volume 1 comes to an end with the only one chapter of section 6, chapter 19, a very short chapter by the title "The View from Now". In it we encounter not only the names of the colleagues of Richards's peer group, with whom he "continued my postgraduate education at the Madison Delicatessen at Madison Avenue and 86th Street in New York City" (p.408), meeting there for lunch every Friday, but also how the work and legacy of the Polish pathologist and philosopher of science Ludwig Fleck (1896–1961) also contributed to him becoming "more ecumenical" (p.409) as it also did his work of editor-in-chief of the *JAPA*. His last word goes to his work in China, in Wuhan, and to how this makes him "optimistic about the long-term survival and future of our psychoanalytic discipline" (p. 411).

Since reporting in detail the articulation of volume 1 of Arnold Richards's *Selected Papers* has allowed me to help our readers be able to visualize and understand well enough the value of his work and legacy, my report of the contents of the following volumes will be much more selective.

As far as Volume 2 is concerned, *Psychoanalysis: Perspectives on a Thought Collective*, I can say that its most important topic is the above mentioned work of Ludwig Fleck, in terms of the light it throws upon our psychoanalytic "thought collective," with particular regard for the German concept of *Bildung*. After articulating both concepts in the first two chapters of the volume, we find them again and again in the course of the whole book, actually centered on the complex topic of psychanalytic politics. Who was Ludwig Fleck? Born in Lemberg (Lvov) as a Polish Jew on July 11, 1896, he grew up in the Austrian province of Galicia, graduated from his Polish lyceum in 1914, and received his medical degree in 1922, in his home-town. From 1920 to 1923 he was assistant to Dr. Rudolf Weigel, well known for his research on typhus, and then worked till 1935 in the department of internal medicine at the general hospital of his home-town. Forced to give up his position, he set up his own microbiological laboratory, and after having directed his former laboratory under the Russian occupation, in 1942 he was arrested by the Germans together with his family, who also forced him to produce his anti-typhus vaccine for their armed forces. Liberated by the US army at the Buchenwald concentration camp, he went to the Polish town of Lublin, where he became an associate professor of microbiology in 1947. In 1957 he and his wife could join their son in Isarel, where he died on June 5, 1961, after having chaired the section of experimental pathology of the Israel Institute of Biological Research.

And what about his fundamental contribution to the field of the sociology of scientific knowledge (SSK)? The first thing we can say is that it was the famous historian and philosopher of science Thomas Kuhn to first mention his work and its importance, in his 1970 ground-breaking book *The Structure of Scientific Revolutions*—presenting Fleck as a pioneer of his own kind of research. What I have understood by reading about him in Richards's volume 2 and also through other sources is the following: working as a microbiologist in various research teams, and having a personal interest in the history and philosophy of science, Fleck started to collect data and to do research on how a research group, a "thought collective," conceptualizes new scientific facts, struggling not only on the level of discovering new facts, but even more on the level of better articulating its own way of thinking, its own "thought style," that is, its way of defining the nature of a scientific fact, including its permeability to other points of view. In other words: a pure and direct observation can not exist, since in the act of perceiving objects the observer, i.e. the epistemological subject, is always influenced by the epoch and the environment to which he belongs, that is, by what Fleck calls the "thought style."

Going now back to Arnold Richards, one of the reasons why he discovered Fleck had to do with the different "thought collectives" and "thought styles" he had personally experienced at interdisciplinary oriented Menninger Clinic during his residency, and at the analytically one-sided New York Psychoanalytic Institute during his analytic training. Furthermore, his Jewish identity allowed him to recognize in the German concept of *Bildung*, that is, the classical education that Freud had gone through in his Viennese *Gymnasium* (with the study of Latin and Greek, of German literature and philosophy) as the "thought style" of Freud and his early disciples. In other words, the kind of love for knowledge and openness to new discoveries and ways of thinking which he himself identified with, and/or has tried to make more and more his own. A first practical application of Fleck's perspective is the following: we go to psychoanalytic congresses more in order to feel confirmed in what we already know and believe than in order to expose ourselves to new points of view, which we might experience as a threat to our professional identity.

From my point of view, I can even confirm Lawrence Friedman's feeling (see above) of Richards living the concept of a "thought collective ... even before he discovered Ludwig Fleck", in terms of my own case, being it similar to what Friedman thinks Richards's case to have been. Having graduated from medical school in Florence in 1981, at a time in which the number of applications for analytic training in the Società Psicoanalitica Italiana (SPI) was very much bigger than the number of training analysts, I did not apply to it. I had the feeling that I lacked the necessary *raccomandazione* (a necessary practice at the time, but not only then), and that I did not want to run the risk of being rejected, being such a vocational and professional choice so important for me. This is how I devised my own alternative analytic training, undergoing a series of three personal analyses, with three analysts whose common denominator was ... multilingualism, that is what I must have imagined as being the "thought style" of the "thought collective" of Freud's psychoanalysis and of his "psychoanalytic movement." My first analyst, a woman, was an Italian trained in French Switzerland; my second analyst was an Italian-Argentinian man trained in Argentina; and the third a North American man trained in London, and practicing in Munich in English and German. Only many years later did I discover the beautiful paper that Didier Anzieu (1923–1999) presented at the 1985 IPA Hamburg Congress, "The place of Germanic language and culture in Freud's discovery of psychoanalysis between 1895 and 1900" (Anzieu, 1986), in which he presents Freud's multilinguistic experience as a child in Moravia (speaking Yiddish, Czech and German) as the basis of psychoanalysis—for example of the structural model, of the languages of the *Ich, Es* and *Überich*. This is how, having started my first personal analysis in the year 1983, I became a member of the IPA only in the year 2010, but with the advantage of being in a situation in which I thought to have belonged to its "thought collective" from much earlier. As far as Richards is concerned, he himself grew up bilingual, he writes—English and Yiddish.

Not to talk about the fact that I believe that we should all have... at least two trainings, that is, an orthodox one centered around the model of the high frequency analytic work, and a second, un-orthodox one, centered around working in analytic psychotherapy with all the patients who ask for our help—or the other way around. In fact, this was exactly the first direction in which I went, through the Milan Scuola di Psicoterapia Psicoanalitica (SPP), a member society of the International Federation of Psychoanalytic Societies (IFPS)—which had been co-founded by the W.A. White Institute and by the Deutsche Psychoanalytische Gesellschaft (DPG) in 1962, and to which I belong since the mid-1990s. In other words, before becoming a member of an analytic organization, my priority was to become a competent psychotherapist and a competent psychoanalyst— what Richards calls *Bildung*.

Coming back to Richards's second volume of his *Selected Papers*, the concept of *Bildung* occupies—as I wrote above—center stage in several of the chapters of the second section, "Freud and his Followers". We find it for example in chapter 4, "Freud's Jewish Identity and Psychoanalysis as a Science", and in chapter 5, "The Need Not to Believe: Freud's Godlessness Reconsidered". At the center of the following three chapters Richards' focus includes the larger history of Freud's inner circle, as it is the case in his 2013 review of Elizabeth Danto's *Freud's Free Clinics: Psychoanalysis and Social Justice* (2005), in his 2008 review of George Prochnik's *Putnam Camp: Sigmund Freud, James Jackson Putnam, and the Purpose of American Psychology* (2006), and in his 2016 review of Joseph Berke's *The hidden Freud: His Hassidic Roots* (2015).

Psychoanalytic politics being the second main topic of volume 2, "Perspectives on the Psychoanalytic Organization" is the topic of the second section, whose first chapter is chapter 9, "The History of Membership And Certification in the APsaA: Old Demons, New Debates" (2005), co-authored with Paul Mosher—a topic very close to the author's heart. Not being a member of the ApsaA (but only a so-called Research Associate), I am not able to give the reader a detailed report of such a complicated history, but I can say that its common denominator is the conflict started in 1946 between the Board of Professional Standards (BoPS) and the rest of the association, consisting of the main role of BoPS in certifying for membership in the APsaA the graduates of all institutes. The consequence: from a paper on the problem of membership published in 1976 by Anton

Kris we learn that of the 2.200 graduates come out of all the APsaA institutes between 1950 and the mid-1970s only 1.400 (64%) applied for membership! No wonder that the authors conclude their detailed report by defining certification in the ApsaA in terms of an "exclusionary attitude... deeply embedded in the history of American psychoanalysis, beginning with A.A. Brill's ironclad conviction that only medically trained psychoanalysts should be allowed to treat patients in the United States" (p.159).

Similar, if not even more preoccupied, is the tone we find in the following chapter, chapter 10, "Psychoanalysis in Crisis: The Danger of Ideology" (2015), at whose end we can read: "Psychoanalysis in this country has seen one ideological war after another ... But we can not go on this way. If we continue to hide from the scrutiny of outsiders, they will continue to distrust us" (p. 176). In chapter 11, "The Politics of the American Psychoanalytic Association," we even learn about the rejection of Arlene Kramer Richards's application for membership in the ApsaA, as a member of an IPA New York institute. Historically very interesting is also chapter 12, "The Left and Far Left in American Psychoanalysis: Psychoanalysis as a Subversive Discipline," in which we learn how many members of the New York Psychoanalytic Institute, including for example Kurt Eissler (1908–1999), were personally against a psychoanalysis promoting social adjustment, and more interested in its "subversive leverage... to safeguard individual freedom" (p. 208). A central role in the last chapter of this section chapter 13, "The Identity of Psychoanalysis and Psychoanalysts" is played again by Fleck's sociology of scientific (SSK), in terms how it inspired the author in his desire and mission of changing the "thought collective" and the "thought style" of the APsaA, that is, from the politics of exclusion to a politics of inclusion. In it we even find the following suggestion:

"The social history of psychoanalysis has so deeply informed its theory—and continues to do so—so that we recommend that mandatory courses in the social and political history of psychoanalysis should be part of the educational curriculum of psychoanalytic training centers" (p. 221).

As far as the four chapters of section 4, "Perspectives of Pluralism: Paradigm and Politics", of volume 2 are concerned, I will limit myself to chapter 14, "The Future of Psychoanalysis: The Past, Present and Future of Psychoanalytic Theory" (1990), that is, report to the reader how the author's approach is all centered around the dialogical dimension of his own work and legacy.

And the same is true also of chapter 19, the last chapter of this volume (and the second chapter of section 5), "Opening Doors: Reflections of a Former JAPA Editor" (2011), centered as it is upon the way in which Fleck's SSK helped the author change the editorial profile of the *JAPA* in the years 1994–2003. But let me here have the author speak, at sufficient length, for himself:

"During this time of stimulus and ferment, I discovered the work of Ludwig Fleck, the founder of the discipline we now call the sociology of science. Like Freud, Fleck was a Jewish scientist-physician from Hapsburg Austro-Hungary—in Fleck's case, from Poland. In 1935 he published *The Genesis and Development of a Scientific Fact*, in which he maintained that scientific discovery is conditioned by social, cultural, historical, personal and psychological factors (Thomas Kuhn credits his work as an inspiration for his own hugely influential work on scientific paradigms and revolutions)" (p. 331).

And a little below:

"He believed that scientific knowledge emerges out of communities of persons exchanging ideas—what he called *thought collectives.* The shared attitudes and assumptions that characterize a thought collective he called its *thought style....* In his view, facts not only emerge in the context of thought collectives; they *change over time* in that context as well. It seems to me that Fleck's vision had a special elegance when applied to psychoanalysis.... His book crystallized my reflections on the different psychoanalytic atmospheres of Topeka and New York, and illuminated how our politics seemed to be contributing to our increasing isolation. Fleck's work gave me an organizing context for what I was seeing, and for thinking about how to respond constructively as editor of *JAPA*" (p. 332).

In other words:

"We were taking very little advantage of the (largely denied) diversity among ourselves that Fleck considered a ready-made engine for scientific progress. We were essentially refusing to cooperate—or even to engage—with non-analytic thought collectives except on our terms... Our own thought collectives were at best ignoring each other and more often trying to push each other out of the tent. Freudians, Sullivanians, and relationalists were barely on speaking terms... I began to envision a role for *JAPA*, after the delinkages and the lawsuit, of promoting a higher level of integration, rather than possible fragmentation and implosion" (p. 333).

Before taking up volume 3, I can also make a personal example of how the politics of exclusion still prevail over the principle of inclusion, as far as the training analyst status in the IPA is concerned. Having been a full member of the DPG (the German Psychoanalytic Society) since 2002, thanks to a reform of the statute of the SPI (the Italian Psychoanalytic Society) I could automatically become a full member of the latter in 2012. Last May I became a training analyst of the DPG and the IPA, and I know that up to now there is no way through which I can have such a title automatically recognized outside of my society. Both the German and the Italian Society belong to the IPA, but the training analyst status—as I know from many other colleagues in a similar situation—seems to be still a national (as opposed to an international) matter. In the field of medicine, there are today recognized treating protocols for every possible disease, but not in the IPA, for the training analyst status. In other words, every IPA society seems to be more interested in controlling what a training analyst trained abroad might teach to its own candidates, as opposed to extending its national tradition, thus realizing the full potential of an international organization. By the way, this is also a reason why I still value very much the professional and scientific context of the IFPS (the International Federation of Psychoanalytic Societies), in which it was possible for me, back in 1994, to be invited by our founding editor Jan Stensson (1935-2024) to join the editorial board of this journal. Exclusively on the basis of my competence.

From this point of view, I can also add the fact that my choice of doing my fist training —in psychoanalytic psychotherapy—at the above mentioned Milan institute can be further contextualized in the following way: it had been founded in the early 1970s by Gaetano Benedetti (1920-2013), and by Joahnnes Cremerius (1918-2002), both trained at the Zurich IPA institute, and both university professors, the former in Bale, and the latter in Freiburg (see Conci, 2014). Both of them regularly met with the members of my class for group and individual supervisions, through which they brought us in contact with the international psychoanalytic debate in which they had been trained, and in which they actively participated. Both of them had spent a year in the United States in the early 1950s, where they had come in touch with both the Washington School of Psychiatry (Benedetti), and the New York Psychoanalytic Institute (Cremerius), being Eugenio Gaddini (1916–1985) one of the few members of the Italian Psychoanalytic Society to have done so. In other words, the level of international connection of the Milan SPP (the institute) and ASP (the society) was at the time higher than the average of the Italian IPA group. Not to talk about the fact that both Benedetti and Cremerius had been analytically socialized in German, the language of Freud—whose knowledge is not of secondary importance for understanding his work.

Coming now to Volume 3 of Richards's *Selected papers*, I can mention both the words of appreciation for him formulated by Judith Logue, and the introduction to it by Arthur Lynch. Logue speaks of Richards as "a man for all seasons", ready "to test the limits of whatever and whomever he encounters, and to expand our horizons" In the eyes of Lynch, in this volume Richards

"continues to carve out a special place for his contributions from the second generation of Contemporary Conflict Theories. In these five sections he has provided an organized view of how the mind works and has heard the suggestions from others that Unconscious Fantasy should be included with compromise formations and unconscious conflict in any definition of how the mind works" (pp. 22–23).

In what follows I will hint at the contents of most of the 20 chapters of the volume, and concentrate only on what I believe to be its most interesting contributions.

Section 1 bears the title "Antecedents" and includes four chapters: chapter 1 deals with "Jacob Arlow (1912-2004)" (2004) and was written with S.M. Goodman; chapter 2 deals with the "Symposium: The Clinical Value of The Concepts of Conflict and Compromise Formation" (1994) held at the New York Psychoanalytic Institute in November 1990; chapter 3 deals with "Technical Consequences of Object Relations Theories" (1980), a symposium of the Fall Meeting of the APsaA of December 1978; and chapter 4 is the "Afterword" to *The Rangell Reader,* edited in 2013 with Lynch and Bachant. Particularly touching and significant I find the words with which the three editors remember Leo Rangell (1913–2011):

"A book is often a metaphor for how one has lived life. Here the students and friends of Leo Rangell have gathered together once more to commemorate the countless contributions from a man who had a life well lived. We, the authors of this afterword, have worked with Leo Rangell separately and together for many years. His work has touched our lives in an enduring way and we are grateful to make this small contribution to a very significant work.

Leo Rangell was interested in all things human. Throughout his career Leo Rangell was a major contributor to the psychoanalytic literature. He was a devoted advocate for the unification of psychoanalytic theory. He was a man on a mission—the development of what he called—the total composite psychoanalytic theory. In this pursuit he stood at the crossroads that defined some of the greatest shifts in psychoanalysis, for the past 60 years. He had witnessed and contributed to the great debates of our time and added significantly to our understanding of clinical and theoretical issues, as well as providing sensible input on complex group, organizational, and political dilemmas.

As you have seen, his contributions were prolific. His works include: 9 books; 438 professional publications; 25 reprints in other languages; 23 written, delivered but as yet unpublished articles; and of the three projects under his supervision that were in progress, the current book is the first to reach completion" (pp. 59–60).

Coming now to section 2, "Views On Clinical Data", I can say that it consists of 4 chapters, being the first of them, chapter 5, "The Narcissistic Patient" (1995), written with Arlene Kramer Richards, the one I liked the most. I admired both the scientific and the clinical competence of the authors, that is, both their open and pluralistic theoretical perspective, and their presentation of a complex clinical case, treated using a classical analytic technique—with balanced interpretations of transference and affect clarifications. Very interesting, from a clinical point of view, are also chapter 6, "The Replacement Child: Variations on a Theme in History and Psychoanalysis" (2000; with Leon Anisfeld), and chapter 8, "Self-Mutilation and Father-Daughter Incest: A Psychoanalytic Case Report" (1988).

The most interesting papers of the following section have a particular historical relevance. I am referring to chapter 11, "Psychoanalytic Theories of the Self" (1982; with Ernest Ticho), and chapter 12, "Unconscious Fantasy: An Introduction to the Work of Jacob A. Arlow, MD, And To The Symposium In His Honor" (1992).In it we can read:

"For me, Jack Arlow is the Richard Feynman of psychoanalysis. Like the brilliant theoretical physicist acclaimed for his ability to solve the problems of engineers and applied scientists .... Arlow is the analyst called on by colleagues and candidates when an analysis in intractable or when efforts at clinical formulation have left lesser heads spinning. His confident ease in approaching problems rests on an utter mastery of psychoanalytic theory and method, though to the undiscerning this mastery may be obscured by his consistent use of jargon-free and experience-near terminology. These qualities typify his papers and in large measure account for their immense popularity among students. Almost all of his many contributions to the literature contain extensive case material well-integrated into the text. If there has been some neglect of Arlow's status as a theoretician of psychoanalysis, it is only because of his accessible writing style, his clinical directness, and the fact that his considerable body of work has up to now appeared primarily in the journal literature, making difficult its assessment as a coherent whole.... The publication of *Psychoanalysis: Clinical Theory and Practice* (1991), a volume containing 22 of Arlow's most important papers provides us with ready access to the seminal contributions that account for Arlow's pervasive impact on our field" (pp. 219–220).

In section 4, "Views and Reviews," we find four book reviews including a review of Robert Wallerstein's *Forty-Two Lives in Treatment. A Study of Psychoanalysis and Psychotherapy* (1986) written by Richards for the *International Journal of Psychoanalysis,* in which he expresses to the author his gratitude for his unique project and work. Understandably critical is his review of Robert Stolorow's and Bernard Brandchaft's 1987 book *Psychoanalytic Treatment: An Intersubjective Approach:* centered on "a sound clinical approach to rich clinical material," the authors exaggerate the relevance of their innovative point of view, founding it as they do on "a caricature of contemporary analytic technique" (p. 285).

We thus come to the last chapter of this volume, chapter 20, "Politics and Paradigms" (1998), occupying a section, section 5, of its own. Through his words Richards celebrated the publication in the *JAPA* of a series of papers by relational authors such as Charles Spezzano, Dianne Elise, Lewis

Arion and Annabella Bushra, that is, the realization of the turn from exclusion to inclusion mentioned above (see volume 2). I believe it makes sense to report here the concluding words of such an important message:

"Aron and Bushra, as well as Spezzano, point in this issue of *JAPA* to interesting and unexpected convergences between contributors from different schools. Most striking is the similarity they note in the views of states of unconsciousness in the analytic situation held by Philip Bromberg, a relationalist, and Sheldon Bach, a Freudian. Is it not possible that whether a shift from a so-called 'drive' paradigm to a relational one is viewed as revolution or evolution is a question determined in large measure by political considerations? There are even those who maintain that the shift itself is a political artifact. My own sense is that these theoretical distinctions will become less clear-cut (and will be advanced less insistently) as dialogue between the various schools continues. I am pleased that this journal can contribute to that process" (p. 295).

Volume 4 of the *Selected papers of Arnold D. Richards*, by the title *The peripatetic psychoanalyst,* accompanied by the already mentioned words of introduction by Daniel Benveniste, and of appreciation by Jane Hall, contains 18 chapters for a total of 304 pages. Chapter 1, "The Organizational Structure of the American Psychoanalytic Association: The Politics of Exclusion", is the text of a paper given by the author in 2014 at the NPAP, the National Association for the Psychoanalysis, the New York City analytic group founded by Theodor Reik (1888–1969), after he was refused membership in the New York Psychoanalytic Society—being he a lay analyst. In it Richards talks of the foundation of NPAP in 1948 in terms of "the beginning of the 'Balkanization' of American psychoanalysis" (p.

29), and reconstructs the renunciation of the W.A. White Institute to apply for membership in the APsaA, after Merton Gill had "made clear" to Clara Thompson (1893–1958) "that the issue was more their ideology than the other old bone of contention, analytic frequency" (*ibidem*). Worthwhile reporting are also the concluding words of this paper:

> "But APsaA has come a long way from the politics of exclusion enshrined in 1946 and defended since, despite BoPS's protestations to the contrary, at great cost to psychoanalysis as a profession. It is on its way to becoming a fully democratic and participatory organization. The decisions that the newly-vested members of the Association make in the next few years will determine whether APsaA can be renewed as a vibrant and forward-looking professional organization, or whether it will wither away as new and more flexible organizations of younger psychoanalysts develop and come to dominate the profession" (p. 37).

Unfortunately, I am not up to date with whatever happened with the APsaA in the last ten years. All I know is that the participation of the North American colleagues in the last elections of the IPA board was percentage-wise lower than the percentage of the European and of the South American colleagues, that is, less than 30%. From this point of view, I very much support the fact itself that Arnold Richards decided to call his publishing house "International Psychoanalytic Books". I have been the coeditor-in-chief of the *International Forum of Psychoanalysis* since June 2007, and I am very much aware of how true it unfortunately is that, although we might have good international networks, we do not certainly yet have enough "international psychoanalysts." The IPA training programs themselves are more self-referential than internationally oriented.

But here is what we can read in the following chapter, chapter 2, "The Politics of Exclusion: Institute Stagnation", about the reception of Richards's political work at his own institute and society

> "I am not sure 'bullying' is the right term to describe how I am treated at my Institute. A better term would be *persona non grata,* which is what I have become there. Since the 90s, I have not been asked to teach, supervise, or analyze, although I am a sought-after teacher, supervisor, an and analyst in non-APsaA institutes" (p. 42).

Incredible! I know that this Book Review Essay is becoming far too long, but I believe in psychoanalysis as an international network, that is, in the necessity for all of us—outside of the United States—to be well informed about what Arnold Richards stands for.

He, for example, stands for good teaching, that is, for an open and pluralistic rendition of central concepts of psychoanalysis such as transference, countertransference, interpretation and supervision, as we can learn from the chapters 4 to 8, that is, the texts of classes he must have prepared for his Chinese students. Not to mention the fact that everything he says is very well distilled through his personal experience, with particular regard for what the tells us concerning his own experience of supervisand of three supervisors (Beres, Lipin and Gero) during his own analytic training.

A central place in his scientific production is also played by chapter 8, "The Spectrum of Analytic Interaction: A Contemporary Freudian Perspective", written together with Lynch and Bachant, and in which the authors set forth "a contemporary Freudian perspective proposing that interaction be viewed as a spectrum of distinct yet overlapping clinical phenomena: acting in/acting out, transference actualization, enactment, countertransference actualization, and boundary violation" (p. 153). Very interesting and worth quoting are the following final considerations:

"We have endeavored to show that interaction has always been a part of the psychoanalytic landscape, though it has been known under different names and guises. Conceptually, enactments and actualizations seek to provide a sophisticated and nuanced elucidation of interaction in the analytic process. Both are forms of repetition whose aim is the fulfillment of a wish, which is often archaic and unconscious to the participant. How much the analytic interaction is a product of the conflicts and fantasies of these enduring psychic structures and how much it is constructed by factors in the present remains a topic of debate.... The object relation, interpersonal, relational, and contemporary Freudian traditions have all made major contributions in expanding our theoretical perspectives on interaction" (pp. 174–175).

Reading these words out loud to myself, I can see what a long way we, as an analytic community, have gone since the time (1997) of Stephen Mitchell's *Influence and Autonomy in Psychoanalysis*—whose premise was that the concept of "interaction" did not have a place in the Freudian system, and that post-Freudian psychoanalysis was still going in the same direction.

That such a debate, around's Mitchell's 1988 "relational turn," is still alive, is what we learn through the following chapter, that is Richard's 2020 Foreword to the book edited by Jon Mills *Debating Relational Psychoanalysis: Jon Mills and His Critics.* I do not personally know Jon Mills, but from what I know of his contributions I have the feeling that he never met Mitchell, and that his critique of relational psychoanalysis is of a philosophical nature, that is, exclusively based on what Mitchell has written—without any reference to the person he was, and to the context in which he was active. My own position would be the following: the dichotomy (which Mills attributes to Mitchell) is already present in Freud, theoretically bound to his drive-based one-personal model, but clinically aware of the relational dimension of his clinical work, a dimension he was allergic to formulate as such, because of his fear of being accused of using suggestion instead of such a scientifically noble instrument as interpretation; it was a brilliant idea for Greenberg and Mitchell to base their 1983 book on such a contradiction; but it was a "politically based move" for Mitchell in 1988 to attribute to post-Freudian psychoanalysis as a whole such a lack of interest for the relational dimension of our work, as if he did not know, for example, Paula Heimann's 1950 paper on "Countertransference", and the technical and theoretical turn which came out of it. In other words, I do not think that Mitchell himself really believed in the dichotomy between drive and relational, such as it is attributed to him, in the form of a belief; it was merely a scientific hypothesis which allowed him to bring about a political turn in American psychoanalysis, in the direction of a new and better balance between the medical and the psychological points of view and/or professional categories. Mitchell himself—in my experience—knew Freud well enough to know how multidimensional his work is, as opposed to it being reducible only to his drive model (which, again, also for Freud was a scientific hypothesis, and not a belief). Or, in other words, and as Arnold Richard convincingly demonstrates in all of his 5 volumes, I can imagine that the debate initiated by Mitchell was too heavily influenced by the very long and destructive lack of dialogue between North American Ego psychology and Interpersonal psychoanalysis. I can imagine that, in such conditions, no really serene debate could take place.

But, since the author keeps surprising the reader with the wealth of his contributions, I am happy to go on with one of the best and original contributions of volume 4, that is, chapter 14, "Dreams and the Wish for

Immortality", leaving again the word to him, for the sense of discovery that Richards's words transmit:

> "In his work on dreams, he [Freud] cast a great light upon a universal and mysterious human experience, and it is in a spirit of appreciation that I avail myself of the opportunity here to shine that light into a corner that he missed. I suggest that the wish for immortality shares the childhood origin, and the fate, of early sexual and aggressive oedipal wishes, and I propose that they be added not to the inventory of primary dream wishes. I hope profoundly that as we further explore this topic, both theoretically and clinically, we will find the evidence for a greatly enhanced understanding of immortality wishes and their place in, and contribution to, our dreams" (p. 270).

Before taking up volume 5, I find it important to report the words with which the author presented to the readers the first issue of his *International Journal of Controversial Discussions (IJCD)* in February 2020, as we can read in chapter 17 of volume 4:

> "The *IJCD, International Journal of Controversial Discussions,* is a new online journal launching in February 2020 and will be distributed free by subscription. Our intention is to create a forum for discussion and debate about controversial issues within psychoanalysis among colleagues with a variety of different approaches. It will offer a meeting place for analysts with diverging theoretical and clinical attitudes whose path might otherwise not cross.... The journal is a work in progress, and we welcome input from the larger mental health community" (pp.291–292).

Volume 5 of Arnold Richards's *Selected Papers* bears the title *The World of Psychoanalysis and Psychoanalysts,* and consists in two sections, section 1 under the title "Clinical Papers", with ten chapters, and section 2 under the title "Views and Reviews", with twenty-two chapters. The most interesting chapter of section 1 is chapter 5, "China on our Minds: An Educational Initiative," written with his wife Arlene, and previously unpublished. From it we learn how the original invitation from China came about, that is, it was originally meant only for Arlene, but, once he heard about it, Arnie also applied, and was accepted, having thus the chance of sharing with his wife a totally new dimension of their life and work —which seems to have kept them younger. What he writes about his work with his Chinese supervises sounds also like an introduction to the kind of democratic exchange that we connect with our Western world. Here are his words:

> "Supervisees were reluctant to tell me of their failure, needing to save face, they often showed their understanding of theory rather than report an hour. Gradually, by accepting their reluctance, I managed to convince them that they were the authorities on what happened in the hour and they could teach that to me. Over time, they began to present both hours and questions, mirroring the questions I asked them. Now they are criticizing me and each other without fear of losing face or insulting the person whose work is being discussed. This has been profoundly satisfying as well" (p. 73).

The other chapters of section 1 deal with topics already articulated in the previous volumes—dreams and the wish for immortality, Jacob Arlow and unconscious fantasy, and the clinical value of the concepts of conflict and compromise formation.

As far as section 2 is concerned, I particularly enjoyed reading the reviews of the books I also know and value. Here are some examples: Lawrence Friedman's 1988 book *The Anatomy of Psychotherapy;* the anthology edited by Lew Aron and Adrienne Harris in 2005 under the title *Clinical Theory: Relational Psychoanalysis. Volume 2, Innovation and Expansion;* Emily Kuriloff's 2014 book *Contemporary Psychoanalysis and the Lessons of the Third Reich. History, Memory and Tradition;* and Kenneth Eisold's 2018 book *The Organizational Life of Psychoanalysis: Conflicts, Dilemmas, and the Future of the Profession.* It was a pleasure to compare Richards's reaction to these books to the ways I had reacted to them.

Last but not least, very significant, touching, and in tune with what I have written so far are the words which the author addresses to the future analytic candidates, in the last chapter, chapter 32 of volume 5, "Letter to a candidate":

"Every analysis is a voyage of discovery for the patient and the analyst.... The psychoanalyst should be a *gebildeter Mensch.* It is a field that one never tires from. The clinical and scientific challenges never end. Even though the times have changed and psychoanalysis is no longer sought after as a profession as it is when I was growing up, its intellectual and clinical satisfactions remain for a dedicated few. To all prospective candidates, welcome!" (p. 308).

When Antonino Ferro had the chance to eventually have a book by him translated into English at the beginning of the 1990s, the publisher must have said that, if the author's name had been "Iron" (the English equivalent of "ferro"), he would have sold many more copies of it. In fact, the book by Ferro was the first Italian psychoanalytic book to have ever been published by an English-speaking publisher—after Eugenio Gaddini's (1916–1985) anthology of papers (see Gaddini, 2016, for the second edition). The colleagues who already know Arnold Richards, and have their own opinion about him and his work, will probably not read this Book Review Essay. And the same is true for all those who will think that our names, Conci and Richards, can not have anything in common. As far as I am concerned, I deeply believe that the kind of dialogue that Arnold Richards developed with his colleagues and with his readers in the course of his long and successful career deserves to be widely known and appreciated by as many of our readers as possible. This is why I have created the dialogue with him around which this Book Review Essay is centered. In other words, it is my belief that the essence of Freud's work and legacy is its self-taught nature, which is what brought him to keep having new free associations, formulating new hypotheses, and making new discoveries—till the end of his life. From this point of view, both psychoanalytic training and the continual dimension of our training are too complex a business to be delegated to an institute, and can be handled at best only by developing our own research projects. This is also the way in which Arnold Richards goes about psychoanalysis, and which I have tried to reproduce in this Book Review Essay.

REFERENCES

Anzieu, D. (1986). The place of Germanic language and culture in Freud's discovery of psychoanalysis between 1895 and 1900. *International Journal of Psychoanalysis, 67*, 219–226.

Berke, J. (2015). *The hidden Freud: His Hassidic roots.* London: London: Karnac Books.

Arlow, J.A. (1991). *Psychoanalysis: Clinical theory and practice.* Madison, CT International Universities Press.

Aron, L., Harris, A. eds. (2005). *Clinical theory: Relational psychoanalysis. Volume 2, Innovation and expansion. Hillsdale, NJ:* Analytic Press.

Berke, J. (2015). *The hidden Freud: His Hassidic roots.* London: Karnac.

Bergmann. M. (1993). Reflections on the history of psychoanalysis. *Journal of the American Psychoanalytic Association,* 41, 929–955.

Conci, M. (2000). Rezension des Buches von T. Müller "Von Charlottenburg zum Central Park West. Henry Loewenfeld und die Psychoanalyse in Berlin, Prag und New York. Frankfurt, Edition Déjà-vu, 2000 [Review of the book by Thomas Müller "From Charlottenburg to Central Park West. Henry Loewenfeld and psychoanalysis in Berlin, Prague and New York. Frankfurt, Edition Déjà-vu, 2000]. *Luzifer-Amor. Zeitschrift für dieGeschichte der Psychoanalyse,* 13 (26), 153–158.

——— (2014). Gaetano Benedetti, Johannes Cremerius, the Milan ASP; and the future of the IFPS. *International Forum of Psychoanalysis,* 23, 85–95.

——— (2019). *Freud, Sullivan, Mitchell, Bion, and the multiple voices of international psychoanalysis.* New York: IPBooks.

——— (2023). Harry Stack Sullivan and Stephen Mitchell in Italy: A historical and a personal account. *International Forum of Psychoanalysis,* 32, 180–91.

Danto, E. (2005). *Freud's free clinics: Psychoanalysis and social justice,* 1918–1938. New York: Columbia University Press.

Eisold, K. (2018).*The organizational life of psychoanalysis: Conflicts, dilemmas, and the future of the profession.* . Abingdon, England; New York, NY: Routledge.

Fleck, L. (1979). *Genesis and development of a scientific fact.* The University of Chicago Press. Original German edition, 1935.

Friedman, L. (1988). *The anatomy of psychotherapy.* Hillsdale: NJ: Analytic Press.

Freud, S. (1933). *New introductory lessons to psychoanalysis.* W.J.H. Sprott translator. New York: Norton.

Gaddini, E. (2016). *A psychoanalytic theory of infantile experience. Conceptual and clinical reflections.* A. Limentani ed. . Abingdon, England; New York, NY: Routledge.

Greenberg, J.R. (1991). overcome by Jay Greenberg with his 1991 book *Oedipus and beyond: A clinical theory.* Cambridge, MA: Harvard University Press.

——— (2001). The analyst's participation: A new look. *Journal of the American Psychoanalytic Association,* 49, 359–380.

——— Mitchell, S.A. (1983). *Object relations in psychoanalytic theory.* Cambridge, MA: Harvard University Press.

Heimann, P. (1950). On counter-transference. *International Journal of Psychoanalysis,*31, 81–84.

Hirsch, I. (2000). Interview with Benjamin Wolstein. *Contemporary Psychoanalysis,* 36, 187–232.

Hoffman, I.Z. (1998). *Ritual and spontaneity in psychoanalysis: A dialectical-constructivist view.* Abingdon, England; New York, NY: Routledge.

Kalish, B.W. (2009). An interview with Leo Rangell, Los Angeles, California, July 2008. *International Forum of Psychoanalysis,* 18, 107–115.

Kris, A.O. (1976). The problem of membership in the American Psychoanalytic Association. *Journal of the Philadelphia Association for Psychoanalysis,* 3 (1 and 2), 22–36.

Kuhn, T.S. (1970). *The structure of scientific revolutions.* Chicago: University of Chicago Press.

Kuriloff, E. (2014) *Contemporary psychoanalysis and the lessons of the Third Reich. History, memory and tradition.* Abingdon, England; New York, NY: Routledge.

Mills, J. ed. (2020). *Debating relational psychoanalysis. Jon Mills and his critics.* . Abingdon, England; New York, NY: Routledge.

Mitchell, S.A. (1988). *Relational concepts in psychoanalysis. An integration.* Harvard University Press. Italian edition: *Gli orientamenti relazionali in psicoanalisi. Un modello integrato.* Bollati Boringhieri.

———(1997). *Influence and autonomy in psychoanalysis.* Hillsdale, NJ: Analytic Press.

Prochnik, G. (2006). *Putnam camp: Sigmund Freud, James Jackson Putnam, and the purpose of American psychology.* New York: Other Press.

Richards, A.D. (2022). *Up close and personal: The poems and pictures of Arnold David Richards.* New York: IPBooks.

——— & Richards, A.K. eds. (1993). *The spectrum of psychoanalysis: Essays in honor of Martin Bergmann.* Madison, CT: International Universities Press.

——— Willick, M.S. eds. (1986). *Psychoanalysis, the science of mental conflict: Essays in honor of Charles Brenner.* Hillsdale, NJ: Analytic Press.

——— ——— Ahumada, J., Olagaray, J. eds. (1994). *The perverse transference: Essays in honor of Horacio Etchegoyen.* Lanham, MD: Jason Aronson.

——— ——— Blum, H., Kramer, Y. eds. (1988). *Unconscious fantasy, myth and reality: Essays in honor of Jacob Arlow.* Madison, CT: International Universities Press.

——— Lynch, A.A., Bachant, J.L. eds. (2013). *The Rangell Reader.* New York: IPBooks.

Rudnystsky, P.L, & Mitchell, S.A. (2000). Between philosophy and politics. In: P. Rudnystsky, P.L, Mitchell, S.A. (2000). Between philosophy and politics. In: P. Rudnytsky ed., *Psychoanalytic conversations. Interviews with clinicians, commentators and critics,* pp.101–136. Hillsdale, NJ: Analytic Press..

Stolorow, R.D., Brandchaft, B. (1987). *Psychoanalytic treatment: An intersubjective approach.* Hillsdale, NJ: Analytic Press.

Wallerstein, R.S. (1988). One psychoanalysis or many? *International Journal of Psychoanalysis,* 69, 5–21.

——— (1986).*Forty-two lives in treatment. A study of psychoanalysis and psychotherapy. New York:* Guilford.

Wolstein, B. ed. (1988). *Essential papers on the countertransference.* New York: New York University Press.

CHAPTER 5

Book Review: *Psychoanalysis: Critical Conversations (Selected Papers by Arnold D. Richards, Volume 1)*

[(2016). Tuch, R., *Journal of the American Psychoanalytic Association* 64(5):1075–1081][3]

What becomes apparent as one makes one's way through this collection of well-written and well-reasoned papers, chapters, and book reviews written or co-written by Arnold Richards is the fact that Richards has a bone to pick with analysts who make a habit of dismissing, to the point of condemning, the work of colleagues whose approach is largely informed by modern conflict theory. What particularly galls Richards is the way in which these

---

3 Dr. Tuch has been in practice for over 40 years. He is a Training and Supervising Analyst at both the NCP and the PCC, Clinical Professor of Psychiatry at the David Geffen School of Medicine, UCLA, former Dean of Training at the NCP and is presently Head of the Scholarship Section of the Department of Psychoanalytic Education (American Psychoanalytic Assn.) He has published extensively in the areas of interpersonal relations and clinical technique. His papers appear in all three of the major psychoanalytic journals and his work has been translated into four other languages. He is the recipient of the Karl Menninger Award for Psychoanalytic Writing, the Edith Sabshin Award for excellence in teaching, and the Leo Rangell Award for psychoanalytic writing. Dr. Tuch relishes the privilege afforded him by patients who take the risk of entrusting him with their innermost demons.

critics unkindly, unfairly, and reductionistically misrepresent the work of contemporary Freudians, which they see as singularly mechanistic, drive-oriented, oedipally focused, and conflict-obsessed while touting their own "evolved" approach as being more humanistic, caring, experience-near, and antiauthoritarian. These detractors celebrate their own brand of psychoanalysis as a truly revolutionary, game-changing paradigmatic shift that effectively replaces the old, tired, misguided ways of analysts, hailing from a different era, who were indoctrinated in a style that has now fallen by the wayside; they pray for the day these unenlightened analysts open their eyes and accept the coming of a new age—the ascendancy of the relational approach heralded by the publication of Greenberg and Mitchell's *Object Relations in Psychoanalytic Theory* in 1983. Most who'd lived through this unfortunate period in American psychoanalysis know of what Richards speaks when he complains that "by elevating the antithesis between drives and relationships into a theoretical shibboleth, the relational turn made it difficult to engage in a nuanced debate regarding their interaction" (p. 55). In an effort to rectify this state of affairs, Richards calls for "adherents of the various analytic traditions to forgo a discourse of dichotomy and polarization and instead approach one another in a dialectical spirit" (p. 46)—to abandon tendencies to see opposing schools of thought as irreconcilable and hence incapable of being integrated. Richards prays for the day when discourse about theoretical differences becomes less impassioned as analysts cease to take their differences personally.

It appears that the rhetoric of self psychology got Richards's goat the most. In two papers written in the early 1980s and another in the mid-1990s, Richards is particularly critical of certain of that school's adherents, though he admits at the tail end of the book that "I have since become more positive about self psychology and I recognize that judging one theory as superior to another is problematic." In this collection of papers, one also sees Richards poking holes in the reasoning of select relationalists, most evident in his review of a book by Stephen Mitchell. In the meantime, Richards demonstrates an affinity for Mitchell's co-author, Jay Greenberg, who "distanced himself from the 'narrow' relational point of view and shifted to a position closer to traditional classical thinkers who see the relational and drive perspectives as mutually enriching." Richards likewise appreciates the writings of Irwin Hoffman, whom he sees as exhibiting a laudable capacity to think dialectically rather than dichotomously, "a satisfying skepticism [toward current trends in thinking], and an independence of thought" that led Hoffman to be critical of relationalists who display positivist tendencies (believing it possible to objectively and accurately read the patient's experience) rather than adopting a social constructivist stance. The latter, Hoffman suggests, is more likely to be apparent in the work of modern conflict theorists. To underscore Hoffman's claim, Richards quotes Greenberg (2001) as having wondered "why the examples in so many of the important relational texts sound so much the same, even as the very idea of a standard or uniform technique is debunked by the relational critique." To Greenberg "it seems we are being offered two parallel messages working at cross-purposes" (p. 365).

To be sure, there is more to this book than Richards's defense of contemporary Freudian theory. He pays homage to Charles Brenner, masterfully summarizing the breadth of his work. He showcases the work of Leo Rangell and Merton Gill as well, and respectfully reviews Hoffman's *Ritual and Spontaneity in the Psychoanalytic Process* (1998). Included is an introductory paper on psychoanalytic theory for novices and another for those interested in learning more about the evolution of contemporary conflict theory. But the theme of responsive defense figures prominently in these pages. And well it might, given the tendency by some in the wider relational school to engage in straw man arguments ignoring the evolution of the thinking of contemporary Freudians.

This tendency may well be the result of relationalists having been unjustifiably excluded for so long from the mainstream of American psychoanalysis that righteous indignation finally set in with a vengeance.

It's at this point in my review that readers might be trying to determine my theoretical orientation. This fruitless exercise would merely serve the purpose of leading the reader to dismiss, or embrace, what I have to say on the grounds I am or am not a fellow traveler. I'm not blind to injustices on both sides of the aisle, and I feel I can recognize instances when the pendulum has swung too far in either direction (Tuch 2015). And—speaking of aisles—when did our professional discourse begin to sound like American politics, with competing sides failing to put their best foot forward in favor of tripping up the opponent by finding fault? Thankfully for our field, times have changed and we are much less likely to see closed-minded attacks on those who think or practice differently, though vestiges of such tendencies clearly persist. These days the field seems less populated with "true believers," and signs of inclusiveness are to be seen everywhere: witness the welcomed inclusion of the William Alanson White Institute by the American Psychoanalytic Association. And while stragglers who remain committed to waging war continue to bicker, the rest of us realize that the relational school has "arrived"—maybe not by replacing other ways of thinking but by having earned a healthy respect and a rightful place in American psychoanalysis.

Richards and his co-authors respond to the arguments lodged by self psychologists and relationalists in a studied, serious, and mostly unemotional manner, offering a catalogue of effective rebuttals encyclopedic in scope. Alas, given the present state of affairs in our field, it remains unlikely this book will be read by those whose views are being challenged. Naturally, this cuts both ways. Richards is quick to note that contemporary Freudian practitioners are equally likely to remain relatively ignorant, and hence prejudiced, about the thought of prominent figures whose work lies outside the scope of mainstream journals. In chapter 13, Richards and his wife, Arlene Kramer Richards, reflect on the fact they'd known next to nothing about the work of Benjamin Wolstein, a highly acclaimed interpersonal psychoanalyst whom they refer to as having been "way ahead of his time" (p. 242). For whatever reason, Wolstein's work appeared almost exclusively in *Contemporary Psychoanalysis*, which Richards and Richards believe "attests to the great divide that has existed since the 1940s between interpersonal psychoanalysis and the rest of the psychoanalytic world.... we are trying to convey a sense of what has been *lost* to the psychoanalytic community as a whole by these decades of estrangement" (pp. 233–235). The authors hope is that this rift will be remedied by what they see as signs of a "new ecumenicism" (p. 234).

In chapter 2, Richards locates the roots of this regrettable estrangement, in part, in the exclusionary politics of A. A. Brill—the "father of American psychoanalysis"—whose policy of restricting training at the New York Psychoanalytic to those with medical degrees (justified as necessary to protect and promote psychoanalysis on these shores) had the dual effect of alienating scores of would-be psychoanalysts who thenceforth would show little interest in psychoanalysis. Richards believes this created an environment that gave rise to a "deplorable penchant for dichotomous thinking, with the tendency to brand interpersonalists and others outside of the institutional fold as 'not analysts'" (p. 28).

Richards sees the causes of such estrangement as issuing from other sources as well. Sometimes analysts come away from their training analysis deeply disappointed, if not seriously scarred, and thereafter dedicate themselves to practicing in a manner decidedly different from their analyst's; this is what Rangell (1982) called "transference to theory." In chapter 18, Richards and Richards suggest that an analyst may adopt a given treatment approach in an effort not only to find more efficacious ways of working but also to protect patients from the potentially injurious effects of a treatment that might lead them to feel ashamed and inferior for not having already figured out what the analyst comes to surmise about their situation, which Richards and Richards find hard to imagine. As to why individuals gravitate to one particular school of thought rather than another, they offer an intriguing possibility: "an analyst creates a theory of clinical practice that corrects for those aspects of her or his character that would thwart the analytic enterprise" (p. 238). I'm not so sure that's true, but it's an interesting theory, nonetheless.

The chapter I personally find most problematic is this same chapter 18, in which Richards and Richards attempt a "thought experiment" by first presenting case material seen from their own theoretical perspective and then imagining how analysts with differing points of view might intervene. This experiment in comparative technique seems deeply flawed, though it issues from the laudable if elusive goal of seeing how theory affects technique and comparing clinical approaches to see whether one might prove more efficacious than others. In the first place, the case presentation is sketchy and does not accomplish what the authors seem to think it does—demonstrating the efficacy of their approach. The authors then attempt to imagine how a self psychologist, for example, would address the material. This results in what I see as a limited, even mocking portrayal meant to demonstrate how limited the self psychological approach, in particular, tends to be. I find this experiment dubious and unfair, and I find myself in agreement with Paul Ornstein (1995), who, in a rebuttal of the paper when it first appeared in the *Journal of Clinical Psychoanalysis*, faults the experiment for not having provided more detailed verbatim notes that might have allowed self psychologists themselves to weigh in on how they might have intervened—though even that proposed experiment is limited in that an analyst who's not in the room, intersubjectively immersed in the process, is necessarily blinded to the extent that he's in no position to be receiving data on all channels, verbal and nonverbal.

In chapter 11 Richards, in conjunction with Janet Lee Bachant, critically reviews Mitchell's *Relational Concepts in Psychoanalysis: An Integration* (1998). They take issue with Mitchell's relational view of sexuality, which sees it as driven from without (in response to the environment) rather than endogenously from within. They see oedipal dynamics in Mitchell's view as "stripped of... genitality" and being more about "a struggle for self-definition" (p. 191). They take Mitchell to task not only for his inability to see the extent to which individuals exhibit a readiness to respond to the analyst in predetermined ways that predate the outset of the analytic relationship (not everything is co-constructed!) but also for his "rejection of early experience as exercising a critical role in the formation of psychic structure" (in their view an attack on the core of psychoanalysis). They also take issue with the notion that "analysis heals because we are more honest, more authentic, or more intimate" (p. 199), an idea they call "naive and grandiose" (p. 199). Their debate with the relationalists carries over into the following chapter (with Arthur Lynch as an added author), arguing that many relationalists who set their sights on observing how the analyst's subjectivity influences that of the patient fail to exercise the sort of free-floating attention needed to bring into focus unexpected types of material that become apparent in surprising ways in the patient's associations.

No review of Richards's work would be complete without acknowledging his place in American psychoanalysis. Richards describes himself as having an orthodox upbringing—meaning, he was trained at the New York Psychoanalytic. He is a publisher extraordinaire. He began as editor of APsaA's newsletter, *The American Psychoanalyst* (*TAP*), did a ten-year stint as *JAPA*'s editor-in-chief, and has since gone on to create his own publishing house—International Psychoanalytic Books (IPBooks), which publishes works from a diverse array of analytic perspectives. He founded a psychoanalytic blog (www.internationalpsychoanalysis.net) that helps facilitate communication between analysts worldwide. He's been involved in promoting the study of Jewish history and has been active in the YIVO Institute, which helps preserve and promote the Yiddish language. Room does not permit mention of his many other accomplishments, though I'd be remiss if I failed to mention that a defining aspect of his being is his presence—his personality—a person Lawrence Friedman aptly likens to "a character in a novel—maybe a Russian novel." It should also be noted that Richards's defense of modern Freudian thinking by no means indicates a blind acceptance of the status quo within the halls of American psychoanalysis. Nothing could be further from the truth.

"The winds of change that have swept through American psychoanalysis in recent decades have had some beneficial effects," he offers, adding: "I share Wallerstein's conviction that contemporary Freudians should reject nostalgia and stagnation in favor of adaptation and growth. There can be no turning back. The question is, where do we do from here?" (p. 159). Richards appeals to analysts to open themselves up "to an exploration of the personal and political roots of adherence to any particular psychoanalytic viewpoint" (p. 38). "Our plea in these matters," he writes, "is for a measure of dispassion, a willingness not to take our theoretical preferences personally, and to consider them in the context of the broader analytic community whose achievements as a whole are only just becoming available" (p. 239), thus alerting us to our ultimate concern: "our shared need to promote the hard-won gains of our science in an increasingly hostile environment" (p. 40).

Charles Fisher Interview Part 2

AR: But then you were still in elementary school, not high school.

CF: I was in the fifth grade and I stayed there through high school. When the new institution was built, this beautiful place was not good enough for the rich Jews of Los Angeles. They wanted more of a showplace; they wanted something that didn't look or sound like an institution. It was a beautiful place out near Culver City. Do you know where that is? It's hills. You could see the ocean. It was called Vista Del Mar, which means "view of the sea." It was 20 miles away but on a clear day you could see the ocean . It had been laid out like a city street and it would curve around so you wouldn't know you were in an institution. There were beautiful stucco houses. Each house housed 20 kids, ten girls and ten boys, and they had house numbers. It was on a paved street so people wouldn't think they were in an institution. I was only there a year. They kept me until I entered college. I was still 16, so they kept me there a year and a few months until I was almost 18, by which time I was a sophomore.

AR: So you were in an institution, then, from nine to eighteen. And your brother—how did he react to the idea that you would go to college and he wouldn't?

CF: That was traumatic to my brother. When my mother was alive, my brother and I did everything together, we played together, we got along nicely. But I had contempt for him because he was a bed wetter. When we got to the orphanage, I began to dislike him. I was ashamed of him. He wet the bed, and he didn't have much dignity about him, and then he was not one of my best friends. Harry Stack Sullivan said you had to have a chum not to be schizophrenic.

AR: I didn't know that. He had a close friend, this other psychiatrist.

CF: Sullivan was homosexual.

AR: But he had a male friend who was a mentor and friend.

CF: He was a strange man. There was an article by Leslie Farber in the London Times Supplement about Sullivan and how he didn't tell the truth about having had a schizophrenic episode, he was a psychopath, a liar.

AR: He was expelled from school for something terrible, from college.

CF: He may have been. But I knew him and I disliked him. He was interesting to listen to but there was more heat than light. He had a mordant humor and a peculiar, interesting, garbled way of talking. He gave you the illusion that he was saying something important. But he was a tremendous influence. He was a very disordered man; he kept most of his life secret. Farber said he was uneducated, no one knows where he went to medical school, and he was an ignorant person, but he had some curious charisma; not for me, though, I didn't care for him. Anyway, I'm losing the continuity. One of the things that led me into psychiatry was that I was a neurotic child and I knew that I was, because I knew that I had things wrong with me and I had no way of rationalizing and I knew that I had something that could be called pathology, whatever I called it. It was mostly what could be called social anxiety. I didn't have any habit disturbances. I had a poor appetite because I didn't like the food there. There were fruit orchards, melon patches, fruit trees, a real paradise, and I used to steal fruit, but I had social anxieties that were increased by the fact that I was in an orphan home. Even before I got to the orphan home, when I was six I discovered that I had public speaking anxieties of severe proportions. I'd go into a panic if I had to perform. It started when I was in first grade, the first time I remember having such a panic reaction. When you had to go to the toilet, you had to raise your hand and go up to the teacher and say, "Can I go to the toilet?" I remember I had to pee, so I observed that I was afraid on certain occasions; I sat in my seat trying to hold my urine. We had rows of benches in those days, not the individual desks and chairs they have now. You'd see a pool of urine on the floor and know that some kid had peed in his pants. So, I sat there and tried to make up my mind, should I say, "May I go to the toilet?" or "Can I go to the toilet?" and I knew that whichever one I chose, I would stammer, so that the anxiety was that I would stammer. I didn't stammer much, but I was in a panic. Finally, I would reach the point where I couldn't go on any longer and I would get up the courage and I'd ask the teacher. Whichever one I would use, I would stammer a little, not a lot, it was an apprehension that I would. However, any performance situation I was faced with, I would panic. I was bright enough that I was always getting into some situation that I would get called upon to do something. However, in class I discovered that if I volunteered, I didn't have any trouble, so I was always dangling my hand.

AR: Turning passive into active.

CF: That's right. So, the teacher would call on me. If no one else knew the answer, I didn't have to be afraid that I was stupid or something, so I didn't have too much trouble. At any rate, I had a terrible speaking problem for many years. It finally got much better. I got into analysis with Edith Jacobson and I got so I could perform. It's very important in becoming known to be able to speak. In my old age, though, some of the anxiety has come back. I still have some trouble when I speak.

AR: You spoke at some significant occasions. Didn't you give the Freud Lecture?

CF: That was years ago. By that time, I was very good. I gave the Brill Lecture and the Freud Lecture. I could do it very well.

AR: And with Sam Atkins you were wonderful.

CF: You missed the thing out in San Diego. That was two years ago and I did very well, so I can do it but there are still situations where I can't . Anyway, it was the bane of m existence and when I graduated high school— between the two institutions we: lived right in Los Angeles; this paradise I was talking about was in a suburb of Los Angeles. In the intermediate institution we lived closer to the center of town. I went to one of the local high schools called Los Angeles Polytechnic High School. That's where I was in my second and third years; I finished high school in three and a half years.

AR: You must have been about 16 then, since you skipped a grade.

CF: When I finished high school I was still 16 by a couple of months, but I was a year ahead, most kids finished at 18. We had something that was called students' day at high school, where they had a student teach a class, so in every one of my classes I was asked to teach. I almost died, but I managed. And I was asked to be valedictorian, but I couldn't do that and I ran away. Most of the time I would face these things out—at tremendous cost. If I didn't do it, I was overwhelmed with anxiety; if I did it, it was the same. So, amongst my motives for wanting to become a psychiatrist was self-cure. It wasn't as simple as that because I also had a profound curiosity about mental disease. I had a mother who was no doubt manic-depressive and a father who was schizoid, affectively so, and I was a little crazy myself. At the institution there was a kid with Tourette's Syndrome, an epileptic kid, a few psychopathic kids, and I was always fascinated by them. Anyway, where am I? I got lost.

AR: You're starting college, your first year in college, you still lived in the orphanage.

CF: I went to the University of California, Southern Branch. In those days there was just Berkeley and then there was Los Angeles and the University of California, Southern Branch, which was a state college, where the tuition was $300 a year. When I got out of high school, I was accepted at the University of California, and in my first year they let me stay in the orphanage. They had no provision for taking care of you after you left. They had begun to get some kids jobs but I was still 17, and I was on my own. So, I got a scholarship of $150 a year and I got a job in the registrar's office. When I was very young, 13, I learned how to type because I was canny enough to know, because I was a canny child, that the only thing that differentiated me from the other kids or anybody else was that I had something of a brain so if I was not to become like my father— my father whom I admired when I was little gradually became a terrible disappointment. He lived a whole life of regret. Once when I was about the age of four he was in business with a man who had a tin business, a man named Brown. The person he went into business with became an extremely rich man, dealing in sheet metal, a contractor, and another irony was that he did the tin work for the new orphanage. My father didn't like this man, he said he was a crook and my father was an extremely honest person, whatever else he was. Where was I?

AR: You've gotten a scholarship and you're in college.

CF: Oh, yeah.

AR: Did your brother go to college?

CF: No, he left high school at 16. In high school he had taken up printing and he didn't do too badly with his life. He worked for a Los Angeles paper box company where they did very complex color printing, like for color printed chocolate boxes. It was a very skilled thing, so he ultimately had a business of his own and did quite well. He got married and had a couple of kids plus some tragedies. He had two sons, one of whom died when he was about 18. The other one is a professor of economics at Rutgers with a reputation in the computer field.

AR: So, you got a scholarship and then were able to leave and live on your own.

CF: In my second year in high school, I enrolled in a course in shorthand, and I learned shorthand. I was in a class with 30 big, beautiful California girls, the only boy. That was an odd thing, a male stenographer. Billy Rose was a world Gregg champion, and President Wilson was, too, both role models. I had to make a living. I enrolled in college as a prelegal because I had the fantasy I would overcome my speaking difficulty and become another Clarence Darrow. I was 16.

AR: A modest ambition.

CF: A modest ambition. So, I actually took a couple of legal courses and I just couldn't comprehend what a tort was. I couldn't tell a tort from a tart. And so, I dropped that and I took a course in public speaking. I almost died. I was never called on. It was a great big class. Anyway, I went there for two and a half years and I did very well. I got good grades. I took general liberal arts courses. I was now getting to be 18 or so. After my sophomore year I took half of my junior year. At this point there was no intellectual direction.

AR: But a lot of practical skills, typing and shorthand.

CF: That's all. However, in my last year in the orphanage, in this cottage with 20 kids, there appeared a new housemother. Her name was Mrs. Riskin. She was about 40. She was a Russian intellectual, a 1905 socialist, altruistic, idealistic, somewhat puritanical. She was one of those. Her husband had died in the 1918 flu epidemic. She had a son my age, named Al. She had a big influence on me. She would give me things to read. I was going to college, but I was not educated in that way. So, she gave me *The Nation* and I can't tell you what a thrill that Nation was.

AR: There was Ingersoll.

CF: No, it wasn't Ingersoll. Anyway, she opened up the world. Then she gave me novels by Gorky, it was Gorky.

AR: Was she educating you or raising your political consciousness?

CF: She was just educating me. She was a lonely woman; she had lost her husband. Her son, whom she loved very much, was away and when all the other kids would go to bed, we'd stay up and talk, and gradually she began to kiss me, and I was fairly sophisticated in a way, but I was aware that she was kissing me too passionately. Anyway, it was an interesting thing. She was a sad woman.

AR: You were special.

CF: Yeah. She gave me one of Schnitzler's novels, which was about a woman who has a son who is 17 years old and is away at school. He brings home with him during a vacation period his boyfriend, who is also 17, and this woman has an affair with the son's friend. I don't think she had any idea that it had anything to do with us. Anyway, when I left the orphanage, her son had come back, and he and I got a little apartment together. In those days you could get an apartment for $20 a month. This was 1926. I didn't particularly like her son.

AR: So, you were in college and.....

CF: I was still in the orphanage. That last year I was in the orphan home. There was another housemother then, a 20-year-old Russian girl, absolutely stunning. She had a boyfriend who would come and visit her. He was a young man of about 24, a very attractive man, and they were in love. His name was Sigmund and he said he was a Viennese. During World War I, he witnessed his father being shot to death in a pogrom. He and his mother and his sister escaped. He was about 18 when he left Europe and came to this country, and he tried to get work. This was during the Depression. Anyway, he drifted across the country to Los Angeles, and I think he was a shoe salesman. He was very intelligent and a great reader and he used to give me books to read, Ben Hecht, Dreiser. He married this Russian girl but later they got divorced. Anyway, Al Riskin decided to go back to Berkeley, and I went to live with Sigmund, who was six and a half years older and not exactly innocent, but a very worldly man, a great womanizer. We were very close and it wasn't exactly good for me in many ways. I'm coming to how I met Betty. His girl, Jessica, lived in a certain section of town and she and her mother had a little dry goods store, notions store, and on that same block Betty lived with her family. Betty comes from a family of nine children, two sets of twins, of which she was one. She knew Jessica.

She had met Sigmund and a couple of times he took her out, and one day Sigmund said to me, "I met a girl you might like." I was desperate for a girl. Anyway, Betty and I met and we fell in love immediately. Betty was a couple of years older. She was tiny, an extremely pretty girl. She weighed 92 and I weighed 106. By that time, I was in a very bad state. I was in a major depression. For the first time I thought of leaving school. I was headed for a lot of trouble. Anyway, Betty wanted to leave home. I thought she wanted to run away from me because I was pressing her too hard. We arranged to meet in New York. She had some friends in New York. She wanted to run away to New York, so I helped her run away in the spring of 1927. When June arrived and school was out, I put a pack on my back, and I just left the city without seeing anybody or saying goodbye. At that time, I wasn't seeing my father or my brother. I had no ties holding me there. My father had become a recluse. He worked a little. He lived in the rooming house section. There's a square there called Central Park, which is the equivalent of Union Square. I came back in 1930. I had not been in touch with my father. In 1930 I saw my father for the last time. The last thing he said to me was, "Your mother was no good. I was too passionate." In 1932 or 1934 he died. They found him sitting on a bench in Central Park; he had had a massive coronary. He was 64.

I'm back to June 1927. I bummed across the country. It is a hard thing to do. There were certain parts of the country where I couldn't get a ride but I had read books that romanticized bumming; there was nothing romantic about it; was dangerous. In a period of 16 days, I had a sensation that I was running all the way to get to Betty.

AR: And, of course, your father had run from Romania to Hamburg and he also ran across the United States the other way.

CF: So, I ran back to New York. Betty was living in New York and not getting along with her friends. By the time I got to Chicago I had spent my $30. I didn't beg on the streets. I bummed a meal in a restaurant. I was in jail for two days.

AR: Really? For vagrancy?

CF: No, I was riding the rails. That was a dangerous.

REFERENCES

Greenberg, J. (2001). The analyst's participation: A new look. *Journal of the American Psychoanalytic Association 49:359–381.*

Greenberg, J., & Mitchell, S.A. (1983). Object Relations in Psychoanalytic Theory. Cambridge: Harvard University Press.

Hoffman, I.Z. (1998). Ritual and Spontaneity in the Psychoanalytic Process: A Dialectical-Constructivist View. Hillsdale, NJ: Analytic Press.

Mitchell, S.A. (1988). Relational Concepts in Psychoanalysis. Cambridge: Harvard University Press.

Ornstein, P. (1995). Self psychology is not what you think it is. *Journal of Clinical Psychoanalysis 4:491–506.*

Rangell, L. (1982). Transference to theory: The relationship of psychoanalytic education to the analyst's relationship to psychoanalysis. *Annual of Psychoanalysis 10:29–56.*

Tuch, R. (2015). The analyst's way of being: Recognizing separable subjectivities and the pendulum's swing. *Psychoanalytic Quarterly 84:363–388.*

CHAPTER 6

Review: *The World of Psychoanalysis and Psychoanalysts. Selected Papers of Arnold Richards*, Vol. 5. Reviewed by Nathan Szajnberg, MD[4]

Dayenu! Is a familiar Passover song at the end of the Seder, translating as "Enough," as in had God only brought us out of Egypt, "*Dayenu*"; had he parted the Red Sea,

Dayenu; had he given us the Torah, *Dayenu*." Arnold Richards first essay in this book, "Dreams and the Wish for Immortality," brings to mind "*Dayenu*." Had he written only this essay, it would be enough. But, like the Passover jingle, he has written thoughtful, critical book reviews and made poignant remarks about his first psychoanalytic home, The New York Psychoanalytic Institute, that we offer repeated "*Dayenus*."

The first essay adds a wish to Freud's list of wishes in dreams: the wish for immortality (or at least, longevity). Richards also modifies Freud's distinction between wish fulfilling dreams versus trauma dreams; that the distinction is not so discrete. Richards reminds us that dreams are

---

4 Ret. Freud Prof. The Hebrew University; Israel and New Center for Psychoanalysis (LA) Societies.

about desire and its dangers. He reminds us of Freud's metapsychological assertions about dreams: 1. Psychic determinism; 2. Unconscious exists; 3. Manifest and latent content; 4. Its sleep-preserving function, among others. And of psychoanalysis? It is a science of motivation.

Like Freud, Richards documents his discovery of dream's wish for longevity/ immortality with his own dreams. Only by twelve years old, do children develop understanding of four principles of death: it's irreversible, universal, functional and has causality.

Freud chose as his epigraph, "Flectere si nequeo superos, Acheronta movebo," which Strachey translated as "If I cannot bend the higher powers, then I shall move the Infernal Regions." from Virgil. We are reminded of another story from Virgil. Aeneas, before he is "permitted" to discover his new home of Rome, goes to the underworld and visits his recently deceased father. They embrace. We can speculate: in shaking the underworld, is Freud also shaking his father back to life, the father whose death precipitated Freud's preoccupation with dreams and its discoveries? And *this* psychoanalyst, Richards, we learn becomes a book lover, a book publisher, a book seller, as his father once was in Revolutionary Soviet Union. We will recall that Freud's epigraph from Virgil was spoken by Juno, that mother goddess (also cuckolded by Zeus, her husband). She says this for she will intervene in Aeneas's actions, correct him as he is about to enter the netherworld. If we can then speculate, it is the union of mother god and father that results in Freud's great discovery of dreams in his netherworld. And, as Aeneas brings his father briefly back to life before he can continue his life's journey, so too, Richards demonstrates that our dreams include the wish for longevity, immortality. Freud's patient, the father who dreams of his dead son calling to him to extinguish a fire: Freud understood the "wish" here is to at least for moments of a dream, the father's wish to bring his son back to life. Richards offers multiple examples of his own dreams' Lazarus moments, reviving beloved friends and colleagues.

In this same essay, Richards alludes to his vicissitudes with his (once- and perhaps still-) beloved New York Psychoanalytic Institute. He enters the recently renovated building (or is it cathedral) on East 82d Street, next to the restaurant where Richard's recently deceased friend and colleague Richard Gottleb would entertain NYPSI speakers (and where Gottlieb offered the restauranteur his prime mutton from his sheep in Western Massachusetts). He muses (and later dreams) that he wished he could be young again to have an office in the now-renovated building, mingle with candidates and colleagues; turn back the clock. (The wish to return to a time when he was thriving and before he was extruded for his strong opinions about Training analyses, for instance.) It is a moment of writing that is personal, vulnerable and moving.

CHAPTER 7

Psychoanalytic Discourse at the Turn of Our Century: A Plea for a Measure of Humility[5]

[(2003). *J. Amer. Psychoanal. Assn.*, (51)(Supplement):73–89]

Since Freud's death in 1939, American psychoanalysis has grown from a small, homogeneous, and hierarchical community that resolved disputes primarily by ostracizing dissidents to a larger and more democratic one notable for its intellectual and cultural diversity. Theoretical pluralism and an increasingly heterogeneous population of practitioners have precipitated a renewed struggle for equilibrium between subversive energies and older traditions and have tested the civility of our discourse as perhaps never before. Although these challenges should not be underestimated, the present moment affords analysts in the United States a unique opportunity for mending fences and building bridges. To this end, I would urge adherents of the various analytic traditions to forgo a discourse of dichotomy and polarization and instead approach one another in a dialectical spirit. Just as the essence of science is to be open

---

5 his paper was presented in the Distinguished Lecturer Series, Contemporary Center for Advanced Psychoanalytic Studies, Fairleigh Dickinson University, October 26, 2003. Submitted for publication May 2, 2001.

to evidence that might refute one's preconceptions, so too is it the essence of the psychoanalytic wisdom to which we all aspire to avoid defensiveness and to acknowledge our mistakes. Human nature being what it is, a counsel of perfection is not what I have in mind; a plea for a *measure* of humility on all sides, however, seems eminently worth making.

Given the long shadow cast over the psychoanalytic movement by Freud's powerful and paradoxical personality, it is an indication of how far we have come in our collective journey that few analysts today find it necessary to idealize him. If we turn back to the mid-century writings of Heinz Hartmann, whose ambition to make psychoanalysis a "general psychology" remains exemplary, it is clear that his vision of Freud requires qualification. Seeking to minimize the role played by emotional or unconscious factors in Freud's work, Hartmann (1959) wrote that Freud's "striving for scientific discipline, his patient accumulation of observational data, and his search for conceptual tools to account for them have reduced [their] importance to a stimulus factor in psychoanalytic theories" (p. 339). In a similar vein, he praised Freud's case histories "because they show the constant mutual promotion of observation and hypothesis formation, the formation of definite propositions which make our knowledge testable, and the attempts to validate or invalidate them" (p. 342).

To be sure, Freud's case histories still have much to teach us, and at his best moments Freud indeed displays the "scientific discipline" that Hartmann prized so highly. In introducing the case of Little Hans, for example, Freud (1909) warned that "it is not in the least our business to 'understand' a case at once; this is only possible at a later stage, when we have received enough impressions of it. For the present, we will suspend our judgement and give our impartial attention to everything that there is to observe" (pp. 22–23). Similarly, he advised analyst readers "not to try to understand everything at once, but to give a kind of unbiased attention to every point and to await future developments" (p. 65). These admirable precepts, however, are often contradicted in his actual clinical practice. In his single consultation with Hans, Freud informed the boy that even before his birth he "had known that a little Hans would come who would be so fond of his mother that he would be bound to feel afraid of his father because of it" (p. 42). Indeed, at the conclusion of the narrative, Freud avowed, "Strictly speaking, I learnt nothing new from this analysis" (p. 147); it simply confirmed his findings from adult treatments.

To call into question Hartmann's vision of Freud as a cautious scientist and to see him instead as a Faustian figure largely in the grip of preconceptions is not to diminish his genius. It is simply to recognize that Freud is important to us today as much because of the questions he raises—and the contradictions he embodies—as because of the answers he provides. This more nuanced, even critical, attitude toward Freud has long been taken by revisionists such as Erich Fromm, Theodor Reik, Karen Horney, and Clara Thompson. What is new is the degree to which it has of late become accepted even by analysts within the American Psychoanalytic Association. If contemporary Freudians have learned to become more iconoclastic, the converse is that relational and other analysts are willing to give Freud his due. Stephen Mitchell (1993) spoke for many when, invoking Hans Loewald, he urged that Freud be transformed from "an improperly buried ghost who haunts us into a beloved and revered ancestor" (p. 176). Analysts of all persuasions can now agree that Freud is owed an immense debt, but our loyalty is no longer (if it ever was) to a single fallible human being; rather, it is to a psychoanalytic mode of thinking and working that has undergone continuous evolution in the more than sixty years since Freud's death.

When, as fate would have it, both Melanie Klein and Anna Freud settled in London during World War II, a conflict broke out in British psychoanalysis centering on these two formidable child analysts, each claiming to be Freud's legitimate heir (King and Steiner 1990). Through the mediating influence of figures such as Ernest Jones, Sylvia Payne, and D. W. Winnicott, a compromise was worked out that established three parallel training tracks in the London Institute. Because a schism was averted, psychoanalysis in Great Britain developed more dialectically than elsewhere, and the postwar period was exceptionally rich and exciting. Indeed, the "relational turn" that has exerted such a powerful hold on late-twentieth-century thinking originates in large measure with analysts in the Independent (that is, non-Kleinian) object relations tradition—Fairbairn, Winnicott, Balint, and Bowlby—who mounted a systematic challenge to the assumptions of what they took to be Freud's libido theory. Ironically, however, because no faction was excluded and thereby forced to found a separate institute, there is even today only one institute belonging to the International Psychoanalytic Association in all of Great Britain, and this lack of diversity has had adverse long-term consequences. Surely in the larger cities of the United Kingdom, it would be healthy to have greater competition for candidates and patients, which is the norm is in other European countries and the Americas.

Although some refugees from Nazi persecution came to England, by far the greatest number immigrated to the United States, where a new version of psychoanalysis began to take hold, severed from the past both by the expanse of the Atlantic Ocean and by the traumas of recent history. From the 1940s through the 1960s, American psychoanalysis was dominated by these Continental figures, most from Central Europe, who though dispersed in various cities were concentrated most heavily in New York. Some were sponsored by the New York Psychoanalytic Society's Rescue Committee, led by Lawrence Kubie and Bettina Warburg, while others came on their own. Among those brought to our shores by this wave of immigration were Hartmann, Ernst Kris, Rudolf Loewenstein, George Gero, Andrew Peto, Hermann Nunberg, Robert Bak, Edith Jacobson, and Kurt and Ruth Eissler. These and other old-world analysts established themselves as the predominant theoretical and political force at the New York Psychoanalytic Institute, whence their influence radiated to institutes across the country.

Whereas object relations theory took hold primarily in Great Britain and only later converged with the American interpersonalism of Harry Stack Sullivan, the mainstream tradition of ego psychology was forged jointly by Central European analysts in the United States and the group led by Anna Freud in London. Although Hartmann and his colleagues sought to use Freud's structural theory in a flexible and pragmatic fashion, they never questioned its metapsychological assumptions, particularly Freud's model of the drives and his view of the ego as simply one system in the personality rather than as synonymous with an overarching "self."

Strikingly, whereas most of the architects of ego psychology came from Vienna, the repudiation of metapsychology in the United States was promoted mainly by students of the Hungarian-born David Rapaport— Merton Gill, Roy Schafer, George Klein, and Robert Holt. (Trained as a psychologist, Rapaport was a brilliant theorist of psychoanalysis, but he never had an analytic practice. Nor did he become a member of the American Psychoanalytic Association.) This divergence between the legacies of Vienna and Budapest goes back to the creative tension between Freud and Ferenczi, and it underscores Ferenczi's importance as the progenitor of many of the innovative trends in contemporary psychoanalysis. More recently, though Heinz Kohut and Otto Kernberg— the two analysts who have gone furthest in recasting Freud's explanatory system—were both born in Vienna, Kernberg's analytic formation in Chile immersed him in the object relations tradition, whereas Kohut developed self psychology in the United States as a continuation of ego psychology. Not by chance, Kohut's first two references in *The Analysis of the Self* (1971) are to Hartmann's work.

Aside from their calling into question such speculative notions as the death instinct, the theorists of ego psychology countenanced no deviation from the axioms of individual depth psychology. A fault line thus opened in American psychoanalysis in 1942 when a group of early interpersonalists, who had begun to examine what hitherto had been regarded skeptically as the social epiphenomena of intrapsychic processes, left the New York Psychoanalytic Society in protest against Horney's removal from her faculty position. This group, which included Fromm and Thompson, formed the American Institute of Psychoanalysis, now known as the American Institute of Psychoanalysis-Karen Horney Clinic. But as with the Lacanians in France, a series of further rifts occurred within the schismatic group. William Silverberg and other interpersonalists left the American Institute of Psychoanalysis to found a more medical, university-affiliated psychoanalytic group at New York Medical College. Fromm and Thompson left to establish the William Alanson White Institute, whose disciplinary orientation was a mixture of medical and psychological, and where Harry Stack Sullivan played a leading role. In the 1960s, Bernard Kalinkowitz, Erwin Singer, and Avrum Ben-Avi in turn moved from the White Institute, where they had trained, to found the New York University Postdoctoral Program in Psychotherapy and Psychoanalysis, which has since become an important center of relational thought. They did so in part because of their sense that psychologists were not accorded equal status at the White Institute and because they wanted to offer a less rigid training program.

Schisms are qualitatively different from ordinary disagreements because the parties break off contact and thereafter develop in isolation. Because they cease to know each other personally, the factions then construct fantasies of the rival group based on ignorance and fear. Horney's ouster set the stage for a half-century of struggle in American psychoanalysis in which issues of power and authority ran parallel with—and often took precedence over—theoretical debates. Although skirmishes continued to flare up periodically in the American Psychoanalytic Association, none led to a crisis on the order of the 1942 schism (Richards, 1999). Even Sandor Rado's resignation from the New York Institute to found the Columbia Center, where his distinctive form of adapational psychoanalysis became ensconced, did not lead to an exodus of his group from the medically based umbrella organization of the American; nor did the self psychology promulgated by Kohut and his colleagues result in a split at the Chicago Institute. Thus, in political terms, these two later controversies have more in common with the clashes between Anna Freud and Melanie Klein in British psychoanalysis than with the original Horney schism in America.

The series of rifts among Horney's adherents furnishes an important lesson for students of psychoanalytic history. For if divisions within the rebel camp replicate the one that generated the initial schism, this suggests that the two warring sides—the Greeks and the Trojans, as it were—are mirror images of one another, whatever substantive differences they may appear to have. In an interview with Peter Rudnytsky (2000), Stephen Mitchell stated that "the internal politics and the generational battles" he witnessed at the White Institute and the NYU Postdoctoral Program "were just as pernicious and crushing" as any at Freudian institutes; "often," he added, "underneath an ideology of openness, there was an enormous concern with political correctness and control" (p. 115). Similarly, Rado asserted in an interview with Bluma Swerdloff (Roazen and Swerdloff 1995) that when a group leaves an institute it considers authoritarian, the new institute established by the group frequently turns out to be no less authoritarian than its predecessor. As Milton warned against the tendency of revolutionary Puritans to reimpose the oppressive institutions of the Anglican church, "*New Presbyter is but Old Priest* writ Large" (Hughes 1957, p. 145).

The persistence of exclusionary behavior in dissident analytic groups exposes the inadequacy of any simple opposition between Freudian

315

authoritarianism and interpersonal egalitarianism. Until recently, the White Institute did not provide full training for social workers with a master's degree. As long ago as 1948, this marginalization of their discipline prompted a nucleus of social workers and their supporters to withdraw from the White and align themselves with Theodor Reik's grouping to found the National Psychological Association for Psychoanalysis. Freud, of course, had in 1926 written *The Question of Lay Analysis* to defend Reik in the Viennese context, but nonetheless, when Reik arrived in this country in 1938 as a refugee from the Nazis, he was denied full membership in the New York Psychoanalytic Institute because he had a Ph.D. in psychology rather than a medical degree. He was instead offered a research membership, which he refused.

If what I have recounted is in one respect a gloomy history, from another vantage point it gives us grounds for hope. Since there is enough blame to go around, there is no longer any good reason for one analytic tradition to feel superior to another. With a measure of humility on all sides, we might begin to lower the barriers between competing groups.

As I suggested at the outset, the world of psychoanalysis today is irrevocably pluralistic. In addition to the ubiquitous contemporary Freudians and relationalists, we have Kleinians, Bionians, Lacanians, self psychologists, intersubjectivists, and interpersonalists. And contemporary Freudians are themselves not all of a piece. Among them we can distinguish conflict theorists (Jacob Arlow, Charles Brenner, Dale Boesky, Leo Rangell), defense analysts (Paul Gray, Fred Busch), and developmentalists (Margaret Mahler, Fred Pine), to name only some of the more prominent subspecies. An organizational pluralism both reflects and informs this theoretical pluralism. At one time the American Psychoanalytic Association was virtually the only game in town. Now, however, a thousand flowers have bloomed: the Independent Psychoanalytic Societies, a federation of four groups that joined the International Psychoanalytical Association as a result of the lawsuit against the American and the IPA; Division 39, with its many affiliated but autonomous institutes; the Academy of Psychoanalysis, limited to medical psychoanalysts; the National Committee of Psychoanalytic Social Workers; and the International Federation for Psychoanalysis, an independent organization. Most recently, the International Society for Relational Psychoanalysis has come on the scene.

An accurate census of the psychoanalytic population even in the United States is difficult to come by. One estimate is that the members of the Academy, Division 39, and the Psychoanalytic Committee of Social Workers together number about 7,000. Section 1 of Division 39 has about 500 members, while Section 4 has thirty local chapters with over 3,000 members, of whom only 500 belong to Division 39. Of the psychoanalytic journals, about 1,500 people subscribe to *Contemporary Psychoanalysis*, the organ of the William Alanson White Society, while 2,400 are subscribers of *Psychoanalytic Dialogues*, the journal of relational perspectives. Psychoanalytic Psychology, the Division 39 journal, has 4,500 subscribers; *Psychoanalytic Review*, sponsored by NPAP, has 2,700. The *Journal of the American Psychoanalytic Association* has approximately 5,600 subscribers, and of that number approximately 3,000 belong to neither the American nor the IPA.

How are diverse groups to coexist in today's psychoanalytic world? The choice comes down to whether they choose to hunker down in entrenched positions or to embrace the challenges of pluralism. Obviously, I am in favor of reaching out; but in order to take that risk we must be prepared to listen to and learn from one another. There is, of course, a paradox in proposing oneself as a spokesperson for humility, since anyone claiming to be humble may well be perceived to be self-righteously claiming instead to be wiser than those whose pretensions are being deflated. It was for this reason that Socrates was put to death by the outraged citizens of Athens. But something of the same paradox inheres in the very practice of psychoanalysis, in which all of us—flawed though we are—take it upon ourselves to offer help and guidance to others. There is no escape from this dilemma except to recognize that we are imperfect messengers of the causes we espouse and to reconcile ourselves to accepting as gracefully as possible the criticism that comes with the territory.

There is, then, an interplay between the political history of psychoanalysis and the nature of psychoanalytic discourse. Because of the breakdown of the organizational structures that once ensured the hegemony of the American Psychoanalytic Association, we have an opportunity to discuss our differences in a genuinely scientific and open-minded spirit. As every psychoanalyst knows, the traumas of the past often continue to exert a hold on the present even when there seems no reason for them to do so; intellectual insight into the causes of a repetition compulsion may not suffice to free a patient from its grip. Like everyone else, psychoanalysts are not immune from the law that those who do not remember the past are condemned to repeat it; or rather, to put it analytically, that those who have not worked through the past are condemned to repeat it *instead of* remembering it.

In contrast to the groups led by Rado and Kohut, which never broke away from the American Psychoanalytic Association, (and were never in danger of being expelled), those who formed the White Institute had to seek recognition as a component society but were persistently rebuffed. The committee appointed to settle the matter included Merton Gill, who told the White delegation that the real reason for their exclusion was not the requirements imposed by the Board on Professional Standards but an entrenched hostility on the part of the powers-that-be. At one point, the American Psychoanalytic Association even sued the White Institute in an attempt to enjoin it from using the word *psychoanalysis* in its name. The White countersued, hiring the prestigious Washington antitrust firm of Fortas and Porter, and the American eventually dropped its suit.

This skirmish foreshadowed the successful lawsuit brought by clinical psychologists against the American and the IPA in the late 1980s, which was financed in large measure by members of the White.

As a consequence of the politics of exclusion practiced by the American, those in the interpersonal tradition developed their form of psychoanalysis in isolation—on a kind of intellectual Galapagos island—and at times even seemed to cherish their outsider status. If the authoritarianism of the American bore the lineaments of Freud's personality, the truculence of the interpersonalists was consistent with the style of Sullivan, who cultivated a deliberate nonconformity. Although the interpersonalists' insularity led to some divergences in their theoretical evolution, there were also many striking parallels with contemporary Freudians, as both analytic species encountered similar clinical challenges. What was lost by this unfortunate severing of contact was the chance for a healthy cross-fertilization, a situation only now being redressed, with representatives of the groups meeting on a regular basis.

Although ignorance of the other's work has at times led both Freudians and interpersonalists to reinvent the wheel, such seemingly superfluous labors have at least the value of showing the extent of the convergence between erstwhile rival traditions. Charles Spezzano (1998), for instance, has pointed to the emphasis placed by both Paul Gray and Harry Stack Sullivan on anxiety in analytic work. In Freudian fashion, Gray argues that anxiety initiates maneuvers of "defense," maneuvers that Sullivan refers to as "security operations." The basic principle, however, is the same. There is likewise a meeting of minds between the Freudian Sheldon Bach and the interpersonalist Philip Bromberg in their conceptualization of narcissistic states of consciousness. Arlene Kramer Richards and I (Richards and Richards 2000) have also recently discussed an exchange between Irwin Hirsch and the late Benjamin Wolstein for a memorial tribute to the latter in *Contemporary Psychoanalysis*. Recognizing that Wolstein makes an unlikely ally for contemporary Freudians, we argue that Otto Fenichel's belief in the centrality of affect to the therapeutic process and Charles Brenner's approach to countertransference as the transference of the analyst are both consistent with Wolstein's point of view. On a broader level, both interpersonalists and Freudians have shown a heightened interest in the phenomenology of subjective experience and a corresponding decline in their concern with abstruse matters of metapsychology. Both groups have reopened fundamental questions about the ground rules of the analytic situation and how the dynamics of authority and power impinge on the analyst's functioning.

A turning point in recent psychoanalytic history came with the founding of the relational track at the NYU Postdoctoral Program in 1988. Having initially offered courses from Freudian, Sullivanian, and Frommian points of view, the NYU program had by the 1970s moved from theoretical eclecticism to a system of three specific tracks—the Freudian, the interpersonal/humanist, and the unaligned—an arrangement reminiscent of the "gentleman's agreement" reached by the British Society in the 1940s. But, as Lewis Aron (1996) has chronicled, the emergence of self psychology, together with the rapidly increasing popularity of the British object relations school, destabilized that arrangement by introducing new alternatives to both the Freudian and the interpersonal/humanist tracks.

The founders of the relational track—Emmanuel Ghent, Stephen Mitchell, James Fosshage, Bernard Friedland, and Philip Bromberg— took advantage of the publication of Greenberg and Mitchell's *Object Relations in Psychoanalytic Theory* (1983) five years earlier to make a definitive break with psychoanalytic orthodoxy. Relying on the "drive/ relational dichotomy" postulated in that volume as a road map through the theoretical landscape, the NYU relationalists endeavored to unite under a single roof interpersonalism, object relations, Kleinianism, self psychology, and intersubjectivity. By connecting American interpersonalism with

British object relations theory, this strategy effectively combatted the marginalization of the Sullivanian tradition and integrated it with a larger body of psychoanalytic thought.

But this positive achievement was not without its unintended consequences. First of all, the interpersonal/humanist track was effectively deprived of its reason for existence, though it managed to hobble on with a nominally separate identity. More profoundly, the struggle for power against what was deemed the common enemy—the Freudian establishment—was waged on two interconnected fronts: a theoretical and clinical one on behalf of the relational perspective, and a political one on behalf of antiauthoritarianism. As Aron observed, the political agenda to a large extent drove the intellectual debate. "One way of viewing Mitchell's achievement," he wrote "is to think of his having forged a multinational combination, consolidating diverse nations, some of which have conflicting interests in regard to other matters, but uniting them against a common adversary—classical theory. He has brought into one relational confederation a wide variety of alternative (non-classical) analytic schools, in the hope that even in their individual weaknesses, together they would be able to overcome the force of classical theory" (1996, p. 33).

This strategy was not only successful but also understandable in light of the injustices perpetrated as late as the 1980s by entrenched forces in the American Psychoanalytic Association. In the turmoil of the Vietnam War era, those with strongly left-wing leanings tended to see classical Freudian theory as an expression of the climate of social conformity of the preceding decades. The struggle for power in psychoanalytic organizational life had as its counterpart an attack on the alleged authoritarianism of classical analytic practice. Although the settlement of the lawsuit opened up the American and the IPA to several nonmedical groups (the Institute for Psychoanalytic Training and Research, the New York Freudian Society, and the Los Angeles Institute and Society for Psychoanalytic Studies), as well as to one predominantly Kleinian medical group (the Psychoanalytic Center of California), it ironically left both the White Institute of the interpersonalists and the Karen Horney Institute—the result of the original 1942 split—still on the outside.

Credit must be given to Greenberg and Mitchell for their articulation of the intellectual synthesis that lay the groundwork for a new political alliance, as well as to the founders of the relational track at NYU for using that synthesis to shape curriculum. A dozen years later, however, it is possible to see that their success came at a price. The energy of the dissidents was fueled at least in part by a sense of their status as victims, and the fundamental premise of a dichotomy between drive and relational theories fails to withstand scrutiny. Melanie Klein, for instance, was classified by Greenberg and Mitchell (1983) as an object relations theorist, though she endorsed the concept of the death instinct. Some in the relational camp, however, including Jessica Benjamin (1999), have questioned the binary opposition between drives, seen as nonrelational, and the need for relationships, seen as lacking instinctual urgency. In his later work, Greenberg (1991) made room for a concept of drives within a relational matrix when he proposed safety and effectance as primary motivations of human behavior.

In short, by elevating the antithesis between drives and relationships into a theoretical shibboleth, the relational turn made it difficult to engage in nuanced debate regarding their interaction. Relationalists hail what they consider their more empathic two-person psychology as the expression of an epistemologically sophisticated constructivism, while they fault the psychology of Freud and contemporary Freudians as noninteractive and as maintaining an allegiance to an outmoded scientistic objectivism. Stuart Pizer (1998), for example, asserts that all classical analysis is characterized by a "a nondisclosing analyst, who arrogates to himself the nonnegotiable position of arbiter of reality, who sits as a neutral observer outside the one-person dynamic situation, [which] is inherently humiliating to the patient, and may iatrogenically embed resistances to negotiation.... it may well be that the maximized power asymmetry of the classical (patriarchal, patronizing) analytic position in its very structure actually incites aggression by dichotomizing power in ways that inherently humiliate the patient with its a priori terms for negotiating the treatment" (p. 188).

Pizer's sketch of what he takes to be classical analysis is, however, a caricature of contemporary Freudian practice. Every analytic style has its dangers and excesses, just as every school has its share of bad analysts and doctrinaire thinkers. If, on the one hand, the Freudian ideals of neutrality and abstinence entail the risk of hardening into authoritarianism, so, on the other, do the relational ideals of empathy and participation risk yielding to inappropriate gratifications. Pizer makes no allowance for the fact that analysts of all persuasions proceed as they do because they believe they are acting in the best interest of their patients. For Pizer, it would seem, negotiation is possible with everyone except a contemporary Freudian analyst. This irony is reminiscent of the tendency of postmodernists to take for granted the truth of their own beliefs, while remaining condescendingly skeptical about the assertions of those with whom they disagree.

The fundamental problem with Pizer's claim that the classical analyst "arrogates to himself the nonnegotiable position of arbiter of reality" can be seen by contrasting his outlook with that of the late Merton Gill. Like Hans Loewald, Gill has the distinction of being revered by contemporary Freudians and relationalists alike, and he is acknowledged as a seminal influence on analysts in both traditions. Lacking political ambitions and belonging to no school, Gill was devoted to exploring psychoanalysis in theory and in practice. He also recognized the limitations of thinking in terms of mutually exclusive polarities. "To speak of internal and external factors as though they were a simple dichotomy," he wrote in his last book, "is false. In human psychological functioning the external world is significantly constructed by the internal world and the internal world is significantly constructed by the external world. In short, we deal with the mutually interactive constructivist circle" (1994, p. 16). As if anticipating Pizer's objection that the classical analyst "sits as a neutral observer outside the one-person dynamic situation," Gill recognized that "the analyst is always influencing the patient, and the patient is always influencing the analyst. This mutual influence cannot be avoided; it can only be interpreted. It is the analyst's awareness of the unremitting influence of patient and analyst on each other and his attempt to make that influence as explicit as possible that constitutes his 'neutrality'" (p. 50).

Gill's emphasis on the virtues of dialectical thinking in psychoanalysis has been carried forward by Irwin Hoffman (1998). Although Hoffman shares the widespread belief that an irreversible paradigm shift has recently occurred in psychoanalysis, he holds that the decisive shift is not from a drive to a relational model, but rather from a positivist to a constructivist one. This leads Hoffman to question the customary alignment of drive theory with positivism and relational theory with constructivism. As Hoffman notes, relational theories, including interpersonal psychoanalysis and self psychology, frequently retain an objectivist cast, whereas classical Freudian theory contains at least the seeds of a constructivist point of view. By clearing the ground for a meeting of opposing camps, Hoffman fosters intellectual exchange and helps heal old resentments. Once areas of agreement are established, any remaining differences can be addressed in a positive, even pleasurable, spirit.

Although, as I have argued, the success of the relational turn has been limited both by a penchant for dichotomies and by a lingering sense of resentment at having been oppressed, it was undoubtedly detrimental to American psychoanalysis to have had a single school hold the reins of power for so long. Historically, the responsibility for what I have termed the "politics of exclusion" in American psychoanalysis (Richards, 1999) rests with the then dominant group. As the editors of the *Journal of Clinical Psychoanalysis* have admitted, theory in the late 1950s and early 1960s was stuck in a "blind alley" of remote abstraction and "seemed unable to progress" (Wyman and Rittenberg 1994, p. 315). What is more, in their zeal to defend classical theory, some distinguished analysts went too far, advancing an argument that echoed Ernest Jones's notorious claim that Ferenczi at the end of his life developed "psychotic manifestations that revealed themselves in, among other ways, a turning away from Freud and his doctrines" (1957, p. 45). By this logic, orthodoxy would be permanently immune to challenge and diagnosis substituted for reasoned discussion.

Thus, it must be recognized that relationalists and self psychologists have performed a valuable service in bringing to the fore issues that with few exceptions had been insufficiently addressed in the literature of ego psychology and structural conflict prior to the 1980s. That literature had focused on other aspects of mind, development, and technique and itself proved of lasting importance. My problem with some relational theorists is that they want not only to celebrate the relational school but also to dismiss the entire contemporary Freudian tradition as anachronistic, and to parlay the emphasis on interaction in the relational literature into a claim that even today no one else understands its importance as they do.

More than a decade has passed since the end of the lawsuit against the American Psychoanalytic Association (and the IPA) and the founding of the relational track at NYU. Taken together, these events mark the entry of American psychoanalysis into a new era. For better or worse—but mostly for the better—we are no longer faced with a cold war between monolithic powers, but with widening rifts on both sides of what once was an insurmountable barrier—a Berlin wall—between Freudians and interpersonalists. Differences within one's own group become muted and can be overlooked in the face of a common enemy, but they quickly reemerge once the external threat disappears.

But if the present situation might be viewed pessimistically as the balkanization of psychoanalysis, I prefer to think that it affords the prospect of creating a new intellectual and political order that allows all of us both to acknowledge our differences and to affirm our common psychoanalytic heritage. As Greenberg (2001) has written, "There are very few psychoanalysts around these days, only Freudians, or Kleinians, or Lacanians, or self psychologists" (p. 361). Because an analyst's subjectivity is his or her instrument, all of us are drawn to a school we find congenial to our temperament. But good analysts, I think, also try to cultivate a style antithetical to their innate disposition, in order to reach a golden mean between the conflicting tendencies of self-disclosure and self-restraint. In short, there is nothing wrong with being a Freudian, a relationalist, an interpersonalist, a self psychologist, or whatever, as long as the analyst does not succumb to the delusion that his or her school has a monopoly on the truth and that there is nothing to be learned from other approaches.

As we forge a new psychoanalytic identity, let us not renounce the discourse of dichotomy and polarization among ourselves only to allow it to creep into our dealings with other mental health professionals and the culture at large. Although we may be convinced that only those who have had personal experience of the unconscious, whether as patients in analysis or simply through reading and self-reflection, are likely to be persuaded of its existence, it does little good to accuse our detractors of resistance if they fail to see the light. For if we adopt this strategy, dialogue grinds to a halt. The only recourse is to speak with the quiet voice of reason, to try to learn as much from our critics as possible, to survive their destructive attacks if necessary, and to trust to time to sort out the merits of our competing claims.

It is the abiding lesson of psychoanalysis to be skeptical of utopian blueprints and protestations of a sudden conversion. The more exaggerated the promises of transformation, the more acute will be the disillusionment as reality sets in and life goes on much as it did before, though under altered circumstances. To a psychoanalyst, the dawn of a new millennium is simply another day, though one to which unusually intense fantasies may be attached. But this skepticism about revolutions does not mean that genuine change, usually as a result of long and painful struggle, is not possible. There are plastic moments in history—and in a person's life—in which, after a prolonged incubation, something new is hatched. For us in the American psychoanalytic community, this is such a moment, and it happily coincides with the turning of a page in the calendar.

Although I call myself a contemporary Freudian, my loyalty, as I said at the outset, is not to Freud as a human being, who for all his greatness had his share of frailties, but to psychoanalysis as a method of thinking, working, and living. This method, though it originated with Freud, has been enriched by Klein, Winnicott, Sullivan, Hartmann, Kohut, and all the other figures who form the tradition to which we are heir and to which we have the opportunity to contribute in our turn. In Winnicott's profound words (1971), "in any cultural field it is not possible to be original except on the basis of tradition" (p. 99). Psychoanalysis is a coat of many colors. Let us cease fighting over our inheritance and resolve instead to share it and to wear it with both humility and pride as we enter the twenty-first century.

REFERENCES

Aron, L. (1996). *A Meeting of Minds: Mutuality in Psychoanalysis.* Hillsdale, NJ: Analytic Press.

Benjamin, J. (1999). Review of I.Z. Hoffman, *Ritual and Spontaneity in the* Psychoanalytic Process. *J. Amer. Psychoanal. Assn.*47:883–891.

Freud, S. (1909). An analysis of a phobia in a five-year-old boy. *Standard Edition* 10: *5–149.*

——— (1926). The question of lay analysis. *Standard Edition* 20:*83–258.*

Gill, M.M. (1994). *Psychoanalysis in Transition: A Personal View.* Hillsdale, NJ: Analytic Press.

Greenberg, J. (1991). *Oedipus and Beyond: A Clinical Theory.* Cambridge: Harvard University Press.

——— (2001). The analyst's participation: A new look. *J. Amer Psychoanal. Assn.* 49: 359–381.

——— & Mitchell, S.A. (1983). *Object Relations in Psychoanalytic Theory.* Cambridge: Harvard University Press.

Hartmann, H. (1959). Psychoanalysis as a scientific theory. In *Essays on Ego Psychology: Selected Problems in Psychoanalytic Theory.* New York: International Universities Press, 1964, pp. *318–350.*

Hoffman, I.Z. (1998). *Ritual and Spontaneity in the Psychoanalytic Process.* Hillsdale, NJ: Analytic Press.

Hughes, M.Y., ed. (1957). *John Milton: The Complete Poems and Major Prose.* Indianapolis: Odyssey Press.

Jones, E. (1957). *The Life and Work of Sigmund Freud.* Vol. 3. New York: Basic Books.

King, P., & Steiner, R. Eds. (1990). *The Freud-Klein Controversies 1941–1945. London*: Routledge.

Kohut, H. (1971). *The Analysis of the Self: A Systematic Approach to the Treatment of Narcissistic Personality Disorders.* New York: International Universities Press.

Mitchell, S.A. (1993). *Hope and Dread in Psychoanalysis.* New York: Basic Books.

Pizer, S.A. (1998*). Building Bridges: Negotiation of Paradox in the Analytic Process.* Hillsdale, NJ: Analytic Press.

Richards, A.D. (1999). A. A. Brill and the politics of exclusion. *J. Amer .Psychoanal. Assn.* 47:9–28.

——— & Richards, A.K. (2000). Benjamin Wolstein and us: Many roads lead to Rome. *Contemp. Psychoanal.* 36:255–266.

Roazen, P., & Swerdloff, B. (1995*). Heresy: Sandor Rado and the Psychoanalytic Movement.* Northvale, NJ: Aronson.

Rudnytsky, P. L. (2000). *Psychoanalytic Conversations: Interviews with Clinicians, Commentators, and Critics.* Hillsdale, NJ: Analytic Press.

Spezzano, C. (1998). The triangle of clinical judgment. *J. Amer. Psychoanal. Assn* .46:365–388.

Winnicott, D.W. (1971). *Playing and Reality.* London: Tavistock.

Wyman, H., & Rittenberg, S.(1994). The contributions of Charles Brenner, MD: Psychoanalysis rebooted. *Journal of Clinical Psychoanalysis* 3: *15–316.*

CHAPTER 8

Commentary on "Psychoanalytic Discourse at the Turn of Our Century: A Plea for a Measure of Humility" by Jay Greenberg[6]

[(2003). *J. Amer. Psychoanal. Assn.*, (51)(Supplement):89–98]

Arnold Richards has invited his discussants to participate in a project that many would consider daunting: to comment critically on a "plea for a measure of humility." Humility, of course, is a commodity that has been in notoriously short supply throughout the history of psychoanalysis. Introducing it, even at this late date, is bound to seem as if it will be a balm for all that ails us: it will simultaneously enhance our intellectual credibility and contribute to the civility of our discourse. In light of all this, having reservations about such a proposal—and Richards is psychologically canny

---

6 Jay R. Greenberg (born October 3, 1942) is a psychoanalyst, clinical psychologist and writer. He holds a PhD in Psychology from New York University. He is a Faculty Member of the William Alanson White Institute, where he is also a training analyst and supervisor.

Greenberg was one of the originators of relational psychoanalysis, though he is now less closely identified with it. Since 2011 he is the Editor of The Psychoanalytic Quarterly. He is the 2015 recipient of the Mary S. Sigourney Award for Outstanding Achievement in Psychoanalysis

331

enough to recommend not that we be abjectly humble but that we strive for a *measure* of humility—is likely to mark the discussant as a curmudgeon.

And yet, churlish though it may be, I can't help thinking that Richards's plea entails more than meets the eye. Let me begin with his reading of Freud. Quoting from his introduction to the Little Hans case, (1909) Richards approvingly cites Freud's statement of intention that "for the present, we will suspend our judgement and give our impartial attention to everything that there is to observe." (p. 22). Acknowledging—in the spirit of humility—that Freud himself often honored this sentiment in the breach, Richards nonetheless considers it an "admirable precept." It is, then, a small step for Richards to ask that we import Freud's openness into the pluralistic world of contemporary psychoanalysis, urging us "to forgo a discourse of dichotomy and polarization and instead approach one another in a dialectical spirit." We are all tilling the same field, Richards tells us, and polarization and the resultant rancor compromise the quality of our crop.

But the problem with Freud's admirable precept is that it prescribes the impossible, a truism that renders it less than fully admirable. We cannot suspend judgment, and we cannot give our impartial attention to everything there is to observe. The critiques of postmodern thinkers aside, a few years after publishing the Little Hans case, Freud himself tacitly acknowledged the impossibility of suspending judgment in the way he had once hoped and believed he could. "Even at the stage of description," he wrote in introducing "Instincts and Their Vicissitudes" (1915), "it is not possible to avoid applying certain abstract ideas to the material in hand, ideas derived from somewhere or other but certainly not from the new observations alone" (p. 117). This is an admirably cautious, uncharacteristically humble acknowledgment coming from Freud (or from anybody with ambitions as large as his). But the statement suggests an epistemological conclusion that Freud never quite got to himself: the abstract ideas that we apply to the material do not simply give shape to our findings; they define what will become the data of observation in the first place. It is a commonplace these days to point out the density of what is going on in even a single psychoanalytic session—the words, acts, thoughts, sensations, feelings, histories, etc. of both participants. Which of these is seen as salient, and how the various pieces fit together, is always a function of the observer's preconceptions.

This is where polarization is most likely—at the level of preconception. By definition preconception precedes observation, and so can never be confirmed. Take "Man is a social animal," as an example, or "Man is essentially selfish and self-serving, submitting to socialization only as a compromise in the name of self-protection." Sweeping preconceptions tend to generate equally sweeping, dichotomously alternative preconceptions. This is an historical truth; more interestingly, this polarization can be healthy for all concerned. Anyone who approaches the task of observation with a new, dichotomously alternative preconception has the potential to create data that previously were unrecognizable. This opens up the possibility of investigating entirely new arrays of phenomena: before he could undertake any systematic exploration of unconscious processes, Freud had to adopt a dichotomous alternative to the generally accepted preconception that the mental and the conscious are coterminous.

The history of psychoanalysis offers many examples of ways in which the most far-reaching inquiries depend on polarizing preconceptions. Consider an early sweeping, unprovable preconception of Freud's: the principle of psychic determinism, with its implication that both inner experience and interpersonal behavior are invariably meaningful. Freud frequently alludes to this principle in his discussions of symptoms, dreams, and the psychopathology of everyday life, making clear that without it there are simply too many escape hatches that provide a way out of the hard work of investigating the unconscious. The preconception of psychic determinism makes data where otherwise there would be chaos; consider

Freud's dogged refusal to ignore even the most apparently trivial details of his dreams. The argument about the inevitability of meaningfulness still rages; some neurophysiologists, rejecting Freud's preconception without fully recognizing that the rejection itself constitutes an equally unprovable preconception, have tried to debunk the claim that dreams have any meaning at all.

Without Freud's tenacity there could have been no psychoanalytic theory of dreams, but the zeal that opened his eyes to some data blinded him to others. Consider another, less central preconception that shaped his approach to the interpretation of dreams: he declared that every reproach of another person in a dream is at bottom a self-reproach. With this assumption, Freud set out on a path that revealed a great deal about his own guilty self-criticism, but that inevitably clouded his awareness of the involvement of others in the dreamer's experience. Thus, he missed his indictment—deserved but deeply painful to Freud—of the extravagantly idealized Fliess in the dream of Irma's injection (1900, pp. 106–120). Similarly, when he dreamt on the night of his father's funeral that "you are requested to close an eye," he uncovered much about his guilt at not having given his father an adequate funeral, but he overlooked the possibility that respect for the dead required him to wink at disturbing aspects of his father's life history (1900, p. 318).

Controversies arising from analysts' differing preconceptions continue both to plague and to enrich contemporary psychoanalysis. Consider Thomas Ogden's concept of the "analytic third" (1994), which rests on the preconception that any experience that an analyst has during (and sometimes outside of) an analytic session is significantly influenced by the intersubjective field created by the analyst and the analysand. This is dichotomously alternative to the idea that eruptions from the analyst's personal life interfere with the analyst's ability to observe the patient. Ogden's idea has crucial technical implications: it tells the analyst to pay attention to thoughts and feelings that he or she would otherwise tend to suppress. But there is more to the concept: like psychic determinism itself, it is a preconception that creates data out of what otherwise would be unwanted, random intrusions into the session of the analyst's preconscious thoughts and feelings.

The problem that preconceptions like the analytic third pose for Richards's argument is that the controversy about them will not go away, and neither will dichotomous thinking or polarized debate. But, perhaps contra Richards, I believe that this is healthy for psychoanalysis. Debate should be respectful, of course, but respect requires that irreconcilable differences be acknowledged. I would suggest, for example, that it is important that some analysts embrace Ogden's assumption that paying close attention to the content of the analyst's reverie is a central element of data collection. Ogden's clinical vignettes suggest the possibility that this can enrich the analyst's understanding of what is going on in the treatment. Only by holding tenaciously to the preconception that such reverie is meaningful, however, will we have any chance to observe— much less to make use of—this source of information. We all tend to feel guilty or ashamed about falling into apparently narcissistic preoccupations during sessions, and in the service of pulling ourselves out of our self-absorption, we work hard to dismiss and thus overcome them. But if we accept Ogden's preconception, we will pay attention to whatever comes up, much as Freud's assumption of psychic determinism taught us never to dismiss any association to our dreams.

But at the same time, we need other analysts to hold on to the traditional idea (equally based in preconception) that the kind of eruptions that Ogden describes interfere with the analyst's ability to observe. It is always tempting to assume that we are doing what we are doing in the service of the analytic process, and it is difficult to accept that we are caught up in satisfying our own needs (for powerful descriptions of the way countertransference can silently undermine analytic observation, see Abend 1982; Jacobs 1991). We need to know more about both faces of the analyst's reverie, and we will learn most from those who hold tenaciously to dichotomously alternative preconceptions.

I say all this because I think that in a deep sense Richards understands neither that fundamental disagreement is inevitable, nor that it can also be productive. There is, I believe, a hidden paradox in his argument: he endorses difference and dialogue, but he can't seem to find any fruitful differences in his exploration of alternative theoretical approaches. Thus, he praises those who find similarities in the sensibilities of authors anchored in different theoretical traditions, and he reduces to a political strategy the kind of comparative psychoanalysis that trades in the articulation of contrast.

Here let me pause to spell out what I think is the structure of Richards's argument. In the bad old days, a hegemonic American Psychoanalytic Association (and, on the larger stage, the International Psychoanalytical Association) excluded and even punished dissidents. Kept out of the conversation, interpersonalists and other outcasts developed their own language. Comparative psychoanalysis came to the rescue of the dissidents by uniting—somewhat spuriously and perhaps even disingenuously— various theorists who had little in common save their exclusion from the psychoanalytic mainstream. If history is written by the victors, Richards seems to be saying, comparative psychoanalysis is written, if not by the losers, at least by disenfranchised outsiders.

Richards's argument goes on: the political climate has changed dramatically over the past fifteen or twenty years. Not only is the dominance of the American Psychoanalytic less absolute than it once was, but the organization itself has changed, welcoming new voices and encouraging conversations that would previously have been unthinkable. On the basis of my own experience I tend to agree with Richards, or at least my disagreements are minor enough that highlighting them would seem like carping, even to me. And I want to make clear that Richards himself has played an enormous role in bringing about the changes within the American; his political courage, and that of a handful of other leaders, has been exemplary, and his efforts have been quite effective.

But having noted the political changes of which he has been so much a part, Richards seems to conclude that comparative psychoanalysis—at least the sort of comparative psychoanalysis that (in his view) trades in dichotomies—is no longer necessary. That is, he sees no valid intellectual project in this way of approaching psychoanalytic theory. Whatever conceptual value it might have had—and it's hard to imagine on the basis of what he has written that Richards believes that the approach ever had very much intellectual credibility—the enduring impact of comparative psychoanalysis is its contribution to an obsolete political battle.

Perhaps my reaction to this aspect of Richards's paper is shaped by the fact that in the process of goring the oxen of psychoanalytic polarizers, this piece of his argument pointedly gores one of my own, and a favorite ox at that. Consider: "Credit must be given to Greenberg and Mitchell for their articulation of the intellectual synthesis that lay the groundwork for a new political alliance.... " (for a perspective similar to Richards's, see Gedo 1999).

But this way of putting things reveals Richards engaging in some quite striking polarization of his own, because he implies that there is no abiding intellectual value in approaching the history of psychoanalytic ideas with the preconceptions that Mitchell and I brought to bear. And preconceptions are indeed the point: Mitchell and I argued that organizing theories around their take on the fundamental concept of drive would provide an interesting vision of the history and current status of psychoanalytic thinking. We believed that this preconception—like the drive concept itself—would be generative because it would give meaning to what otherwise might seem random developments.

Richards evidently believes that our application of this preconception, whatever its political efficacy, is of little or no intellectual interest. This, of course, is a polarizing perspective in its own right. For example, he believes that Mitchell and I distorted the history of psychoanalysis for the sake of alliance-building: "A dozen years later, however, it is possible to see that their [political] success came at a price.... the fundamental premise of a dichotomy between drive and relational theories fails to withstand scrutiny. Melanie Klein, for instance, was classified by Greenberg and Mitchell as an object relations theorist, though she endorsed the concept of the death instinct." Here Richards is arguing that the putative failure of our "fundamental premise"—that is, of our organizing preconception— supports some preconceptions of his own. First, he believes that the history of psychoanalysis is more accurately understood if we begin with the assumption that we are all more alike than different and that we are always reinventing each other's wheels. And a second preconception is that Mitchell and I used an intellectual facade to cover a political project.

This may lead to a reading of psychoanalytic history that interests some, and to a vision of our book that some find appealing. But, unsurprisingly, I take issue with Richards's assumptions. He is, of course, correct to say both that we classified Klein as a relational theorist and that she endorsed the death instinct. But in order to support his own preconceptions, he ignores the central points of our argument: that the core of Klein's theorizing addressed the nature of the object and its function in the child's development; and that she introduced a dramatically—even dichotomously—new vision of the nature of drive itself. It was in these innovations that we found the essence of Klein's contribution, as well as the affinities between her work and that of other relational theorists.

Our reading of Klein is admittedly strong and potentially controversial (once again, Gedo [1999] agrees with Richards that we forced Klein into an uncomfortable mold). However, I find considerable support for our view in the subsequent development of thinking among the "contemporary Kleinians." A group that was just coming into its own at the time Mitchell and I were writing our book, these authors have largely abandoned the death instinct (along with other instinctually based elements of Klein's thinking, such as her emphasis on the role of part-objects). In its place they have stressed concepts derived from Klein's vision of the transactions between people—children and parents, analysts and analysands—interpersonalizing those concepts in the process of updating them. Evidently, Klein's most influential followers read the essence of her contribution much as Mitchell and I did. That is not to say, of course, that they would happily join interpersonalists and others under the umbrella of relational theory. But that's another matter altogether.

Intriguingly, the fate of drive in contemporary Kleinian theory is quite different from the fate of drive among contemporary conflict theorists, the group with which Richards identifies. This difference, in my view, is evidence for the value of placing Klein and the ego psychologists in different theoretical camps, despite Klein's use of some of the language of drive theory. While energic explanatory concepts have largely disappeared from the discourse of both groups, the death instinct as a theme is no longer prominent among the Kleinians. In contrast, the ubiquity and irreducibility of sexual and aggressive motivations remain central in contemporary conflict theory; primitive sexual and aggressive wishes are always an element of every compromise formation. This suggests to me that Mitchell and I were on to something—at least that there was an important heuristic point to be made—when we aligned Klein with the relational theorists and suggested that taken together these authors were working with preconceptions that were both dichotomously and fruitfully alternative to the preconceptions of Freud's drive model.

Before leaving the immediate territory of Richards's critique of my own polarizing tendencies, consider what he has to say about the problematic legacy of the conceptual structure that Mitchell and I imposed on the history of psychoanalysis: "by elevating the antithesis between drives and relationships into a theoretical shibboleth, the relational turn made it difficult to engage in nuanced debate regarding their interaction." This certainly makes it seem as though we performed a disservice, but note the two sentences that appear before the one just quoted: "Some in the relational camp, however, including Jessica Benjamin, have questioned the binary opposition between drives, seen as nonrelational, and the need for relationships, seen as lacking instinctual urgency. In his later work, Greenberg (1991) made room for a concept of drives within a relational matrix when he proposed safety and effectance as primary motivations of human behavior."

Some might say, on the basis of Richards's reading of Benjamin's work and my own, that the drive/relational dichotomy, by highlighting competing preconceptions, has been heuristically effective. Certainly, it has not inhibited a committed relational thinker like Benjamin from trying to find a middle ground. Nor has it kept me from trying to find a theoretical synthesis that embraces what I believe to be the most salient clinical sensibilities of the two models.

Generative preconceptions work precisely because they invite alternatives. Thus, an important aspect of Freud's power as a thinker was his extraordinary ability to come up with polarities that led—often immediately—to objections and alternatives. And then the debate— advocates of each perspective adducing evidence based on data generated by their own preconceptions—began.

Which leads to the central question I am left with after reading Richards's plea: Where in his psychoanalytic universe does he find room for genuine difference? Or, to put it more bluntly and to withdraw the question in favor of a suspicion, I suspect that he doesn't feel that contemporary conflict theorists have very much to learn from anybody else. This, needless to say, is a position that falls somewhat short of true humility, but consider Richards's claims. He approvingly cites Charles Spezzano's idea that Sullivan and Paul Gray both emphasize, in interestingly similar ways, how anxiety affects patients' experience. This, of course, supports Richards's idea that we are more alike than different. Spezzano goes on to make a creative point when he suggests that this similarity can lead us to think in new ways about the nature of psychoanalytic process—but he knows full well (and I suspect that Richards does too) that this is hardly the last word on the subject of Sullivan's interpersonal theory and Gray's ego psychology. Telling the whole story, which was never Spezzano's purpose, would certainly turn up more differences than similarities.

More tellingly, perhaps, Richards cites his own argument that the interpersonalist Benjamin Wolstein was an (admittedly strange) bedfellow of Fenichel and Brenner. Again, finding convergence can be interesting and illuminating. But doing so imposes strong preconceptions about just what is most salient in the writings of each author; it is at least equally true that Wolstein was an iconoclast and a renegade who saw himself as advocating a technique that was radically alternative to anything classical psychoanalysis had to offer. On Richards's version, Wolstein's dissent is muted and his acquiescence highlighted. My own hunch is that if Wolstein had seen himself in that light, he wouldn't have bothered to write at all.

So, in the end—not to mention at the beginning—Richards too has preconceptions. I understand his preconceptions this way: The seeds of virtually everything that psychoanalysts say can be found in Freud, and the most comprehensive elaboration of Freud's ideas can be found in contemporary conflict theory. Theorists of other persuasions emphasize one or another element of conflict theory, but they don't really introduce anything new. Thus, the need for humility, because only by being humble will these theorists realize how little they are adding to what is already there.

Perhaps. But I have to admit to being afraid that Richards's way of looking at things ties one hand behind my back—and, beyond that, that insisting on our similarities might well preserve a theoretical monolith even as the efforts that Richards himself has spearheaded hold out the possibility of a more vital, pluralistic political climate in which future psychoanalytic debates can take place.

REFERENCES

Abend, S. (1982). Serious illness in the analyst: Countertransference considerations. *J. Amer. Psychoanal. Assn.*30: *365–379.*

Freud, S. (1900). The interpretation of dreams. *Standard Edition 4/5.*

——— (1909) Analysis of a Phobia in a Five-Year-Old Boy. *Standard Edition* 10:1–150.

——— (1915). Instincts and their vicissitudes. *Standard Edition* 14:*117–140.*

Gedo, J. (1999). *The Evolution of Psychoanalysis: Contemporary Theory and Practice.* New York: Other Press.

Greenberg, J. (1991). *Oedipus and Beyond: A Clinical Theory.* Cambridge: Harvard University Press.

Jacobs, T. (1991). *The Use of the Self.* Madison, CT: International Universities Press.

Ogden, T. (1994). The analytic third: Working with intersubjective clinical facts. *Int. J. Psycho-Anal.*75:3–19.

CHAPTER 9

Up Close and Personal by Arnold Richards–A Review by Steven Ellman[7]

Since I am aware of Arnie Richards (Dr. Arnold Richards) iconic analytic career I was startled to see a volume of his entitled "Up Close and Personal" which contained elements of his poetry and photography. I know his psychoanalytic writing and his work as an editor involving saving journals and creating a new publishing company, but I had no idea that he wrote or even read poetry. I must admit that I was dubious that I would be captivated by either his poetry or photography. However, a distinguished poet/psychoanalyst Eugene Mahon wrote in glowing, actually quite poetic terms, about Richard's poetry both being artful and more importantly being able to arouse the readers emotions without being sensational or

---

7 Steven Ellman was Professor in the Graduate School of City University of New York (CUNY) where he was Director of the Ph.D. program in Clinical Psychology. He is now, after 30 years as a Professor at CUNY, Professor-Emeritus. He has published more than 70 papers in psychoanalysis, sleep and dreams the neurophysiology of motivation. He has published several books including *Freud's Technique Papers: A Contemporary Perspective* and *The Mind in Sleep* (with Antrobus). He has been President of IPTAR twice, Program Chair and he is training and supervising analyst at IPTAR. He is also Clinical Professor at New York University Post-Doctoral Program in Psychoanalysis and Psychotherapy. He was the first President of the Confederation of Independent Psychoanalytic Societies (CIPS). CIPS is the national professional organization of the independent International Psychoanalytic Association (IPA) societies of the United States. He is a member of the IPA and was previously on the Executive Council of the IPA.

falsely theatric. Mahon tells us that Dr. Richards has poetically pieced together perceptual elements that allow the reader to feel the world he has lived in and created.

Of course, who believes these types of excerpts especially when they appear from Richard's colleagues. I then entered this poetic and visual world with my characteristic skepticism. It is rare, but Mahon has understated what Richards has accomplished. His poetry at times artistic is always moving and engaging. Irene Willis the poetry editor (of his website, InternationalPsychoanalysis.net) describes Richards as a humble Brooklyn boy, but clearly, she is not sufficiently acquainted with Brooklyn boys; few of them are humble. It is also clear that Arnie as she noted has become close to both Eros and Thanatos with a lingering closeness to Thanatos. Do not fear, death does not overshadow his love of life or his appreciation and love for his friends and family. As an illustration, in Elegy for Muriel, he visits the unfortunate death of a colleague and is able to bring us to a new sense of her tragic death while at the same time celebrating both her prideful and accomplished sonatas and sauces.

Janet Lee Bachant has written that Richards's photography helps us delve more deeply into our own reveries. I am annoyed that I read her description since I was about to describe how the meaning of reverie could be ascertained by detailing one's experience in viewing the photographs assembled in this volume. One might then investigate the experience of the viewer as they gradually allow the visual images permeate their experience of the old and new in these intriguing pictures from around the world and around Arnie's moving world. The volume allows us to admire Arnie's continued explorations of his inner world and the differing worlds he has encountered.

CHAPTER 10

Finding Integration in a Splintered World: Contemporary Psychoanalytic Thoughts on Clinical Work

Janet L. Bachant[8] & Arnold D. Richards

[(2024). *Psychoanalytic Review*, 111(3):233–251]

Practitioners interested in the process of helping people change are confronted today with such a burgeoning array of perspectives, theories, and treatment modalities that even the most diligent can feel overwhelmed by the number of choices. This plethora of approaches calls into question whether there is *anything* that can tie them together. Asking if the psychoanalytic field is destined to be splintered into fragments that defy cohesion or if it is possible to generate a way of thinking and working that is more inclusive, this paper takes a historical and integrationist

---

8 Janet Bachant has worked as a psychologist, psychoanalyst, and photographer in New York City for over 40 years. After September 11, she developed a coalition of over 350 mental health workers who donated services to disaster responders and their families. After studying photography, she found a way to express her artistic sensibilities. Her teaching has engaged students at various psychoanalytic institutes in New York and China. She has written numerous journal articles and co-authored (with Elliot Adler) *Working in Depth: Framework and Flexibility in the Analytic Relationship*. Her book, *Exploring the Landscape of the Mind: An Introduction to Psychodynamic Psychotherapy* is available from Amazon.com

approach, grounded in a clinical focus on mental organization and Leo Rangell's total composite theory. It discusses trends in the development of psychoanalysis and argues for the importance of integration of the findings from neuropsychology and neuropsychoanalysis into psychoanalytic clinical work.

Patients come to treatment because they are suffering. Their need for help structures the therapeutic situation in significant ways, most notably mandating the creation of the asymmetrical slant (Adler & Bachant, 1996; Freedman, 1985; Freud, 1915; Loewald, 1960; Pine, 1993) in which the treatment is primarily focused on the patient. Built into the patient's appeal to the clinician is a bias toward seeing them as a parental figure. The need for help and the biases this need creates are inevitable parts of the structure of the therapeutic situation, which engenders conflicts and intensities, and must be countered by a collaborative mode of relating.

All therapy is grounded in the reality of the patient's conflicted desire to change and the therapist's focus on helping patients better understand themselves. Changing established habits, defenses, relational styles, and ideas about self and others is a formidable task. Human beings are extraordinarily complex, motivated by many bio/psycho/social factors. The clinician's task to *facilitate* change is exacerbated by the fact that some of the early mental organizations are highly *resistant* to change.

Because we all perceive and interpret the world uniquely, important differences between schools of thought have been present since the beginning of psychoanalysis. Some of these differences cannot be theoretically combined. Certain perspectives have core principles—related to motivation, therapeutic action, change, human development, the genesis of pathology—that render integration unworkable. Perspectives that prioritize cognition over emotion, for example, are a case in point. Clinicians need to decide which are the foundational perspectives that work for them. These decisions are complex and unique, having different determinants for each clinician. It is widely observed (e.g., Sandler & Rosenblatt, 1962) that we often integrate techniques and ideas of different schools of thought in our daily work; taking a pragmatic approach, we "borrow" from different perspectives. Consciously or unconsciously, working from a single theoretical point of view is often not what goes on in the clinical encounter.

Nevertheless, there is a body of knowledge that most clinicians, across a range of theoretical orientations, use in their work. We can therefore identify areas of overlap and contributions that have provided us with important and enriching additions.

THE NEED FOR AN EVOLVING MODEL OF PSYCHOANALYSIS

Models of psychoanalysis must grapple with the fact that no one perspective may be able to provide the solution for every patient-clinician collaboration. Fred Pine (1990) attempted to illuminate different perspectives, but we argue that his approach is not integrative enough and even encourages pluralism. Other perspectives have made contributions that highlight different therapeutic processes and offer useful approaches to clinical work (Rangell, 1990, 2004, 2007; Wallerstein, 1998, 1990).

The danger of pluralism is that it moves us toward fragmentations rather than integrations. Rangell (1990) noted that many of the concepts that form the basis of pluralistic perspectives have been represented in the psychoanalytic corpus from the beginning, evolving over time: "The self, and the object, as whole entities, have always had a firm place in central unified psychoanalytic theory" (p. 6). Examples of new findings include the understanding that the severity and persistence of trauma is critically tied to early childhood experience; the value of working from *both* one-person and two-person perspectives; the profound consequences of lack of emotional connectedness in early childhood; the importance of mirroring; and the value of applying learning principles to work through entrenched, automatic mind/brain-driven maladaptive patterns as well as attending to the intersubjectivity of ongoing relatedness between parents and children, patient and therapist, patient and self. D. Benveniste (personal communication, 2024) comments on the value of using different *lenses* at different times, as patients' needs and growth change. Contributions from different perspectives through more than 100 years of clinical and theoretical development of psychoanalysis and related fields have made this possible.

Although Sigmund Freud began to think about psychic life within a clinical context, the treatment of hysterical patients rapidly shifted his interest to theoretical issues—to how the mind is organized (the patterns of defenses, wishes, and fears that structure the conscious and unconscious narratives that develop in childhood), symptom formation, dreams as representations of mental organization, and the larger view of metapsychology. Powerful transferences to Freud caused some of his followers to relate to him as a guru or authoritarian leader, and others profoundly invested in demonstrating his omissions and flaws. The history of psychoanalysis—as is the case with all sciences—is inevitably characterized by dissent, conflict, accommodation, and clarification, leading to knowledge of increasing complexity. Leo Rangell (2004, 2007) was an early and principal promoter of the need for these processes. An advocate for inclusion and syntheses, he (1974) also warned of dangers involved in developing a pluralistic perspective: "The alternative systems utilize the mechanism of *pars pro toto*—and their followers prefer the part to the whole" (p. 6). As we look at the possibilities of integration, we must ask ourselves if we are developing a theoretical system that accommodates larger and larger streams of data, replacing old observations with new ones when both are valid, or if we are substituting a part for the whole.

We argue against the idea that there has been a paradigm shift in psychoanalysis, either from the drive model to the relational model, or from a model of *guilty* to *tragic* man. Our position is that psychoanalysis has been enriched by the tensions that emerge as the visions and voices of various contributors are developed, explored, and incorporated into the corpus of analytic thinking. These tensions have not been smooth or without questions about core beliefs and principles. The development of psychoanalysis has proceeded with passionate debate, and, indeed, there are some core beliefs that defy integration such as those that prioritize human interaction at the cost of diminishing the importance of biological and psychological factors; or a system that prioritizes developmental deficit over inner conflict. Our way of thinking privileges the notion of interactive variables, rather than the dichotomies that often organize the field. Developmental deficits *do not* exclude inner conflict; the intersubjectiveness of all experience *does not* render psychological and biological determinants less relevant.

There were historically important reasons why a number of thinkers rightfully focused on areas that Freud did not consider. These contributors included Harry Stack Sullivan (1953/1968) and other interpersonalists (Erich Fromm, 1941, 1947; Edgar Levenson, 1972; Benjamin Wolstein, 1959/1995; Irwin Hirsch, 2014), who concentrated on the impact of social determinants on human development; Heinz Kohut (1971) and other Self Psychologists (Ernest Wolf, 1984; Paul Tolpin, 1988; Michael Basch, 1991; Paul and Anna Ornstein, 2003; Arnold Goldberg, 2017), who focused on developmental deficits and lack of attunement in the creation of pathology; the Intersubjectivists (Stolorow, Brandchaft, & Atwood, 1987; Thomas Ogden, 1994; Irvin Hoffman, 1995; Donna Orange, 1995), who emphasized the idea of co-construction and intersubjectivity; Object Relations theory,

349

whose prominent representatives — W. R. Fairbairn (1952), Melanie Klein (1958/1975), D. W. Winnicott (1960/1995)—addressed the importance of internal self and object relations; and Jacques Lacan (1966/2007) and Merton Gill (1982), who are each in a category of their own. Karen Horney (1924, 1950/1991) and Clara Thompson (1964) deserve special mention as theorists who have significantly impacted our understanding of the psychology of women and the influence of social forces on development. Finally, we are also aware that perspectives outside psychoanalytic thinking have made important contributions to our understanding of therapeutic effectiveness.

TRENDS IN PSYCHOANALYSIS

Understanding the trends in the development of psychoanalysis is an essential precondition for navigation of the contemporary labyrinth of models and for development of the clinical ability to work with different lenses. It should be apparent that these trends are a matter of degree, rather than of kind, always *more or less*, rather than *all or nothing at all*. Hopefully, always in the service of clinical work, they involve a movement toward more inclusive thinking and a willingness to forgo dichotomies.

Trend 1

Perhaps the most obvious trend is a change in thinking about the nature and quality of the therapeutic relationship. When Sigmund Freud started practicing psychoanalysis, he related to his patients in a way that was probably not very different from the way he related to friends, colleagues, and ordinary people in his life. He then went on to develop a special set of analytic methods and techniques that involved the use of the couch, free association, "evenly hovering attention," neutrality, and anonymity. These constraints were emphasized over time and culminated in the blank screen model of the 1940s and 50s, commonly linked with American Ego Psychology. Yet, even during those years, some psychoanalysts understandably found this way of relating to patients problematic. Consequently, some of them argued for a much more personal stance, which they considered more therapeutic. The "one-person" model was replaced with a "two-person" model, in which the concept of enactment was central; the concept of coconstruction, developed by Gill and Hoffman (1982) and others (e.g., A. D. Richards, 1999) suggested that everything that occurs in the analytic situation is co-created by the patient and analyst.

Lynch, Bachant, and Richards (2020) argued that these models are not mutually exclusive. Each is important and relevant at different times in the clinical encounter. According to Zetzel (1956), Loewald (1960, 1970), Greenson (1965, 1967), Greenberg and Mitchell (1983), and S. Mitchell (1984), the relationship is important and therapeutic in various ways, but the structure of the therapeutic engagement is a vital and indispensable aspect of working therapeutically (Adler & Bachant, 1996). There are times when focusing on understanding how the patient's mind is organized (what pattern, fantasy, fear, anxiety, or defense is driving behavior) is critical to deepening the treatment. Other times require a more sustained analysis of the interaction between the participants. Each perspective can be understood as an oscillating figure and ground that enrich each other, providing context and content on different planes of experience.

Working on understanding patients' mental organization gives them an opportunity to reflect on how their minds are organized. The patient's mental organization is *brought to* the therapeutic interaction (Bachant & Adler, 1997). For example, when only children are confronted with the birth of a younger sibling at an early age, it is not uncommon for them

351

to experience (because of the dominance of the fear system and the right hemisphere in early life) the loss of the world they knew in a blaming way, as their fault. This psychological organization, anchored in the functioning of an undeveloped brain, can generate a mindset dominated by a blaming of the self for the change in his or her world. This organization is one that the patient *brings to* the therapeutic interaction, not one that is co-constructed *in* the therapeutic interaction. The ability to reflect is critical for the emergence of insight and for the capacity to ward off being hijacked by acute emotional arousal. This ability can be compromised by early emotionally dominated right hemisphere functioning, an unconscious mental organization that brings a sense of conviction to inner experience. Such "convictions" include mental organization consequent to growing up female in a culture where females are devalued; experiencing ruptures in attachments due to early problems with nursing; early loss of siblings or parents; and the experience of bodily threatening injury or illness at an early age. They always bear the imprint of the child's early interactions with caregivers. As the structuring of the mind becomes intrapsychically organized very early, it will be brought to subsequent interactions with more or less flexibility and openness to learning something new.

On the other hand, a focus on an interactive level of experiencing enables patterns of relating to be seen and felt in the immediacy of the present, generating a sense of recognition and belief in both participants (Lynch et al., 2020). This emotional immediacy helps patients identify intrapsychic patterns, wishes, fears, and fantasies in an interactive context.

At the heart of the relational critique of the Freudian approach is the notion that Freudian analysts are cold, distant, and not personally forthcoming, thereby characterizing them as less humane, friendly, and accepting—"not as nice" as the Self Psychologists, the Interpersonalists, the Relationalists, and their cohorts. To support this critique some authors cite blank screen, therapist's anonymity, and the proscription against self-disclosure in Freudian practice, sometimes contending that we have only two dichotomous choices: "psychological meaning is either regarded as inherent and brought to the relational field, or as negotiated through interaction" (S. Mitchell, 1988, pp. 4–5). In their review of this position, Bachant and Richards (1993) contend that a false opposition limits our view of mental organization. It is imperative to decide if the criticism of Freudianism is valid and useful theoretically and, more importantly, clinically. But, is being "nice" what counts, or is helping patients understand themselves, their conflicts, and what motivates them at the core of analytic work? An integrative approach values both the relationship and the importance of focusing on the patient's mental organization.

Trend 2

Another trend involves a movement *away from* the clinician being theory-driven *toward* being experience-driven. It places less emphasis on the metapsychology and more on the centrality of conflict and fantasy. Instead of favoring a rigid application of theory, it focuses on the immediacy of "who is doing what to whom" (Arlow, 1991; Benjamin, 1988; Brenner, 2006, 2008; Freud, 1937; Isaacs, 1948; Klein, 1958/1975; S. Mitchell, 1988; A. K. Richards, 2013) and on the "what's going on around here" way of interacting clinically (Levenson, 1972). It involves a recognition of the many layers of meaning in the therapeutic process, and argues that staying close to the patient's experience, *intrapsychically and interpersonally*, is central to therapeutic work.

Trend 3

What clinicians do in the consulting room is something that patients cannot do on their own: develop a better understanding of how *their* mental experience is organized. Informing our listening, and critical to the process of developing narratives with patients, is the question of how patients' communications with us (through language, tone, styles of relatedness, and actions) represent how their minds (fears, fantasies, transferences, conflicts, defenses, and desires) are *organized*. This enables patients and therapists to gain access to underlying and often unconscious modes of relating; patterns that deepen an understanding of what makes change challenging. This framework of focusing on how patients' minds are structured provides therapists with a blueprint that guides interventions. Central to generating this framework is an understanding of the patient's developmental history on biological, social, and psychological levels.

The historian Yuval Harari (2015) contends that it is the development of narratives, the stories we tell each other, the belief in common myths, that drove the explosion of civilization and the massive, rapid development of our brains. Harari writes: "Any large-scale human cooperation—whether a modern state, a medieval church, an ancient city or an archaic tribe—is rooted in common myths that exist in people's collective imagination" (p. 17). By extension, only by understanding *how and when* certain individual myths were conceived that culminate in patterns of experiencing and relating can we help patients develop a narrative that enables them to address the challenges of changing their behaviors and accepting their unique lives. Importantly, this focus provides patients with an ability to work on their wishes, fears, defenses, and impulses on their own, outside analytic sessions.

Trend 4

A growing acknowledgment of the importance of very early experience, especially the experience of relational trauma and its direct connection to brain development, is a trend that pervades many contemporary therapeutic approaches, including neuropsychology, neuropsychoanalysis, contemporary classical psychoanalysis, cognitive-behavioral therapy (CBT), dialectical behavior therapy (DBT), eye movement desensitization and reprocessing (EMDR), mindfulness, relational psychoanalysis, and somatic therapies (Beck et al., 2012; Cozolino, 2002; Gomez et al., 2017; Hayes & Wilson, 1994; Kabat-Zinn & Chapman-Waldrop, 1988; Linehan, 2018; Van der Kolk, 2014). Patients' efforts to change enduring patterns of behavior are significantly enhanced by developing the narrative of when, how, and why their maladaptive impulses occurred. Clinicians' knowledge of how brains develop and how minds are structured is an essential aspect of developing these narratives and helping the healing process (Bachant, 2019; Solms, 2003a; Solms & Turnbull, 2002). Integrating the insights generated by the emerging fields of neuropsychology and neuropsychoanalysis is not only a necessary and vital part of understanding patients and working effectively with them, but a subject area that should be an integral part of psychoanalytic training.

These trends have enabled us to address omissions in early psychoanalytic thinking and to develop new areas of theory and practice. But if we view them through a lens of pluralism, we contribute to a splintering of the field, a drifting of theory (Lynch et al., 2013) with no real efforts at "retention of consistency or intellectual unity" (Rangell, 2007, p. 99). Rangell's solution for the disarray implicit in theoretical pluralism is the proposal of a single unitary theory that is cumulative and cohesive, a blend of all valid discoveries containing all nonexpendable elements and criteria. His vision is that, as new clinical evidence is established, we can continue to evolve by learning to think with a spectrum in mind, each element of the spectrum valued.

We can choose to integrate.

INTEGRATING NEUROPSYCHOLOGY INTO PSYCHOANALYTIC CLINICAL WORK

As we think about integration in psychoanalysis, it is essential to incorporate current research on brain functioning into our understanding of theory, pathogenesis, and treatment. Updated knowledge of how the brain functions and changes during childhood is a core aspect of understanding psychological development (Bachant, 2019; Cozolino 2002; Damasio, 1994, 1999, 2003; Edelman, 2004; Ginot, 2015, 2022; LeDoux, 1996, 2015; Pally, 2000; Panksepp, 1998; Solms, 2003a, 2003b, 2020; Solms & Zellner, 2012). Neuropsychology, the study of the relationship between behavior, emotion, and cognition, *and* brain functioning (Oxford University Press, n.d.), is an essential aspect of psychodynamic understanding and was the impetus behind Sigmund Freud's "Project for Scientific Psychology" (1895)—his effort to establish a scientific basis for the study of the mind. Cristina Alberini (2020) has described it as the cornerstone of the development of neuropsychoanalysis.

For psychoanalytic clinicians, perhaps the greatest impetus for developing neuropsychological understanding comes from working with patients. We have many opportunities to observe that integrated patterns of functioning (especially those related to very early adversity and trauma) point to how the development of defenses, wishes, and fears was shaped by the constraints of brain development during the patient's earliest life. Infants and very young children organize their world with an undeveloped brain, one that is dominated by fear, anxiety, and primitive modes of

356

thinking and feeling. According to Eric Kandel (1998), psychoanalysis, psychiatry, and cognitive psychology "can define for biology the mental functions that need to be studied for a meaningful and sophisticated understanding of the biology of the human mind" (p. 459). In turn, a critical challenge for psychoanalysts is to join with biologists (Kandel, 1999). More than a century ago, the state of science could not enable Freud to complete his "Project," but he consistently envisioned an integration of psychoanalysis with neuropsychology (Alberini, 2020; Jenkins, 2005; Solms, 2003a, 2003b, 2020). Today we understand that mind and body are not separate domains but different expressions of a unified process. We can get closer to understanding the impact of mind/brain processes on psychological development.

Underpinning ideas of how we can help patients change is the bedrock necessity of understanding how the brain develops and how its stages of growth affect psychological development and functioning. Infants are born while their brains are still in the process of formation; neural development is not complete until the mid-20s. Throughout this long time span, emotional experiences and their organization in the developing brain determine the nature of our well-being (Panksepp, 1998). Efrat Ginot, author of *The Neuropsychology of the Unconscious* (2015), argues that we need a concept of unconscious functioning that integrates knowledge in affect theory, cognitive neuroscience, and neuropsychological findings with clinical work. This integration asks us to consider unconscious processing on a continuum, giving expression to integrated patterns of feeling, thinking, and behaving. Ginot's latest research (2022) focuses on the early manifestation of the fear system in the developing brain. This orientation helps clinicians to more fully understand the power of the child's earliest experiences: "Inevitable negative encounters and lack of attunement, *even normative ones*, will give rise to unsettling experiences of hyperarousal and extreme agitation" (Ginot, 2022, p. 000), experiences that patients may not remember directly, but do in their bodies, their expectations, actions, and even the language they use (Adler, 2023; Alberini, 2020; Freud, 1915; Van der Kolk, 2014).

Clinicians need to understand not only the centrality of emotional relatedness in psychological development (Panksepp, 1998; Solms, 2003a, 2003b), but also that because young children's brains are not fully formed, they are uniquely vulnerable to disturbing internal states. Among our innate emotional systems, pro-social instincts, such as needs for attachment and separation anxiety (Panksepp, 1998), safeguard connections between people, particularly between caregivers and infants. Fear and anxiety, especially during a child's early years, possess the power to easily induce internal disturbing states. The fear system not only quickly responds to threats, both real and imagined, but also gives rise to the automatic defenses in order to avoid painful experiences. Early experiences, both positive and negative, underpin all we learn and internalize about ourselves and others. The unconscious expectations and beliefs they engender are the building blocks of our various self-states and automatic patterns (Bachant & Ginot, 2023). Alberini (2020) argues that "understanding mental functions, i.e. the mind, will require us to understand the brain as an organ at a systems level and in the context of its interactions with the whole organism. This is because the brain coordinates the external and internal information processing necessary to create responses that enable the organism to adapt to continuously changing stimulation" (p. 40).

We clinicians also need to understand that patients are unable to recall the formative experiences that shape their mental organization directly. Yet, adverse early experiences, whether generated from internal fantasies or interpersonal interactions, will be represented in the patients' mind/brain organization *whether they can be directly remembered or not* (Adler, 2023; Alberini, 2020; Ginot, 2015; Solms, 2003a, 2003b). Patients may not be able to directly recall these experiences, but therapists have tools with which to help access them: patients' modes of relating to us and to themselves, their language, tone, and the actions they employ. We listen not only to what patients say, we also listen to what they do.

Deeper understanding of brain development and functioning asks us to reevaluate some of the narratives about pathogenesis and treatment. Winnicott's (1960/1995) description of the development of the *true* and *false* self, for example, is very appealing in that it speaks to an experience that many people can recognize. Phenomenologically, it makes a certain sense. But this narrative embodies a misunderstanding about integration itself. Childhood strategies to avoid pain, often spoken of as defenses, are typically understood as part of the "false self," yet these expressions of early mental organization, structured into our minds, are every bit as "true" as other aspects of mental functioning. They are integral parts of who the patients are. Dichotomizing our understanding into a "true self" and a "false self" stops us from seeing the person holistically. It can even augment the patient's tendency to split and to think of a part of themselves as bad. This way of thinking does not help patients understand the development of their childhood strategies, have compassion for their need to develop them, and resolve in the real struggle to change them. It can also encourage a grandiosity on the part of therapists who may prematurely decide that they "know" what the patient's problem is and how it should be solved.

In light of present neuropsychological findings, central psychoanalytic concepts such as the unconscious, resistance, and insight also need an update. Our mind/brains are organized by an innate propensity to automatically enact conscious/unconscious patterns. We perceive, react to, and act on a wide range of external and internal stimuli unconsciously because of the interconnectedness of all mental functioning (Ginot, 2022), with each mode of functioning influencing the other (Alberini, 2022; Damasio, 2010; Isaacs, 1948; Panksepp, 1998; Solms, 2003a). Unconscious processes underlie every aspect of our emotions, cognitions, and actions.

Most importantly, specific *conscious* processes can both trigger and modulate *unconscious* ones. Consequently, we can no longer talk or think of the unconscious as a distinct, separate container of repressed material. Rather, we need to view our mental functioning as an ongoing continuum of interacting conscious and unconscious *processes* (Adler, 2023; Adler & Bachant, 1998; Bachant, 2019; Cozolino, 2002; Ginot, 2015, 2022; LeDoux, 1996, 2002; Pally, 2000; Panksepp, 1998; Solms, 2020).

In a recent reflection on his career, Elliot Adler (2023) talked about the way others have described Freud's *The Interpretation of Dreams* as the indispensable work, without which psychoanalysis would not have developed:

I had puzzled over this assertion as a student, but my subsequent teaching had led me to see that its truth lay in his discovery that the essential way we organize our experience of the internal and external world—giving it meaning by thinking in words— simultaneously expresses and enacts disguised wishfulness from all stages and all forms of our lived experience. In effect, the language of dreams, saturated with the distillates of both immediate circumstance as well as persistent life historical influences—expressed with overloaded metaphoric density—haunts our fundamental sense of reality. (pp. 16–17)

Automaticity is a profound roadblock to change, one that asks us to reconsider how we understand insight. Understanding the brain's tendency to automatically enact conscious and unconscious patterns, we need to appreciate that insight is a necessary but not sufficient factor in therapeutic action. Change involves retraining the brain, consciously directing the interruption of automatic modes of relating and consciously practicing the patterns that patients want to incorporate into their lives. This does not diminish the centrality of transference and resistance in psychoanalytic work. It does, however, ask of us to expand the psychoanalytic understanding of resistance with an awareness that some of its aspects are a manifestation of the automaticity of brain functioning. This modification of our thinking and technique gives patients more opportunities to practice and reinforce different neuropsychological patterns that can then underpin new, more adaptive ways of feeling, thinking, and behaving. In the consulting room, we do this by helping patients understand that changing maladaptive behaviors involves opportunities to practice learning something new and taking effective action that benefits the integrated self (Bachant, 2019). According to Jiménez (2006), therapeutic change is generated by means that include changing the strength of synaptic connections and inducing structural changes that alter the anatomic pattern of the interconnections between neurons.

CONCLUDING REMARKS

Psychoanalysis is a method of understanding and a mode of treatment as well as a theory of how the mind works. Engaging with people therapeutically has been evolving since its inception through the contributions from many perspectives. This paper emphasizes some of the major trends in this evolution and highlights important clinical issues. Our focus has been on integrating and incorporating the relevant additions as they emerged in the course of more than a century of our history, while respecting the differences between varied psychoanalytic perspectives. We have made a case for the need to integrate contemporary findings from neuropsychology and neuropsychoanalysis into clinical work. Only by understanding the biological constraints on brain development can we appreciate the psychological strategies our patients developed to deal with an unsettling world. We argue against the idea that there has been a paradigm shift in psychoanalysis and against dichotomous thinking: conflict and deficit, biology and lived experience—to name only two such dichotomies—are interactive variables, not exclusive explanations. There is no doubt that, after Freud, there are many theories that offer clinically useful approaches, but a part can never substitute for the whole.

Integration involves working with both the here and now *and* unconscious processes. It involves acknowledging the importance of the relationship in the clinical encounter, just as the clinicians' conviction that helping patients understand the way their minds work is essential to change. Such an understanding must include recognition of the role of development and early relational trauma. Neuropsychology continues to contribute to our quest to integrate theory and practice, illuminating how its insights can enhance the psychoanalytic enterprise.

REFERENCES

Adler, E. (2023). *Learning to listen: My career in psychoanalysis* [Paper presentation]. Westchester Center for Psychoanalysis and Psychotherapy.

——— & Bachant, J. L. (1996). Free association and analytic neutrality: The basic structure of the psychoanalytic situation. *Journal of the American Psychoanalytic Association, 44*(4), 1021–1046. https://doi. org/10 .1177/000306519604400403

——— ——— (1998). *Working in depth: A clinician's guide to framework and flexibility in the analytic relationship.* Lanham, MD: Jason Aronson.

Alberini, C.M. (2020). Commentary: Rethinking the framework of the Project for a Scientific Psychology. *Neuropsychoanalysis, 22*(1–2), 37–41.

https:// doi.org/10.1080/15294145.2021.1878604

Arlow, J.A. (1991). *Psychoanalysis: Clinical theory and practice.* Madison, CT: International Universities Press.

Bachant, J. L. (2019). *Exploring the landscape of the mind: An introduction to psychodynamic therapy.* New York: IPBooks.

——— & Adler, E. (1997). Transference: Co-constructed or brought to the interaction? *Journal of the American Psychoanalytic Association, 45*(4), 1097–1120.

——— & Richards, A. D. (1993). Review essay [Review of the book *Relational concepts in psychoanalysis: An integration*, by S. Mitchell]. *Psychoanalytic Dialogues, 3*(3), 431–460. https://doi.org/10.1080/10481889309538986

Basch, M.F. (1991). Are selfobjects the only objects? Implications for psychoanalytic technique. *Progress in Self-Psychology, 7*, 3–15.

Beck, AT. (1967). *Depression: Causes and treatment.* University of Pennsylvania Press.

——— Haigh, E. A.P., & Baber, K.F. (2012). Biological underpinnings of the cognitive model of depression: A prototype for psychoanalytic research. *Psychoanalytic Review, 99*(4), 515–537. https://doi.org/10.1521/prev.2012 .99.4.515

Benjamin, J. (1990). An outline of intersubjectivity: The development of recognition. *Psychoanalytic Psychology, 7*(Suppl), 33–46. https://doi.org/10.1037 /h0085258

Brenner, C. (2006). *Psychoanalysis or mind and meaning.* New York: Psychoanalytic Quarterly.

——— (2008). Aspects of psychoanalytic theory: Drives, defense and the pleasure/unpleasure principle. *Psychoanalytic Quarterly, 77*(3), 707–717. https://doi.org/10.1002/j.2167-4086.2008.tb00357.x

Cozolino, L.J. (2002). *The neuroscience of psychotherapy: Building and rebuilding the human brain.* New York: W.W. Norton.

Damasio, A.R. (1994). *Descartes' error: Emotion, reason, and the human brain.* New York: Grosset/Putnam.

——— (1999). *The feeling of what happens: Body and emotion in the making of consciousness.* New York: Harcourt Brace Jovanovich.

——— (2003). *Looking for Spinoza: Joy, sorrow, and the feeling brain.* New York: Harcourt Brace Jovanovich.

Edelman, G.M. (2004). *Wider than the sky: The phenomenal gift of consciousness.* New Haven: Yale University Press.

Fairbairn, W.R. (1952). *Psychoanalytic studies of the personality.* Abingdon & New York, Routledge & Kegan Paul.

Freud, S. (1895). Project for scientific psychology. *Standard Edition 1,* 283–397.

——— (1915). Remembering, repeating and working through. *Standard Edition 12,* 145–156.

——— (1937). Analysis terminable and interminable. *Standard Edition 23,* 209–254.

Freedman, N. (1985). The concept of transformation in psychoanalysis. *Psychoanalytic Psychologist, 2*(4), 317–339. https://doi.org/10.1037/0736 -9735.2.4.317

Fromm, E. (1941). *Escape from freedom.* New York: Henry Holt.

——— (1947). *Man for himself: An inquiry into the psychology of ethics.* Greenwich, CT: Fawcett Publications.

Gill, M. (1982). *Analysis of transference, Vol. I: Theory and technique.* Madison, CT: International Universities Press.

——— & Hoffman, I. Z. (1982). *Analysis of transference, Vol. II: Studies of nine audio-recorded psychoanalytic sessions.* Madison, CT: International Universities Press.

Ginot, E. (2015). *The neuropsychology of the unconscious: Integrating brain and mind in psychotherapy.* New York: W.W. Norton.

——— (2022). *Our anxious selves: Neuropsychological processes and their enduring influence on who we are.* New York: W.W. Norton.

Gomez, J., Hoffman, H.G., Bistricky, S.L., Gonzalez, M., Rosenberg, L., Sampaio, M., Garcia-Palacios, A., Navarro-Haro, M.V., Alhalabi, W., Rosenberg, M., Meyer, W.J. 3rd, & Linehan, M.M. (2017). The use of virtual reality facilitates dialectical behavior therapy. "Observing Sounds and Visuals" mindfulness skills training exercises for a Latino patient with severe burns: A case study. *Frontiers in Psychology, 8,* 1611. https://doi.org/10.3389fpsyg.2017.01611

Greenberg, J.R., & Mitchell, S.A. (1983). *Object relations in psychoanalytic theory.* Cambridge, MA: Harvard University Press.

Greenson, R.R. (1965). The working alliance and the transference neurosis. *Psychoanalytic Quarterly, 34,* 155–181.

——— (1967). *The technique and practice of psychoanalysis, Vol. 1.* Madison, CT: International Universities Press.

Harari, Y.N. (2015). *Sapiens: A brief history of humankind.* New York: Harper Perennial.

Hayes, S.C., & Wilson, K.G. (1994). Acceptance and commitment therapy: Altering the verbal support for experiential avoidance. *Behavior Analyst, 17*(2), 289–303. https://doi.org/10.1007/BF03392677

Hirsch, I. (2014). *The interpersonal tradition: The origins of psychoanalytic subjectivity* Abingdon & New York: Routledge.

Hoffman, I.Z. (1995). *Ritual and spontaneity in the psychoanalytic process: A dialectical-constructivist view. .* Abingdon & *New York:* Routledge.

Horney, K. (1924). On the genesis of the castration complex in women. *International Journal of Psycho-analysis, 5,* 50–65.

——— (1967). *Feminine psychology* (H. Kelman, Ed.). New York: W. W. Norton.

——— (1991). *Neurosis and human growth: The struggle towards self-realization.* W.W. Norton. (Original work published 1950.)

Isaacs, S. (1948). The nature and function of phantasy. *International Journal of Psycho-analysis, 29,* 73–97.

Jiménez, J.P. (2006). After pluralism: Toward a new integrated paradigm. *International Journal of Psychoanalysis, 87*(Pt 2), 1487–1507. https://doi.org/10.1516/aebf-qqc1-e0eh-68wn

Kabot-Zinn, J., & Chapman-Waldrop, A. (1988). Compliance with an outpatient stress reduction program: Rates and predictors of program completion. *Journal of Behavioral Medicine, 11*(4), 333–352. https://doi.org/10.1007 /BF00844934

Kandel, E. (1998). A new intellectual framework for psychiatry. *American Journal of Psychiatry, 155*(4), 457–69. https://doi.org/10.1176/ajp.155.4.457

——— (1999). Biology and the future of psychoanalysis: A New Intellectual Framework for Psychiatry revisited. *American Journal of Psychiatry, 156*(4), 505–524. https://doi.org/10.1176/ajp.156.4.505

Klein, M. (1975). On the development of mental functioning. In *Envy and gratitude and other works, 1946-1963* (pp. 236–246). New York: Free Press. (Original work published 1958)

Kohut, H. (1971). *The analysis of the self.* Madison, CT: International Universities Press.

Lacan, J. (2007). Écrits (B. Fink, Trans.). New York: W.W. Norton. (Original work published 1966.)

LeDoux, J. (1996). *The emotional brain: The mysterious underpinnings of emotional life.* New York: Simon & Schuster.

——— (2015). *Anxious: Using the brain to understand and treat fear and anxiety.* London: Penguin.

Levenson, E.A. (1972). *The fallacy of understanding: An inquiry into the changing structure of psychoanalysis.* New York: Basic Books.

Linehan, M.M. (2018). *Cognitive-behavioral treatment of borderline personality disorder.* New York: Guilford.

Loewald, H.W. (1960). On the therapeutic action of psychoanalysis. *International Journal of Psycho-analysis, 4*, 16–33.

——— (1970). Psychoanalytic theory and psychoanalytic process. *Psychoanalytic Study of the Child, 25,* 45–68. https://doi. org/10.1080/00797308.1970 .11823275

Lynch, A.A., Richards, A.D., & Bachant, J. (2013). Afterword. In B. I. Kalish & C. P. Fisher (Eds.), *The Rangell reader* (pp. 269–280). New York: IPBooks.

——— Bachant, J. L., & Richards, A. D. (2020). The spectrum of analytic interaction: A contemporary Freudian perspective. *Psychoanalytic Review, 107*(5), 435–455. https://doi.org/10.1521/prev.2020.107.5.435

Mitchell, J. (1974). *Psychoanalysis and feminism: Freud, Reich, Laing, and women.* New York: Vintage Books.

Mitchell, S.A. (1988). *Relational concepts in psychoanalysis: An integration.* Cambridge, MA: Harvard University Press.

Ogden, T.H. (1994). *Subjects of analysis.* Lanham, MD: Jason Aronson.

Orange, D.M. (1995). *Emotional understanding: Studies in psychoanalytic epistemology.* Guilford Press.

Ornstein, P.H., & Ornstein, A. (2003). The function of theory in psychoanalysis: A self psychological perspective. *Psychoanalytic Quarterly, 72*(1), 157–182. https://doi.org/10.1002/j.2167-4086.2003. tb00125.x

Oxford University Press. (n.d.). Neuropsychology. In *Oxford English Dictionary.* Retrieved February 20, 2024, from: https://www.oed.com/ search/dictionary/?scope=Entries&q=Neuropsychology

Pally, R. (2000). *The mind-brain relationship.* London Karnac.

Panksepp, J. (1998). *Affective neuroscience: The foundations of human and animal emotions.* Oxford: Oxford University Press.

Pine, F. (1990). *Drive, ego, object, self: A synthesis for clinical work.* New York: Basic Books.

——— (1993). A contribution to the analysis of the psychoanalytic process. *Psychoanalytic Quarterly, 62*(2), 185–205.

Rangell, L. (1990). *The human core: The intrapsychic base of behavior.* International Universities Press.

——— (2004). *My life in theory.* New York: Other Press.

——— (2007). *The road to unity.* Lanham, MD: Jason Aronson.

Richards, A.D. (1999). [Review of the book *Ritual and spontaneity in the psychoanalytic process: A dialectical-constructivist point of view* by I. Z. Hoffman]. *Psychoanalytic Psychology, 16*(2), 288–302. https://doi. org/10.1037 /0736-9735.16.2.288

Richards, A.K. (2013). Primary femininity and female genital anxiety. In N. R. Goodman (Ed.), *Listening to understand: Selected papers of Arlene Kramer Richards* (pp. 91–110). New York: IPBooks.

Sandler, J., & Rosenblatt, B. (1962). The concept of the representational world. *Psychoanalytic Study of the Child,* 17, 128–145 . https://doi. org/10 .1080/00797308.1962.11822842

Solms, M. (2003a). Preliminaries for an integration of psychoanalysis and neuroscience. In M. Leuzinger-Bohleber, A.U. Dreher, & J. Canestri (Eds.), *Pluralism and unity? Methods of research in psychoanalysis* (pp. 184– 206). IPA.

———. (2003b). Do unconscious phantasies really exist? In R. Steiner (Ed.), *Unconscious phantasy* (pp. 99–115). London: Karnac.

——— (2020). New project for a scientific psychology: General scheme. *Neuropsychoanalysis, 22*(1–2), 5–35. https://doi. org/10.1080/15294145.2020 .1833361

——— & Turnbull, O. (2002). *The brain and the inner world: An introduction to the neuroscience of subjective experience.* New Yorik: Other Press.

——— & Zellner, M.R. (2012). The Freudian unconscious today. In A. Fotopoulo, D. Plaff, & M.A. Conway (Eds.), *From the couch to the lab: Trends in psychodynamic neuroscience* (pp. 209–218). Oxford: Oxford University Press.

Stolorow, R.E., Brandchaft, G., & Atwood, B. (1987). *Psychoanalytic treatment: An intersubjective approach.* Abingdon &; New York: Routledge.

Sullivan, H.S. (1968). *The interpersonal theory of psychiatry.* New York: W.W. Norton. (Original work published 1953)

Thompson, C. (1964). *Interpersonal psychoanalysis: The selected papers of Clara M. Thompson.* New York: Basic Books.

Tolpin, P.H. (1988). Optimal affective engagement: The analyst's role in therapy. *Progress in Self-Psychology, 4,* 160–168.

Van der Kolk, B. (2014). *The body keeps the score: Brain, mind, and body in the healing of trauma.* New York: Viking.

Wallerstein, R.S. (1988). One psychoanalysis or many? *International Journal of Psychoanalysis, 69*(Pt 1), 5–21.

_____ (1990). Psychoanalysis: The common ground. *International Journal of Psychoanalysis, 71*(Pt 1), 3–20.

Winnicott, D. W. (1995). Ego distortion in terms of the true and false self. In *Maturational processes and the facilitating environment: Studies in the theory of emotional development* (pp. 140–152). Madison, CT: International Universities Press. (Original work published 1960.)

Wolf, E. S. (1984). Self psychology and the neuroses. *Annual of Psychoanalysis, 12,* 57–68.

Wolstein, B. (1995). *Countertransference.* Jason Aronson. (Original work published 1959.)

Zetzel, E. R. (1956). Current concepts of transference. *International Journal of Psychoanalysis, 37*(4–5), 369–375.

CHAPTER 11

Review of *Gray Matters: A Biography of Brain Surgery* by Theodore H. Schwartz (2024). New York: Penguin Publishing Group Reviewed by Arnold D. Richards

This is an awesome book, not only a detailed account of the training and work of one of the foremost neurosurgeons in the United States, but also an in-depth history of the development of the field of neurosurgery itself. My review will be autobiographical because Dr. Theodore Schwartz's (who I will call Teddy) parents were my closest friends. When I returned to New York to start my analytic training from Petersburg, Virginia, where I was the medical director and the chief psychiatrist at the federal reformatory, my first job was with the psychiatric OPD at Montefiore Hospital where Lester Schwartz, Teddy's father, was the director. That began my wife and I's relationship to Lester and to Mara, Teddy's mother, which continued as long as they lived. Teddy has included in this book sections on both Lester and Mara which are very moving. I found it very sad to read again about Lester's illness and his passing, as well as about Mara's history. She was hidden in Belgium during the World War II. Lester and Mara introduced us to the Society for the Advancement of Judaism, which became our synagogue, and I was on the board of directors.

We have known Teddy since he was two years old. We always used to say that he was brilliant at birth and in fact was first in his class in elementary school , middle school, and high school, and graduated magna cum laude from Harvard Medical School and Harvard College. He participated in the most prestigious neurosurgery residency in the United States, the Neurological Institute. In his book, Teddy describes the most important neurosurgeons in the history of the profession starting with Harvey Cushing, Wilder Penfield, Leo Davidoff (who was a chairman at Montefiore who I knew) and many others. But I would propose Teddy, needs to be added to that list. Additionally, I need to mention that Mara and Teddy saved my life. I am writing this review because of them. In 2002 I developed an ataxia. I went to many doctors and no one could diagnose it, including my internist and neurologist and many others. This went on, I would say, for at least a month. My wife told Mara about this condition and mentioned that I had two other symptoms: computer apraxia and dysgraphia, as well as the ataxia. Mara told Teddy and Teddy told her to tell me that I needed to go to the ER immediately. I did. They did a CAT scan which visualized a massive subdural hematoma in one side of the skull. I was immediately sent to the operating room and Teddy removed the hematoma. I recovered without sequalae, although I did go into status epilepticus after they removed the brain hematoma. I had seizures for four or five days and was hooked up to an EEG.. The book makes me more aware of how serious this situation was. It describes the lucid interval, the amount of time in distress from which the brain can still recover. It often happens that is no more than four or five days. I came very close to that, as I said earlier.

The book presents the history of Teddy's training and practice and development as a neurosurgeon, as well as the history and the development of the field of neurosurgery, which has gone from a very primitive state to a situation now in which the most advanced techniques, surgical approaches, and technological tools are used. Teddy has been involved in all these developments, removing tumors through the nose to the orbits and electrode implantation in the treatment of seizures. The descriptions gives you a sense of the science, but also of the society, as when he describes athletic trauma in baseball and football. What stands out most is Teddy's personality. His dedication is as awesome as his humanity. The patient comes first, always; and his honesty, because he is willing to acknowledge the mistakes he has made, and recognizes his responsibility in each case. He also talks about the impact of growing up in a psychoanalytic family has had on his work on as a neurosurgeon and his willingness to consider factors which are out of awareness, like the unconscious. In every chapter one learns something that we didn't know before. Most striking to me was to find out that Evita Perón had a prefrontal lobotomy before she died, which was arranged by her husband, and I presume he instigated that because he was concerned about her developing a political reputation and because she became an icon with the Argentinian population. I have a friend who grew up in Argentina at that time who remembers when that surgery was revealed, but many felt it was uncertain whether it was for medical or primarily political purposes. A very important section of the book is concerned with prefrontal lobotomy, starting with Rosemary Kennedy, which was arranged by her father, Joseph Kennedy, who in my opinion was a very bad man. He was ambassador to England from 1938 to 1940 and a supporter of Adolf Hitler.

The chapter on frontal lobotomy is very nuanced. Most of us have a very negative view of the procedure, but Teddy does describe some double blind studies which demonstrate that it can be beneficial, and at the same time he shows how it was misused. He tells us about a neurosurgeon at Colombia who was exiled because he allowed too many German Jewish refugees to join his department. This had a personal resonance for me because when I was applying to medical school, my college dormmate was the son of the director of the admissions of the department of psychiatry of PNS and he told me that I should not apply because I would be rejected because I was Jewish. I read the book once, I would now like to read it again. I recommend that everyone who can do so read it. You will learn a lot about neurology anatomy and how the brain works. What I found very edifying is Teddy's philosophical discussions, for example, his considerations of the mind brain issue, dualism versus monism, and free will. Teddy tells us that he majored in philosophy in college, which may relate to the sophistication of the discussion of these issues. I understand that Teddy has done a podcast about his book and is giving lectures as well. Read the book and run, don't walk, to wherever you can hear him interviewed.

CHAPTER 12

The Influence of Personality of Psychoanalytic Technique

Part 1: Kohut
by Arnold Richards

Our fundamental thesis is that a psychoanalytic theoretician develops a theory of technique to counter his or her own anti-analytic proclivities. This idea can be located within the broader perspective advanced by Ludwik Fleck that the development of scientific ideas is influenced by historical, sociological, cultural, and psychological factors. We believe this thesis has significant heuristic value and that the dynamics it refers to can be recognized in the work of many, but certainly not all, psychoanalysts. My focus will be on Heinz Kohut but first we can illustrate our approach by way of a very abbreviated survey of some well-known analysts.

First, of course, is Freud, for whom abstinence was foundational for technique. There is ample evidence that he had to struggle to not interfere in the lives of his patients. The most egregious example is the case of Horace Frink, who he urged to divorce his wife and donate money to psychoanalysis. Fenichel was an extremely obsessional individual. He kept records of every play or concert he attended and every assignation as well, but in his book on psychoanalytic technique stressed "going for the affect." Henry Stack Sullivan, who grew up as an isolate in a rural New York community and had few friends as a child, developed an interpersonal theory of technique. Jack Arlow, who could listen to a single session and live out the operative unconscious fantasy, always stressed in his writing on psychoanalytic technique the importance of waiting for evidence before making interpretations. Kurt Eissler, who was, like Freud, an interventionist by personality, wrote about parameters. Paul Gray, who functioned in a very authoritarian manner at his psychoanalytic institute, emphasized helping the patient soften his own superego. A psychoanalyst, still living, who became known as the terminator because he would terminate patients and supervisees (and his own personal relationships as well), wrote about how to manage termination in brief psychotherapy.

These examples should suggest the robustness of our hypothesis. Arlene will consider the life and theory of Melanie Klein; Art, the life and theory of Karen Horney; and I will talk about Heinz Kohut.

Two central technical concerns for Kohut are empathy and authenticity. I have spoken to many of his colleagues and almost all agree that Kohut was extremely narcissistic and was hardly empathic with his friends and colleagues. I can cite many anecdotal examples that were provided to me by those who came to know him well. But I can also add that, on the other hand, his patients experienced him as being a very empathic psychoanalyst. Charles Strozier interviewed many of his former patients; the common report was that he was rarely unempathic in their sessions. I spoke to two of his former analysands myself who gave the same report.

Another point that became clear from the reports of his former patients was that he never acknowledged or indicated in any way that he was Jewish. One of his patients who had been in analysis with someone who was not Jewish and left the treatment because the analysis was not going well went to Kohut for a new analysis. He told me that after he lay down on the couch he said to Kohut, "By the way, are you Jewish?" Kohut did not respond.

After a long silence Dr. S. said, "I guess that subject is off the table." And indeed, it never came up again. My other colleague never asked and never was told and only learned from Kohut's obituary that he was Jewish. He was an immigrant like Kohut and noted that issues concerned with being an immigrant and making a life in a new country, a situation he shared with Kohut, never came up.

In sum, Kohut, who knew he had a problem with empathy in his personal relationships, made the empathic attitude of the analyst central to therapeutic action. And Kohut, who went out of his way to deny that he was Jewish, saw self psychology as an approach which helped the patient achieve authenticity. It is evident that Kohut maintained a false self all his life, considering his background, which was very Jewish.

Some details. His parents belonged to the assimilated Viennese Jewish elite. The name Kohut was a fairly common Jewish name derived from the Hebrew name Kohah, son of Levi. There was a distinguished line of Rabbi Kohuts from Hungary and several other Kohuts who were leaders of the Jewish community. Kohut insisted that Kohut was the Czech word for rooster and that the Kohuts were Bohemian Christians. His mother was descended from Jews in Slovakia. Her name was Lampl. Kohut, according to his biographer, never commented on this fact. He, of course, was circumcised and Bar Mitvahed, according to Strozier, on April 20, 1926; and he recited the Kiddish in Hebrew at his father's funeral. Keep in mind that in those days for a Jewish boy to get Bar Mitvahed, he had to know a fair amount of Hebrew, read from the Torah (the Haftorah) and recite the blessings. So, we can note, in Stozier's formulation, "deeply conflicted and split off attitudes towards his identity as a Jew."

Strozier continues, "Further, there is no reason to believe that just because he grew up as an assimilated Viennese Jew, he failed to consolidate a core sense of self as a member of the larger Jewish community of which he was an integral and formally initiated member. Kohut was not a believing or observant Jew but that begs the question. It would seem that Heinz Kohut negotiated a number of contradictory elements concerning his religious and ethnic identity within which he constructed a personal myth that even in adolescence was moving toward self re-creation."

It was when Kohut was at Billings hospital in the late 40's that, according to Strozier, he began to present himself as "ethnically half Jewish" at most (and not Jewish at all if he thought he could get away with it). Strozier describes the "empathic current" he created for Miss F, a very diffident patient he treated in the 1950's and early 60's. A less successful case was Peter Barglow, Mr. W in Kohut's Restoration of the Self. Barglow, who was a European Jewish immigrant, like Jorge Schnieder, thought he was Christian because he never mentioned Jews or made Jewish jokes. Barglow thought Kohut talked in "a clearly Christian rhetoric." Paul Tolpin had what he considered a classical analysis with Kohut but nevertheless felt that Kohut was empathic throughout.

But we should keep in mind that the issue is not how empathic Kohut was as an analyst with his patients; the issue is how central maintaining an empathic stance was in his theory of technique. I contend that it was central. Strozier characterizes Kohut's paper on empathy as a jewel of his early writing. Freud located empathy in a spectrum from identification to imitation to empathy, but did not discuss the place of empathy in the therapeutic process. For Kohut it was central. Kohut was described as a narcissist; Freud was not. Would we agree that narcissistic individuals lack empathy? Kohut's early work in empathy, according to Strozier, represented a radical departure from the then regnant psychoanalysis, which emphasized drive theory, instincts, ego psychology, and interpretation. His landmark paper on empathy was presented at the 1957 IPA Congress in Paris and published in JAPA in 1959. In it he writes that empathy is the vicarious form of introspection, and that introspection and empathy are the essential ingredients of the investigation of psychological phenomena.

Strozier writes that Kohut "more than any other psychological theorist in recent decades wrote in general about humans in ways that grew intimately out of his own experience (while never doubting that his ideas were in turn historically conditioned)" (Strozier 2001. p. 260). The centrality of introspective-empathic method in data gathering (experience near) and cure defined self psychology for Kohut and other self psychologist like Paul Ornstein, Kohut, according to Strozier, maintains that empathy cures. Kohut writes, "Without anything else happening, without a single interpretation or explanation occurring, empathy in a therapeutic setting has a healing effect on a patient. The experience of prolonged empathic immersion even for those more traditionally dismissed as "unanalyzable" is curative. Some patients require prolonged periods of "only" empathy before they can benefit from interpretive work."

The centrality of empathy for Kohut is evidenced by his four crucial points:

1. Empathy is the oxygen or psychological life. We cannot breathe without it. Therapists who seriously employ empathy see things differently and change the world they encounter
2. It is not gender related
3. Empathy is a more important unifying force than sex
4. Narcissism can be transformed into creativity and empathy and humor.

And about Kohut's narcissism nothing more needs to be said. But I will say more. Glen Gabbard told me that he asked Karl Menninger what he thought of Kohut? Karl replied that he was the most narcissistic human being that he had ever met. Martin Stein told me another story. He and Heinz were in CAPS Group One. CAPS is the Center for Advanced Psychoanalytic Studies which meets in Princeton, New Jersey. Admission is by invitation only and includes the crème de la crème of American psychoanalysis. At their first meeting Kohut took the floor and spoke without interruption from more than half an hour. He only stopped when Stein began swinging his watch chain as Kohut spoke. Kohut never returned to the group.

John Gedo, who had been a close associate of Kohut until they split in the mid seventies, invited Kohut to the last session of the Chicago Institute course he taught on new directions in psychoanalysis. Kohut presented a case with of a patient who prided himself on his sexual performance. After about half an hour Gedo offered that he had a similar case which supported Kohut's thesis. Kohut responded in a dismissive manner, accusing Gedo of trying to aggrandize himself by talking about his own patient. Gedo said he broke with Kohut because Kohut would never give him a straight story about anything, not just about whether or not he was Jewish. Gedo felt that his dissembling tendency increased after he was diagnosed with leukemia in the mid seventies. Kohut experienced this as a narcissistic blow to his sense of omnipotence and for years would frequently change the story about his diagnosis and alter the specific details.

About Kohut playing fast and lose with the truth Strozier writes that Kohut "never seemed to let reality get in the way of a good story." When Kohut was acknowledging his Jewish origins he claimed to be half Jewish (on his father's side), but there is no evidence that his mother converted to Catholicism early in his life. Kirsner writes, "But he went further than being assimilated, he actively disidentified with his Jewish background and became a Christian." As Ernest Wolf put it, "Jewish culture, Jewish food, Jewish jokes were alien to him" (p. 39). He would even feign not understanding Jewish expressions or jokes.

It was Kristallnacht (November 8–9, 1938) that convinced Kohut that he had to leave Austria. And in March 1939 he was able to lead a group of 125 Jews on a transport out of Vienna. It is hard to understand, given his experience fleeing Vienna, why Kohut could deny that he was Jewish and forsake his Jewish identify. I would propose that Christian identity was a false self and his Jewish identity was his disavowed true self. This awareness, perhaps unconscious, made him sensitive to the identity issues of his patients, and he developed self psychology as a mode of helping patients achieve authenticity. There are many examples in his case material about patients reassembling or reconstituting by vocational choices or adopting other ideals.

But we might consider that becoming Christian for Kohut was a gesture in the service of repairing or healing a fragmented self. Strozier maintains that Kohut also was conflicted about his sexual identity and had an important homosexual experience in adolescence with a tutor. We do not know whether these issues were addressed with his first analyst, August Eichhorn in Vienna or his second, Ruth Eisler in Chicago.

Kohut after the early fifties decided to present himself as Christian, gave sermons occasionally at the Unitarian Church, brought up his son Tom as Christian, and hid his Jewish origins from him as he proclaimed he was not Jewish because his mother was not Jewish but his mother converted to Catholicism in 1948. (Kohut's mother died in 1972 after she became paranoid). Another indication of Kohut's narcissism his failure.

Charles Strozier's book, *The Making of a Psychoanalyst,* is a treasure trove of data supporting my thesis: vignettes, descriptions of his behavior, comments about his personality, his relationship to himself and to others. It is a fact that sometime in the late fifties he decided that he was Christian, and that he had never been Jewish, began to attend the Ukrainian Church, became close to the Pastor, and continued his relationship with the Pastor and the Church to the end of his life. He certainly was not the first or the last Viennese to leave Judaism for Christianity. But his insistence that everything Jewish was foreign to him is another matter. Strozier writes that at his birthday party on May 3, 1981, Kohut pretended that he did not know what a bris was and asked his friend Robert Wadsworth to look into the matter, which Wadsworth dutifully did. He told his friend Jerry Biegler that he did not know what Halvah was. At Biegler's first session with Kohut, Beiger, who was concerned with own Jewish identity asked Kohut whether he was Jewish. Strozier writes, "Kohut evaded the question and muttered something about who was Jewish anyway." He told Biegler that he could teach him some Yiddish expressions and that they could manage that way. By the way Biegler had a very good analytic experience with Kohut. David Solomon told a similar story. He had been in analysis with Ann Bergman who was not Jewish and went to see Kohut looking for a better experience. He began the session by asking Kohut if he was Jewish and Kohut said nothing. And after a long pause David said, "'Well, I guess that is off the table' and the subject never came up." Jorge Schneider was very upset when he learned after Kohut had died that he was Jewish. He felt badly that there might have been much that could have been shared because not only were they both Jewish, they were both immigrants starting out in a new country.

Strozier's book is replete with examples of Kohut's self-centeredness. He recounts in great detail Kohut's unwillingness to give his student David Terman any credit for coming up with the theory of a single line of development before Kohut had written about it. He never gave him any credit or talked with him about it, and he did not come to Terman's defense when Terman was attacked for these ideas. Gedo also felt that Kohut had taken Gedo's ideas about self structure but Gedo's of Kohut was much less benign than that of Terman who accepted Kohut's failure to give him credit

Strozier points out that authenticity became an obsession with Kohut. Yet Strozier writes, "Yet in his personal life he harbored secrets and lies." The most striking or flagrant examples is of course the Case of Mr. Z, which has the case of himself. Kohut seemed to enjoy getting away with this deception. His son referred to the case as a "giant prank, which he loved."

I would propose that our hypothesis about the relationship of personality to theories of technique and cure is quite robust in the case of Kohut as I have presented in the forgoing.

Part 2: Melanie Klein and Clinical Theory
By Arlene Kramer Richards[9]

Of all the women who learned, practiced, wrote about and taught psychoanalysis in the years from 1920 to 1960, Melanie Klein was one of the most influential. She contributed highly original and generative ideas. She added theoretical concepts and created radically new techniques. Her life was devoted to her work from her early adulthood to her death. How did the life and the work mesh? What did her new concepts mean for her own way of seeing the world? Did she invent ideas to cover her blind spots?

First, her clinical theory. Among her most important contributions were:

---

9 Arlene Kramer Richards, Ed.D., is a psychoanalyst and a poet. She is a Training and Supervising Analyst with the Contemporary Freudian Society and the International Psychoanalytic Association and Fellow of IPTAR. She is currently faculty at the CFS and Tongji Medical College of Huazhong University of Science and Technology at Wuhan, China. Her psychoanalytic writings have helped clarify and bring to life issues of female development, perversion, loneliness, and the internal world of artists and poets. Most recent publications include "Gambling and Death" in E. Ronis and L. Shaw (Eds.), *Greed, Sex, Money, Power and Politics,* (IPBooks, 2011) and Little Boy Lost. In A. Adelman and K. Malawista (Eds.), *The Bereaved Therapist: From the Faraway Nearby.* (Columbia University Press, 2012), "The Skin I Live In" In A.K. Richards, L. Spira and A.A. Lynch (Eds.) *Encounters With Loneliness: Only the Lonely* (2013) and a book of her papers, *Psychoanalysis: Listening to Understand: Selected Papers of Arlene Kramer Richards* (IPBooks, 2012) *Myths of the Mighty Women* edited by Arlene Kramer Richards and Lucille Spira (Karnac, 2015), Psychoanalysis in Fashion edited by Arlene Kramer Richards and Anita Weinreb Katz (IPBooks, 2019), and Pedro Almodovar: A Cinema of Desire, Passion and Compulsion edited by Arlene Richards and Lucile Spira (IPBooks, 2019). She also published a book of poetry *The Laundryman's Granddaughter: Poems by Arlene Kramer Richards,* (IPBooks, 2011). She is a former representative from North America to the IPA. She is in Private Practice in Palm Beach, Florida.

1.   The importance of investigating the first year of life;

2.   The idea that disorganized and disorganizing anxiety fueled by aggression in the first year must be tamed in the adult treatment by interpretation;

3.   The importance of the <u>analyst</u> taming aggression by interpreting it; and

4.   Interpreting the defensive splitting of love objects into a good object and a bad object with the intent of integrating an image of a partly good and a partly bad object which results in the depressive position;

5.   Recognizing and interpreting to the patient the process of projective identification;

6.   Focusing on the affects of envy and gratitude as opposites.

These contributions were made over time, taught to generations of child and adult analysts, and found helpful by patients and their analysts. What follows in the way of seeing these contributions as reactions to her own failures and lacks is not meant to diminish her achievements in any way. Rather, it is meant in the spirit of admiration for the overcoming of personal shortcomings in the service of helping others to overcome theirs.

1. The importance of the infant's feelings in the first year of life and the importance of the mother's presence at that time was her first great contribution and her first break with Freud's idea that the third through sixth years were the crux of personality formation. Klein came to this idea after she had been absent from the first year of life of her son Hans who later died in what Klein's daughter Melitta insisted was suicide. Klein had been away visiting Budapest, Rosenberg and Abbazia when Melitta was a three year old and Hans was a baby. She left them again when she went to a sanatorium in Switzerland two years later. It is interesting that Erik, the only one of her children who remained on speaking terms with her as an

adult was sent out to be wet-nursed as an infant. He had not experienced her as a mother in the first year of his life. Thus, she was advising clinicians what she had to remind herself: that attention must be paid to the infant in the first year of life even when it is impossible for the infant to put her feelings into words and for the adult to remember what happened in that year. Reconstructing what might have happened to account for the way the infant felt was then the only road to becoming interested in the infant's experience.

2. The idea of disorganizing aggression aroused by loss of the mother, delay of feeding and/or maternal un-involvement reflects clearly Klein's experience of having been an unavailable mother. The effects of maternal intrusiveness are similarly echoed in the intense and insistent interpretations of very early traumas interpreted early in the treatment in the classically Kleinian clinical theory. Maternal intrusiveness is evidenced by the intrusiveness that Klein's own mother. Grosskurth (1986) concludes her description of Melanie's mother's intrusiveness: "Libussa felt compelled to arrange her children's lives like pawns on a chessboard" (p. 20).

3. The importance of the analyst taming aggression by interpreting it is central to Klein's clinical theory. This is in great contrast to her personal reaction to those who disagreed with her. Whether her children or her disciples, her tolerance for their disagreement was not sufficient to prevent breaks in the relationships that lasted for decades, and in some cases for life. For example, according to Grosskurth (1986): "Many British analysts regarded Klein as ruthless in the way she discarded people if they did not subscribe wholeheartedly to her person and her ideas—not only Heimann, but also Rickman, Winnicott, Riviere, Eva Rosenfeld, and Clifford Scott." (P.424). Klein's own daughter pleaded with her to overcome this implacable attitude toward difference and to stop interpreting every difference as an

attack on her when she wrote to her mother: "I certainly can, with your help, retain a good and friendly relationship with you , if you allow me enough freedom, independence, and dissimilarity, and if you try to be less sensitive about certain things" (p. 199). She signed the letter "With love, yours, Melitta" (p. 199). Despite this overture, Klein remained so angry with her that she effectively forced her out of London and out of Klein's life. By contrast, Klein's account of her clinical theory emphasizes the analyst's acceptance of the child's negative feelings toward her and the clinical efficacy of doing that. In her own words: "I may discover, in a child's mind, while he is in my playroom, that the strong anxiety revealed is due to the fact that in phantasy I, the analyst, am an awful witch who is going to cut him in pieces. Through my interpretation I resolve this special anxiety, the child begins to play happily, and I may then become a nice fairy to him. This would mean that through my interpretation I have been able to resolve the negative transference, and that has resulted in the positive transference coming up" (p. 235).

4. The fourth contribution, that of integrating the bad and good in the object rather than splitting objects into bad and good was a problem throughout her life for Klein herself. Most notably she was unable to maintain relationships when the other person seemed to her to be totally bad because of a disagreement or a failure to be useful to her or her group. In her terms, the other person became the bad mother when that person did not do what Klein wanted or disagreed with Klein's ideas. She divorced her husband, feuded with her daughter and never reconciled with her; she publicly feuded with each of her proteges Edward Glover, Paula Heimann, Donald Winnicott, John Rickman, W. Clifford Scott and Winifred Bion and never reconciled with any of them. She was clearly not a person who could see the good in those close to her once they aroused her aggression.

Therefore, she had to remind herself that treating her patients required exactly that: mastering aggression.

5. Recognizing and interpreting to the patient the defense of projective identification. This clarification of who is experiencing an emotion and who is reflecting the experience of the other is an important part of the analytic process that requires the constant monitoring of one's own feelings, tracing them back to one's prior experience and separating them from what is being experienced by the other person and attributed to oneself. This process takes time and thinking. It is counter to the rapid intuitive responses that were characteristic of Klein's interactions with others; Winnicott had once described her as "a Eureka shrieker." The possibility that the analyst is mis-perceiving the interaction between analyst and patient is too great to be ignored. Klein needed to be careful of her own proclivity to blame others and the idea of projective identification brought this danger to the fore in both her own analyses and those she supervised.

6. The opposition of envy and gratitude is more complex than her other contributions. It involves painful feelings. For Klein the envier, the infant who has nothing and needs everything is the victim of envy. The feeling of wanting and not having causes the baby to hate the mother. Here again her need to be the mother she could not be for her own babies resulted in a clinical insight. She understood the need to present to the patient for the feelings of anger, even rage, at the mother for having the breast to give or to take away which the patient had a baby and persist into the present. Her need to protect herself from the envy she had experienced as child when she was the youngest and unwanted baby in her family, when her mother preferred her sister and brothers to her and continually criticized her for her demanding-ness had to have created a kind of envy that arises out of competitiveness. By pushing the envy back to an earlier

time in development, the pain of her own later envy was partly assuaged by attributing it to an earlier stage and the baby rather than the small child. Her theory also left out the pain of being envied, an experience that had to arise out of her being her father's favorite, the beauty of the family and the most talented of the children. According to Grosskurth (1986) her biographer, Klein had reason to envy her daughter when Melitta was a medical student, in analysis with Eitingon, who was also a doctor, and was being courted by a handsome, charming man who was the benefactor of the Freud family. Yet Klein only wrote about the girl's envy of her mother, not of the mother's envy of her daughter. I presume that since her theory came from her practice, she only interpreted the daughter's envy as well. So, looking at the transference and soft pedaling the counter-transference was a way to avoid the pain of acknowledging her envy of her daughter and, even more crucial, her mother's envy of her. Could one see this as protecting the analyst from the unbearable and thus safeguarding the analytic situation? Protecting the mother and the mothering function when the baby was little was not something Klein learned from her own mother. When Klein had her first baby Melitta, Klein's mother, according to Grosskurth, "showed only the slightest interest in the baby, and her recital of her problems would have disturbed any possibility of Melanie's serenity while looking after her little girl" (p. 43).

This attitude was in contrast to Freud's advice to the family of a woman who had just given birth that they were to feed her the most elegant foods, pamper her and encourage her feelings of wanting to give to her baby. Ironically, that baby may have been Anna Freud. My point here is that Melanie Klein had to remind herself that taking care of the mother and the new baby was important because she herself had not had that care when she had a new baby. Libussa, Melanie's mother sent her away to a spa after her second child was born telling Melanie that her husband, her children and her mother were much happier when she was gone. Clearly she had to remind herself that a mother was essential to a baby's development to counter such denigration of her maternal function.

While Klein talked of the relationship between envy and gratitude as opposites, she was specifically referring to a baby's envy of its mother and her capacity to give and withhold the breast, the source of warmth, food, and tenderness. If the baby envied the mother this power, then the mother became the hated trigger for that envy. The alternative was for the baby to feel gratitude toward the mother for these comforts. Klein believed that this characterized the clinical situation which brings back the feeling of being with someone who holds the power to soothe, but also the power to withhold that soothing.

REFERENCE

Grosskurth, P. (1986). *Melanie Klein: Her World and Her Work.* New York: Knopf. Sayers, J. (1991). *Mothers of Psychoanalysis.* New York: Norton.

Part 3: The Work and Times of Karen Horney by Arthur Lynch.[10]

INTRODUCTION

Karen Horney was perhaps one of the most courageous psychoanalysts of her time. Born in 1885 and raised in Hamburg, Germany she: challenged

---

10 Arthur A. Lynch, PhD is President of the Board of Directors, Senior Faculty member, Training and Supervising Analyst at the American Institute for Psychoanalysis. He is an Adjunct Professor at Columbia University School of Social Work and is Board Certified in Psychoanalysis by ABECSW. Dr. Lynch has authored and co-author numerous articles on

male privilege, broke with social norms, modified and extended psychoanalytic theory against the father of the field and against the norm. She also bore the consequences that this courage often brings and was politically minimized while in New York.

To get an appreciation of Karen Horney's work, insight into her life and times is essential. One way to look at her life is through the lens of rejection by another; as well as the need to respond to that rejection through attempts at reparation and repairing contact with the rejecting other; or, by devaluing and dismissing them. This was a major painful emotional motif in her life and work.

Biographical information

Karen Horney was born in Hamburg, Germany in 1885. She grew up in a tumultuous family. Her father Berndt Henrik Wackels Danielsen (a.k.a. Wackels) was a steamship captain who charted the seas between Hamburg and Chile and was absent most of each year. His nature was to complain and bully but he relied on his wife "Sonni" (Clothilde Marie Danielsen, Horney's mother) to take care of him. (Q. p. 22). This was Wackels's second marriage, at age 44, and Sonni's first at age 28. Sonni was unhappy in her marriage. She had two children of her own with Wackels. The first was Berndt adored for his looks and charm. The second, 3.5 years younger, was Karen who was known as the smarter one, as well as "the character." There were also four more adult children from Wackels' prior marriage. The marital unhappiness divided the family loyalties along parental lines. Karen and her brother Brent sided with their mother who would burden

psychoanalysis. He is co-editor of Encounters with Loneliness, Only the Lonely with Arlene K Richards and Lucille Spira (2013), and editor of five volumes of The Selected Papers of Arnold D. Richards. Dr. Lynch is in private practice in New York City.

them with the responsibility for her happiness until she separated with her husband 24 years later. This took its toll on both children.

Even in a house divided where there are conscious alliances and devaluations of the other side, there are often unspoken yearnings and desire, as well. Karen longed to be close with her absentee-father, but this would never have happened. This environment left Karen not only feeling rejected and searching for solutions but also hating to be left out.

One way she dealt with the pangs of being rejected was through denial. Another way she dealt with feeling rejected was to devalue and reject first. The final way, to deal with feeling rejected was to create a better imaginary father in the figure of one of her teachers —Herr Schulze. This is a form of idealization and the pining for an internal ideal father/object acted to compensate for her missing real father. This last coping strategy—an idealizing tendency—played an important role in her theory and in her future relationships with men. But at this young time in her life, she turned to Herr Schulze and took on an intellectual quest. "School", she would say in her diary "is the only true thing after all." (Diaries, 22).

Karen had a good deal of luck. As Fate would have it, Gymnasium study for women was spreading in Germany beginning in 1897. Karen was ready to go but her father did not want to pay. Women, after all were not supposed to be intellects or professionals. Karen would eventually propose a contract that once she finished her education her father would no longer have to do anything for her. Both parties agreed. Karen went through the Gymnasium and received her medical degree from Berlin University in 1915. During this time, she met and married Oskar Horney (1909) and had three children: Brigitte (1911), Marianne (1913) and Renate (1916). She entered analysis with Karl Abraham in the summer of 1910 and continued through 1911 at 6 times a week. In May 1910 Karen's father, Wackels, dies and he is shortly followed by her mother in early 1911. By 1912 she was in Abraham's evening clinical seminars as well as, conducting her first analysis.

Professionally Horney was underway. In 1917, she wrote her first paper "The Technique of Psychoanalytic Therapy" and becomes a founding member of the Berlin Psychoanalytic Institute in 1920. By 1926 here marriage to Oskar, which had been strained, ended.

As her interests in psychoanalysis grew she joined the teaching staff at the Berlin psychoanalytic clinic, developed its training program and curriculum, and began writing her controversial papers on femininity. Abraham dies in 1925 and she stayed on as a major presence until 1932.

A Word about the Berlin Psychoanalytic Institute

In spite of economic and political turmoil, the period in Berlin between 1920 and 1930 saw a cultural renaissance. What happened in Berlin provided the spirit that gave the Berlin psychoanalytic community its very special character of challenging its members to extend and improve psychoanalytic theory. Six analysts founded the Berlin Psychoanalytic Institute in 1920; five men (Karl Abraham, Hans Sachs, Max Eitingon, Sándor Radó, and Carl Müller-Braunschweig) and one woman, Karen Horney. A wide array of talent was drawn to Berlin to join the early founders including: Franz Alexander, Helena Deutsch, Ernst Simmel, Siegfried Bernfeld, Heinz Hartmann, Otto Fenichel, Rudolf Loewenstein, Edith Jacobson, Theodor Reik, Annie and Wilhelm Reich, Melanie Klein, and Alice and Michael Balint. The circle around Freud in Vienna tended towards promoting Freud's developing theory, while the members in Berlin were involved in bringing psychoanalysis to the community at large and providing public educative lectures to social workers, educators, and others. The Vienna group emphasized the inevitable tension between libido

392

and civilization. The Berlin analysts viewed psychoanalysis as a force that would free the human creative potential and allow it to unfold. Once again, Karen Horney was in the right place at the right time.

In 1932 Franz Alexander wrote and invited her to be his Associate Director at the new Chicago Psychoanalytic Institute. She held this post for two years before she moved to New York to become a training analyst at the New York Psychoanalytic Institute.

In 1937 she wrote *The Neurotic Personality of Our Time* where she clearly stated her beliefs and the importance of culture and environment on the development of neuroses. In 1939, she wrote *New Ways in Psychoanalysis* where she detailed her disagreements with Freud. This led to the loss of her teaching appointment and her resignation at NYPSI. In 1941 she founded both the American Institute for Psychoanalysis, as well as the *American Journal of Psychoanalysis*. Here she was Dean and guiding spirit of the Institute and the Journal until her death on December 4, 1952.

Honey's Major Contributions

Horney made her contributions to clinical theory by challenging areas of restriction and oppression, a battle she had been waging since her childhood, with an austere father and a restrictively demanding mother.

Her main contributions fall into four major areas that traverse three phases:

1. Model of the mind: Gender theory, True self.
2. Model Development: Basic anxiety, Character theory, Cultural theory.
3. Model of Pathology.
4. Model of Psychoanalytic technique.

Horney's earliest works (1920ish–1930s) in psychoanalysis were dedicated to feminine psychology. She wrote a series of 20 essays in which she tried to modify these ideas while staying within the overall Freudian framework[11]. She had just come out of a period of giving birth to and raising three daughters, as well as maintaining her training and practice. These were positive experiences for Horney that did not match the prevailing theory of penis envy nor Freud's belief that healthy women enjoy suffering and are biologically predestined to be masochistic and submissive. These experiences combined with a restrictive cultural credo from her childhood "Kinder, Küche, Kirche" (translated: children, kitchen, church),[12] defined the role and values of women, in Germany. Horney resented women defined by these criteria (3 Ks). It was this restrictive thinking that erected unnecessary barriers in her life simply because she was a woman. It was this insult to women that prompted her to reevaluate this part of the early psychoanalytic theory.

Childbirth, according to Freud, was only a substitute and partial compensation for the lack of a penis. Horney wondered: "I, as a woman ask in amazement, and what about motherhood? And the blissful consciousness of bearing a new life within oneself? (1926) Both Freud and Abraham insisted that little girls had penis envy, a deep-seated desire to be boys. Jones who supported Horney's view thought that: "Freud saw girls as nothing more than damaged little boys." (Jones, 1927, vol 8, p. 459-472 *IJP*)

Horney's response to both Freud and Abraham's point of view is telling:

---

11 She engages the topic with an investigative methodology that she will use for several of her later books. First, she evaluates each of Freud's concepts pertaining to women and identifies the debatable portions. Next, she checks the theory with her clinical experiences. Finally, she contrasts the knowledge with her own experience as a woman.

12 Kinder, Küche, Kirche also known as the 3 Ks, was the slogan many men and women proudly defined as the female role model in the 19th Century. The phrase started to appear in writing in the early 1890s.

In this formulation we have it assumed as an axiomatic fact, that females feel at a disadvantage in this respect of their genital organs, without being regarded as constituting a problem in itself—possibly because to masculine narcissism this has seemed too self-evident to need explanation. Nevertheless, the conclusion so far drawn from the investigations—amounting as it does to an assertion that one-half of the human race is discontent with the sex assigned to it and can overcome this discontent only in favorable circumstances—is decidedly unsatisfying, not only to feminine narcissism but also to biological science.

She went on to argued that penis envy was not a given but the result of restrictions placed on girls for instinctual gratification. She also employed the new "I" psychology to make a different argument, one with large ramifications for gender identity. She reformulated the production of a girl's penis envy as a secondary result of the frustration of any child's early sexual life, her/his Oedipal defeat. It was the little girl's recognition that she was not her father's primary love that led some girls to a repudiate their own sexuality and create a defensive desire to become identified with the father and be a boy. Only in this fantastic retreat did girls encounter penis envy. Similarly, she argued that boys could be subject to the same dynamics. Boys can identify psychologically with their mothers and develop castration terrors. Horney went on to write about the unpredictable course of character development in light of the Oedipal complex in her papers on masculine women. In her later papers, she takes it a bit further and notes that there is an unconscious tendency to devalue women by men because of "womb-envy," a male envy of pregnancy, childbirth, and motherhood, and of the breasts, and suckling. In these she introduced one of her greatest contributions—the role of culture. She insisted that Freud was mistaking as biological many matters that were essentially cultural.

Ultimately, she modifies Freud's thinking about penis envy, female masochism, and feminine development, which were all controversial at the time. Horney proposed a "primary femininity" indicating that females have intrinsic biological constitutions and patterns of development that must be understood in their own terms. In proposing this she wonders whether the entire foundation of psychoanalytic theory had tended to neglect female psychology and may be only half correct. Freud had to concede to her criticism that for those who considered his ideas the result of his male subjectivity, he stood "defenseless" (Female Sexuality, Freud. 1931).

But Horney's contributions thus far were a testament to the freedom and encouragement of the Berlin Institute. In these papers, Horney took her place as one of Berlin's major thinkers besides her two Hungarian colleagues Sándor Radó and Franz Alexander. Rado and Horney were both analyzed by Abraham, around the same time. Both contributed creatively to the theoretical area between Abraham and Freud. Both extended and modified the new Psychoanalytic theory. It is unfortunate that only 30 years later, at the New York Psychoanalytic Society and Institute (NYPSI), Horney would become severely marginalized in a broader struggle for power between Lawrence Kubie and Sándor Radó; as Kubie moved to reduce the influence of all the Berliners at the NYPSI. Meanwhile it was Alexander the first candidate and first graduate of the Berlin Institute that attempted to forge a new theoretical consensus on this middle ground. Perhaps one might say that, the third attempt at a Total Composite Psychoanalytic Theory can be found in his 1927 book *Psychoanalysis of the Total Personality*. The first two were Freud's Topographical Model and his Structural Model.

Model of the Mind and Development

Horney's theory of human behavior and character structure was ultimately based on the humanistic theme that saw the person as continually striving to evolve and realize a sense of self. This theme highlights the importance of the culture, the family, and the environment as the source of both healthy and neurotic behavior.

Horney in her second phase of theory building begins by critiquing Freud's basic concepts with the aim of extending Freud's and Abraham's theory. In *New Ways in Psychoanalysis* (1939), she chose the debatable ideas and listed her objections to 14 of Freud's basic concepts. These list includes: libido theory, the Oedipus complex, narcissism, feminine psychology, the death instinct, emphasis on early childhood, transference, culture & neurosis, the ego & id, anxiety, the superego, neurotic guilt, masochism, psychoanalytic treatment. She makes it clear that she is not attempting to refute psychoanalysis. She says: "the purpose of this book is not to show what is wrong with psychoanalysis, but, through eliminating the debatable elements, to enable psychoanalysis to develop to the height of its potentialities.... As a result... I believe that the range of problems which can be understood is enlarged considerably.... "(1939, p. 8). Here she is trying to extend her earlier thinking on Femininity and the work she has been engaged in since 1917 on broadening her understanding around the models of human developmental and psychopathology. She defines her solution in a nutshell:

> ... psychoanalysis should outgrow the limitation set by its being an instinctivistic and a genetic psychology. As to the latter, Freud tends to regard later peculiarities as almost direct repetitions of infantile drives or reactions; hence he expects later disturbances to vanish if the underlying infantile experiences are elucidated. When

we relinquish this one-sided emphasis on genesis, we recognize that the connection between later peculiarities (inhibitions & symptoms) and earlier experiences is more complicated than Freud assumes: there is no such thing as an isolated repetition of isolated experiences; but the entirety of infantile experiences combines to form a certain character structure, and it is this structure from which later difficulties emanate. Thus, the analysis of the actual character structure moves into the foreground of attention. (Horney, 1939, p. 9).

Model of the Mind–The Self

From birth, each human being is composed of a unique combination of biological endowments that are given expression through living in a specific and distinct environment of family and culture. Horney found that basic to all human development was the principle of growth, a powerful force driving individuals towards the development of their own particular potentialities.

> You need not, and, in fact, cannot teach an acorn to grow into an oak tree… the human individual, given the chance, will develop the unique alive forces of his real self…. that central inner force, common to all human beings and yet unique to each, which is the deep source of growth. (Horney, 1950, p. 17).

Her concept of the "real self", is her model of the mind, and is basic to her theories of health and of neurosis. A person's real self is the source of that person's energy, aliveness, and spontaneity; it is one's sense of whom one is. The self that is referred to when one speaks of finding oneself. The dynamic core of one's being provides a sense of identity. Hartmann (1950) clarified Freud's use of "das Ich," ego or self? Hartmann redefines narcissism as a libidinal cathexis of the self and not the ego, which distinguishes three specific and different domains of Freud's concept of das Ich: as ego, as self-experience, and as self or person (i.e., identity). This refinement Richards (1982 Superordinate) showed, offered analysts a new way to designate the complex nature of wishes, fantasies, identifications, and attitudes; of the "representational world" (Sandler and Rosenblatt, 1962).

MODEL OF HUMAN DEVELOPMENT

Horney suggests that developmentally favourable conditions allow personal growth to occur according to one's own capabilities, skills, desires, and capacity, giving rise to the emergence of the Real Self. This development is lost in pernicious conditions. The idea of an actualizing life force is similar to Aristotle's "entelechy"; the actuality opposed to the potentiality. It is the "élan vital." the creative force within an organism, that is responsible for growth, change, and vitality. For Horney, self-realization is the process of allowing the real self to unfold and is synonymous with the healthy growth, which she calls the "constructive forces." It is the result of loving and respectful relationships from childhood. It is the outcome of these relationships that determines how far the self-realization process will evolve to create an unshakable inner sense of integration. This process directs the individual in healthy activities, during which one *moves toward others* to express love and trust, *moves against others* to express healthy friction and mastery of the environment, and *moves away from others* to express one's needs for autonomy and self-sufficiency. These same interpersonal moves when trying to stem the tide of "basic anxiety" have a very different flavour.

To the extent that the child feels secure and develops genuine self-esteem, all is well. To the extent that he struggles with sustained damaging influences, deep insecurities, or "Basic Anxiety" lead to feelings of helplessness and isolation. This is the feeling of being alone in a hostile world. Basic anxiety is intolerable if it is intense and sustained. The child must act to alleviate it. Horney captures the child's possibilities noting the child can: seek affection and approval, get angry, or retreat. When this happens, the moves are in the service of mitigating anxiety and not serving self-realization. When basic anxiety occurs "moving toward others" now becomes whatever appears to be the most satisfiable tactic to obtain safety. It may appear as a demonstrated compliance, clinging dependence or neediness, or a form of self-deletion or effacement. Similarly, "moving against others" may become aggressive, exploitative, inflated, contemptuous, competitive, arrogant or controlling. These are found in tendencies of perfectionism, vindictiveness and grandiosity. Finally, "moving away or detaching from others" is now in the service of avoidance. Avoiding any conflicts that are characterized by submission, acquiescence, resignation or domination, isolation, desolation. In short, basic anxiety leads to a search for "safety," whether by searching for love and approval, becoming angry and combative, or by retreating internally or externally.

Ingram (2001) has pointed out four characteristics of these "moves" 1) They begin in a simple form in infancy, traceable to mother-child interactions, and develop into complex behavioural patterns over the course of maturity. 2) These "moves" are not only in connection to another person but also develop intrapsychic representations of the other and of the self. 3) Health is determined by the individual's capacity to move appropriately and flexibly when circumstances demand change. It is this plasticity that allows for multiple coping strategies. 4) It is when the strivings of the alternate moves are repressed and replaced with the emergence of a dominant style that unconscious conflict emerges. If these unconscious conflicts become dominant (i.e., rigid, demanding and generalized) they form the "basic conflict." The basic conflict is the perceptual set that the anxious person filters reality through. When this lens become the dominant filter the other two alternatives are repressed. The result of this is a narrowing of the person's coping ability and what Horney called the emergence of "the neurotic solution." The aim of the neurotic solution is to provide immediate relief and safety from anxiety. The relatively healthy individual can exercise authority while expressing affection and trust in others. He can also maintain a healthy friction and while withdrawing or detaching from his affection when necessary. He is able to thrive in an environment because he has the means to manage conflicting impulses and feelings.

The potential for healthy growth, Horney believed, is always a present possibility. It is a constructive force. If the individual develops neurotic solutions, blockages form to interfere with their growth, and these have to be worked through before the individual can continue making gains in self-realization. For Horney however, no matter how isolated and out of touch a person becomes from their sense of self; no matter how alienated they are, she believed deeply that one "can change and go on changing as long as they live." (Horney ,1945, p.19). It is this inner force that helps the individual endure even in the most difficult of times.

Model of Psychopathology

Horney saw neurosis as culturally induced and therefore subject to modification. She further viewed the neurotic process as a warped form of human development, which interfered with the realization of a person's own potential. She states:

Under inner stress, however, a person may become alienated from his real self. He will then shift the major part of his energies to the task of moulding himself, by a rigid system of inner dictates, into a being of absolute perfection. For nothing short of godlike perfection can fulfil his idealized image of himself and satisfy his pride in the exalted attributes which (so he feels) he has, could have, or should have (Horney, 1950, p. 13).

When the individual has been forced to rely on neurotic solutions to attain a sense of safety, pathological forces have come into play. Now the child must restrict his actions to what is acceptable in his environment. Where this restriction offers a sense of safety it is compromised by the growing sense of anxiety, which acts as a constant inner danger. This requires the child to be on alert and restricts further expression of genuine feelings. As long as this threatening circumstance remains, a solution is required to repress and rid the child of his anxious feeling. The power of these solutions comes from their ability to provide the child with a sense of safety. A toxic cycle ensues of anxiety, partial relief and uncertainty. The conflicted feelings are pushed further and further away from consciousness creating a sense of dissociation, discomfort, dread and an overall uncertainty of one's sense of self. What began as an attempt to reduce anxiety has become a demanding and rigid pattern of behaviour that is fueled by fear. This pattern hardens not only in behaviour but also the specific attitudes and beliefs which support the behaviour and this further restricts the possibility for growth. Horney (1945) noted:

The neurotic is not flexible; he is driven to comply, to fight, to be aloof regardless of whether the move is appropriate in the particular circumstance, and he is thrown into panic if he behaves otherwise.... [Those attitudes] do not remain restricted to the area of human relationships but gradually pervade the entire personality. They end by encompassing not only the person's relation to others but also his relation to himself and life in general.

Horney agreed with Freud that the unconscious is characterized by hidden conflict, which ranges from mild to severe, from symptom formation to character pathology and a profound sense of alienation. She suggested that the neurotic trends tend to fall into ascribable character types that are molded around a core attitude towards the self and other. This core attitude is deeply rooted in experience and supported by a system of secondary approaches to tension relief. She suggested that the neurotic trends tend to fall into three main character types. These are grounded in the individual's prominent form of relating. These character types are: the compliant, self-effacing type; the aggressive, expansive type; and the detached, resigned type.

The Compliant, self-effacing character type moves towards others to manage his anxiety. This individual is pursuing approval and appreciation, at any cost. Because of these needs, the individual strives to avoid rejection and disapproval. Some common terms identifying these kinds of individual's are: backslapper, bootlicker, doormat, flatterer, groveler, parasite, politician, puppet, brownnoser. These individuals are often sensitive to the needs of others, basically agreeable and unselfish. Any assertiveness, becoming the center of attention, or hostility, produce anxiety and are driven from consciousness. Their primary considerations are informed by a guiding principle "that love conquers all."

These individuals are so alienated from their true feelings that they often cannot protect themselves. This leaves them vulnerable to be taken advantage of and frequently in a state of inner turmoil. As a result, they desperately seek partners who will take care of them and organize their lives. Interpersonal friction is unbearable as it brings the possibility of rejection and being alone. These individual's usually present in the couple as the self-effacing member.

The aggressive, expansive character types are individuals who move against others to manage their anxiety. They strive for dominance over others, and perfection in themselves. Their primary considerations are informed by a guiding principle that "it is a dog eat dog" world we live in where "only the strong survive." These individual's need to achieve and feel superior to others. As such, there is no room for tender or loving feelings even in intimate relationships, where they do demand admiration and submission but not love or compassion. These latter feelings are seen as weaknesses to be exploited in others. This group can be separated into three subgroups: the narcissistic person; the arrogant-vindictive person; and the perfectionistic person. Individuals in this large group typically present for treatment due to some failure in their lives that leaves them feeling powerless, e.g., an unexpected job loss or demotion, the failure of a marriage.

The Detached, resigned type of individual moves away from others to manage their anxiety. Their primary considerations are informed by a guiding principle "no muss no fuss." This individual avoids conflict at all costs. This includes relationship or work commitments or any activity (e.g., competition, asking for help) that stimulates feelings of involvement. They often develop compensatory feeling of superiority based on their feelings of self-sufficiency, safeguard their need for privacy, and hold their freedom as the greatest value. Clinically individuals in this group seek treatment far less then other character types but may enter treatment when they become aware of their needs for others.

AUXILIARY APPROACHES TO ARTIFICIAL HARMONY (1945)

When the individual promotes one of the basic moves the other two become repressed. Although no longer available to consciousness these alternate moves are active and continue to create psychological stress and strain, which is called "basic conflict" (Horney, 1945). The individual uses these auxiliary methods to reduce the inner tensions created by the basic conflict. There are general measures to relieve tension and to further defend against disruption of the neurotic solution and the sense of wholeness it provides, however, fragile. These include compartmentalization, automatic control, supremacy of the mind, blind spots, rationalization, arbitrary rightness, elusiveness, cynicism, narcotization, and externalization (projection).[13] We can each add or subtract from these as we see needed.

When the neurotic process is underway, restrictions are imposed and these moves—toward, away, and against—become increasingly rigid and inflexible. Here the person's "primary move" is elevated and activated and the "alternate moves" that are in conflict with the primary move remain unconscious but in a constant struggle for expression, against the primary move. The constant flux of the pressure created by these alternate moves provides the dynamics that are so crucial to understanding the person in clinical context and making sense of inconsistencies. The internal conflict generated by these opposing strivings, which have become not only rigid and fixed, but demanding, repetitive, and generalized, was called the "basic conflict." This constitutes for Horney the "neurotic solution" to the underlying problem of "basic anxiety." (Horney, 1945)

---

13 The person may take some action to ward off or control the imagined danger, perhaps by humiliating or abandoning or even destroying the other.

In order to retain a sense of integration and wholeness, the neurotic person must avoid awareness of conflict. Of course, these solutions are actually partial solutions because the person is relying on a quick fix for their anxiety. When the neurotic process is underway, restrictions are imposed. Ways of feeling, thinking, and acting that are experienced as at odds with the primary solution are automatically and unconsciously rejected; the person is alienated further from them.

The neurotic process supplants self-realization, and the person becomes more and more alienated and impoverished. In order to retain a sense of integration and wholeness, the neurotic person must avoid awareness of conflict. When awareness threatens it is internally rejected or questioned rather than acknowledged as valuable. The person must act immediately to get rid of the feeling or thought. The person is just affirming, more strongly, his or her neurotic solution is not enough, and more profound measures become necessary. What else does the person in the thrall of the neurotic process do to protect the solution? To bolster the neurotic solution to the basic conflict by use of externalization, the person may unconsciously elect to experience internal attitudes, feelings, and impulses as occurring outside the self—or may respond with disproportionate intensity to certain external events. The defenses, plus externalization, plus alienation, plus the neurotic solution are "like bands of steel holding together the person's psyche," (Ingram, 2001) keeping it from exploding outward. That should be enough, but it isn't. Yet another structural support is necessary to sustain the increasingly complex personality of the neurotic.

Depending on which orientation one has selected, that vision is elevated to a status of utter grandiosity. The person is not merely kind, tough or one who enjoys freedom but the kindest, or fiercest, or freest person one could imagine. With the idealized image, the neurotic solution becomes a comprehensive solution. The neurotic seeks the transformation into this "idealized-self," a transformation that is the very antithesis of self-realization. The quest to actualize the idealized self is unconscious and we may catch only a brief glimpse of its shadow. To the extent that the neurotic images he or she has become an idealized self, there is a "sense of pride" in the neurotic's search for glory. Glory is the quest to become one's idealized self, finally, for once and for all. Catching a glimpse of his actual self, perhaps when a "claim" is frustrated or when a "should" is not achieved, the neurotic may fill with self-hate. The person hates himself for falling so far short of the idealized self. In hating oneself for failing to fulfil inner dictates the person further endorses those same dictates and the neurotic process.

The Model of Psychoanalytic Technique

On a close read we will see that this theoretical shift for Horney had a greater impact on her thinking about the mind, development and pathogenesis than it did on her theory of technique. In this way she retained much of Freud's basic technical concepts (unconscious process; psychic conflict and the essential features of existing psychoanalytic technique: resistance, defense, transference, countertransference and interpretation). What changed was the focus of what was being analysed by the analytic method. As we will see, she did not only analyse, but she also added other features to the analytic relationship. Horney's model of technique is taken from her theoretical framework. Since 1917 she stressed the unity of theory and practice.

All psychoanalytic theories in their entirety have been formed out of observation and experiences which were made using the psychoanalytic method. These theories in turn exert their influence on psychoanalytic practice. The intimate interrelationship of theory and practice makes it difficult to appreciate or understand one without the other.

Horney (1937) stressed the focus of her work on the unceasing neurotic process of the patient. She rejected the idea that we repeat childhood experiences and did not believe that discovering childhood memories had therapeutic value.

She said: "the attitudes we see in the adult patient are not direct repetitions or revivals of infantile attitudes, but have been changed in quality and quantity by the consequences which have developed out of the early experiences."

Instead, Horney emphasized in her work that neurotic individuals expressed self-perpetuating dynamic structures that caused them anxiety, fears and blockages. These require careful analytic work to free the patients and return them to healthy growth. In treatment, Horney understood and emphasized the constructive use of the analyst's feelings in the analytic relationship. She also emphasized the use of dreams in the analytic process.

Horney shapes her treatment approach with a philosophical view that there are inherent constructive forces, as well as an inborn capacity to make choices and change in one's life. She saw psychoanalysis as a relationship with the aim of helping rid the patient of their compulsive character structure and to mobilize the forces of creative living and self-realization. It is the analyst's responsibility to assist patients in the process to overcome the obstructive forces that retard healthy growth, which she called "blockages."

Blockages are patient efforts to thwart the analyst's help. They resist and prevent change by maintaining the status quo. Even though the patient has sought help for their suffering they simultaneously defend the delicate mental unity that the neurotic character structure offers. After all, on some level this is all they know. All blockages serve defensive purposes.

David Rapaport (1944) wrote in *The Scientific Methodology of Psychoanalysis* that Karen Horney's discussion of the defences had anticipated Anna Freud's influential book *The Ego and the Mechanisms of Defense*. He wrote:

> Horney really was the one who, possibly somewhat earlier than Anna Freud, pushed the investigation of defense mechanisms to the fore, justifiably so, because the psychoanalytic method allows and obliges the analyst to investigate both the unconscious material the patient prevents himself from communicating and the defense mechanisms by which he chooses to prevent, or to get by without such communication (p. 206).

This protective reaction is particularly true in the initial phase of therapy when the blockages are uncovered, identified, examined and clarified. Horney calls this the "disillusioning process." As the patient becomes aware of these blockages, they often intensify. There are two main groups of blockages. First, there are those that primarily serve a sense of safety. These are called the "protective blockages" and are activated to prevent anxiety caused by self-awareness. These defences are used to resist the analyst's efforts to examine the compulsive nature of the patient's present behaviour patterns, e.g., silence, lateness, cancellations, narcotizing, expressed disappointment or depreciation of the analyst's values, pseudocompliance, self-accusations to produce further insights. The second group of blockages are those that serve the deceptive aim of self-satisfaction of the idealized image. These are called the "positive-value blockages" and are actively used to make the patients feel integrated and whole. These defences are used to prevent self-awareness by promoting a state of satisfaction with themselves as experienced by the ideal image. Patients use these to reinforce their claims on others, to justify their exploitation of others, and to permit acts of vindictiveness.

Horney notes that in the first phase of treatment—the disillusioning process, the analyst is quite active in identifying and clarifying either of those two groups of antagonistic forces. Protective blockages can be explored with the patient early in the analysis without too many negative repercussions. Clarifying the defences used to protect the idealized image, however, requires a bit more tact. This image represents the overall solution for well-being. Any premature exploration of the values that support this image is responded to with terror and feeling of annihilation.[14]

Horney stressed the importance of the patient-analyst relationship. She saw analysis as a human relationship in which the analyst helps the patient to free themselves from their neurotic conflicts and to further activate their constructive forces towards self-realization. The analyst should come to the analytic situation with maturity, a belief in the constructive resolution of conflict; an ability to communicate a state of hopefulness to patients overwhelmed with self-hatred and hopelessness; a respect for the patient's struggles by, listening, clarifying, and illuminating; an ability to provide direction without guidance; and a desire to help the patient develop alternative solutions to their conflicts. There are two important goals for this phase:

1. To assist the patient to own their feelings
2. help the patient to recover his spontaneity.

Horney was flexible with the application of technique. Because she saw the person as the unique blend of hereditary, endowments and environmental influences; rules and regulations of technique could not be rigidly applied.

---

14 This first phase requires both a good analytic relationship and special qualities in the analyst. These are necessary to enable the patient to free himself from the stranglehold of the positive-value blockages and the pride system without feeling that their self-esteem and self-confidence are being destroyed.

She stressed flexibility in technique based on the analyst's sensitive perceptions of where the patient was at any moment. The emphasis in analysis was always on the reduction of obstructive forces toward healthy growth made the rigid adherence to the frequency of sessions and the use of the couch less important.

Horney recognized that true durable change required attitudinal change and this relied on a revaluation of values.[15] To achieve true attitudinal change required a thorough reorientation and reassessment of values in consonant with their real self. This process begins after the first phase of analysis (the disillusioning phase) as the patients begin to question their present set of values and goals. Here as the idealizing process begins to fade in its intensity and compulsivity, they are ready to revise their values and to develop alternate sets of values that are less rigid and more appropriate to their lives as they are in actuality. Dreams continue to play a prominent role in this later phase of the analysis. In 1950, Horney stated:

> In dreams we are closer to the reality of ourselves. They represent attempts to solve our conflicts either in a neurotic or healthy way, and in them constructive forces can be at work even at a time when they are hardly visible.

It is in the later phase of the mobilization of the constructive forces that the patient experiences central inner conflict that is, the struggle between the pride system and the real self. This working through period is often stormy, filled with painful and hateful affect, which demands all of the analyst's special qualities and skill. When there is successful resolution of

---

15 Change is not achieved by simple behavioural change in the patient. Behavioral change can occur coercively, through imitation or devotion, or from fear of the analyst's disapproval.

central inner conflict, patients can move toward the final phase of analysis, the discovery and creative use of their spontaneous real inner self..

REFERENCES

Alexander, F. (1935). *The Psychoanalysis of the Total Personality: The Application of Freud's Theory of the Ego to the Neuroses.* New York and Washington, DC: Nervous and Mental Disease Publishing Company.

Freud, A. (1936). *The Ego and the Mechanisms of Defense.* New York and London: Routledge, 1992.

Freud, S. (1931). *Female Sexuality Standard Edition* 21:221–244

Horney, K. (1980). *Adolescent Diaries of Karen Horney.* New York: Basic Books.

Ingram, D. H. (2001). The Hofgeismar Lectures: A Contemporary overview of Horneyan Psychoanalysis. *American Journal of Psychoanalysis* 61:113–141

Jones, E. (1927). The Early Development of Female Sexuality. *International Journal of Psychoanalysis* 8:459–472.

Hartmann, H. (1950). Comments on the Psychoanalytic Theory of the Ego. *Psychoanalytic Study of the Child,* 5:74–96.

Horney, K. (1937). *The Neurotic Personality of Our Time.* New York: W. W. Norton & Company, 1994.

——— (1939). *New Ways in Psychoanalysis, New* York: W.W. Norton, 2000.

———. (1945). *Our Inner Conflicts: A Constructive Theory of Neurosis.* New York: W.W. Norton, 1992.

——— (1950). *Neurosis and Human Growth:* The Struggle Towards Self-Realization, New York: W.W. Norton, 1991.

Hartmann, H. (1950). Comments on the Psychoanalytic Theory of the Ego *Psychoanalytic Study of the Child* 5:74–96. `

Rapaport, D. (1944). The Scientific Methodology of Psychoanalysis In *The Collected Papers of David Rapaport,* ed M.M. Gill. New York: Basic Books, 1967.

Richards, A. D. (1982). The Superordinate Self in Psychoanalytic Theory and in the Self Psychologies. *Journal of the American Psychoanalytic Association* 30:939-957

Sandler, J. & Rosenblatt, B. (1962). The Concept of the Representational World. *Psychoanalytic Study of the Child* 17:128–145

Strozier, C.B. (2001). *Heinz Kohut: The Making of a Psychoanalyst.* New York: Farrar, Straus and Giroux

Commentary on *The Need Not to Believe* and some Thoughts on the Significance of Antisemitism in Freud's Life by David Lotto[16]

[Merle Molofsky, ed. (2022). *Jew-Hating The Black Milk of Civilization.* New York: IPBooks]

Dr. Richard's paper gives us a comprehensive and insightful account of the role of Judaism in Freud's life. He describes three strands of Freud's Jewish identity: his commitment to cultural assimilation, the tradition of *Bildung;* his response to antisemitism; and his militant godlessness. I think they are all important components but I would argue that it is the second—his response to antisemitism that is predominant and which underlies the other two strands. My thesis is that the overarching and

---

16 David Lotto is a Psychoanalyst in practice in Pittsfield, Massachusetts and is the editor of the Journal of Psychohistory. He has written on a number of papers on a variety of Psychoanalytic and Psychohistorical subjects. He has a long-time interest in Freudian biography, particularly the importance for of battling against the antisemitism that pervaded his milieu. He can be contacted at dlotto@nycap.rr.com.

unifying theme that pulls the three strands together is antisemitism. With regard to the *Bildung*—with its valorization of a thoroughly westernized education, particularly the fealty to "science"—the main reason for his strong loyalty to it was that he saw it as the best path toward combating antisemitism. In general, science, and a scientific attitude toward the world was the best hope for countering antisemitism. In particular, his science, psychoanalysis, would hopefully prove to the world that, there was no Jewish science or Aryan science but one science that applied equally to all; we all share the same schmutz. And, as mentioned in the paper, his theory was an argument against those who saw the origin of psychopathology in inherited "traits." Such theories were used by antisemites, along with the idea of "racial differences" to justify viewing Jews as being hereditarily marked with a variety of psychopathological conditions and character flaws.

I also think that for Freud, and many others, the connection with, and to, science implied or even required a rejection of religion mostly because it embodied a world view that was antithetical and totally incompatible with that of science as they understood it. From the paper:

> If there is anything Freud did believe in, it was science; science, in his view, will go as far in alleviating man's condition as it is possible to go. But by the same token, a true scientific stance, if it is informed by the insights of psychoanalysis, dictates that religious belief must go—an outworn and no longer needed illusion (Richards, 2009, p. 563).

Most of the paper is devoted to the third strand—Freud's godlessness, along with his antipathy to religion. Dr. Richards raises the issue of why Freud was so vehemently antireligious—where does the passion come from? I would answer that it comes chiefly from the two sources—the first, the commitment to the scientific view of the world, which is logically inconsistent with religion, which was that scientific psychoanalysis could stand as a bulwark against antisemitism. The science of psychoanalysis had discovered the secret of the source which powers the delusionary belief in the existence of a supreme being—the infant's wish to be taken care of by all-powerful parents. The truth shall set us free from the bonds created by our infantile wishes. When we discovered why we wanted there to be a benevolent supreme being, we would no longer need to believe that there was one.

The second source of the anti-religious passion is the belief that adherence to the old religious ways of Judaism was throwing red meat to the antisemites. The rituals, dress, and the observances of traditional Judaism were, for Freud, markers that were frequently used by anti-Semites to denigrate Jews. Freud saw Jewish religiosity as a mortal danger to his people because it could encourage antisemitic acts. As it came to pass, there was more than a kernel of truth to his fear for his people.

The history of religiously inspired Christian antisemitism was another reason for his detesting religion. Both Meissner and Yerushalami think that Freud's rejection of religion has a protesteth too much quality that requires a search for hidden motivation. But if one takes the scientific nature of psychoanalysis as Freud understood it seriously, then atheism is where one starts. There is no supreme being and any belief or suggestions that there may be something of value in traditional religion, which is tied to such a belief, is nonsense.

Back to antisemitism. From the paper: "The specter of antisemitism, which became increasingly virulent in Vienna from his adolescence and early adulthood onward . . . evok[ed] in him a defiant commitment to retain his identity as a Jew." (Richards, 2009, p. 572). His writings and public statements are explicit on this. In Gymnasium: "In the higher classes I began to understand for the first time what it meant to belong to an alien race, and anti-Semitic feelings among the other boys warned me that I must take up a definite position" (Freud, 1900, p. 229). In University: "When, in 1873, I first joined the University, I experienced some appreciable disappointments. Above all, I found that I was expected to feel myself inferior and an alien because I was a Jew. I refused absolutely to do the first of these things. I have never been able to see why I should feel ashamed of my descent or, as people were beginning to say, of my 'race.' I put up, without much regret, with my non-acceptance into the community" (Freud, 1900).

Then there's Freud's statement, which is also quoted in the paper: "My language is German. My culture, my attainments, are German. I considered myself German intellectually, until I noticed the growth of anti-Semitic prejudice in Germany and German Austria. Since that time, I prefer to call myself a Jew". (Richards, 2009, p, 573, quoted as being cited in Gay, 1987, p. 139). For me, this quiet courageous declaration is one of the things I admire most about Freud and is one of the reasons I think refusal to bow to antisemitism was such a central feature of his life as well his identity as a Jew.

In regard to Freud's denials of being able to understand or speak Yiddish or read Hebrew, along with his vehement opposition toward all forms of religious ritual in his life, I think these are both aspects of his militant godlessness rather than any sort of rejection of his Jewish identity or faith in the tenets of the kind of Judaism he respected.

I think the reason the childhood memory of his father's unheroic response to his hat being knocked off while walking in the street and his wish to take revenge for this antisemitic act played such an important part in his inner life is that it is one of the sources of his lifelong passion to refuse to accept the brunt of antisemitism. Another instance is his changing his name from Sigismund to Sigmund because Sigismund had become a favorite name used in antisemitic jokes.

And one last point. My take on what was at the heart of his deep love and loyalty to Judaism was what he learned from his father and the Phillipson Bible but mostly from Hammerschlag—to quote from Dr. Richards' earlier paper on Freud's Jewish identity: "Religious instruction served him [Hammerschlag] as a way of educating toward a love of the humanities..." (Richards, 2014, p. 989, cited as Freud, 1904, p. 255). This was not the "dark emotional powers" he mentions in his remarks at the B'nai B'rith, which I assume refers to his long ancestral chain going back to biblical times, but what he was proud of about his Jewish heritage was its universal ethics where all humans are judged worthy of respectful treatment, along with the hard-earned experience of being able to see things in a different or new way that came from generations of living as outsiders.

I also see battling antisemitism as the source of the vehemence of his dislike of America. Freud had an intense dislike of much about America and Americans, by which he meant the United States and its denizens. His opinion of America remained steadfast throughout his adult life. In letters to many of his correspondents he fired off an unending barrage of disparaging remarks on a broad variety of things American. After returning from his only trip to the United States in the fall of 1909, he blamed his time in America for causing a number of physical ailments including stomach problems, "my colitis," and prostate trouble; and the blaming of the deterioration in his handwriting to his visit to America.

Freud made many negative comments concerning Americans. At various times he characterized them as prudish, having no time for libido, being savages, anti-Semitic, and cultural philistines.[17] He also disagreed strongly with the American Psychoanalytic Association's stand against lay analysis, was quite resentful of the popular success that both Jung and

---

17 Gay, p. 567, 211, 570, 563.

later Rank achieved in the United States; and after 1919, he displayed considerable anger at Woodrow Wilson and the Americans for abandoning their pledged commitment to Wilson's fourteen points.

But the vast majority of his criticisms, complaints, and characterizations of America had to do with money. Freud was repulsed by the excess materialism of Americans, their preoccupation with the pursuit of the almighty dollar.[18] In Freud's opinion America suffered from an anal fixation, which was the cause of their obsession. In a 1930 letter to Oscar Pfister, he referred to the United States as "dollaria,"[19] presumably a pun on the German and English for diarrhea.

In a 1921 letter to Jones, he gave a succinct summary of his view of Americans:

> ... competition is much more pungent with them, not succeeding means simple death to everyone, and they have no private resources apart from their profession, no hobby, games, love or other interests of a cultured person. And success means money.[20]

There are also a number of references to Americans routinely cheating and engaging in shady business deals.[21]

Various biographers have speculated concerning the sources and surprising strength, along with the apparent irrationality of Freud's negative views of the United States.[22] It is certainly an interesting question. Gay (1988) suggests that Freud may have envied the relative ease with

---

18 Ibid., p. 562–569.

19 Freud-Pfister, 147 p. 135.

20 Gay, p. 564.

21 Ibid., p. 562–564.

22 Gay & Jones, for example.

which one could make a living as a medical professional in the United Sates as compared to anywhere in Europe. One could easily suspect some component of defensive reaction formation behind his vehemence against the supposed crass materialism of Americans.

But consider that Freud's accusations about Americans' alleged preoccupation with making money and using dishonest methods to acquire wealth are uncomfortably close to the traditional antisemitic accusations made about Jews. Thus, Freud's' passionate prejudice against Americans can be seen as an attempt to distance himself from the stereotypical antisemitic canard and demonstrate that he, a Jew and by extension other Jews, were not like that; it was the Americans who were.

REFERENCES

Freud, S. (1930) Letter from Sigmund Freud to Oskar Pfister, August 20, 1930. Psychoanalysis and Faith: The Letters of Sigmund Freud and Oskar Pfister 59:135.

Gay. P: (2006). *Freud: A Life for Our Time.* New York: W.W. Norton.

Jones, E. (1964). *Life And Work Of Sigmund Freud.* L. Trilling & S. Marcus,. eds. New York: Basic Books, 1975.

Richards, A,D. (2017). *Psychoanalysis: Perspectives on Thought Collectives.* New York: IPBooks.

CHAPTER 14

Witnessing the Death of Yiddish Language and Culture: Holes in the Doorposts

[(2012). In *The Power of Witnessing*, eds. Goodman, N.R. & Meyers, M.B. New York: Routledge]

This was the end. This was the sum total of hundreds of generations of living and building of Torah and piety, of free thinking, of Zionism of Bundism of struggles and battles, of the hopes of an entire people—this empty desert.

I Iooked around me at what had been the Jews of Warsaw. I felt one hope and, I feel it now., May this sea of emptiness bubble and boil, may it cry out eternal condemnation of murderers and pillagers, may it forever be the shame of the \civilized world which saw and heard and chose to remain silent—(Goldstein, B., 2005).

To bear witness to the Holocaust is to look both ways. We must acknowledge heartbreaking destruction and loss, but we must also celebrate the enduring power of life. Not every individual witness is privy to both perspectives, however. Some witness only destruction; some are themselves destroyed. Some witnesses come so close to destruction that they can endure their experience only by separating as much as possible from what they have seen, keeping it to themselves and passing it on (if at all) as a tale told at a remove. Some manage to continue to grow even with traumatized roots; they put out new shoots and look to the future. Destruction and creation- witnessing includes both. So, when Nancy and Marilyn asked me to contribute to this volume a personal view of what the Holocaust meant to Yiddish culture, I found myself contemplating that tension between absence and presence, death and life, destruction and creation. I grew up in a family that did not hide what was happening, which allowed me to be openly interested. At the same time, I saw the intensity of pain the events of the thirties and forties caused in my family and my community, and I learned to appreciate why some people felt the need to separate themselves from it, and why others were disconnected from it by fiat, because their parents couldn't bear to engage with their experience intimately enough to pass it on.

I think that my choice of profession had a lot to do with my own issues about coming to terms with the past. I'm a psychoanalyst, committed to helping people find ways to discover and tolerate their own histories (whatever they may be) so as to be free to build their futures. I grew up bi-lingual in Yiddish and English in Brooklyn, New York and have been involved since 1978 with YIVO, [footnote] an organization dedicated to the preservation of Yiddish language documents and cultural history I served as Chairman of the Board of Directors between 1987 and 1990. I have gained an expansive, intricate, and very privileged view, not only of the catastrophe of the Holocaust, but of the extraordinarily creative ways that the Jewish people had found and continue to find to develop.

In this essay I act as a witness to honor the history of Yiddish culture and memorialize some the writers and poets who were killed. There is absence where a vast wealth of literature and a tradition formerly flourished.

Traveling To Krakow: Holes Where Mezuzahs Used To Be

In the early 1980s I traveled to Krakow with a YIVO group for a special showing at the Jagiellonian University there. That exhibit gave rise to the collection published as *Image Before My Eyes: A Photographic History of Jewish Life in Poland,* 1864-1939. (Dobrosczycki & Kirshenblatt-Gimblett, eds. 1977) and also to Josh Waletsky's 1981 documentary of the same name. There was an official opening ceremony for our contingent, followed by a tour of the displays documenting Jewish life in the Polish territories before the Holocaust. The Polish visitors to the exhibit, of all ages, responded to the photographs as if they were archeological documents, records of an ancient civilization. They didn't seem to feel any close connection between these pictures and their history—in some cases, their lives. But to those of us from YIVO it was a moving and gripping evocation of the vibrancy of Jewish life in Poland not so very long ago—certainly within our parents' memories, and for many of us, our own.

I thought about this as we drove from Krakow to Warsaw, stopping off to visit the formerly Jewish villages—the shtetlach—we passed through along the way. On the doorposts of houses formerly occupied by Jews there were nail holes you could see and touch, ghosts of mezuzahs that were no longer there. But it wasn't all that long ago that they had been there, and I felt the connection acutely, looking at those photographs in Krakow, and walking through those once Jewish, now Polish, villages. My mother came from a village like these. She spoke the language that the people who lived here; she read the books that the people who lived here read. I read them too. We had them at home while I was growing up in Brooklyn. My father's story is different, but that's part of the point of my assignment for this volume, which is to bear witness to the fate of the Yiddish literary culture in Eastern Europe from a personal point of view, in the context of my own history.

A Brief Biography

I grew up in Brooklyn in the thirties and forties, hearing and reading about the Holocaust in English, Yiddish, and Russian. My parents' marriage was a microcosm of the sociological stew that was Eastern European Jewry. They came from towns that are very close together on the map, and their Yiddish was very similar. But my father spoke Russian and my mother spoke Polish. My father's family had been more or less integrated with the Russian world for generations—his great-grandfather, who was killed in the Crimean war, was the only Jewish noncommissioned officer in the Russian army, and his grandfather was manager of the Russian estate of an absentee Polish landowner. My father graduated from a Gymnasium where he had been excused from religion classes because he was Jewish. My mother came from an Orthodox shtetl family; her family kept Kosher, and the schools there were traditional kheyders[23]. My mother left Galicia with her family in the 20s. She was eleven years old. She worked as a milliner and learned English in night school. My father came here by himself in 1924. He was a Bolshevik atheist, who joined the Russian revolution and became a librarian in the Red Army. It was the job of the librarian of each unit of Trotsky's army to drive the horse and the cart full of books for the soldiers to read. That was my father's job. Guns weren't enough, Trotsky thought. You had to know Marx too.

My earliest lexical memory dates from 1939. I was five, reading the *Yiddish Forward*[24] and there was a picture of a bearded man and a caption: "Barimpta yiddisher professor geshtorben." Freud had died. Yiddish culture was an integral part of my growing up, as I know it was not for many Jewish

---

23 School room for Jewish children in Eastern Europe.

24 Yiddish Forward, c. September 24, 1939,

children at the time. But it wasn't until I was an adult that I became really aware of the magnitude of what ad been lost.

Yiddish: A Lost Language

So let me start with the language in question, Yiddish. The origins of Yiddish aren't absolutely clear, but it's thought to have arisen in the 10th or 11th century, in the Rhineland, the fruit of generations of migration back and forth between Palestine and Europe after Rome destroyed Judea in the first century AD. It was an inclusive language, open to elements of the various other Jewish linguistic traditions that intersected with it, and so it grew in time into a communicative thread that connected a lot of Jews of very different backgrounds.

But its universality—as a language, and as the marker of a traditional and separate Jewish culture—was on the wane long before the Holocaust. There were various reasons for this, but they mostly had to do with pressures for assimilation. Convenience was one of these pressures. Yiddish was still the main, and often the only, language of the provincial Jews living in shtetls in the Pale of Settlement. Many of these people, for religious reasons, kept themselves apart from the "secular" world, and perpetuated their isolation with the traditional religious kheyder education that followed a curriculum centuries old. But an increasing number of Polish Jews spoke Polish as well; it was a necessary tool for doing business with the Poles. My mother's father by traditional lights was a rather worldly person, and he spoke German as well as Polish and Yiddish

Some Jews just wanted to feel like part of the world that surrounded them; this was true all over Eastern Europe and elsewhere. The great Sholem Aleichem wrote in Yiddish because his audience spoke and understood it. But he wanted his children to be part of Russian civilization and Russian society, and to them he spoke Russian. Fear was another reason for assimilation and the thinning out of the population of Yiddish speakers in Eastern Europe leaving it less concentrated than it had once been. In the wake of the financial crisis that followed the Panic of 1873, pogroms became more frequent within the Pale of settlement. Times were hard after the booming mid-eighteen-hundreds and in some quarters the Jews were blamed for it. This was the same period in which the term anti-Semitism came to prominence with the publication of a propaganda pamphlet by Wilhelm Marr in 1879, *Der Weg zum Siege des Germanenthums* über *das Judenthum* (*The Way to Victory of Germanic over Judaism*). Many Jews felt the need to distance themselves from the distinguishing cultural, religious, and linguistic markers that made Jews so easily recognized—and so easily demonized. Another reason was pride. Yiddish was kept very carefully under wraps by many of the Jewish urbanites who settled in Europe's great cities, or who grew up there as the children of immigrants, and wished to assimilate themselves as perfectly as they could to their cosmopolitan surroundings.

Sigmund Freud was an example of this. Like many Austrian Jews, he aspired to membership in what he saw as a great cultural tradition, and certainly this possibility was becoming ever less remote as the Enlightenment progressed. But every movement that Freud and Jews like him made toward establishment culture meant a movement away from the culture of their parents. They were ashamed of their parents—with their odd dress and odd appearance and odd language—and guilty for being ashamed. I think that Freud's much-vaunted "godlessness" had as much to do with embarrassment as with religion. His wife's grandfather was the chief rabbi in Hamburg, and he didn't want his status as an enlightened Jew in sophisticated Viennese society to be undermined by identification with those scruffy and primitive Jews from the shtetl. He unabashedly acknowledged his prejudice against them, saying once of a play about Yochanan the Prophet that "I'd rather be the Jew in the tuxedo than the Jew in the caftan." (Grinwald 1941).

Freud later said that it was anti-Semitism that made him a Jew: "My language is German. My culture, my attainments are German. I considered myself German intellectually, until I noticed the growth of anti-Semitic prejudice in Germany and German Austria. Since that time, I prefer to call myself a Jew." [Gay, 1988, p. 448]. But some prosperous German and Austrian Jews actually came to blame the shtetl Jews for the Holocaust, believing that it was their foreignness that attracted such dangerous attention. I heard this said by German Jews in the United States and by some of the Viennese psychoanalysts who I knew in New York City. They didn't recognize this as anti-Semitism themselves, nor did they recognize that the very success that they thought would insulate them had made them envied, and that when hard times returned again in the thirties envy contributed a great deal to conventional anti-Semitism and support for Hitler's Final Solution.

Sociological factors like these shaped the Yiddish literary and intellectual world, in which the traditional, the assimilationist, the religious, the worldly, the political, the highbrow, the trashy, and the avant-garde were all represented. Assimilationist pressures and temptations being what they were, the halcyon days of the 1930s would likely have been the peak of Yiddish literary culture even if there had never been a Holocaust. But while they lasted, they were glorious. If not for the destruction, this literary tradition would have influenced the development of the arts for generations to come.

Eastern Europe before the war was rich with gifted poets, novelists, playwrights, journalists, historians, artists, musicians, and philosophers. In 1931, Poland had the highest percentage of Jews anywhere, more than three million of the 17 million Jews worldwide, about 18%. I'll be using Poland here as a focus, partly because it was home to the greatest number of Jews in Europe, and partly because its cities were centers of the Yiddish literary life that I'll be discussing. Poland's Yiddish literary culture was the largest and most active in the world; it was the only country in which successful Yiddish authors could support themselves by writing. Isaac Bashevis Singer has talked about the intellectual life of Warsaw, its newspapers, the coffee houses where patrons could sit and talk about the great Yiddish and Western writers for hours at a time. Many of those great writers died before World War II—the likes of Y.L. Peretz, Sholom Aleichem, and Mendele Mocher Sforim, who has been called the grandfather of Yiddish literature. These men were read everywhere within the Pale of Settlement, and I read their work myself as a child here, in my Yiddish school. At home we had a bound set of the collected works of Sholom Aleichem, and a volume of Peretz as well.

By 1906 there were five Yiddish dailies in Warsaw with a circulation of 100,000; and double that circulation by the end of the decade. They serialized the work of Yiddish writers, and published theater reviews and schedules. There were Jewish literary magazines. There was an Association of Jewish Writers and Journalists in Warsaw, and a PEN club in Vilna. So Yiddish speakers in Eastern Europe between the wars had plenty to choose from. Readers could find everything from serious novels to avantgarde poetry to escapist junk. Theater repertoires included not only musical comedies and tear-jerkers, but also drama, and performances in Yiddish translation of Shakespeare and such modern playwrights as O'Neill and Dreiser (/Forgresert und farbessert/—"bigger and better" "enlarged and improved meant as a boast).There were Yiddish movies, cabarets, and marionette theaters. A Yiddish version of the Pushkin/Tchaikovsky opera Eugene Onegin was produced in Vilna in 1920. Clearly not all of these offerings were by Yiddish authors or composers, but a vast number of them were, and the fact of the others attests to the appetite, and the cosmopolitan temperament of Polish urban Jewry.

Destruction

But, by the middle of the 1940s Yiddish civilization was almost completely destroyed by the Germans, with the collaboration of Ukrainians and Poles. And the question to which I will address the rest of this paper is: What happened to the Yiddish writers? We can divide the Yiddish literati into groups according to the date of their deaths. The first group includes the early greats, who were dead by the time the war began. A second group survived the Holocaust and developed a Yiddish readership (significant, if dwindling) in the United States and Israel. Among these were the likes of Itzik Manger, Chaim Grade, and Abraham Sutzkever. There also had been a very creative and vibrant group of Yiddish poets called the Yunga, the young ones, who were developing an avant-garde Yiddish poetic sensibility. Some of these survived the war in the Soviet Union, but were subsequently killed by Stalin. In Joseph Leftwich's anthology (1987) *Great Yiddish Writers of the 20th Century*, both of these groups are generously represented. Leftwich includes many of the early giants who died before 1940, including Y.L. Peretz, Sholom Aleichem, and Isidor (Yisroel) Eliashev. Among the postwar greats who survived the Holocaust, Leftwich includes, for example, Grade, Sutzkever, and Sholem Asch.

The group I want to speak of and memorialize here is barely represented among Leftwich's 81 authors, or in any other anthology or classification that I know of. These are the Yiddish writers who were murdered in

Eastern Europe between 1940 and 1945, particularly those who were not granted the time to fully develop their craft, or to establish enduring reputations. They were acclaimed and reckoned significant among the Jewish Eastern European literati of their time. But their work had not yet been disseminated widely, and it was lost, for the most part, when the audience of readers and play-goers who knew it best disappeared. It is these writers who call up so poignantly the bittersweet awareness of what might have been.

Of the group who were murdered during the war years Leftwich included only three, and two of them were old men who had fully developed their skill and renown. Simon Dubnov, who wrote a many-volumed history of the Jews was killed by Germans in Riga in 1941 at the age of 81 and Hillel Zeitlin, the scholar, writer, and journalist, died in 1942 in the Warsaw Ghetto at the age of 72. Leftwich's third choice is the poet and critic Yisroel Shtern, who perished in Treblinka 1942 at the age of 46.

These three, however, are only a few of the dozens, perhaps hundreds, of Yiddish poets, novelists, playwrights, historians, philosophers, and journalists who were lost between 1940 and 1945, dying of starvation in the ghettos of Poland and the Pale, shot in the fields and forests of Russia and Lithuania, or otherwise murdered in concentration camps. They are only a few of the people whose names we don't recognize, whose productions we've never heard of, whose books aren't fondly remembered by our parents. They hadn't written enough, or written long enough, before the war to be known outside of their immediate community, and they didn't survive the war to promote their work afterwards to the world's tragically destroyed audience of Yiddish speakers, readers, and theater-goers.

Leftwich's list is sobering, and it's very hard to add to it. I hope I've made clear that this isn't because there wasn't much going on in the arts in Yiddish-speaking Europe. It's because the documentation of the period was decimated along with the people themselves. What little we know comes from material saved from the conquering Nazi armies by courage, guile, and luck, and then in some cases saved again from the tightening grip of Stalin. These efforts at preservation are yet another aspect of witness, and I'll mention two of them here: YIVO and Ringelblum.

YIVO was founded in Vilna in 1925 by Max Weinreich and other European Jewish intellectuals (Edward Sapir, Albert Einstein, and Sigmund Freud were among the trustees) who wanted to make available for study the history, language, and culture of the Jews of Eastern Europe before they were swamped by change and assimilation. YIVO sent emissaries throughout the Pale of Settlement, to collect the stuff of the culture. Its initial mission was collection and scholarship, not preservation. But given what happened so soon afterward, their foresight turned out to be a great blessing.

When the German army took Vilna in March 1942, the Einsatzstas Rosenberg task force, started by Nazi ideologue Alfred Rosenberg for looting the Jewish world of its cultural treasures, established a sorting center in the YIVO building. It was supposed to identify the most valuable materials there and ship the plunder to Rosenberg's Institute for the Study of the Jewish Question in Frankfurt. Rosenberg's functionaries could not distinguish between the gold and the dross, however. They impressed Jews who knew the material into this bitter task, but their unwilling accessories soon set their minds to saving YIVO's most valuable holdings. Dubbed di papir-brigade, the Paper Brigade, they disguised, removed, and hid as many important documents as they could. They were led by the poet Abraham Sutzkever and the writer and cultural historian Shmerke Kaczerginski, and they risked their lives to cache materials in the ghetto, in YIVO's attics, and with non-Jewish contacts for safekeeping.

In 1987, despite the ravages of war and Communism, a huge collection of YIVO materials that had been spirited into the hands of gentiles were discovered in a book depository the Lithuanian National Book Center.

Approximately 170,000 documents were saved at the Lithuanian Center, E. Fishman has told this story in his book *Embers Plucked from the Fire: The Rescue of Jewish Cultural Treasures in Vilna* (YIVO, 2009). Perhaps most miraculously, or at least most ironically, the materials dispatched from YIVO to the Nazis in Frankfort were discovered in 1946 by a US Army officer in a freight car at a railway siding outside of Frankfort. These were sent to New York, and reconstituted as the American YIVO collection.

Emanuel Ringelblum the organizer of relief in the Warsaw Ghetto and of Oneg, the Warsaw Ghetto archive, tried to accumulate materials that would portray all facets of Jewish life from many different perspectives. He also wanted to document the destruction of Polish Jewry, to which he was an eyewitness. He and his colleagues collected questionnaires, memoirs, and interviews administered by amateur field workers, as well as input from professional historians and sociologists. David Roskies (*The Jewish Search for a Usable Past,* Indiana University Press, 1999, p. 24) includes him among the eyewitness chroniclers of modern Jewish catastrophe. His work is an example of what Roskies calls "the Literature of Destruction," another name for the tradition of witnessing that is the subject of this volume.

By some estimates, about half of what was written by Jews during this time was saved through the efforts of committed individuals like Ringelblum, who had opportunities to escape but who chose to remain the Warsaw ghetto to continue his work. Ringelblum finally left the ghetto on the eve of the uprising, but he was discovered by the Gestapo and killed, along with his family and the Gentiles who had hidden them. The archive was maintained unit February 1943. Two of the three Oyneg Shabes Caches were found after the war; the last is still missing. My mother was still alive at the time of the discovery of our YIVO materials in Vilna; when I told her about this discovery and the amazing accomplishments of the Papir-Brigade, she said in Yiddish, "Better they had saved fewer papers and more people." That wasn't within their power. But mindful of my mother's comment, my intent in the rest of this piece is to speak of the Yiddish poets, playwrights, and novelists of Poland who were murdered between 1941 and 1945. In some cases, at least, thanks to those who documented their lives and to those who courageously managed to preserve the documents, their names will live on.

Yet there are others whose names do not live on—whose names, even, have been lost, along with their lives and their work. Witnessing works both ways—we witness what is present, "before our eyes," as the Krakow exhibition had it, and we witness also the fact of absence and the fact of the loss of the future. Some of these names are lost to us because it was not only the people who vanished, but those who knew them, as well. They too might have grown into greatness had their world not been destroyed. But like the mezuzahs that once graced the doorposts of village homes, they are gone; we can know that they were there only by the holes they left behind.

A Community Eradicated: Creative Voices Lost

Some of the holes in the doorposts are large and deep; some are small and barely discernible. But they all attest to a community destroyed, to an irreversible loss of life and of creative force. What follows here are two lists. The first is a list of Yiddish writers murdered between 1940 and 1945 about whom a significant amount is known. I offer it to establish a more detailed picture of these people and the lost riches that can never be recovered. I will then follow with a Yizkor list, a list of remembrance, of those whose names we know but whose work we do not. All this material is excerpted from the wonderful YIVO Encyclopedia of Jews in Eastern Europe website (www.yivoencyclopedia.org). Anyone interested in this vanished world will find a visit there very rewarding. Yet the list still is not complete, and it never will be. Part of the tragedy we are witnessing here is the fact that we do not even have names for so many of these people, and yet surely many of them contributed in measure as full as those who are remembered. The names we do have, the ones I am memorializing here, are listed with the little information available about them on the YIVO site, at http://www. yivoencyclopedia.org/article.aspx/Yiddish_Literature/Yiddish_Literature_ after_1800#id0qbg My hope is that anyone with historical connections to this vanished civilization will look at that list, and offer to YIVO any further information they may possess, either of names that should be added, or of knowledge about the people who are already included there.

Mordkhe Gebirtig, poet and songwriter. Born 1877, Krakow. Died 1942, by random German fire while being marched to the Krakow train station for transportation to the Belzec death camp. Gebirtig is best know for his song "S'brent" (It is burning), which was written in 1938 in response to a pogrom, and became a favorite of the Jewish Resistance movement. The first collection of Gebertig's songs, *Folkshtimlech (In the Folk Style)*, was published in 1920, and a second, *Mayne Lider (My Songs)*, in 1938. In 1940 or 1941 he wrote Atos fun nekome (A Day for Revenge), a song about hope for the downfall of the perpetrators of the Holocaust.

Shimen Horontshik, novelist. Born 1889, Wieluń. Died 1939, Kałuszyn, a suicide, to forestall being murdered by German troops engaged in a pogrom. Horontshik lived in Lodz during World War I and in France and Belgium during the early thirties. He wrote eleven novels, five of which were primarily autobiographical. Two—*In geroysh fun mashinen (Amid the noise of the machines*, 1928), and *1905* (1929)—are set in the lace-making district of Kalisz, where industrialism and capitalism are making inroads upon shtetl life. *Bayn shvel (At the threshold*, 1935/36) looks at the conflicts between Jews and Poles and among Jews themselves, as seen through his young eyes. In other novels he considered the damage to the Jewish way of life wrought by greed and the loss of moral structure.

Alter-Sholem Kacyzne, novelist, playwright, and photographer. Born 1855, Vilna. Died 1941, Tarnopol; killed with thousands of other Jews who were fleeing the German advance. Kacyzne's great two-volume *novel Shtarke un Shvakhe (The Strong and the Weak)* was published in 1929/1930; it dealt with the 1905 Polish uprising and the conflict between Bohemian Jews and the rising generation of Poles. He also wrote three plays, *Dem Yidns Opera* (The Jew's Opera), *Ester (Esther)*, and *Shvartsbard* (about Sholem Schwartzbard, who assassinated the Ukrainian nationalist Symon Petliura in 1926). [25]

Kacyzne was probably one of the most prolific of the pre-war Yiddish writers in Poland, and considered by many the literary heir to Y.L. Peretz. Despite these accomplishments, he is better remembered as a photographer than as either novelist or playwright. In 1921 he was commissioned by the Hebrew Immigrant Aid Society to photograph Jewish life in Poland, and his work was published regularly in the New York *Forverts.(Forward)*. Kacyzne's photographic archive in Warsaw was destroyed in the Holocaust, but the 700 photographs he had sent to New York are at YIVO.[26]

Yitzhak Katzenelson, poet, educator, writer. Born 1885, near Minsk. Died 1944, Auschwitz. Katzenelson was a major Hebrew and Yiddish poet, (called by some the Poet of Destruction.) His first anthology of Yiddish poetry, *Die zun fargeyt in flamen (The sun sets in flames)* was published in 1909. He was a man of many accomplishments. He established a network of private Hebrew schools that continued until 1939, and for it wrote children's literature and Hebrew textbooks. He started a Hebrew theater company, and wrote plays on contemporary and biblical themes. He translated the poetry of Heinrich Heine into Hebrew. He published

---

25 https://en.wikipedia.org/wiki/Sholem_Schwarzbard

26 http://polishjews.yivoarchives.org/archive/index.php?p=collections/controlcard&id=22442&q=photogallery

his collected Hebrew poems in three volumes in 1938. These were much darker in tone than his early work.

But at the time of publication the political situation made for poor distribution, and few copies survived the war. Later, however, they revealed Katzenelson to be what the YIVO Encyclopedia calls "the great eulogist in verse of the murdered Jewish people."(http://www.yivoencyclopedia.org/article.aspx/Katzenelson_Yitshak; In December 1939 Katzenelson escaped from Lodz, and became a central figure in the pedagogic and cultural life of the Warsaw Ghetto. He continued to teach, direct plays, and write, and he contributed to the underground press. Forty of his own works were composed in the Ghetto, including two long poems (Dos lid vegn Shloyme Zhelikhovsky [The poem about Solomon Zhelikhovsky] and Dos lid vegn Radziner [The Poem about the Radzhin Rebbe]). Both of these were about heroism in the face of death. He was now writing in Yiddish, seeking to reach the largest audience he could in his current circumstances. But August 1942 his wife and two younger sons were deported to Treblinka, and his poetry turned very dark again. He took part in the first Warsaw Ghetto uprising and escaped briefly, but was caught and sent to a German detention camp in Vittel, France, and then to Auschwitz, where he and his son were murdered. In Vittel, Katzenelson wrote two of the Holocaust's most important works: *Pinkas Vitel* (*The Vittel diary*) in Hebrew, and *Dos lid fun oysgehargetn yidishn* folk (The Poem about the Murdered Jewish People). These capture the terror, pathos, and rage of his people, and lament his own impending death.

Miryem (nee Manya Hirshbeyn), poet and journalist. Born 1890, Lodz. Died 1944, Auschwitz. Ulinover was a prolific poet and active in Yiddish literary circles during the 1920s. Her first poems were published in Polish when she was 15. She also wrote in Russian and German. Her Yiddish work began to appear ten years later. Her best-known collection of poems is *Der bobes optser* (*My Grandmother's Treasure*, 1922). There is disagreement among literary critics about whether Ulinover is a modernist or a naïve folk poet, and about whether her poetry is secular or religious. Kathryn Hellerstein writes in the YIVO encyclopedia that "Miryem Ulinover wrote poems designed by a modern sensibility that sought to preserve the folk diction, sayings, and customs of pre-modern Jewish life in Poland." (Hellerstein 2008).

Oyzer Varshavski, novelist. Born 1898, Sochazcew. Died 1944, Auschwitz. Varshavski's first novel, *Shmuglars (Smugglers)*, published in 1920, is considered the finest example of Yiddish naturalism. It is a raw tale of Jews in a Polish town trying to make a living during World War I by distilling illegal whiskey and smuggling it into German-held Warsaw. Varshavski portrayed the implosion of shtetl life as it came into increasing contact with the outside world. In his *study In the Mirror of Literature: The Economic Life of the Jews in Poland as Reflected in Yiddish Literature (1914-1939)*, William Glicksman (1966) describes Varshavski's vision as the vortex of a world at the brink of an abyss. His second novel, *Shnit-tsayt (Harvest Time, 1926)*, was about shtetl life in the years between the outbreak of World War I and the beginning of the German Occupation. There is a tragic irony to Varshavski's last book, *Rezidentsn (Residences; Résidences: On ne peut pas se, 1944)* which describes the efforts of various Jewish characters to escape the Nazis in occupied France. Varshavski settled in Paris in 1924, but after the occupation fled first to Vichy France and then to Italy, where he and his wife were seized and sent to Auschwitz.

Dvora Vogel, philosopher and art critic. Born 1900, Burshtyn, Galicia. Died 1942, together with her husband, mother, and small son, in the Lvov ghetto during the Great Action of 1942. Vogel was educated in Vienna, in Lvov, and then at Jagiellonia University in Krakow, where she completed a dissertation on Hegel's aesthetics. She was an accomplished academic as well as a writer; she taught psychology at Hebrew Teacher's Seminary in Lvov, and was a central figure in the Polish literary and artistic avant-garde.

She corresponded widely with other writers in a circle of mutual influence. Her first volume of poems, published in 1930, (*Tog-figurn Lider, Figures of the Day*) are free verse poems on concrete and abstract themes. *Manekin Lider* (*Mannequin Poems,* 1934), were openly constructivist in principle. Her work was little regarded in her time; if she and her audience had lived long enough to become familiar with the new literary forms, her literary fate would likely have been very different.

Grieving the Death of Writers Lost

Finding this list has changed what was intellectual insight to a profoundly emotional feeling. The sadness and sense of loss to all of us must be overwhelming.to me. The number and the details of who they were and what they had written follows.

[The following list identifies and briefly describes Yiddish writers who are not the subject of an independent biographical entry.]

Apshan, Hertsl (1886–1944), prose writer and journalist. Hertsl Apshan was born near Sighet, Hungary; as an adult he was a businessman and insurance agent in that city. After 1918, he lived in Romania. Apshan's depictions of Hasidic life in Transylvania were praised for their artist observations and soft irony. He was murdered in Auschwitz.

Aronski, (Zak) Moyshe (1898–1944), prose writer and educator. Born in Ovruch, Ukraine, Moyshe Aronski (originally Zak) graduated from Kiev University in 1930 and subsequently taught literature and history in Yiddish schools in Ukraine. From 1926, his prose appeared in periodicals in Kharkov, Kiev, and Moscow. Aronski enlisted in the Soviet Army and was killed in action. He published more than 15 novels and collections of stories about Jewish life in the Soviet Union.

Beylin, Moyshe-Zisl (1857–1942), scholar and folklorist. Born in Novogrodek, Belorussia, Moyshe-Zisl Beylin served as a crown rabbi in Rogachev (Belorussia) and Irkutsk (Siberia), and from 1920 lived in Moscow. Throughout his life he collected and studied Yiddish proverbs, songs, and children's rhymes and riddles; his studies appeared in Russian, German, and Yiddish scholarly and literary periodicals. Beylin's last collection of Yiddish folk jokes and anecdotes was ready to be published in 1941 but was not released because of the war. Some of his unpublished materials are preserved in the YIVO archives. He died in Siberia.

Dreyfus, Leybush (Leon; 1894–1941), prose writer, journalist, and actor. Born in Lwów, Leybush Dreyfus began to publish poetry in the *Po'ale Tsiyon* press in1911. After World War I he went to Czechoslovakia, where he founded a traveling Yiddish theater company. He returned to Lwów and contributed short stories, essays, and poems to the Yiddish press under various pseudonyms. Living in Riga and Warsaw, Dreyfus edited Yiddish and Polish periodicals, published a novel about actors *(Kulisn [Behind the Stage]; 1927)*, worked in theater and on the radio, and in 1939 returned to Lwów. He died in the Janów concentration camp.

Dua, Yankev-Kopl (1898–1942), writer and journalist. Yankev-Kopl Dua was born in Warsaw and attended a Russian school. He became involved in socialist politics and contributed numerous articles on art, theater, literature, and music to the left-wing Yiddish press. His novels about Polish Jewish history were reprinted in installments by Yiddish newspapers in the United States, Argentina, and South Africa. He was the main editor and author of *Groshn-bibliotek* (*Penny Library*), which published popular brochures and produced numerous translations from world literature. Dua continued his literary work in the Warsaw ghetto; a German officer shot him on the street.

Dubilet, Moyshe (1897–1941), literary critic and educator. Born in Ekaterinoslav province, Ukraine, Moyshe Dubilet served in the Red Army during the Russian Civil War and later graduated from the Yiddish department of the Odessa Pedagogical Institute. He taught Yiddish language and literature in Yiddish schools and in 1933 began graduate studies at the Kiev Institute of Jewish Proletarian Culture, researching nineteenth-century Yiddish literature (Yisroel Aksenfeld, Shloyme Ettinger, Sholem Yankev Abramovitsh, Sholem Aleichem). Dubilet's collection *Kritishe artiklen* (Critical *Essays)* was published in 1939; in 1941, he enlisted in the Soviet Army and was killed in action.

Eliashev, Ester (1878–1941), literary critic, journalist, and teacher. Ester Eliashevwas born in Kaunas, and studied philosophy at the universities of Leipzig, Heidelberg, and Bern (receiving a doctorate in 1906), and taught at the Higher Women's Courses in Saint Petersburg. She returned to Kaunas in 1921, where she worked as a teacher and was a prolific literary critic and journalist. Eliashev died on the eve of the German invasion. She was the sister of Isidor Eliashev (Bal-Makhshoves).

Gilbert, Shloyme (1885–1942), prose writer and poet. Born in Radzymin, near Warsaw, Shloyme Gilbert began to publish neoromantic poetry and novellas in1907. His first collection of stories appeared in Warsaw in 1922, followed by two additional books of poetry and drama inspired by religious and mystical motifs. He was deported from the Warsaw ghetto to Treblinka.

Glik, Hirsh (1922–1944), poet. Born in Vilna, Hirsh Glik began to write under the influence of his older friends from Yung-Vilne; he issued his first publications in 1940. Glik is famous for his ghetto poetry, especially the "Partisaner lid" (The Partisan Hymn; 1943), which became a symbol of Jewish resistance.

Goldshteyn, Moyshe (1900–1943), prose writer. Moyshe Goldshteyn was born near Siedlec, Poland, and lived in Warsaw. In 1923, he immigrated to Argentina and published short stories in the Yiddish press. In 1932 he arrived in Birobidzhan, worked in an agricultural colony, and published reports about Birobidzhan and Argentina in the Yiddish press. Two collections of his short prose works were published in Moscow. He served as an officer in the Soviet Army and was killed during World War II. A number of his war stories were published posthumously.

Gotlib, Yankev (1911–1945), poet. Yankev Gotlib was born in Kaunas, and received at traditional education. His first poem was published in 1925 and subsequently he published four collections of poetry and a book about H. Leyvik; he also edited literary publications in Kaunas. He died under evacuation in Central Asia.

Grin, Yerakhmiel (1910–1944), prose writer. Yerakhmiel Grin was born in a village near Kolomyya, Ukraine; he lived in Warsaw. He wrote stories and novels about Jewish life in the Carpathian Mountains, and died in the Janów concentration camp together with his wife Hinde Naiman-Grin (1916–1944), a Polish and Yiddish writer and journalist.

Grodzenski, Arn-Yitskhok (1891–1941), poet and journalist. Arn-Yitskhok Grodzenski grew up in Vilna and published his first poem in 1906. From 1910 to 1913, he lived in Antwerp, and then returned to Vilna, publishing his first collection of poetry in 1914. In 1916, Grodzenski fled to Ekaterinoslav, where he lost his legs in an accident. He contributed to various Yiddish publications in Ukraine as well as translated Russian and German poetry. In 1921, he again settled in Vilna, where he worked as an editor and translator. His most popular work was the novel *Lebn* (*Life*; 1923). Tchaikovsky's opera Eugène Onegin was performed in his Yiddish translation in Vilna in 1923. Grodzenski was murdered in Ponar.

Hartsman, Motl (1908–1943), poet. Born in Berdichev, Motl Hartsman attended the Yiddish school headed by Nina Brodovskaya, who encouraged his first literary and theatrical attempts; he received his higher education in Odessa and Moscow, and completed graduate study in Kiev with Maks Erik. Hartsman's first poems were printed in Berdichev's Yiddish newspapers and quickly became popular; a few collections of his poems were published in the 1930s. His last long poem, Der toyt-urteyl (The Death Sentence), was written during the war while he served in the Red Army. He was killed in action.

Hershele (1882–1941), poet, prose writer, and journalist. Hershele (pseudonym of Hersh Danilevich) was born in Lipno, Poland. As a textile worker in Warsaw, he joined the socialist Zionist movement, was arrested, moved to Switzerland, and then came back to Poland, where he eventually settled in a town near Warsaw. His first publications, in 1904, were greeted warmly by Y. L. Peretz. Beginning in 1910, Hershele contributed poetry, short stories, children's literature, and translations to various Yiddish periodicals; he collected and published Yiddish folklore; and some of his poems became folk songs. His earliest book of poetry came out in 1907; he also published and edited several other collections. His poetry from the Warsaw ghetto appeared in illegal publications. He also published a collection of plays and dramatic poems, titled *Bayopgruntn* (*By Abyss*;

1930). He participated in Yung-Vilne and served as chair of the Yiddish PEN club. In 1938 he moved to Palestine.

Heysherik, Kalmen-Khayim (1900–1941), prose writer. Kalmen-Khayim Heysherik was born near Łódź, Poland. As a prisoner of war in Germany during World War I, he kept a diary that later served as the basis of his memoirs and fiction, which became popular during the 1920s. He published stories and essays in major Polish Yiddish newspapers. After the occupation of Warsaw in1939, he fled to Vilna. He was murdered in Ponar.

Kava, Shloyme-Leyb (1889–?), critic and journalist. Born in Warsaw, Shloyme-Leyb Kava (main pseudonym of Moyshe-Yosef Dikshteyn) served as Y.L. Peretz's secretary and later became vice president of the Association of Jewish Writers and Journalists in Warsaw. From 1905, he published numerous articles and essays in the Yiddish press, some of them sharply satirical and critical. In 1923, he published a collection of Yiddish folklore and was involved with various Yiddish publications in Poland. He died in the Warsaw ghetto.

Kirman, Yosef (1896–1943), poet. Yosef Kirman grew up in Warsaw in a poor family and was a worker; his first poetic publication appeared in the collection *Ringen* (*Rings*; 1919), he later contributed to various periodicals and published one collection of poems. He was arrested for his political activity by the Polish police. In the Warsaw ghetto he continued to write poetry and prose, which was partly preserved in the Ringelblum Archive. He was murdered in the Poniatów concentration camp.

Kreppel, Yoyne (1874–1939), journalist and writer. Born in Drohobycz, Galicia, Yoyne (Jonas) Kreppel was active in the Zionist movement and later became a leader of Agudas Yisroel. He also participated in the

Czernowitz Conference. Beginning in 1914 in Vienna, he served for many years as an adviser for the Austrian Foreign Ministry. He contributed to *Deryud* and other Yiddish publications in Galicia and from 1919 was a Vienna correspondent for New York's *Yidishes togblat.* A prolific Yiddish-language author of crime and historical fiction in Poland and America, he published more than 100 small books of stories and novels that were popular among a mass readership. He composed a comprehensive overview of contemporary Jewish life in German with *Juden und Judentumvon Heute* (*Jews and Judaism Today*; 1925). Kreppel died in the concentration camp at Mauthausen.

Olevski, Buzi (1908–1941), poet and prose writer. Born in Chernigov, Ukraine, Buzi Olevski's primary focus was on the economic and social transformation of shtetl youth; he also wrote for children. He wrote his dissertation on the poetry of Dovid Hofshteyn in Kiev, and later lived in Moscow and Birobidzhan. As an officer in the Soviet Army, Olevski fought in World War II and was killed in action. His autobiographical novel *Osherl un zayne fraynd* (*Osherl and His Friends*) was published posthumously in 1947.

Pitshenik, Moyshe-Leyb (1895–1941), writer and journalist. Moyshe-Leyb Pitshenik was born in Złoczew, Galicia, spent 1920–1922 in Katowice, and was the director of the Jewish school in Łowicz from 1923 on. He published poetry, stories, and articles in the Polish Yiddish press as well as historical novels about the Haskalah and Hasidism. He was murdered by the Nazis near Chełmno.

Rashkin, Leyb (1903?–1939), prose writer. Born in Kazimierz (Kuzmir), Poland, Leyb Rashkin (Shaul Fridman) began writing stories in the 1930s. His major work, *Di mentshn fun Godl-Bozhits* (*The People of Godl-Bozhits*;

1936),a realistic panoramic portrait of the Polish shtetl, was one of the most important Polish Yiddish debut novels in the 1930s and was awarded a literary prize. Rashkin was murdered while attempting to escape from German occupation to the Soviet Union

Shaevich, Simkhe-Bunem (1907–1944), poet and writer. Born in Tęczyce, Poland, Simkhe-Bunem Shaevich grew up in Łódź. From 1933 he published poetry and short stories, mostly in left-wing papers in Łódź and Warsaw; his first collection of stories was ready for publication in 1939 but was not issued due to the start of the war. In the Łódź ghetto, Shaevich composed profound Holocaust poems that explored traditional concepts such as exile and martyrdom. These works were preserved by survivors and published, posthumously, in 1946.

Shalit, Moyshe (1885–1941), journalist and communal activist. Born in Vilna to a well-off family, Moyshe Shalit was actively engaged in a wide range of public and philanthropic activities in Russia, Poland, and abroad, among them the PEN club and the Association of Jewish Writers and Journalists. In 1906, he published a historical study of the BILU movement in Russian (translated into Yiddish in 1917) as well as articles and reviews in the Yiddish and Russian press, and he edited a number of books and periodicals on politics, culture, and education. He was arrested and murdered immediately after the German occupation of Vilna in July 1941.

Sito, Fayv (1909–1945), prose writer. Fayvl Sito was born Rovno, Volhynia, lost his family during the civil war, and grew up in an orphanage. He studied in Odessa and at the Kharkov Conservatory. His stories about the lives of Jewish orphans in postrevolutionary Russia were based on personal experience, written with warmth and humor, and made him popular with a Yiddish readership. Also popular were his parodies of various

Soviet Yiddish writers that were collected in two books (1934, 1938); he additionally wrote plays and translated from Russian and Ukrainian into Yiddish. In 1939–1941, Sito edited a Yiddish magazine for teenagers in Kiev. During the war, he edited an army newspaper and worked for the Moscow Yiddish newspaper Eynikayt.

Tumru, Dovid (1910–1941), prose writer. Born in Alitus, Lithuania, Dovid Umru lived in Kaunas. He began to publish short stories in the Yiddish press in the 1930s; two collections of his short stories appeared in Kaunas in1937 and 1938. In 1940–1941 he edited the newspaper *Vilner emes* and served as the director of the Vilna State Yiddish Theater. He was murdered by the Gestapo in July 1941.

Varshavski, Yakir (1885–1942), writer and journalist. Born in Mława, Poland, Yakir Varshavski contributed to the Hebrew press (from 1908) and to Yiddish periodicals (from 1909); he also taught Hebrew in Warsaw's schools. Varshavski published his travelogue to Palestine and Egypt (1919), as well as a number of other books in Hebrew in Poland, including short stories for children. His two Yiddish collections were ready for publication in 1939 but did not appear due to the outbreak of World War II. He continued writing in the Warsaw ghetto until the Nazis murdered him in the summer of 1942.

Vaynig, Naftole (1897–1943), literary critic and folklorist. Born in Tarnów, western Galicia, Naftole Vaynig studied philology at Kraków University and art in Vienna. He also taught in Polish and Jewish schools. From 1917, his critical essays appeared in the press of Vienna and Warsaw, and he contributed studies of Jewish folklore to academic Yiddish publications in Poland. From 1941, he was in the Vilna ghetto, where he continued to teach, write, and collect folklore. His study of Leyb Naydus's poetry won a literary prize of the Judenrat.

Vulman, Shmuel (1896–1941), prose writer. Shmuel Vulman was born in Kaluszin, Poland. From 1917, he lived in Warsaw and contributed poetry, articles, reviews, and translations to numerous Yiddish periodicals in Warsaw, Lwów, and Czernowitz. He published collections of poetry, memoirs of the German occupation during World War I, an autobiographical novel, and a number of popular books on history, literature, geography, and other subjects. He was murdered by the Nazis in Kremeniec, Volhynia, where he had fled from Warsaw.

Zhitnitski, Hersh-Leyb (1891–1942), writer and journalist. Hersh-Leyb Zhitnitski was born in Szeradz, Poland, and lived in Łódź. From 1920, he lived in Warsaw, and fled to Lwów in 1939. He fell into the hands of the Nazis in 1941, and was deported to a death camp a year later. His first short story appeared in 1913 in *Lodzer morgnblat*. Zhitnitski worked as an editor of the *Warsaw Haynt,* contributed to the Yiddish press of Poland, the United States, Argentina, and Palestine, and published two collections of novellas and a novel about World War I in installments. His last book was ready for publication in 1939 but was never published due to the outbreak of the war.

Zilburg, Moyshe (1884–1941?), literary critic and translator. Born in Molodechno, Belorussia, Moyshe Zilburg took part in revolutionary activity, was arrested, left Russia, and moved to Galicia. He lived in Kraków, Lwów, and Vienna, where he edited the Yiddish literary magazine *Kritik* (1920–1921). In 1923, he returned to Vilna and worked on various Yiddish literary publications. He began to publish literary criticism around

1908 and later produced several translations from Hebrew, German, and Russian. After the German occupation of Vilna, he was killed in Ponar.

The contribution of this paper is to bring to our awareness the Yiddish writers listed in an Encyclopedia but otherwise not widely recognized and their loss not mourned. This is my Kaddish for them.

REFERENCES

Dreyfus, Leybush, a novel about actors (*Kulisn* [*Behind the Stage*]; 1927) .

Dubilet, Moyshe Dubilet's collection *Kritishe artiklen* (Critical *Essays)* was published in 1939.

Dubnov, S. (1915), *Jews in Russia and Poland From the Earliest Times Until the Present Day Vols. 1–3*, Forgotten Books, 2018.

Fishman, D.E. (2009). *Embers Plucked from the Fire: The Rescue of Jewish Cultural Treasures in Vilna.* New York: YIVO.

Gay, P. (1998). *Freud: A Life for Our Time.* New York: W.W. Norton.

Grinwald, M, (194) Lunch with Freud. *Ha'aretz.* September 21, 1941.

Gershon, D.H. ed, (2008). *The YIVO Encyclopedia of Jews in Eastern Europe: 2 Volumes,* New Haven, Yale University Press.

Gebirtig, Mordkhe *Folkshtimlech (In the Folk Style),* was published in 1920, and a second, *Mayne Lider (My Songs),* wrote Atos fun nekome (A Day for Revenge),

Glik, Hirsh (1922–1944), "Partisaner lid" (The Partisan Hymn).

Grodzenski, Arn-Yitskhok (1891–1941 *Lebn (Life*; 1923).

Glicksman, W, (1966) *In the Mirror of Literature: the Economic Life of the Jews in Poland as Reflected in Yiddish Literature (1914-1939).* Berlin: De Gruyter Mouton,

Hartsman, Motl (1908–1943), Der toyt-urteyl (The Death Sentence),

Hellerstein, K. (2008). Miryem Ulinover in *The YIVO Encyclopedia of Jews in Eastern Europe: 2 Volumes,* ed. D.H. Gershon. New Haven, Yale University Pres.

Hershele (1882–1941), poet, prose writer, and journalist. Hershele (pseudonym of Hersh Danilevich) a collection of plays and dramatic poems, titled *Bayopgruntn (By Abyss;* 1930).

Horontshik, Shimen.m (1889–`939). *In geroysh fun mashinen (Amid the noise of the machines,* 1928), and *1905* (1929) .

Kacyzne, Alter-Sholem. *Shtarke un Shvakhe (The Strong and the Weak)* was published in 1929/1930; *Bayn shvel (At the threshold,* 1935/36 Plays , *Dem Yidns Opera* (The Jew's Opera), *Ester (Esther),* and *Shvartsbard*

Katzenelson, Yitzhak *Die zun fargeyt in flamen (The sun sets/ in flames)* was published in 1909. Dos lid vegn Shloyme Zhelikhovsky [The poem about Solomon]. Shlomo Zhelikhovsky and Dos lid vegn Radziner [The Poem about the Radzhin Rebbe] Katzenelson wrote two of the Holocaust's most important works: *Pinkas Vitel (The Vittel diary)* in Hebrew, and *Dos lid fun oysgehargetn yidishn* folk *(The Poem about the Murdered Jewish People).*

Image Before My Eyes: A Photographic History of Jewish Life in Poland (1864–1939) (1977). edited by Lucjan Dobrosczycki and Barbara Kirshenblatt-Gimblett .

Leftwich, J. (1987), *Great Yiddish Writers of the 20th Century,* Lanham, MD: Jason Aronson.

Marr, Wilhelm (1879). *Der Weg zum Siege des Germanenthums* über *das Judenthum (The Way to Victory of Germanic over Judaism),* 1979.

Motl (1908–1943). Der toyt-urteyl (The Death Sentence),

Oyzer Varshavski, *Shmuglars (Smugglers), In the Mirror of Literature: Shnittsayt (Harvest Time,* 1926 *Rezidentsn (Residences; Résidences: On ne peut pas se 1944).*

Olevski, Buzi (1908–1941). Novel, *Osherl un zayne fraynd* (*Osherl and His Friends*).

Rashkin, L, (1903?–1939). His major work, *Di mentshn fun Godl-Bozhits* (*The People of Godl-Bozhits*; 1936).

Roskies, D.G. (1999), *The Jewish Search for a Usable Past,* Indiana University Press.

Ulinover, Miryem (nee Manya Hirshbeyn), *Der bobes optser* (*My Grandmother's Treasure,* 1922).

Vogel, Dvora published in 1930, (*Tog-figurn Lider, Figures of the Day*). *Manekin Lider* (*Mannequin Poems,* 1934).

CHAPTER 15

Review by Paul H. Elovitz: The Unorthodox, Interesting, and Productive Life of Arnold Richards. *Unorthodox: My Life In and Outside of Psychoanalysis: A Memoir by Arnold D. Richards.*

[(2024). *Clio's Psyche*, 31(1):128–130].

The word *Unorthodox* in this book's title is clearly appropriate for Arnold Richards' life and autobiography. When this most accomplished psychoanalytic editor and publisher came to my attention, I was immediately impressed and set up the December 2013 interview "Arnold Richards: Disseminating Psychoanalysis" in *Clio's Psyche* with him. I developed enormous respect and admiration for Dr. Richards and his talented wife, Arlene Kramer Richards. His energy is all but astounding, and I hope that at his age, I can come close to matching it and his productivity. Among his many achievements, he fought effectively for the inclusion of non-psychiatrists into psychoanalysis, healed many as an analyst, did yeoman service as an editor, and created International Psychoanalytic Books (IPBooks), which has brought some wonderful titles to the psychoanalytic community while providing creative employment for his daughter and son-in-law.

Unorthodox starts with a fine introduction by Daniel Benveniste and the reflections of Nancy Goodman. Benveniste gets to the heart of the matter when he writes that "Psychoanalysis is inherently subversive, and Arnold Richards is a psychoanalytic guerrilla warrior." Amidst Daniel's other insights are over three pages of short biographies in "Richards' Personal Thought Collective" (p. xxx-xxxii). These are very helpful for the reader, especially since the author's thesis is "that personal relationships determine politics and are affected by politics" (p. 123). Without this, the reader might get lost among the New York psychoanalysts he references. Additionally, Richards has made a great commitment to bring psychotherapeutic training and insights to China, provided crisis counseling to New York survivors of 9/11, brought psychotherapy to prisoners in Virginia, and generally worked to expand the application of psychoanalysis. All of these important contributions are covered in his book.

Richards' memoir covers his family history, childhood and youth in Brooklyn, stellar education at all levels, sparkling career, and turning against the politics of exclusion in the psychoanalytic community. His father was a Bolshevik atheist, and his mother an orthodox Jew. His life mirrors the extremes of his parents. Much of Richards' unorthodoxy may come from his father, who went to the movies on Yom Kippur. Still, unlike this sad man who lost a brother and his mother in the Russian Civil War and saw the failure of his dream of a wonderful communist society, Arnie's life has been better, and his zest for life is enormous. Although Arnold had a bar mitzvah, he wandered from his religion and later became passionate about being Jewish, identifying strongly with Yiddish culture and language. A daughter points out that when she was young, her father was always curiously asking where his fellow Jews or their families were from.

Richards had a solid psychiatric and psychoanalytic education, and he advanced rapidly in the orthodox Freudian New York psychoanalytic community after spending time at the Menninger Clinic in Kansas. Arnie fell in love with editing. First, he had turned the dull *Bulletin of the American Psychoanalytic Association* into the lively *The American Psychoanalyst* (*TAP*), and then, for a decade, greatly improved *JAPA* as its editor. "For those ten years, *JAPA* was my life," he says (p. 177).

As noted by Benveniste, Richards has been a maker of "good trouble" for necessary change, to use the term of the late Congressman John Lewis. His most important "good trouble" started with wanting his psychologist wife, Arlene, to be accepted by the New York Psychoanalytic Society (NYPSI). This led him to focus on the psychoanalytic politics of exclusion from the NYPSI. Aside from the unfairness of this policy to non-psychiatrists like his wife, he pointed out that psychiatrists were no longer opting for psychoanalytic training because, as prescribers of drugs, they can make $1,000 an hour rather than being paid for one analytic session. To Richards, they are becoming drug dealers. Without opening up the field to lay analysts, as Freud had wanted, the practice of psychoanalysis might have died.

One of many unorthodox aspects of this memoir is that his children write about the lives of their parents, and his wife suddenly interjects as well with her own recollection. There is no index, but his book is adorned with documents, photos, and poems. I especially enjoyed his "Father's Day" poem about his father's sad life. There are various interesting tidbits, such as Marianne Kris being the analyst to Jacqueline Kennedy Onassis and Marilyn Monroe.

Arnold Richards places great hope on the growth of psychoanalysis in China as it declines as a treatment option in the U.S. I recommend reading this interesting, informative, and insightful memoir about a major figure in psychoanalysis and an important analytic editor.